Love,
Marriage,
and Family
in Jewish Law
and Tradition

Love,
Marriage,
and Family
in Jewish Law
and Tradition

by Michael Kaufman

JASON ARONSON INC.
Northvale, New Jersey
London

First Jason Aronson Inc. softcover edition—1996

This book was set in 11 pt. Baskerville by Lind Graphics of Upper Saddle River, New Jersey.

Library of Congress Cataloging-in-Publication Data

Kaufman, Michael.
    Love, marriage, and family in Jewish law and tradition / by Michael Kaufman.
      p.   cm.
    Includes bibliographical references and index.
    ISBN 0-87668-515-7 (hardcover)
    ISBN 1-56821-884-2 (softcover)
    1. Marriage—Religious aspects—Judaism. 2. Marriage customs and rites, Jewish. 3. Jews—Families—Religious life. I. Title.
    BM713.K34   1992
    296.4'44—dc20   91-38088

Manufactured in the United States of America. Jason Aronson Inc. offers books and cassettes. For information and catalog write to Jason Aronson Inc., 230 Livingston Street, Northvale, New Jersey 07647.

To my children

Miriam
Zvi Hirsch
Naomi Deena
Rena
Avraham
Sasson Yisrael Eliezer
Simha Yosef Yaakov
Rachel Freda
Ora Ruth

and their children
and their children's children after them

"And when all of your children shall be taught God's way, great shall be the peace of your children." (Isaiah 54:13)

Talmudic comment: "Read not *banayich*, your children, but *bonayich*, your builders." (*K'ritut* 28b)

"Grandchildren are a crown to their grandparents." (Proverbs 17:6)

Rashi's comment: "[They are a crown] when grandparents see their grandchildren continuing in the proper [Jewish] way."

Contents

Part II LOVE

Part VI   THE MARRIED STATE

Foreword

Rabbi Nachman Bulman

Michael Kaufman is not a new name in Anglo-Jewish literature. He has authored a significant study on Jewish art in the context of Jewish history and Jewish thought, and most recently he published a cogent and insightful analysis of the problems facing contemporary Jewish youth.

His grace and felicity of expression, total fidelity to classic Torah tradition, and keen sensitivity to the pervasive assimilation crisis which clearly threatens so many Jews today, have all been brought to fruition in his major work to date, *Love, Marriage, and Family in Jewish Law and Tradition*. The book makes a serious and successful effort to provide an overview of the Jewish approach to the crisis in love, sensuality, and morality that pervades our time.

The author clearly and articulately presents the paradox that confronts many Jews in our day: On one hand, there is a growing *T'shuvah* movement of significant dimensions—many Jews are searching for and discovering their Jewish roots and returning to a Jewish tradition forsaken by their parents and grandparents. At the same time, the modern sexual revolution and its underlying values, which are distant indeed from Jewish ethical norms, have ravaged the values, identity, and general stability of large numbers of Jewish young people.

In this book's chapters, we rediscover the rare harmony between the ritual and the corporeal toward which Torah tradition guides us. Talmud and *Midrash, Rambam,* Rav S. R. Hirsch, and the brilliant

Rosh Yeshivah of Telz in our time, Rav Mordechai Gifter, all speak to us in timeless, organic unity. And they speak to the very soul of an age in ferment, in all its myriad facets.

Dr. Kaufman's deft use of contemporary idiom blends them all in conveying to us how "humane" the sanctity of Torah values is: That Judaism's rejection of promiscuity is light years removed from Christian asceticism; that the patriarchal Jewish family is a supreme safeguard precisely *against* the denigration of women; that love is central to Torah tradition, Christian anti-Jewish polemic notwithstanding; that the sensual drives can lead to life's ennoblement, rather than unavoidably to its animalization; that Torah-based criteria for the selection of a mate are infinitely wiser than those which are now prevalent in the larger society; that commandments and prohibitions in Jewish marital behavior are not constricting of life's genuine needs, but are liberating of its total divine-human potential; that the laws of *nidah, sh'lom bayit,* and the raising of children make us an immortal people, among whom love and truth are enduringly replenished and assured.

Love, Marriage, and Family in Jewish Law and Tradition is eminently useful as a practical marriage guide. The book provides a thoughtful analysis of the unique, ever-timely Jewish insights into love and life and the place of the family in the world, and in the process corrects much distortion of Judaism's wisdom in a most significant area of life.

The family is a fundamental institution in Jewish life upon which the very survival and well-being of the Jewish people is dependent. It is an institution that has been severely buffeted by an array of new concepts and life-styles in recent years and a resultingly high rate of divorce and broken homes. Considerable human and Jewish suffering could be alleviated if only the truth of Torah would be effectively transmitted and its principles widely followed in this area of life.

Michael Kaufman's *Love, Marriage, and Family in Jewish Law and Tradition* is an eloquent work, rich in content. It is a truly outstanding book—a genuine *tour de force.* A wide acceptance of the book by Jews who would pattern their lives upon its ideals would go a long way toward stabilizing Jewish marriage and buttressing the Jewish family. It is a work to read and study—an indispensable book that should be in every Jewish home.

Acknowledgments

It is difficult to credit all of the influences that contributed to this work. However, several should be mentioned.

First and foremost, my parents, Yisrael Eliezer and Freda Kaufman of blessed memory, who were my earliest teachers, established personal examples of elevated Jewish living, *yir'at Shamayim,* and uncompromising devotion to Judaism. They taught me the beauty of the Jewish way of living in a home enveloped in the warm atmosphere of Torah, and enriched with the *mitzvot* of *tz'dakah* and *g'milut hasadim,* charity and acts of lovingkindness. Most importantly, they gave me a proper sense of priorities in life, by providing the intensive Jewish education necessary to enable me to live Jewishly and to transmit the Jewish heritage to my children.

I owe a great debt of gratitude to R. Samson Raphael Hirsch, the nineteenth-century giant of Jewish thought, whose philosophy emphasizing the eternal relevancy of Torah is as valid in our day as it was in his. I am indebted to the example set by my late uncle, R. Shraga Faivel Mendlowitz, who fashioned Yeshivah and Mesivta Torah Vodaath into a major, influential institution of Torah scholarship, and founded Torah Umesorah, the National Society of Jewish Day Schools, and thereby created an educational framework that helped ensure American Jewish continuity and provided a spiritual foundation for the American Jewish community.

I wish to express my appreciation to those who gave generously of their time and suggestions: I am grateful to R. Yaakov Weinberg,

Rosh Yeshivah of Ner Israel Rabbinical College in Baltimore, for his critical reading of the manuscript. I benefited from the considered judgment of R. Nachman Bulman, the esteemed founder and spiritual head of Kiryat Nahaliel in Migdal Haemek, Israel, who provided the Foreword and rendered a critical evaluation regarding the substance and structure of the manuscript. I am grateful to R. Moshe Rom, R. Yitzhak Kaufman, and Greg Smith, who read portions of the manuscript and rendered valuable advice and suggestions.

I am indebted to the students of Aish HaTorah, Ohr Someyach, Neve Yerushalayim, and Hebrew and Tel Aviv Universities, many of whom frequent our home in the Old City of Jerusalem, of whom I made use as sounding boards for various ideas in the book. I wish to express my thanks to Sara Nathan, Linda Kashani, and Miriam Mantel for editorial assistance.

I express my appreciation to my publisher, Arthur Kurzweil of Jason Aronson Inc., who saw the need for this work. Warm thanks are due to Muriel Jorgensen, Editorial Director at Jason Aronson Inc., for her infinite patience and her painstaking concern with every detail of the manuscript.

I am especially grateful to my dear wife, companion and friend, Marcia, who took time out from her many activities to carefully review the text. Her countless suggestions, keen criticism, and insightful observations are reflected throughout the work. She has been a continuous source of inspiration and stimulation. She has also made an immeasurable contribution to the book by living it with me. Her wisdom, infinite patience, and constant encouragement and devotion sustained me during the lengthy preparation of this work and helped make it possible. She thus shares in the book's creation. Her ultimate recompense will be the use that will be made of the book. To the readers I say, *She-li v'she-lachem she-lah hu* — our book, yours and mine, we owe to her. May we merit seeing our children and our children's children occupied with Torah and *g'milut hasadim*.

While acknowledging my thanks to those who have rendered assistance, I assume sole responsibility for the material included herein and its interpretation, and for whatever shortcomings there may be.

Introduction

Jewish Values for Our Time

Jews in the Western world during this century have enjoyed an unparalleled era of personal freedom and economic prosperity. With the enfranchisement of European Jews in the nineteenth century and the gradual opening of society's professional, social, and economic doors to Jews, there has been a flowering of Jewish talent in virtually all realms of human endeavor—in literature, music, art, philosophy, science, medicine, law, government, and business.

So successful have Jews been in areas to which they were previously denied access that, despite the fact that they constitute but a minuscule percentage (about one fifth of one percent) of the world's population, they have earned some of society's most prestigious honors. Their contributions and attainments in every sphere of human thought and endeavor have left an indelible stamp upon humanity.

While Western society at large has profited greatly from this explosion of Jewish talent, Jews have been paying dearly for their freedom. Now, unfettered from the harsh repressions and persecutions that characterized most of their history, Jews have largely assimilated into Western society and have adopted its mores and values. In the process, however, many have abandoned their own heritage, the elevated, age-old Jewish mores and values that have distinguished the Jewish people since their birth as a people.

In recent times, this departure of many Jews from their heritage does not necessarily represent a deliberate, reasoned rejection of it; it stems, rather, from a lack of knowledge of the principles and ethical teachings of Judaism. Many Jews dismiss the age-old traditions of Judaism as moribund and outdated without even knowing them. They are unaware of the beauty and richness of the Jewish way of life, its relevance to the modern world, and the meaningful customs and traditions of Judaism.

They are equally unaware that it is the Jewish way of life and its rich customs and traditions that have helped maintain the Jews as a people through generations of persecution and dispersion in all corners of the world, long after other great and mighty nations have disappeared. They are no less oblivious to the incomparable contributions by Judaism to the moral and spiritual development of mankind and of the extent to which Jewish values and the legal and ethical system of Judaism lie at the very foundation of Western civilization.

The price that Jews are paying for their freedom in this century is becoming higher and higher, threatening even their continued existence and vitality as a people into the twenty-first century. One result of the Jews' assimilation into Western culture is the increasingly high intermarriage rate. Another is the steadily declining birth and fertility rates among Jews. This is the effective influence of contemporary trends and life-styles that, in the pursuit of the narcissistic and hedonistic values in vogue today, place an inordinate emphasis on self-fulfillment and self-realization.

These new trends and life-styles endorse either late marriage or no marriage at all, and small families. These factors, in turn, are closely linked to an approach that views the pursuit of careers by both partners (and the attainment of success in them) as the most important goal in life. The result is a steady diminution of the Jewish population in both relative and absolute terms by forces from within, to a degree that external enemies never achieved.

Nowhere do we see more clearly the results of this adoption of societal values at the cost of abandoning Jewish tradition than in the sphere of the Jewish family. In the past, virtually impervious to degenerative influences from the outside world, the Jewish home was universally respected as a model of stability, wholesomeness, and integrity. This is no longer the case.

The high divorce rate among Jews disassociated from their traditions, and the simultaneous erosion of the Jewish family, are concomitant by-products of the substitution by many Jews of divisive societal values in their lives for the elevated ones of their Jewish legacy. It is not without reason that the Jewish family, as it has existed for thousands of years, represents a bastion of stability for the nation. It is an institution founded on timeless, ever-applicable principles and moral values in which men and women are given clear guidelines on how to value, respect, and treat each other, as well as how to raise their children to be ethical human beings concerned for others. The high rate of divorce among Jews these days, therefore, reflects that of contemporary society in general, inasmuch as it results from the widespread abandonment of elevated Jewish traditions and mores. This is a result of an ignorance of the Jewish heritage and its social and moral teachings.

This work was motivated by a recognition of the immense problems facing Jews today, in view of the increasing disintegration, among large sections of the Jewish population, of the basic institutions of marriage and family. There is a need to reiterate the essential, sturdy, time-honored Jewish principles that have upheld the Jewish family for generations, and to point to those components of the Jewish tradition that have enabled the Jews to persevere for so long—as opposed to certain contemporary trends which, as the statistics show all too clearly, lead only to familial divisiveness and to the erosion of family life.

Life, Judaism teaches, has meaning, but to appreciate life it has to be lived in a meaningful, purposeful way. Judaism is not a religion defined by faith alone—that is, a creed with some rituals. It is an elevated, refined system of living based on faith but defined by concrete actions and deeds designed to make life full of purpose and meaning.

The intent of this work is to present Judaism's views on how best to live a meaningful, purposeful life, specifically in regard to the elemental human instincts and emotions relating to sensuality, procreation, and child-rearing, and to examine the institutions of marriage and family and their central position in the Jewish order of living.

Marriage, in Jewish thought, is a significant medium for attaining fulfillment in life; the married state is considered the ideal state. Judaism perceives marriage as a divinely designed institution created for the contentment of the individual, and for the welfare of society. The purpose of this work is to show how a Jewish man and woman may create a truly Jewish home, fill it with beautiful, meaningful traditions and important social and moral values, and attain genuine personal happiness and fulfillment.

Thus, this work is more than ideas, thoughts, and theory; it is designed to serve primarily as a practical guide. It provides effective guidelines for selecting a marriage partner with whom a proper Jewish home can be built; it describes the traits to look for in a partner, whom one might properly consider for marriage and whom one should avoid; it also describes how to go about finding and choosing the right person with whom to share one's life, in accordance with one's personal goals, and with proper regard for the higher end that marriage is designed to fill.

This book explores the Jewish understanding of love, and underscores how distant it is from the popular idea of romantic love. It goes on to discuss the preparations for the Jewish wedding, and the marriage ceremony itself, its procedures and rituals, and their significance. This work discusses Judaism's unique approach to sensuality and shows how investing the conjugal relationship with sanctity transforms it into an eminently more satisfying, meaningful, and enduring physical and emotional relationship between two partners.

This book outlines the responsibilities of the married couple to each other, and provides important Jewish insights into how one can cultivate a harmonious relationship with one's marriage partner based upon mutual esteem and devotion. It also presents the Jewish approach to what Judaism considers the highest responsibility of a Jewish couple — raising and educating children the Jewish way.

This work is written primarily for Jews: for those who are married, and those who are planning to marry; for those who are close to their heritage — to increase and deepen their understanding of it — and for those who are estranged from their heritage, so that they may be exposed to its richness, beauty, meaning, and applicability to our times. Nevertheless, this work is addressed to a wider audience as well; to all people who are interested in learning about

Jewish thought, practice, mores, and values, and to those who may
wish to incorporate these mores and values into their own lives.

This work is written from the perspective of a broad-based,
historical, traditional Judaism founded on Torah, as expounded by
the Jewish Sages and rabbinical authorities through the ages in their
legal and ethical teachings concerning the life-style Judaism deems
ideal for Jews. This approach, based on Jewish tradition and Jewish
law, contravenes, at times, accepted principles and views of contemporary society. One significant example is Judaism's directive to
the individual to find happiness not through narcissistic and hedonistic pampering of oneself, but through altruistic concern for
others, and by channeling one's energy and drives in the service of
God and humanity. In presenting this book, we refer to the classical
Jewish texts, as well as contemporary ones, and thoughts, points of
view, and quotations gathered from sources ranging over three
thousand years.

I would like to underscore, however, that reading *about* Judaism,
Jewish law, and Jewish ethics is no substitute for studying Torah
and the teachings of the Sages in the original Hebrew texts. For
those who may be deterred by the degree of proficiency in Hebrew
that is required to study the original texts properly, I would refer to
the example of Oscar Block, the Victorian man of letters who
learned Hebrew, so that, in his own words, "if I went to heaven I
could talk to God in His own language."

It is my hope that this book will offer important insights,
guidance, and clarification of Jewish views on love, sensuality,
marriage, and child rearing, so that if these timeless concepts are
put into practice, lives and marriages may be enriched. I will be
especially gratified if this work makes the reader more aware of the
beauty and rich content of the Jewish way of living. If, as a result
of this work, readers are stimulated to delve into their own heritage,
and would learn more fully to apply Jewish principles and practices
to their own lives, I will feel amply rewarded.

I

Deciding on Marriage

1

Marriage:
A Jewish Duty

Procreation, the Fundamental Biblical Command

Judaism's approach to marriage is characterized by the Hebrew word for betrothal, *kidushin,* sanctification — the hallowing of man and woman in a sacred spiritual bond. Its purpose is the sanctification of their life together, creating a *mikdash m'at* (miniature sanctuary) to fulfill the holy tasks of procreation and the education of children, and for mutual companionship and security.

Marriage provides a universally recognized framework for a man and a woman to live together exclusively, in privacy and intimacy. Among other things, it provides public recognition of their transition from one state of existence into another, one greater than their own and hallowed by tradition.

Marriage implies various elements: social, psychological, economic, and biological. Judaism raises marriage above all these basic levels by consecrating the husband–wife relationship on the spiritual foundation of *kidushin,* thereby creating a "sanctuary" out of a worldly institution. Holiness permeates all aspects of the Jewish approach to the married relationship.

The male–female unit is woven into the very fabric of Creation. In the context of the creation of the first woman, the Torah declares: "And the Lord God said: It is not good for man to be alone. I shall make him a helpmate for him."[1]

The Torah goes on to define the relationship in terms of a

3

positive injunction for the male: "Therefore shall a man leave his father and his mother and cleave to his wife and they shall become one flesh."[2]

According to the Talmud, God originally created man and woman simultaneously as one androgynous, hermaphroditic being; only later did He separate part of Adam to create man and woman as separate entities.[3] The Sages derive this from the phraseology of Genesis, "He created *them* male and female,"[4] and "He called *their* name Adam on the day he created *them*."[5] As a separate entity, without his female partner, he was but half a man; through marriage and the union of the sexes he became whole again. When the woman, Eve, joined him, he was returned to his natural state: one single body, as it had been, with one mind, one heart, one soul — two halves together forming a complete being.[6] The Jewish idea is that although each is a distinctly separate entity with specific male or female characteristics, neither the male nor the female entity is truly a whole being without the other. The Sages teach:[7] "Why did God originally create Adam as a single bisexual being? In this way God invested Man with the capacity to fulfill the Torah command 'And he shall cleave to his wife.' "[8]

Since the first couple joined to restore the wholeness of the human being, men and women have been driven to seek similar union and completion of being. The product of their union, their children, are both symbols and a perpetuation of this completeness.

God's Partner in Creation

"Be fruitful and multiply,"[9] the biblical injunction, is God's most fundamental command to human beings. It is a basic Jewish idea that children created in fulfillment of that command constitute the most significant legacy a person can leave after his sojourn on earth.

To fulfill the command of procreation, a Jew must bring at least one male and one female child into the world.[10] This *mitzvah* is usually listed as the very first biblical precept binding upon the Jews. *Sefer HaHinuch,* the thirteenth-century compendium of precepts and their rational basis (usually attributed to R. Aaron HaLevi of Barcelona) teaches:

> The purpose of this *mitzvah* is that the world which God wants to be inhabited will indeed be populated. As it is written: "He did not

create the world to be a waste; He fashioned it to be a habitation."[11] And this is a most important *mitzvah,* for through it all the other commandments may be fulfilled. For indeed, the *mitzvot* were given to humans to fulfill and not to the angels.[12]

According to the Sages, God intentionally left Creation incomplete;[13] in so doing He bestowed upon His creatures the ability to continue the divine process of Creation through procreation. The Torah teaches that man was created in God's image,[14] that is that the Almighty endowed man with His traits. Judaism understands this to mean that man's supreme goal is to exercise these traits after the example of God,[15] which includes the awesome duty of participating in the creation of life. Man on earth has a cardinal duty to populate it.

Marriage in Judaism is not merely a viable *option* to satisfy the human need for companionship — it is a basic religious obligation.[16] Marriage sanctifies man and woman by joining them in a grand partnership with God. In the sublime act of Creation, they sanctify the world by nurturing life. The Sages declare: "No man can enjoy complete happiness unless he has a wife and children."[17]

The medieval Spanish-Portuguese philosopher and biblical exegete R. Isaac Abarbanel (1437–1508) refers to the single state as one of incomplete happiness and illusory joy.

The Marital State: The Norm of Jewish Life

Marriage is considered a required norm of Jewish life by the *Shulhan Aruch,* the *Code of Jewish Law:* "Every man is obliged to marry in order to fulfill the duty of procreation, and whoever does not is as if he had shed blood, diminished the image of God and caused the Holy Presence to depart from Israel."[18]

The *Midrash* states that God himself so greatly desires that marriages take place that He Himself arranges marriages[19] — and He even serves as a witness at weddings.[20]

So important does Judaism consider marriage that Jewish law even permits the sale of a holy Torah scroll if the proceeds will enable a wedding to take place.[21] Indeed, marriage is considered an even greater *mitzvah* than honoring one's parents.[22]

No man, young or old, is excused from fulfilling the biblical command of procreation and bringing at least one male and one female child into the world.[23] Even if a man has been married and has already fathered children, he is forbidden to remain single.[24] The Talmud teaches: "If a man has married in his youth, let him also marry in his old age. If a man has fathered children in his youth, let him also father children in his old age."[25]

Maimonides incorporates this dictum into his codes:

> Even though a man may have fulfilled the *mitzvah* of procreation, it is nevertheless a *mitzvah* of the Sages that he may not cease from further procreation so long as he remains virile, for he who adds a single soul to Israel is as if he has created an entire world. And it is a command of the Sages that no man may remain without a wife.[26]

The rationale behind this is that even though a man may have fulfilled his basic responsibility to have at least one son and one daughter, he cannot know what will happen to his children the next day; by having more than is required, he helps secure his representation in this world by future generations.

Nevertheless, even if procreation is no longer possible, a man may not remain single. Maimonides states unequivocally: "No man may remain without a wife."

If a man is still single after a certain period of his life, Jewish law sanctions the court to compel him to marry.[27] The rabbinic courts were allowed to employ corporal punishment and to exact fines; they could even apply the ban of excommunication to add weight to their verdicts. Such compulsion has not been used since the Middle Ages.[28] Nevertheless, in 1745 the elders of Jerusalem would not permit bachelors of marriageable age to live in the city. They issued a prohibition that male members of the community between the ages of twenty and fifty could not reside in the city without wives. Bachelors were given up to four months to find themselves spouses, failing which, they were to be expelled from Jerusalem.[29]

A Male Is Not a Man

The Sages went so far as to question the effective masculinity of the Jewish male who was determined to remain a bachelor.[30] "A man without a wife is not called a man, as it is written, 'He created them male and female . . . and He called their name Adam (man).' "[31]

No matter how old or otherwise mature, only in marriage does a human male attain the status of manhood. The *Zohar* states simply: "A man is not called a man until he unites with a woman in marriage."[32]

As the Sages see it, if a person stays single because his friends do so or because it is the social norm, he lacks a certain strength or, as it were, a certain manliness, to rise above this and make a mature decision in accordance with God's natural design. The Sages declare: "In a place where there are no men, strive to become a man."[33]

A State of Wholeness

The Sages say that a prerequisite for God's presence is the element of perfection or completion. Therefore, a man without a wife is an incomplete entity, who is denied the presence of God. A single person is perceived as having a fundamental defect in that he lacks the oneness and wholeness ordained by God for mankind. As the Sages put it: "A man without a wife is not a complete human being."[34]

The *Zohar* teaches:

The Holy One, Blessed Be He, does not dwell, nor is He to be found at all with that which is imperfect. He can be found only with one who has attained true oneness. . . . A person can be considered one and whole . . . and without defect[35] . . . when he is joined together with the complementary part of him and is thus hallowed by the elevated sanctification of *kidushin.* He who has not married a woman . . . remains but half a person—and his [intended] life's partner remains but half a person. . . .[36]

In the single, defective state, a person possesses only the *potential* for attaining completion and for giving completion to another. The *Zohar* makes this point clear: "Soul and spirit, male and female, are intended to illuminate together. One without the other does not radiate and is not even termed a 'light.' Only when they are attached to one another are they called a 'light.' "[37]

Man and woman are thus perceived in Jewish thought as essential, even indispensable to one another. Marriage is understood to proceed from the deep-seated memory of man and woman in the primordial state of oneness and a yearning to return to that original state. Judaism understands that in attaining that oneness it is the woman who supplies perfection. It is the man who is seen as imperfect, whereas the woman provides that which is necessary to create wholeness. The Sages emphasize this, saying: "It is impossible for a man to achieve human perfection unless he is married to a worthy woman."[38]

The Jewish idea is that marriage brings a couple to the complete state in which they can establish proper communion with God. It creates out of two individual complementary entities a single, transcendent superentity of mystical significance through which, in the words of the Sages, "heaven and earth embrace."[39]

Naturally, it is not just the man who requires a mate for completion; the woman in equal measure requires a man to achieve her own. The *Midrash* teaches:[40] "A woman has no tranquillity except with a husband, as it is written [in relation to Ruth's seeking a husband, in the Book of Ruth], 'And Naomi said: My daughter, let me seek for you tranquillity, which will be good for you.' "[41]

The Talmud refers to the woman's need for personal fulfillment: "A woman is an incomplete being who concludes a covenant [of marriage] only with the one who can transform her into a complete vessel."[42]

Marriage as Optional for the Woman

Judaism considers marriage as voluntary and optional for the woman, however. Unlike the man, she is exempt from the duty of procreation.[43] There are several reasons for this. Marriage and procreation entail seeking out a mate. A certain boldness and aggressiveness are required; the Sages consider these characteristics more appropriate to the male sex, and are not, the Rabbis feel, in harmony with the more chaste, reserved character of the woman. This view is also shared by most civilized societies. This is the way the process is described in scripture: "Therefore shall a man forsake his father and his mother and cleave to his wife."[44]

It is the man who is bidden to actively search for a wife, not *vice versa*. The Talmud explains:

Why did the Torah state "When a man will take a wife"[45] and why did it not state the reverse? Because it is in the nature of a man to actively pursue the woman and it is not the nature of the woman to actively pursue the man. If a person loses something, who seeks out whom? It is the one who loses something who seeks it out, and not *vice versa*.[46]

In Jewish thought, woman was taken from man. Thus, it is the unmarried man who is the more active in pursuit of a spouse because he feels more incomplete. In every generation it is the man who repeats the saga of Adam, his primal forebear, and follows his instinctive urge to find the woman who will make him whole.

Another reason for marriage being optional for the woman is that the Torah, in principle, does not impose burdens that are too difficult to bear. In the words of scripture: "The ways [of Torah] are those of sweetness."[47]

The Torah would not categorically command a woman to experience discomfort and risk her health. Recognizing that the woman's health is occasionally jeopardized by pregnancy and childbirth, the Torah does not ask her to place herself in a possibly precarious situation. This commitment is based on her own free choice; she is not directed to do so by fiat.[48] Her natural, personal apprehensions are respected. Thus, the command to procreate cannot be equally incumbent upon a woman, and Judaism has exempted her.

However, some Sages in the Mishnah and Talmud maintain that a woman is in fact equally obligated to fulfill the command to procreate,[49] and substantiate their view by citing the verses in Genesis: "Male and female He created them:[50] God blessed them and said to *them*, 'Be fruitful and multiply, fill the earth and master it.' "[51]

They also cite the passage in Isaiah:[52] "For thus says the Lord, Creator of heaven: He is God who fashioned the earth and created it; He did not create it to be a waste: He fashioned it to be inhabited."[53]

The predominant view in the Jerusalem Talmud is that women

are included in the obligation to marry and procreate.[54] This view is also supported by the medieval Tosafists, whose opinion is that the passage in Isaiah has universal implications which include women in the obligation to procreate and populate the world.[55]

However, the final halachic ruling is that women are exempt from the command to procreate.[56] This position is maintained by Maimonides who concludes that a woman may, if she wishes, marry a eunuch or remain unmarried. This conclusion is shared by other codifiers of Jewish law.[57] Yet, Maimonides advises Jewish women to disregard this exemption and marry to avoid having to face male impudence and immorality. He made it incumbent upon a Jewish parent, therefore, to marry off a daughter as well as a son.[58]

Fulfillment through Marriage

Marriage, then, is the preferred state for women, but Jewish law does not make it mandatory. It encourages the woman to marry, but does not condemn her should she choose to remain single.

The Rabbis were aware, however, that women often desire marriage more strongly than do men: "More than a man wants to marry, a woman wants to be wed."[59]

In addition, Jewish women have always opted for marriage and children because of what is called the maternal instinct — a desire for children greater than that experienced by a man. This need overrides any inclination a woman might have to take advantage of her option in *halachah* to remain single.

Few biblical verses are as poignant as Rachel's plea, "Give me children, for if not I shall surely die."[60] Consequently, one might say that while a man has a natural inclination to seek completion when he simply unites with a woman, for a woman this is insufficient. For her personal and creative fulfillment, she needs children as well.

Because of this, Jewish law provides that a woman married to a sterile man may have the rabbinic court force a divorce.[61] Though she is excused from the *mitzvah* of procreation and cannot use her husband's sterility as automatic grounds for divorce, the court respects *her wishes* on this point, and allows both this and her desire for children as valid grounds for divorce. Maimonides explains that the law respects the woman's desires to have children "when she is old."[62]

For the Jewish woman, the decision whether or not to marry is hers alone. Comments one observer:

> The release of the Jewish woman from the commandment of procreation has made possible the evolvement of the concept of woman as a personality and not as a childbearing machine. Certainly woman is involved in the commandment to preserve the race, but it is her *privilege* to determine whether she becomes involved or not. The rabbinic opinion on this subject and its formulation in Jewish law may have been the first stage in the full emancipation of Woman.[63]

While the woman is exempt from the command to marry and bear children, by doing so she enables the man to procreate. Her reward for the performance of the *mitzvah,* therefore, is greater than that of her husband, in accordance with the rabbinic principle, *Gadol ha-m'aseh yoter me-ha'oseh,* "Greater is the enabler of the act than its actual performer."[64] R. Nissim Gerondi, the fourteenth-century Spanish commentator on the Talmud, comments: "Although she is not personally commanded regarding procreation, she nevertheless performs a *mitzvah* in marrying because she thereby assists her husband in the fulfillment of his *mitzvah* of procreation."[65]

Marriage, in Judaism's view, is not for procreation alone; it is also for companionship and fulfillment. A bride is called *kalah,* completion. Jewish tradition considers a wedding to be a commencement ceremony marking emergence from the preparatory cocoon where one has existed in a nascent, incomplete state and a metamorphosis into a new, transcendental, completed state.

It follows that for the marriage to be successful, the two partners in the fused marital entity must learn to think more of their new joint personality than of their former, more primitive, separate selves. This does not mean the loss of their separate individualities, but an incorporation of the two selves. The Jewish idea is that the merger created by the interweaving of two characters allows a confrontation of the outside world from a position of considerably increased strength. This whole marital personality is a greater force than its two constituent parts. The Sages teach: "Husband and wife together are greater as a unit than each of them is as an individual."[66]

The Single State as the Selfish State

In Judaism, the deliberate intent to remain single is regarded as the height of selfishness. A fundamental principle of the Torah[67] (and a pillar upon which the world rests[68]) is selfless love for others. The commandment to perform *hesed,* acts of love to fellow humans, in fulfillment of Judaism's Golden Rule,[69] begins at home, where a man is at all times surrounded by people needing this love and understanding. It is in the home, more than almost any other circumstance, that Judaism requires a man and woman to give their all — time, compassion, love, and strength — selflessly and ceaselessly.

While one may have performed *hesed* while single, marriage marks the entry into a world of ethical loving based on *hesed.* With marriage, one ceases to be essentially a *taker* from parents and from society, concerned primarily with one's self, and opens a door to enter a world of concern for others. In the words of the Sages, "Marriage is the first step toward a man's entry into the community."[70] A contemporary observer comments:

> Marriage is the beginning of *hesed,* for in marriage one is obligated to shift the focus of his concern from himself to his wife and children. A person who refuses to marry . . . wants to live by and for himself. [The Bible teaches:] "it is not good for man to live alone,"[71] for to live alone is to deny the foundation of Jewish ethics, the experience and emotion of *hesed.*[72]

True wealth, the Sages say, is to be married to a pleasant woman.[73] They found it difficult to understand why an individual would refrain from marrying and willfully deprive himself of all the benefits which God gave to human beings through the institution of marriage.

The single person, the Sages teach, lacks joy, blessing, good — and even Torah: all the elements necessary for a decent existence. The *Midrash* says:[74]

> "And the Lord God said: It is not good for Man to be alone"[75]. . . . R. Jacob taught: Every man who has no wife lives without good, without help, without happiness and without forgiveness.

Without good, as it is written, "It is not good for a man to be alone."[76]

Without help, as it is written, "I shall make him a helpmate for him."[77]

Without happiness, as it is written, "And you shall rejoice, you and your household."[78]

Without blessing, as it is written, "To bring blessing to your household."[79]

Without forgiveness, as it is written, "And I shall forgive you and your household."[80]

R. Simon said in the name of R. Joshua Ben Levi: Even without peace, as it is written, "And peace will be with you and peace will be with your household."[81]

R. Joshua of Sichnin said in the name of R. Levi: Even without life, as it is written, "See life with the wife that you love."[82]

R. Hiyya bar Gamda said: He is not even a complete person, as it is written, "And He blessed them and He called their name Adam."[83]

And some say: He even diminishes the Divine Image, as it is written, "For man was created in God's image,"[84] and immediately afterwards it is written, "And multiply."[85]

Men and women who did not marry, or who did not remain married, were soon, by tradition, regarded as unfortunates. The Sages express a deep compassion for the widow and widower. The Talmud declares: "He whose first wife dies experiences as great a tragedy as if the Temple was destroyed in his days. . . . His entire life is darkened . . . his steps are shortened . . . his spine becomes bent. . . ."[86]

Divorce was also regarded as a great tragedy. The Talmud says: "Whoever divorces his first wife — even the Temple altar sheds tears for him."[87]

The Sages declare: "For everything there is a substitute, except for the wife of one's youth."[88]

Those who deliberately refrained from marrying were considered to have failed one of man's essential purposes, propagation. The school of Shammai (end of the first century B.C.E.–beginning of the second century C.E.) maintained that procreation was the purpose of the creation of the world.[89] A childless life is not truly a life; the Rabbis teach: "A childless person is like a dead one."[90]

Judaism and the Single Man

Obviously, the matter of marriage and procreation refers to one who is able to do these things. When natural or other circumstances do not permit fulfillment of these roles, the Sages regard this only with compassion. Judaism's attitude toward the man who chooses to remain single, however, is one of uncompromising severity.

The Talmud states that in the afterlife a man will have to account for not marrying and not having children: "At the end of times when a man is brought before the ultimate tribunal for the final judgment, he is asked. Did you deal honestly in business? Did you set regular hours for the study of Torah? Did you fulfill your duty of procreation?"[91]

R. Eliezer says: He who does not marry and engage in procreation is as if he has shed blood. . . .

R. Jacob says: It is as if he had diminished the Divine Image . . .

R. Ben Azai says: It is as though he has shed blood *and* diminished the Divine Image. . . .[92]

The Sages add that such a man causes the Divine Presence to depart from Israel, and go so far as to declare him to be the equivalent of a murderer, "deserving the death penalty."[93]

The premium that Judaism places upon human life is well-known: bloodshed is the most serious of crimes. A corollary to this is that a person to whom God has given the potential of creating life, but who refrains from fulfilling that potential, causes the diminution of life. He is thus considered in the approximate moral category of a murderer. The *Zohar* says:

> When is a man called complete? . . . When he is joined with his mate in unity, in joy and in affection, and there issues from their union a son and a daughter. Only then is man complete below like the Holy Name above, and the Holy Name becomes attached to him. However, if a man is unwilling to complete the Holy Name below, it is better for him that he had not been born, for he has no portion at all in the Holy Name. And when his soul leaves him in this world it will never join him again, because he has diminished the likeness of his Master. . . .[94]

In Jewish thought, therefore, the murderer and the unmarried individual are viewed as having related character traits: neither is willing to transcend his self-centeredness and to show genuine concern for his fellow human being. A person who deliberately chooses to remain single is erecting a fence around himself. Inside his circle of isolation he creates smaller and smaller concentric circles, becoming increasingly oblivious, more self-involved, and less giving in the context of interpersonal relationships.

The married man, in contrast, must necessarily break down the walls separating him from humanity. There is no space within a marriage for a multiplicity of walls, each enjoying its fortresslike existence; forced contact and friction must eventually bring down these walls. Judaism teaches that human love that is released must flow first toward a spouse and children, then to all of one's people, and last, to all of humanity. In essence, the individual who marries builds a bridge between himself and the human community. His tools are the pure acts of love essential to the Jewish spirit and the Jewish home.

The Sages state that the Jewish people merited their redemption from Egyptian bondage because they married and had children.[95] Thereby, the Jewish slaves showed their faith and trust in God's continued merciful supervision of the universe. In our times, such faith-in-action is sadly lacking. Perhaps the antidote to the selfish egocentrism prevalent in present-day society can be found in a revival of the old institutions of marriage and family. Indeed, in Judaism, these are considered the prerequisites for future redemption. As the Sages say: "Just as Israel was redeemed from Egypt for marrying and having children, so too shall they be redeemed in the future for marrying and having children. Know well that this is so — for Israel will never be redeemed unless they marry and procreate."[96]

2

Whom One May — And May Not — Marry

Judaism's Marriage Taboos

Marriage taboos exist in Judaism. According to *halachah,* Jewish law, every male may not marry every female. There are impediments to certain matches between men and women (refer to the list at the end of this chapter) with considerations of ethical, moral, biological, and mystical significance. Certain unions, the Torah teaches, carry a potentially destructive element. If one of these unions does take place, their legality is contingent on the severity of the proscription. Certain marriages will not be recognized: in legal terms they are null and void from the beginning. Others are recognized after the marriage has taken place, although *a priori* they are undesirable. The latter prohibition provides grounds for divorce as well, if divorce is desired. The *Code of Jewish Law* states:

> These marital unions that are forbidden for reasons of *ervah* [indecency: i.e. incest, and other forbidden relationships] include ones that are biblically prohibited and those that are rabbinically prohibited. They are invalid marriages. Marriages contracted among those rabbinically prohibited are valid and require a divorce to dissolve them.[1]

The concepts of "adultery," "indecency," and "forbidden marriages" are considered by many to be obsolete terms, and may have an archaic ring in our modern, "sexually liberated" world. "If it gives you pleasure, do it," seems to be the guiding principle of the present day's permissive, hedonistic society—a society which celebrates narcissism. In the Jewish perception, the unconcern of that society with the age-old values of marriage and the family is a superficial manifestation of something more deeply amiss: a selfish concern with one's self only, and a disregard for all others, whether they be parents, children, or marital partners. By this philosophy, others exist only to provide the individual with unceasing pleasure.

In Jewish thinking, rejection of the Torah's rules in favor of more selfish living is symptomatic of the present general state of society, and is expressed in a widespread general collapse of human values. The rules of the Torah may be old, but their timeless relevancy can be seen clearly in their emphasis on human decency, and, in particular, in their humanistic approach to marriage.

Decency, declares Judaism, is the very first factor the Jew must consider in his choice of a spouse. That decency must be maintained throughout married life. Judaism understands as well that devotion for life to one's marital partner is not a quaint or archaic notion; it is an essential social value that is incompatible with the concept of adulterous relationships.

The problem is compounded because, as a result of certain kinds of negligence, parents may place upon their children and grandchildren serious stigmas that affect their status as Jews or their legal qualification to marry most other Jews. In brief, they may make their children less than full-fledged Jews, unacceptable as mates to very significant segments of the Jewish community. Many young men and women who are in the process of discovering their Jewish roots learn, to their dismay, that, because of an error on the part of their parents, they are simply not proper Jews in all respects.

A particular problem in our day relates to Jewish youngsters settling in Israel. Since the Israeli Rabbinate, which is the legal authority in charge of marriage procedures, does not recognize many marriages performed outside Israel, a couple wishing to marry in Israel may be surprised to learn that they are forbidden to marry one another because of a misstep on the part of a parent.

It is vital for a couple planning to marry, therefore, to ascertain at an early stage the rules regarding Jewish marriage prohibitions, and to consult a qualified rabbi who is expert in, and observant of, *halachah.*

What's Wrong with Intermarriage?

A basic tenet of Judaism is that the technical "Jewishness" of a prospective marriage partner be clearly verifiable. The marriage of a Jew and a non-Jew is not binding in Jewish law. Such a marriage has no validity even if it should be performed and blessed by many rabbis. To be "in love" or emotionally or sexually attracted to each other is not considered sufficient reason for marrying.

Judaism's prohibition against marrying non-Jews is not based on a lack of esteem for non-Jews or on racial prejudice; sincere converts are welcomed into Judaism. The proscription exists to ensure that the commitment of Jews to the faith of their fathers is not weakened or broken.[2] Intermarriage, in fact, contributes to the destruction of the Jewish people.

Jewish marriage as *kidushin,* a sanctified relationship, is based on the concept of a family in which children are raised in a pervasively Jewish atmosphere and environment, in which all members observe the precepts of the Torah and live the Jewish way of life. Where there is a marriage with one non-Jewish partner, the very foundation of *kidushin* is lacking. It is demonstrably impossible for a person to maintain seriously his or her Judaism when married to someone of a different faith—even though both may be liberally tolerant of each other's devotion to distinctive religious beliefs and practices. Such marriages have generally not proven successful. Where both partners are Jewish there is a far greater chance for a marriage to succeed. According to a published statistical report, divorce among American Jews "is more prevalent among those whose spouses are not Jewish than when both of them are of Jewish origin."[3]

When children are born and hard decisions must be made on the tradition, faith, and manner in which they will be raised, dormant conflicts suddenly arise. Children of such marriages grow up confused by the contradictions of their parents, and sometimes develop serious psychological problems as well. It is essential, therefore, to their children's psychological well-being that both parents are Jewish.

The Jewish view is that if Judaism is worth keeping, it is worth perpetuating. Perpetuation entails education. It follows that parents must be of one mind — and one faith — in order to bring up children who are well adjusted — religiously and psychologically.

"Liberalized" Marriages, Divorces, Conversions

When seeking a Jewish mate one was, at one time, able to rely upon Maimonides' statement that all Jewish families have a *hezkat kashrut;* that is, their claims of Jewishness are ordinarily to be accepted.[4] It was presumed that Jewish families claiming to be authentically Jewish were indeed so, and that all conversions or divorces among a family's ancestors were performed according to Jewish law. This *hezkat kashrut,* or presumptive Jewishness, in effect among Jewish families in Maimonides' day some nine hundred years ago, is no longer reliable because Jewish law is not observed by many Jews, nor even by some rabbis.

During the last two centuries, liberal Jewish movements have emerged whose ideology rejects the eternal validity of *halachah* and its binding nature. Accordingly, they have modified, changed, and abolished many laws and traditional practices of Judaism to suit the times, or to meet what they believe to be the needs or desires of their followers. Very few demands of personal religious observance are made upon their members, and, perhaps for this reason, these movements have succeeded in attracting large numbers of followers.

Whether from a vaguely sensed human need or because society declares it fashionable, many Jews have discovered in these movements a convenient means to maintain affiliations of a loose nature with their Jewish heritage, while not obliging themselves to follow the observances and practices required by traditional Judaism. In this way, they are able to consider themselves Jews belonging to a very strong, ancient, ethnic framework, even while, in fact, they may be abrogating practices and traditions that have been fundamentals of Judaism for thousands of years. Their leaders teach that they are not bound by the *Code of Jewish Law;* that it is an anachronism irrelevant to the modern age. Their Jewishness finds its expression in Jewish social contacts, cultural nostalgia, and ethical philosophy; for those who feel the need, there is the option of an occasional traditional practice of Judaism. Like other socio-cultural modes, and in contrast to traditional Judaism, these movements have manifested their dependence upon the changes of time and fashion.

Among the alterations in Jewish practice instituted by these movements are some affecting personal status, such as marriage, divorce, and conversion. By and large, these changes, which accord with the ideologies of these movements, are not in accord with—and even contravene—*halachah*. Over the years, many Jews affiliated with these movements have undergone changes in personal status or have been affected by such changes within their families.

A Deepening Division within the Jewish Community

This process has gradually created a deep, ever-widening chasm dividing the Jewish people into two quite distinct religious group-ings. The reason for the division is not a mere difference of opinion or ideology in traditional Jewish thinking; the acceptance or rejec-tion of *halachah* is bound up with the fundamental unity of the Jews as a people. Throughout centuries of widespread Jewish dispersion it kept the Jews together, while once-powerful nations were reduced to insignificance or disappeared. Anthropological or sociological studies would certainly have predicted similar extinction for the widely dispersed Jews, who were everywhere subject to severe persecution, constant harassment, and frequent forced migrations. Their survival as a single entity, one widely dispersed over vast distances, is due in no small measure to their common loyalty to ancient, apparently insignificant practices, and seemingly prosaic legalities.

Halachah is thus perceived as having served in some profound way as a binding element for a widely scattered Jewish people. The Jews often shared no common climate, geography, or topography, but only a common ancient history, religion, and an ethical and moral way of life. Wherever they resided they maintained their cultural and intellectual distinctiveness through the bonding power of *halachah*.

Today, Jews committed to traditional Judaism find themselves

strictly forbidden by *halachah* to marry certain followers of nonha-
lachic movements. Before marriage is considered, they are compelled to investigate thoroughly the backgrounds of potential marriage partners whose families are affiliated with these movements,
including any previous changes in personal or family status, to see
that all is in accord with Jewish law. Earlier marriages, divorces,
and conversions must be carefully examined and proven legitimate
according to Jewish law before marriage is considered.

It is possible to find parallels between the growing divisions in the
Jewish community today and those that existed with the development of the Karaite sect some twelve and a half centuries ago.
Karaite theology, the central characteristic of which was the recognition of scripture as the sole source of religious law, with the
rejection of the Talmud and Oral Law, resulted in the Karaites'
eventual schismatic break with Judaism into a separate religion with
whose adherents Jews are forbidden to intermarry.[5]

Members of contemporary Jewish movements aiming to mod-
ernize Judaism are now considered, from the traditional Jewish
viewpoint, of a status superior to that of the Karaites (as far as
marrying their followers is concerned) since normative Jews are
strictly forbidden from marrying Karaites or any of their descendants — even if they convert to normative Judaism. At present, only
the credibility of the claims of members of these movements
concerning personal Jewish status is in question. Unlike the situation with the Karaites, their claims of Jewishness are not automatically presumed by *halachah* to be false. They merely necessitate
arduous and possibly emotionally painful detective work when it
comes to marriage with their members.

However, if the schism within the Jewish community continues to
grow larger in the matter of changes in personal status, it is possible
to foresee a not-too-distant and grim future in which a halachically
observant Jew will be automatically prohibited from intermarrying
with a member of those movements that do not accept *halachah* as
binding even if he or she would wish to "convert" to "normative"
Judaism. Paradoxically, a non-Jew would be able to convert and
marry anyone Jewish. This would mean that followers of these
liberal Jewish movements and their descendants could be *forever*
prohibited as marriage partners for Jews. The resulting split and

decimation of world Jewry would be a catastrophe of incalculably tragic proportions.

Nonhalachic Conversions

In the second half of the twentieth century, especially in the United States, large numbers of interfaith marriages have taken place. Non-Jewish partners have either not converted to Judaism, or have undergone conversion procedures not in accordance with the stringent requirements of *halachah;* marriages have been performed by rabbis who do not observe *halachah* or do not accept its binding nature, or who are not conversant with the relevant regulations of Jewish law. Reform Judaism, for example, which denies the validity of *halachah,* has few, if any, requirements for conversion, and these do not conform to *halachah.* In the words of a leading American Reform rabbi: "In Reform Judaism the offspring of a religiously mixed couple, if he or she celebrates Bar/Bat Mitzvah and/or confirmation, is considered to be in every respect a Jew, without undergoing formal conversion."[6]

In 1983, the Central Conference of American Rabbis, the Reform movement's rabbinic body, adopted a resolution declaring "that the child of one Jewish parent is under the presumption of Jewish descent."[7] Reform Judaism considers a child of a mixed marriage to be automatically Jewish if he participates in acts of formal Jewish identification, such as being given a Hebrew name.[8] While Reform recognizes the children of such religiously mixed couples as Jewish in every respect, *halachah* does not.[9] Jewish law, therefore, strictly prohibits marrying such "Jews" or their descendants.

Nonhalachic Divorces

The problem is more severe with respect to divorce. Of the large and growing number of divorces in recent years among American Jews, most were not conducted in accordance with the procedures of Jewish law. Often they were simply civil divorces—considered perfectly valid by civil law and by Reform Judaism — or were performed by rabbis who do not observe *halachah*. The halachic rules relating to divorce are intricate, requiring specialized knowledge and expertise. A rabbi who is not expert in this area and/or does not subscribe to *halachah* himself, cannot perform a credible halachic divorce.

According to Jewish law, if the couple does not undergo a valid halachic divorce, they are considered still to be married,[10] and thus any subsequent marriage into which either of the partners enters is illegal and void. Further, in Jewish law the partners of such a "remarriage" are considered to be living in an illicit, adulterous relationship. Moreover, they are prohibited by Jewish law from *ever* marrying each other — even in the event that there is a subsequent valid Jewish divorce to legally terminate the first marriage.[11]

The *Mamzer*

As for the children of this second union, Jewish law considers them to be *mamzerim,* or illegitimate "bastards." A *mamzer* is not, as is often erroneously believed, the issue of an unmarried couple. A child born out of wedlock is not, according to Jewish law, a bastard. Although a sexual relationship between an unmarried couple is prohibited in *halachah,* a child born in such a relationship is "legitimate," and neither its status nor its rights are in any way impaired. The parents of such a child are permitted to marry each other.

A *mamzer* is the issue of a *prohibited* (adulterous or incestuous) relationship,[12] or is the child a woman has with another partner when she did not, before marrying the father, terminate her first marriage with a proper Jewish divorce. The parents who commit incest or adultery — or who "marry" following a civil or improper Jewish divorce — are forbidden by Jewish law from ever marrying each other legally — no matter what subsequent steps they might take to try to rectify the previous error.

Jews are strictly forbidden to marry the sons or daughters of such a union.[13] In the words of the Torah, "A *mamzer* may not enter into the community of Israel, even unto the tenth generation."[14] A *mamzer* is only allowed to marry another *mamzer*[15] or a proselyte.[16] Even the descendants of a *mamzer* — children, grandchildren, and great-grandchildren — remain forever proscribed as marital partners. A *mamzer* has a status inferior to that of a non-Jew who converts to Judaism. The non-Jewish convert is considered a normative Jew in virtually every respect. Although in Jewish tradition it is abhorrent to proselytize, sincere converts are welcomed, and Jews are permitted to marry converts or their descendants.[17] However, there is no way that a *mamzer* or his descendants may ever attain normative Jewish status; thus, there is no way that he or his descendants may ever be permitted to marry normative Jews according to Jewish law.[18]

The Talmud asks, *"Mahu mamzer?"* — What is a *mamzer?* — and replies, *"mum zar"* a strange (or alien) blemish.[19] The *Sefer HaHinuch* explains the concept of *mamzer* by contrasting it to the holiness of marriage.[20] A *mamzer* is conceived in a state of impurity and unholiness,[21] through sexual relations forbidden by the Torah and punishable by death. He is therefore perceived by the Sages as an alien implantation,[22] who owes his existence to the physical order of things but not the moral.[23] Since Judaism attaches great importance to the moral strength of the family unit and the *mamzer* is the embodiment of an immoral, antimarriage, antifamily act, the *mamzer* may not marry into the Jewish family and the Jewish community.

Similarly, a man who engages in sexual relations with his mother or sister or another man's wife, violates human decency and embodies human degeneracy. The children of these unions are also *mamzerim*.

In stipulating that the offspring of all such immoral unions are not free of the spiritual blemish of the act, that the act has not ended with them, and that even their children's children will be penalized by society, the Torah provides a powerful social deterrent against aberrant and immoral behavior.[24] It thus provides a bulwark to protect the Jewish family as a cornerstone of Jewish survival.

Marriage and Divorce — For the Specialists

Because of the potentially serious consequences of improper divorce, the *Code of Jewish Law* strictly prohibits rabbis from performing divorces — and marriages — unless they are experts in all the related laws. The *Code* condemns, in the strictest of terms, rabbis who do perform them: "They can easily err and permit forbidden marriages, and thereby cause the proliferation of *mamzerim* in Israel."[25]

Both conversion to Judaism and the dissolution of Jewish marriages constitute major changes in personal status. Jewish law lays down a detailed set of requirements and procedures to ensure that the desired changes are legal and binding.[26] Any ceremony, however elaborate or impressive, which falls short of the strict letter of the law, renders the new status invalid according to *halachah*.

Many European noblemen and former aristocrats can trace their lineage back for centuries. Americans, for instance, like to boast of ancestors who came to America on the Mayflower. But the Jewish people do not define their heritage merely in terms of a physical line of known ancestors. What is important is how well the spiritual lineage has remained intact through the generations. Every new marriage is perceived as having the potential either to reinforce that spiritual lineage, or to dilute it.

Marriages Forbidden to a Man by Jewish Law

• A non-Jewess.[27]
• One whose conversion to Judaism, or the conversion of whose mother, grandmother, or other female ancestors was not performed according to *halachah* by a competent rabbi or rabbinic court loyal to *halachah*.[28]
• A Karaite, even if she converts to normative Judaism.[29]
• A married woman, or one who has not had a Jewish divorce performed according to *halachah* by a competent rabbi or a rabbinic court loyal to *halachah*.[30] (In the latter case, her legal status would be equivalent to that of a woman still married to her previous husband. Her subsequent "remarriage," therefore, is considered invalid in Jewish law, and her relationship with her second "husband" is considered an adulterous one.)
• One who is the child of an adulterous or incestuous union, or of a divorced and remarried woman whose divorce was only civil or was not performed according to *halachah* by a competent rabbi or rabbinic court loyal to *halachah* (a *mamzeret*).[31]
• A woman with whom he committed adultery.[32]

- A woman who has committed adultery with another.[33]
- A childless widow when the brother of her deceased husband is still alive, and a *halitzah*[34] ceremony has not been performed.[35]
- His divorced wife, if she had remarried another man and has, in the interim, been widowed or divorced.[36]
- His former wife, if he had divorced her because she had committed adultery, even if she had not remarried in the interim.[37]
- His mother, his grandmother, his maternal grandfather's mother, his paternal grandfather's mother.[38]
- His stepmother, his father's stepmother, his mother's step-mother.[39]
- His daughter, granddaughter, and their descendants.[40]
- His sister, his half sister.[41]
- His aunt, his paternal grandfather's sister, his maternal grandmother's sister.[42]
- His wife's mother, grandmother, and forebears.[43]
- His wife's daughter, granddaughter, and descendants.[44]
- His wife's son's daughter and his wife's daughter's daughter.[45]
- His former wife's sister, if he is divorced. (However, if his ex-wife had died, he may marry her sister.)[46]
- His brother's wife, his half brother's wife; the sister or half sister of his divorced wife during her lifetime.[47]
- His father's paternal or maternal brother's wife, his mother's paternal or maternal brother's wife, his paternal grandfather's paternal brother's wife, his paternal grandfather's sister, his maternal grandmother's sister.[48]
- His son's wife, his grandson's wife, the wives of all his male descendants.[49]
- His son's daughter, his daughter's daughter.[50]
- If he is a *kohen* he may not marry a divorcee, a *halitzah* widow, a woman who has engaged in adultery, a convert, or a woman who has had sexual relations with a gentile.[51] (If she has engaged in premarital or extramarital sexual relations, a rabbi should be consulted.)

Marriages Forbidden to a Woman by Jewish Law

- A non-Jew.[52]
- One whose conversion to Judaism, or the conversion of whose

mother, grandmother, or other female forebears was not performed according to *halachah* by a competent rabbi or rabbinic court loyal to *halachah*.[53]

• A Karaite, even if he converts to normative Judaism.[54]

• A married man, or one who has not had a Jewish divorce performed according to *halachah* by a competent rabbi or rabbinic court loyal to *halachah*.[55]

• One who is the child of an adulterous or incestuous union, or of a divorced and remarried woman whose divorce was only civil or was not performed according to *halachah* by a competent rabbi or rabbinic court loyal to *halachah* (a *mamzer*).[56]

• A man with whom she committed adultery.[57]

• Her divorced husband, if he had remarried another woman and she had died or they were divorced in the interim.[58]

• Her father, grandfather, and his forebears; her stepfather, the husband of her grandmother and of her forebears.[59]

• Her son, grandson, great-grandson; her son-in-law, the husband of her granddaughter and descendants.[60]

• Her husband's father, grandfather, the father of her father-in-law and forebears, the father of her mother-in-law.[61]

• Her former husband's brother or half brother, if she is divorced.[62] (If her husband had died, she may marry his brother.)

• Her brother, her half brother; her sister's or half sister's divorced husband during her sister's lifetime; her nephew.[63]

• A *kohen*, if she is a convert or a divorcee.[64]

Marriages Permitted to a Man among His Relatives

• His stepsister.[65]
• His father-in-law's former wife.[66]
• His niece.[67]
• His brother's, half brother's, or sister's daughter-in-law.[68]
• His cousin.[69]
• His stepson's wife, since divorced or widowed.[70]
• His deceased wife's sister.[71]

Marriages Permitted to a Woman among Her Relatives

• Her stepbrother.[72]
• Her stepmother's former husband.[73]

- Her cousin.[74]
- Her deceased sister's or half sister's husband.[75]
- Her uncle.[76]

Through the list of prohibited and permissible marriages, the Torah weeds out basically improper candidates for a Jew to marry. Once the general prohibitions are noted, we may now turn our attention to the search for that mate who best fits a person's specific needs, personality, and circumstances.

3

Choosing the Right Mate

The Big Gamble: Society's Guide for Finding a Marriage Partner

Today's high divorce rate and many broken homes should come as no surprise considering the haphazard way most people meet their mates. What is surprising is that, in this modern age of liberation and emancipation, few people question the primitive, but socially accepted tradition of chance meetings which result in marriage. From the low success rate of these marriages, it would seem a new approach to finding marriage partners is long overdue; nevertheless, the belief in random romance persists.

The romantic method of finding a mate is based on chance, unrealistic idealization, and emotion. It is conditional upon two rules: first, you must never admit to an honest interest in marrying or in finding a suitable marital partner; second, you must meet your spouse-to-be by chance, never by design. An organized plan, explicit intent, and premeditation are unheard of.

If anyone should suggest buying a car or a house in this haphazard manner, he would be heartily ridiculed. Purchasing either one requires a systematic search. Selecting a business partner requires a thorough exploration of every aspect of his personality, his assets, his past business record, and his reputation. No thoughtful, intelligent person would enter into a business partnership with another on the basis of a chance meeting and subsequent superficial appraisals.

Yet, when making what is probably the most vital decision of a lifetime, most people do not dream of going about it systematically. Is this not absurd when you consider that a marriage, which involves living with one another in the closest intimacy, raising a family, and establishing a major economic partnership, would be initiated by luck and a chance meeting?

It seems that never do people act as irrationally as when they are choosing a mate. Rarely, in this regard, do they question the absurdity of relying on chance. How many people would risk their money wagering on the successful outcome of so speculative a venture as a marriage resulting from an accidental meeting? Yet, a high percentage of failed marriages are the direct result of the haphazard system that is society's norm for choosing a mate. This system, reinforced by romantic novels, films, television, and the press, deceives people, and prevents them from seeing the obvious — the common-sense idea that selecting a partner for marriage requires a carefully thought-out, systematic plan.

Making a Good Match: Like Splitting the Red Sea

Finding the right mate is far from easy. In fact, the *Midrash* says making a good match is difficult even for God:

A Roman matron asked R. Yossi bar Halafta (second century C.E.): "How long did it take the Holy One to create heaven and earth?"

"Six days," he replied, "as it is written, 'For in six days the Lord created heaven and earth.' "[1]

"All agree that God created the world in six days," she affirmed, "but what has He been doing since then?"

"He matches up couples and makes marriages," replied R. Yossi, "and then He places them in their homes."

"And this is His occupation?" she exclaimed. "Even I can do this. I'll take my slaves and match them up in no time."

R. Yossi replied, "This may seem easy to you, but for the Holy One it is as difficult as splitting the Red Sea."

What did the matron do? She took one thousand male slaves and one thousand female slaves and lined them up in rows. She said:

"You wed that one, and you wed this one." She married them all off in one night. But no sooner did the couples get together than they began quarreling and attacking one another. The next morning, they came before the matron with complaints — and wounds; one with a bruised head, one with an eye missing, another with a fractured hand, and another with a broken leg.

"What is wrong with all of you?" asked the exasperated matron.

"I don't want him," said one.

"I don't want her," said another.

She sent for R. Yossi bar Halafta and told him: "There is no God like your God. You were correct, and your Torah is indeed true, beautiful and praiseworthy."[2]

If making a good match is difficult for God, how much more so is it for humans? Despite all his wisdom, King Solomon confessed that one thing too marvelous for him to fathom was "the way of a man with a woman."[3] The mystery of marriage, the combination of ingredients that make for good "chemistry," lies with God. Humans can "play God" and make matches, but to be successful they need to follow certain guidelines, and to leave the rest in God's hands.

The sensible approach is for two people, before they contemplate marriage, to analyze and evaluate thoroughly their emotional and intellectual traits, to determine if and how they complement each other. Even more difficult, they need to look with foresight into the future to guess how life's ravages might affect their union. That means considering not only how they stand now in their youth and strength, but how they will appear after many years have passed. In difficult times, will they strengthen each other, or will their union crumble under the constant tests of stability that every marriage faces? Do they have the ability to establish a joint, sound, and consistent value system for their future family?

Taken together, this approach requires enormous sensitivity, foresight, and good sense, and must seem a tremendous weight for a young person to bear. Thus, it is no wonder that the Jewish Sages went to great lengths to guide the young person in seeking a mate.

Career versus Early Marriage

In connection with marriage, the Sages expect a man to seek out a woman, because the man is the more outgoing and aggressive of the two sexes. In Genesis, a passage containing the "marriage clause" corroborates this idea: "Therefore shall a man forsake his father and his mother and cleave to his wife."[4]

However, the character traits the Talmud recommends as necessary or desirable in a mate are universal — applicable to both men and women. Among traditional Jews, soberly and diligently, a young man preparing for his future is taught to establish his priorities. Which comes first, a wife and family, or a career? Scripture advises: "Prepare your work outside, and make it fit for yourself in the field; and afterwards build your house."[5]

In other words, a man should first establish himself financially, and then find a wife. The *Zohar* advises:

> These days, when everyone is concerned with earning a livelihood, a person should prepare his house first and his income, and only afterwards should he take a wife. And then he should serve his Creator and occupy himself with Torah, in accordance with what our Sages said: "If there is no wheat, there can be no Torah."[6] . . . One can deduce this from the example the Holy One, Blessed Be He, set: First He prepared a house (the world) and the sources of sustenance (trees, plants, fruits, vegetables, animals) for humankind; and only then did He create man and woman and have them bring children into the world. . . .[7]

The Sages thus caution a man to marry only when he can support his wife and family, as he pledges to do in the *ketubah,* the marriage contract, since to do otherwise would be irresponsible and would place his wife and children in a precarious position. According to Jewish law, a person may not even acquire an animal or a bird if he cannot properly feed and tend it.[8]

In his code of law, Maimonides has this to say: "Intelligent people first establish a source of livelihood, then buy a home and only afterwards marry, as it is written. However, foolish people reverse this order. First they marry; afterwards, if they can afford it, they buy a dwelling. Then, at the end of their days, they seek to learn a craft — or end up being supported by charity . . ."[9]

If a man decides to marry before he has at least partially established himself, he may find himself struggling to complete his studies and to build a profession during the awkward and delicate period of early marriage. Under such conditions, the chances of marital and professional difficulties are seriously escalated.

Conversely, it is common today for a woman to postpone marriage in order to pursue a career. When she finally does marry, she is often more career- than family-oriented. Also, when this occurs, she may find it difficult to set aside her personal ambitions in order to give priority to her family's needs.

Jewish tradition distinguishes between the priorities of a man and those of a woman. A man is told to marry only after he has established his livelihood. The Jewish woman is free to marry or not to marry, as she chooses. However, she is encouraged to marry early and to place family before career.

Let us examine the situation where, upon marrying, the husband is moving in the direction of economic viability. The wife, even if she is working, has made the decision that her family will take precedence over her career. This will reduce the chance for familial stress, whereas the chances for marital harmony are maximized.

Notwithstanding these considerations, however, Judaism does not favor postponing marriages unduly and delaying fulfillment of this *mitzvah*. The Sages urge a man to marry early, setting eighteen to twenty years as the ideal age, expecting that by then he will have established some financial roots. If he is a full-time student of Torah,[10] he may postpone marriage until he is twenty-five.[11] Maimonides explains:

> If one studies Torah and busies himself with it, and is concerned lest his burden of supporting a wife result in a diminution of his Torah study, he may postpone marriage on the basis of the principle that one who is involved in performing one *mitzvah* is freed from the duty of fulfilling another. This is especially true when the *mitzvah* is that of Torah study.[12]

Maimonides' decision is based on a passage in the Talmud: "With a millstone around his neck [the responsibility of supporting a wife and family] how can one study Torah?"[13]

Beginning the Search

Where does one begin to search for the right partner? It may be best to start with prayer. R. Isaac Aboab teaches in the *M'norat HaMaor:*

"Just as a man should pray to God that He should provide for him and protect him, so too is it meritorious to beseech God to find him a good, proper, and peaceable woman."[14]

A great deal of effort, in addition to prayer, is required if a "good, proper, and peaceable woman" is to be found. A person's true nature is not readily revealed. Although early marriage is advocated by the Sages, they caution against hasty marriages. They maintain that a man, before he makes an educated decision, should carefully examine the character of his prospective bride. The Talmud counsels: *"M'ton u'n'siv it'ta*—Wait before you marry a woman[15] [until you can investigate and examine her deeds to determine whether or not she is evil or quarrelsome: *Rashi*]."[16]

According to the Sages, a woman's deeds determine whether or not she will make a good wife, following the premise that a person's nature is determined less by his ideas and beliefs than by his* acts. Not what a person thinks, but how he behaves is important.[17] The Sages advise a man who wants to live a long life to marry a good woman. As Ben Sira says:

> Happy is the man who has a good wife; the number of his days are doubled.[18]

Commenting on this talmudic paraphrase of Ben Sira's advice, Rashi, the medieval exegete, says that such a man's lifetime is not actually doubled, but the quality of his life with such a wife is so rich that it seems as if it is twice as long.[19]

A Woman of Valor

The Sages appear to be stating the obvious: A man should seek a good wife. But what, from Judaism's perspective, consitutes a "good wife"? Solomon, in his description in Proverbs of the *aishet hayil,* the "valorous woman," describes some of her attributes.

> Who can find a valorous woman? Her worth is far above pearls. Her husband's heart trusts in her. . . . She does him good all the days of

---

*Unless specifically referring to a man, the use of the masculine pronouns throughout does not presume maleness but may refer to either male or female.

her life. . . . She extends her hands to the poor and needy. . . . She
opens her mouth with wisdom and the teaching of acts of love is on
her tongue. . . . She looks well after the needs of her household and
eats not the bread of idleness. . . . Her children rise and call her
blessed, and her husband praises her: "Many daughters have done
excellently, but you excel them all". . . . Grace is false, and beauty is
but a superficial vanity: a woman who reveres the Lord — she shall be
praised. . . .[20]

To the young man choosing his life's partner, it is difficult and
bewildering to decide which qualities of character are most important in a woman. In this elegy, the wise king delineates a number of
important qualities a man should look for in seeking his ideal mate.
His final conclusion is that the ideal wife and mother, the *truly*
valorous woman, is she who reveres God.

The ideal quality to be sought, then, is *yir'at HaShem,* reverence of
the Lord (also referred to as *yir'at Shamayim,* reverence of heaven),[21]
one of Judaism's chief virtues. The Sages teach: "Everything
depends on reverence of the Lord, and even the entire Torah is of
no use unless it is accompanied by *yir'at Shamayim,* for it is the very
peg upon which everything hangs. . . . Nothing in the world
outweighs such reverence — neither silver, nor gold, nor pearls."[22]

What makes *yir'at HaShem* supreme is that through it one attains
all other desirable attributes.[23] Scripture directs: "After the Lord
your God shall you walk and Him shall you revere."[24]

By practicing the principle of *imitatio Dei,*[25] a person who "walks
after God" reveres God and emulates His attributes of love, justice,
compassion, truth, and charity; these traits then become ingrained
in a person and are expressed in his daily life.

Yir'at HaShem, then, is the first and foremost characteristic the
Jew is counselled to look for in a marriage partner. External
attractions ultimately fade, but a sound character is impervious to
time. In King David's words: *"Yir'at HaShem t'horah, omedet la'ad —*
Reverence of God is pure, enduring forever."[27]

The Place of Beauty

Although Solomon called beauty in a woman a "superficial vanity,"
it is not, in Judaism, considered undesirable.[28] On the contrary:[29]

the Bible praises the Jewish matriarchs, Sarah,[30] Rebecca,[31] and Rachel[32] for their beauty and comments favorably on the beauty of various other women.[33]

The prospective bridegroom's opinion about his bride's appearance, therefore, is a legitimate factor in his decision. Nevertheless, if his decision to marry a woman is based in large measure on her beauty, the Sages sanction it only grudgingly[34] as a concession to man's frailty and his susceptibility to sensual desire.[35] They go so far as to blame[36] Absalom's premature death[37] on the fact that David married Absalom's mother primarily for her beauty.[38] The *Sefer Hasidim* derives from this that a man who marries a woman for her beauty will eventually pay a heavy price for doing so.[39] The Sages definitely do not consider it legitimate for a man's basic concern to be that *others* should find his wife beautiful.[40]

Beauty is skin deep, and a pretty, graceful exterior can cover serious personal blemishes. An attractive face may reflect inner beauty and kindness — or it can mask vanity and self-absorption. It requires a discerning eye to see beyond a pleasing surface to the quality of the woman within.[41]

The *aishet hayil* of whom Solomon speaks is not a passive figure; she actively and boldly runs her household, cares for her loved ones, and maintains a high moral standard in her home. Most important, as a God-fearing woman, she is committed to Jewish tradition. Ideally, she possesses the formal training and education necessary to prepare her for her role as a wife and mother who is to raise the children in the Jewish tradition. Even if she lacks a formal Jewish education, her husband trusts in her genuine faith and good sense, in accordance with the dictum, *Reshit hochmah yir'at HaShem* — Reverence of God is the beginning of wisdom.[42] Conversely, a woman who is not God-fearing, no matter what her intellectual attainments are, will not be able to give her children a meaningful, traditional, Jewish upbringing.

The Importance of Religious Observance

Naturally, choosing a marriage partner on the basis of *yir'at Shamayim* (piety) works both ways. Judaism advises a woman to study carefully a man's behavior to determine *his* allegiance to Jewish tradition.

It is important for a couple contemplating marriage to be candid with each other regarding their mutual commitment to Jewish observance and practice. This means discussing in advance and in detail their respective levels of observance and commitment to Jewish traditions. What will be the nature of the Sabbath celebration in their home? How will the festivals be celebrated? What kind of Jewish education will they give their children? A less than clear understanding in these areas could be responsible for future marital problems.

In the grip of strong emotional feelings for one's chosen partner, it is easy to disregard his or her religious standards when they are less committed to Jewish observance. It is easy to harbor the illusion that things will work out of their own accord, and that after marriage one will be able to bring one's spouse's views closer to one's own. All too often, however, these expectations are not realized. The resultant discord from these unrealistic expectations could have been prevented by extensive discussion beforehand on each other's views and practices.

What is also important to look for in a partner is not only how he/she relates to matters concerning God, such as prayer and religious Jewish observances, but also in the Jewish laws relating to ethics and conduct toward one's fellow man. In Judaism, piety involves both relations with God and with one's fellow man.

Consistency in views and practices is especially important for a couple contemplating marriage, because of the effect on the children they may have. When the couple presents a united front in their approach to a Jewish life-style and when they serve as living examples of their beliefs, the chances for their children to feel secure, confident, and to be themselves able to pass on that life-style, are naturally much greater.

A business partnership entails dividing responsibilities. Before entering into such a relationship the principals discuss in meticulous detail every aspect of their future relationship. No one would agree to merge his interests with another person's in a supposedly equal partnership if their resulting interests turned out to be substantially different. A marriage is obviously a much more serious partnership. It makes sense, then, for potential marriage partners to discuss thoroughly their religious ideals and practices, as well as their moral and ethical values. A person's religious standards affect his life-partner in innumerable aspects of daily life. Therefore, they should be examined beforehand. A Jewish home, filled with the beauty of the Jewish way of living, can only be built where both partners are equally dedicated to its proper establishment as a spiritually Jewish structure.

How Important Is the Partner's Family?

Solomon's advice to young men to disregard the externals of a woman has historically found an echo among the young women themselves. As a fascinating Mishnah in the talmudic tractate *Ta'anit* proclaims:[43]

> There were no happier days in Israel than the fifteenth of Av and Yom Kippur. On those days the daughters of Jerusalem would all go out in borrowed white garments [— so as not to embarrass those who lacked fine clothes —] . . . and dance in the vineyards. And they would cry out: Young man, raise your eyes and see what you will choose for yourself as a wife. Do not set your eyes on beauty; set them on a good family. For grace is false and beauty is but a superficial vanity; a woman who reveres the Lord, she shall be praised.[44]

In the Mishnah, the notion of the "good family" is often known as *yihus,* pedigree or lineage, and it is considered a significant traditional priority in Judaism. The Talmud states that the *Sh'chinah,* the Divine Presence, rests on the families in Israel with this characteristic.[45]

Seeking a marriage partner from a good family is an old tradition. Scripture records that when Abraham wanted a bride for his son Isaac, he sent his trusted servant Eliezer to seek out a suitable maiden. Upon meeting Rebecca, Eliezer asked her, "Whose daughter are you?"[46] The Sages counsel: "Marry into a good family to ensure good offspring."[47]

Why is family so important? Surely it is the prospective mate (not his parents) who is important. After all, it is the spouse with whom a person will live, not his or her family.

A thorough review of the early influences that shape a person's character helps one to draw some educated conclusions. No one grows up in a vacuum; character does not develop in isolation. Close relatives exert an indelible influence on a child's development, and play a vital role in forming his character. In his earliest years, the family constitutes the child's entire world. Throughout his formative years, the family is the center of his existence.

Throughout a person's life, the influence of the family environment manifests itself in a person's behavior, speech, thought patterns, and attitude to life. These influences of home and family remain with a person long after he has left home. This is why it makes sense to get to know a potential mate's family before determining what kind of spouse he or she will be.

Indeed, the good family is preferable to the successful, prominent one. The Sages specifically advise a young man to seek "the daughter of deeds rather than the daughter of a prominent family."[48]

> Not in every home has proper training been emphasized, and this is expressed in different outlooks . . . in overly rich and wasteful life-styles, in the spoiling of children, and in a lack of proper training of children to enable them to withstand the trials of life. There are also parents who are not accustomed to honoring people properly . . . and one should suspect that they have imprinted their own behavior on their children. It is clear that it is more difficult to get along with a spouse who thinks mainly of himself and not of the next person. It is important, therefore, to determine the nature of the training in the home of the prospective mate, and, in particular, the nature of the behavior of the parents toward one another, for this is a working model for their children.[49]

Looking at Close Relatives

Because children reared in the same home are exposed to similar influences, a woman's siblings can reveal much about her.[50] Traditionally, males are considered to be more outgoing than their sisters, therefore their true character is more readily evident. The Sages thus advise would-be grooms: "He who marries a woman must first examine her brothers."[51]

The *Sefer Hasidim* states that anyone who could have married a woman with righteous brothers but chose instead to marry the sister of wicked men will pay the heavy price of having wicked children.[52]

The Sages also advise women sizing up prospective bridegrooms that: "Most young men resemble their mother's brothers."[53]

The Quiet Family

Rashi has this guideline for the young man or woman seeking a mate:

> Look for the quiet family. As a rule, quarrelsome families may actually be suspect regarding their authenticity as Jews. Because of their questionable descent [from elements which infiltrated the community], a serious defect which they try to conceal, hatred is implanted in them, and they are quarrelsome. However, the authentic Jewish families . . . are known to be quiet ones. Indeed, by their very calm repose, they demonstrate that they are legitimately Jewish. Therefore, whoever wishes to determine the legitimacy of a Jewish family need only ascertain whether the family is quiet or quarrelsome.[54]

According to the Sages, while most nations customarily engage in warfare and altercation, the Jewish people are characterized by a more peaceful and studious nature. A quarrelsome Jewish family reflects, on a smaller scale, the warlike behavior of other nations. Consequently, their very Jewishness is suspect.[55]

Maimonides goes even further, and warns Jews against marrying into certain families if they are considered defective:

> All Jewish families have a *hezkat kashrut* [i.e., may ordinarily be presumed to be Jewish]. However, if you see families that are constantly fighting with others, or a quarrelsome family, or if someone is always arguing with everyone and is insolent—all these are suspect [as not being Jewish], and one must shun them, for the signs indicate that their lineage is not pure. This applies as well to anyone who always casts aspersions on families or individuals and calls them *mamzerim*—illegitimate. He himself, therefore, is suspect of being a *mamzer*.[56] Anyone who is insolent or cruel or hates others, and does not act lovingly toward others is suspect of being a Gibeonite [i.e., non-Jewish].[57]

Three Vital Traits in a Mate

As we have said, it is important to look for a mate who comes from a family with fine qualities. Even more basic, however, is to ascertain that the family is authentically *Jewish*. Maimonides disqualifies families who display insolence or cruelty. The Talmud identifies indigenous "Jewish traits":

> Whoever has compassion for God's creations is of a certainty of the seed of our father Abraham. Anyone who does not have compassion on God's creations is certainly not of the seed of Abraham. . . . Three signs indicate membership in the Jewish nation: Jews are compassionate, they are modest, and they perform acts of love for their fellow humans.[58]

Whether these three qualities: *rahmanut, baishanut,* and *g'milut hasadim*[59] (compassion, modesty, and performing acts of love for others) are "natural" Jewish traits, or characteristics acquired because Judaism obliges Jews to behave morally, they are essential to look for in a prospective marriage partner.[60] The *Sefer Hasidim* declares[61] that these three qualities make up Solomon's proverbial "threefold cord that is not quickly broken."[62] In a similar vein the Talmud adds: "All [sincere candidates for conversion to Judaism] who possess these three traits are worthy of acceptance as converts by the Jewish nation."[63]

What about the Convert?

Judaism perceives intermarriage as a transgression — and tragedy — of immense proportions. Through this act, a Jew in effect cuts himself off from a chain of tradition thousands of years old. Conversion *to* Judaism, however, while not encouraged, is recognized and fully accepted, provided one converts for genuine and not ulterior motives, and that conversion is performed according to strict halachic procedures by a duly authorized, halachically observant rabbi.

Marriage is often the motive behind insincere conversion; if a Jew and a non-Jew wish to marry, conversion to Judaism may make the marriage more acceptable to the Jewish partner and his family. Jews are forbidden to marry such "converts" or their descendants.

A person who sincerely accepts Judaism and whose conversion was not related to marriage with a Jew, is called a *ger tzedek,* righteous proselyte. He is considered Jewish in every respect, and Jews may marry him or his descendants as they would other Jews. In marrying a *ger* or a descendant of a *ger,* one should carefully examine the family's background to determine that they are *rahmanim, baishanim,* and *gom'lay hasadim,* just as when marrying a Jew by birth. While it is forbidden to marry someone who converts to Judaism for the sole purpose of marrying a Jew, the Sages hold that marriage to a *sincere* convert from a good family is preferable even to marriage into a Jewish family which lacks the desirable character traits. The *Sefer Hasidim* declares:[64]

> It is preferable for a good-hearted person to marry a sincere convert who is good-hearted and comes from a family whose members are modest and perform acts of brotherly love and who conduct their affairs honestly and pleasantly, than to marry an ordinary Israelite from a family lacking these attributes.[65] From the proselyte's family will come *tzadikim,* righteous and good people.[66]

The highest ideals of Judaism are manifested through modesty, honesty, compassion, and love that is displayed through acts of kindness. These qualities also embody the ideal attributes of the ideal Jewish life's partner.

Hesed in a Woman

When the time came for his son, Isaac, to marry, the patriarch Abraham set a precedent to which the Sages often refer in their discussion of traits to be sought in a wife. Although Abraham had converted many pagans to monotheism, he preferred to take for his son a wife who came from relatives in a distant land[67] rather than from a family he had converted, because his relatives, he knew, had the desirable qualities of modesty, compassion, and brotherly love.[68] He entrusted his servant Eliezer with the important task of finding a wife for Isaac,[69] the woman who would be no less than the mother of the Jewish nation.

How Eliezer went about his momentous mission and what characteristics he looked for in the prospective wife tell us a lot about Judaism's attitudes and values. R. Samson Raphael Hirsch (1808–1888), the German rabbi and philosopher, comments:

> Purity of character was the dowry the first Jewish bride had to bring with her. . . . Not by her wealth, not by her physical charms, not by her intellectual attainments would he recognize her, but by her character, by the goodness of her heart, by her readiness to help others; in a word, by her *g'milut hesed,* her acts of love extended to others; by that trait which is the outstanding characteristic of the sons of Abraham and Sarah. He would look for a girl whom he would request to give him a drink from her pitcher and who, in her reply, would not only accede to his request, but would also of her own accord offer to give water to his ten camels . . . who could feel not only for humans but also for weary and thirsty beasts . . . and translate [this feeling] into action and speedy help; the maiden in whose heart burns a spark of the holy fire of human love. . . .[70]

When Rebecca demonstrated that vital Jewish trait of *hesed,* Eliezer knew he had found the girl for Isaac. She discerned and empathized with the suffering of both man and animal, and expressed those feelings tangibly by giving water to all of them, although this entailed considerable effort.

Hesed means feeling another's discomfort and pain and demonstrating it through action. A person who has this attribute is a compassionate, selfless, and giving person who would continually be willing to give love to a spouse and children. Selfishness is the opposite of *hesed.* The person who is overly self-concerned will not easily and consistently give love to the marriage partner and children. This is why it is so important to look for *hesed* in a potential mate.

According to the *Midrash,* Abraham's other son, Ishmael, did not do as well as Isaac when he began married life.

> Three years after Abraham sent Ishmael away, he longed to see his son and sought him out in Paran. When Abraham arrived at his son's tent he found Ishmael away. He asked Ishmael's wife for some water,

but she refused to give him any. Abraham said: "When your husband returns home tell him that an old man from Philistia came to see him, but finding him absent, offered this advice — the pegs of your tent should be changed." Ishmael grasped the allusion to his wicked wife, and he divorced her and wed another woman, Fatima.

The following year Abraham again traveled to see his son and found Ishmael absent. Without waiting for his request, Fatima offered him hospitality and urged him to partake of food and drink. Abraham told her: "When your husband returns home, tell him his tent pegs are excellent, and he should retain them." Upon returning home and hearing Abraham's message, Ishmael thanked his gracious wife and blessed the Lord who had sent him so admirable a wife.[71]

In the Footsteps of the Matriarchs

Rebecca is held up as a model for Jewish women, who are expected to follow in her footsteps. The Sage Hillel taught that when fulfilling the *mitzvah* of gladdening bride and groom and dancing before a bride at a wedding, she should be praised with the words, *kalah na'ah vahasudah* — the bride is pleasant and performs acts of lovingkindness.[72]

The Sages teach that *hesed* in a wife supersedes other desirable virtues. A woman possessing only *hesed* is preferable to one who lacks it, but has many other virtues. The Sages declare:

> Although Isaac's wife was required to continue the work of our mother Sarah, to convert women to the belief in one God in the world, nevertheless, Eliezer did not seek a woman who mastered religious philosophy and kindred skills, but one who mastered *hesed*. The one who is a master of *hesed* and is not selfish is prepared to receive all of the truth and to give it to others as well.[73]

The story of Rebecca concludes like this: "Isaac brought her into the tent of his mother Sarah, and he married Rebecca; and she became his wife, and he loved her, and Isaac was comforted after his mother."[74]

Rashi comments that Rebecca continued to observe in her home the same traditions that Sarah practiced.[75] Onkelos (the second-century proselyte who rendered the Bible into Aramaic) translates the passage as follows: "And Isaac brought her into his home, and when he saw that she was practicing those acts that his mother Sarah did, he took Rebecca to be his wife."[76]

Isaac found joy and comfort in his wife because she performed the same good deeds that distinguished his mother. From here we learn that the secret of marital happiness is finding a partner whose deeds are good. R. Akiva expresses this thought: "Who is the man who is wealthy? He who has a wife whose deeds are beautiful."[77]

Commenting on the verse in the Song of Songs, "You are beautiful, my beloved, you are beautiful,"[78] the Sages teach: "You are beautiful in your observance of the precepts; you are beautiful in your performance of deeds of lovingkindness."[79]

Why Modesty Is Desirable

Modesty is known as *tz'niut,* or *baishanut*—literally bashfulness. A *baishan* (m.), or *baishanit* (f.), is one who is easily shamed and embarrassed. In traditional Judaism, *baishanut* is considered an archetypically Jewish trait and is thought to be a major preventative against sin and a sign of good character. If a person feels shame, he can improve; a sense of shame is "a good sign."[80] The Sages declare: "Whoever commits iniquity and is ashamed of it afterwards, is forgiven all his sins."[81]

The *Sefer Hasidim* adds: "If not for the attribute of shame given to man by the Holy One, man would never be free of sin."[82]

Shame signifies an ability—and desire—to improve; you feel ashamed, because you know there is a better way to behave. Shame derives from a conviction of your own essential goodness and strength. The *M'norat HaMaor* teaches: "The most beautiful and most praiseworthy of traits in a woman is that she be modest."[83]

Tz'niut (modesty) is visibly demonstrated in dress and in behavior. Indeed it is that trait of modesty that has kept the Jewish people a distinct, viable nation over the years.

Traditional Jewish standards of dress for women allow for stylishness, and changes of fashions and styles, but include the element of modesty as an important, integral factor. No matter what the time of day or the season, someone immodestly dressed—in revealing or flamboyant clothing—goes against Jewish standards of propriety.

The ideal Jewish woman is neither a high-powered sophisticate nor a prude. In control of herself, she radiates self-respect, dignity, and reserve. Her refined appearance engenders refined speech and behavior.

The Talmud tells of the woman, Kimhit. Her seven sons had attained the high priesthood, she asserted, because of her *tz'niut*. She adds: "In all my days even the walls of my homes never saw the hairs of my head."[84]

From this the Sages derive that a modest Jewish woman is a source of power and wisdom:

> When a woman conducts herself modestly in her home, she is worthy of marriage to a *kohen gadol* (high priest), and also of raising children who would become high priests. When she is modest and in the inner world of her home [she is likened to a holy altar] just as the altar atones, so does she atone for her entire household. . . . When is a woman like a fruitful vine?[85] It is when she is ensconced modestly in the home. And if she is so, she will raise children who are worthy of being anointed with the oil of anointment [of the high priesthood].[86]

The Sages conclude that such a woman's children will grow up to be Torah scholars — "Masters of Torah, Masters of the Mishnah, and Masters of the Talmud."[87]

The opposite trait to *tz'niut* and *baishanut* is *azut*, which is the expression for boldness, vulgarity, lack of reserve, shamelessness, loud speech, grossness and rudeness, brazen or obstreperous behavior. The Sages compare *azut* to idol worship,[88] and blame Jerusalem's destruction on the prevalence of this trait among the Jews.[89]

The Sages teach that an *az panim* (a person with a "brazen face"), will most assuredly come to evil,[90] and end up as a transgressor.[91] They add: "The brazen one ends up in hell; the modest one in heaven."[92]

The major Torah scholars throughout Jewish history were characterized by their modesty and humility. Jewish philanthropists throughout the generations have often taken the quiet, hidden road, giving charity anonymously. Judaism praises the *matan b'seter,* the giving of charity discreetly. The donor's reason for giving is to alleviate the distress of the needy, not to receive credit and honor. Guided by *tz'niut,* he performs the *mitzvah lishmah,* for its own sake, and seeks no public recognition. "Humility," declares the Talmud, "is the greatest of all virtues."[93]

In the past, Jewish women lived within a protected circle where modesty was the rule. Today, however, with more and more women joining the work force, Jewish women must often work in environments antithetical to Jewish standards of modesty, and it is more difficult for them to maintain traditional Jewish standards. This is why it is so important for the man who wants to build a traditional Jewish family life to search for a woman with the moral fortitude and strength of character to remain modest, withstanding the influences of an increasingly immodest world.

It is no less important for a woman to look for a man who reflects the accepted values of Judaism while working where immodest dress, speech, and conduct are the accepted norms. The recent revolution in moral standards has made a life-style based on *tz'niut* a significant challenge.

Torah Study: How Essential Is It?

The Torah, the Jews' repository of wisdom, ethics, and morality, is the key to understanding the Jewish way of life. Traditionally, the Torah student was considered the most desirable husband because he occupied himself with Judaism's greatest calling. The Talmud declares:

> Of the following, a person will enjoy the fruits in this life, but they will remain as abiding riches in the world to come. Honoring father and mother; performing acts of love for one's fellow; hastening to the House of Study, morning and evening; performing acts of hospitality to the stranger; visiting the sick; dowering the bride; accompanying the dead at funerals; praying with devotion; and bringing peace between people. *However, the study of Torah is the equivalent of them all.*[94]

Torah study equals all of these other praiseworthy acts precisely because it leads to their fulfillment. A basic premise of Judaism is that one studies the Torah in order to fulfill its requirements; the scholar is also the doer. The Talmud teaches: *"G'dolah shimushah shel*

Torah yoter milimudah — To use (fulfill) the Torah is greater than to study it."[95]

A Jew is characterized by his deeds. The Torah scholar is not some pious ascetic who is removed from the world, for he, more than anyone else, knows the importance of performing God's will. The scholar is even permitted to neglect *limud Torah* (Torah study) if the opportunity arises to perform certain other *mitzvot*.[96]

The Talmud goes so far as to say that someone who busies himself with and immerses himself in Torah study to the exclusion of the performance of deeds of love is as though he had no God.[97] The Talmud cites two of the leading talmudic Sages, R. Hanina ben Teradion,[98] and Rava,[99] as having been punished severely — R. Hanina with death by immolation, and Rava with having his life cut short by one-third — because they were too involved in Torah study to devote sufficient time to performing deeds for others.

The Mishnah in *Avot* states: *"V'lo hamidrash ha'ikar ela hama'aseh* — Not the teaching is paramount, but rather the action thereon."[100]

Torah study is considered an important *mitzvah,* highly praise-worthy in its own right.[101] However, the emphasis is always on that learning which results in action. Time and again the Sages empha-size that the deed is the goal of study. *Talmud gadol, she'hatalmud mayvi liday ma'aseh* — "Learning is important, for it leads to action."[102] In the words of a daily prayer: *Lilmod u'l'lamed, lish'mor v'la'asot* — "to learn in order to teach, to observe, and to do."[103] The Sages declare that he who toils and labors at Torah study, devoting his life to the task but not devoting time to fulfilling the Torah, will not enjoy life, and on dying will inherit Gehenna.[104]

R. Jacob Emden, the eighteenth-century rabbinic scholar and ethical teacher phrases it like this: "Study and performance of Torah are dependent on one another. . . . One who studies Torah but not with the view of thereby fulfilling its precepts — what is the purpose of his life? If his Torah study is not for the sake of heaven, why does he bother to study altogether?"[105]

R. Samson Raphael Hirsch has this to say: "If our study is to . . . achieve its true purpose, then pursuing it, from the very beginning, must be to fulfill the Law of God.[106] Study and worship are but paths which lead to action. . . . A life of action, pervaded by the spirit of God — such a life is the only universal goal."[107]

The Desirable Son-in-Law

Characteristic of the Jew is his fervent desire to pursue knowledge. It is a derivative of the central place Torah study has always held in Jewish life. The Torah scholar, who had attained wisdom through intensive study of Torah, and who was himself a living model of Torah, was the most honored and respected member of the community. Jewish communities were traditionally headed by scholars. In Jewish protocol, a Torah scholar even takes precedence over a king![108] Maimonides explains: "The Sage is more of an asset to the nation than is the king."[109]

Similarly, according to Jewish law, a high priest who is ignorant must defer to a Torah scholar, even if the scholar is a *mamzer!*[110] R. Akiva even asserts that the verse, "You shall revere the Lord,"[111] means that Torah scholars should also be revered.[112]

It was natural, then, that Torah scholars and students with the potential to be Torah scholars, were traditionally the most sought-after bachelors, far more so than wealthy businessmen or other professional men. Young women dreamed of marrying Torah scholars, and their parents were just as eager for their sons-in-law to come from this Jewish "aristocracy."

The Hebrew for Torah scholar, *talmid hacham* (literally, "wise disciple," or "one who is wise because he always remains a student"), refers also to the aphorism in *Avot.* "Who is wise? He who learns from everyone."[113] The Sages declare: "He who marries his daughter to a *talmid hacham* and he who enables *talmidei hachamim* to continue their studies . . . and he who supports them from his property and wealth, is as if he cleaves to the Divine Presence."[114]

Elsewhere the Sages state: "The prophets only prophesied their prophecies of consolation and hope for the future so as to encourage people to marry their daughters to Torah scholars."[115]

The Sages emphasize, however, that it is insufficient to be a scholar; the *talmid hacham* should also be characterized by the supreme trait of *yir'at Shamayim,* reverence of heaven. They declare, "The Torah is but a portal enabling one to enter into *yir'at Shamayim,*"[116] and this statement is based on the verse in Psalms, *Reshit hochmah yir'at HaShem,* "Reverence of the Lord is the beginning of wisdom."[117] *Yir'at Shamayim* takes precedence over the study of

Torah, and the ideal *talmid hacham* is also a *y'ray Shamayim*, one who reveres heaven.

The Sages were fully aware that having a *talmid hacham* for a son-in-law could be costly, for to pursue his scholarship he must be spared the economic pressure of supporting a family. The Sages teach: "A man should do whatever he can to . . . marry his daughter to a *talmid hacham*.[118] . . . A man should give his daughter in marriage to a *talmid hacham* even if doing so involves substantial expenditure."[119]

In vying with others to gain Torah students for sons-in-law, fathers were quite willing to go to great lengths to provide continued financial support so that the young men could study Torah without economic worries. Jewish society honored such a father for removing the financial burden from his son-in-law. Even if the father-in-law was completely unlearned, he could now possess his share of the reward of the Torah.

A Scholarly Match

Similarly, young men traditionally sought the daughters of *talmidei hachamim* as their brides. The Sages urge men to make great efforts in this direction, even if it involves undertaking substantial expenditures. "A man should marry the daughter of a *talmid hacham*," the Sages say, "even if this should entail giving away all of his money."[120] The Sages teach:

> A man should even sell all that he owns in order to marry the daughter of a *talmid hacham*. If he does not find the daughter of a Torah scholar, he should marry the daughter of one of the outstanding righteous men. If such cannot be found, he should seek the daughter of a leader of the community. If he cannot find one like this, he should seek out the daughter of the one who teaches Torah to little children. However, under no circumstances should he marry the daughter of an *am ha'aretz* [one who is ignorant of the Torah and who reflects that ignorance in gross, boorish, and unethical behavior].[121] A man who gives his daughter in marriage to an *am ha'aretz* is doing the equivalent of throwing her to a lion.[122]

He who marries the daughter of a *talmid hacham* will end up having children of his own who are *talmidei hachamim.* The branches of the vine are like the vine and the other branches.[123]

Maimonides, in his Code, the *Mishneh Torah,* invests this order of priorities listed in the Talmud with the status of law. Nevertheless, if a young man wishes to marry the daughter of an ordinary God-fearing Jew rather than the daughter of a *talmid hacham,* he is permitted to marry her.[124] The young man is assured that his personal needs — and the need for him to have a successful marriage — take precedence in making this most momentous decision of his life. (Incidentally, the great twentieth-century rabbinic authority, R. Abraham Isaiah Karelitz [1878–1953], known as the Hazon Ish, determined that in modern times all girls who receive a proper intensive Jewish education in recognized traditional religious schools, can be considered the equivalent of daughters of *talmidei hachamim;* indeed, he suggested that as a result of their specialized training, they themselves may be the equivalent of *talmidei hachamim.*[125])

In this context, it is easy to recognize the Jewish love of learning and scholarship, a love reflected today in countless spheres. For many generations, Jews have avidly studied the Torah, the written and oral teachings of Judaism, and their rich literature. However, for many Jews whose parents and grandparents did not transmit these teachings to their children, it remains dimly, if at all, in their consciousness. Nevertheless, an inherited love of learning and knowledge is firmly ingrained in the Jewish consciousness, and this is expressed in a variety of ways. Jews occupy leading positions in all areas of scholarship, as a result of their characteristically unquenchable thirst for knowledge.

Among secular Jews whose parents did not provide them with an intensive Torah education, the consuming and infinitely absorbing experience of Torah study is missing and so they satisfy their quest for scholarship in other ways. As admirable as this is, traditional Judaism instructs Jewish women to prefer the student who is firmly entrenched in his *Jewish* scholarly heritage to someone who has achieved success and recognition in the spheres of secular knowledge. Judaism teaches that it is the Torah that represents the Jewish

people. It is the mainstay of the Jewish past, and the guarantee of
the Jewish future.

Why Not Marry for Money?

Traditionally, Jewish fathers, then, have been willing, even eager,
to trade their material wealth for the spiritual returns of supporting
Torah scholars as sons-in-law. At the opposite end of this scale of
Jewish values is the marriage based on financial considerations.
While Judaism neither considers poverty as a desirable state nor
condemns wealth *per se,* the Sages severely condemn one who
marries purely for financial benefit. The Talmud declares:[126]
"Whoever marries a woman for monetary gain shall have improper
children, for it is said: 'For they have acted treacherously against the
Lord, and they have given birth to strange children.' "[127]

Here, the Sages disparage the deep, basic dishonesty which
underlies a marriage based on such motives. Not only is the couple's
relationship adversely affected, since it is based on a lie, but the
children of such a union breathe this tainted atmosphere and,
consequently, are affected by it. To marry for money is an
egotistical act. One subordinates the interest of building a family,
based on sound values, to certain myopically selfish motives, and
denies the basic purpose of Jewish marriage: the merger of two
individuals to create a greater entity of mutual love leading to the
creation of an emotionally and morally healthy family unit. The
acquisition of a spouse as a kind of by-product of a profitable
financial venture obviates the mutual respect, affection, and unity
of purpose upon which a harmonious Jewish home depends.

R. Moses Isserles, the sixteenth-century Polish codifier of Jewish
law, known as the *Rama,* in his gloss of the *Shulhan Aruch,* permits
such a marriage only if the bride's parents, entirely of their own free
will, give money to the groom. If the groom makes the gift a
condition of marriage, and delays the wedding until the money is
forthcoming or until a larger sum is offered, he causes his bride
anguish and paves the way for quarrels. In this case the *Rama*
forbids the gift altogether. He writes:

> He who does this shall not succeed, and his marriage will not be
> successful, for this money that he takes for marrying his wife is not

honest money. He who does so is called "one who marries a woman for monetary reasons" [which is forbidden]. If, however, he will be satisfied with whatever gift he will be given by his father-in-law and his mother-in-law, he will succeed.[128]

R. Judah Ashkenazi, the eighteenth-century German codifier of Jewish law, known as *Ba'er Hetev,* comments: "Whoever quarrels about the dowry will not succeed, and his marriage will not be a good one, for the money that a person takes in marrying a wife is not honest money."[129]

The thirteenth-century French scholar R. M'nahem HaM'iri puts it poetically:

Al tikah ishah l'mamon o l'yofi,
Ki hakol yelech, v'yisha'er hadofi.

If you marry a woman for money or for beauty,
They will all soon disappear,
And what you will be left with is the impurity.[130]

Judaism views the idea of marriage for money with such abhorrence that it allows one, in order to avoid this, to violate the *mitzvah* of respect for one's parents. The *Sefer Hasidim* states that if a man's parents insist that he marry a rich girl while he prefers to marry someone with the qualities recommended by the Sages, he may then disregard his parents' wishes.[131]

The Charm that Captivates

A man is urged to seek the more intangible qualities, one of the most important of which is *chen,* a certain elusive quality in a woman, encompassing charm, grace, and favor—something that makes her attractive to others all her life. A wife with this trait will, long after her beauty fades, continue to provide enjoyment for her husband. The Talmud says that the charm a woman has in her husband's eyes is one of her most captivating qualities.[132] *Rashi* remarks: "A woman's charm will always captivate her husband; even if she may be ugly she remains charming in his eyes."[133]

Judaism encourages single women to make every effort to appear attractive and to use, in moderation, accepted cosmetic aids[134] for this purpose.[135] The Talmud declares, however, that a young woman with *chen* needs neither make-up nor a special hairstyle to attract her man.[136] This quality, beyond surface beauty, is a warm human emanation that enchants a man more than any cosmetic or artifice can do.

Since, as mentioned, *yir'at Shamayim* (reverence of heaven) is considered a highly desirable quality in a woman, it is interesting to note that charm and *yir'at Shamayim* are regarded by the Sages as related traits. The Talmud teaches: "Whoever has charm most certainly has *yir'at Shamayim.*"[137]

The Wise and Worthy Wife

The *Zohar* asserts: "He who has acquired a wise and understanding woman has acquired *everything.*"[138]

However, one who marries an unworthy woman, according to the Sages, transgresses no fewer than five separate precepts of the Torah.[139] In a similar vein, the Talmud warns: "He who marries a woman who is unworthy will have unworthy children[140] . . . and God himself will apply stripes to him."[141]

Whatever fine qualities a young man may bring to his marriage, they are negated by his union with an unworthy woman, for their descendants will suffer from an unfortunate combination of influences. The Talmud says of one who marries an unworthy woman that "it is as if he had plowed all the fields in the world and then seeded them with salt."[142]

The Sages then deliver the ultimate accolade to the man who marries a good woman: "Whoever marries a worthy woman is considered as if he had fulfilled all of the Torah."[143]

Age Difference

Marriages may succeed very well where there is a wide age difference, but they are generally discouraged. The Sages teach: "He who gives his daughter in marriage to a *zaken,* an old man, commits a wrong."[144]

However, if a young woman herself prefers an older man, and is not marrying as a result of pressure by her parents, such a union is acceptable. The same holds true where the woman is older than the man. The *Sefer Hasidim* states: "[The talmudic passage] regarding giving a daughter in marriage to a *zaken* refers specifically to an instance where she does not want him as a husband. However, if she desires the *zaken* because he is a good Jew or because she feels that she can be fulfilled by him, then it is a *mitzvah* for her to marry him. . . ."[145]

Comparative Accomplishments

The Sages feel that the marriage is more likely to succeed if the man has somewhat greater achievements than his wife. The Talmud teaches: *"N'hot darga, n'siv it'ta* — Descend a step when taking a wife."[146]

The Sages express concern, however, that should this superiority of achievement be too great, she may be made to feel inadequate.[147]

On the other hand, they caution that a man could make a serious misalliance by marrying a woman more than worthy of him;[148] that is, so superior to him intellectually that she might become contemptuous of him. A wife with superior accomplishments may initially make a man feel proud, but it is worthwhile for him to look ahead to see if the difference might lead to an unhappy marriage in the end.

In order for a man to make a reasonable, intelligent, and balanced decision as to whether it is a good match, he needs to be honest with himself, and to acknowledge his own strengths and weaknesses.

The Asset of Charitableness

Tz'dakah, the Hebrew word for charity, is related to *tzedek,* justice or righteousness. As Judaism perceives it, a person who gives *tz'dakah* is fulfilling an elementary obligation to do what is just and right by sharing his income with the needy.

Tz'dakah is an attribute God displays toward humans.[149] Therefore, since Judaism instructs Jews to imitate God's ways, they are required to give *tz'dakah;* that means actively seeking out the needy, not waiting to be asked to give. The Torah commands: *Tzedek tzedek tirdof,* "Justice, justice shall you pursue."[150] Charity holds such a central place in Judaism that the Sages consider it to be the significant equivalent of all other Torah precepts combined.[151]

In choosing a life partner, then, Judaism says to look for benevolence and generosity in a person, and to avoid someone who lacks these virtues, or who appears to avoid giving charity. It is true that charity begins at home; one who sincerely wishes to fulfill the *mitzvah* of *tz'dakah* provides first for his own family, and then for his community. However, to keep the *mitzvah* completely requires reaching out and showing compassion to those beyond one's family circle.

Charitableness also includes the capacity to judge others charitably, and to give another the benefit of the doubt. The Sages say: "Do not judge another until you have been placed in his situation."[152]

One who judges other people harshly is also likely to be overly critical of his own spouse and children. Therefore, an inability and an unwillingness to understand and to empathize with others is, in a marriage partner, a significant deficiency. Such a person, in order to foster the illusion of his own importance, may behave in an autocratic and tyrannical manner toward his spouse and children.

Avoiding Certain Negative Traits

Similarly undesirable is one who has a strong capacity to hate others. The Torah says: "You shall not hate your brother in your heart."[153]

The Sages teach that the First Temple in Jerusalem was destroyed because of three sins: idolatry, bloodshed, and immorality.[154] The Second Temple was destroyed because of one sin: *sin'at hinam,* needless hatred.[155] The Sages deduce from this the seriousness of the sin of hating others: "This teaches that needless hatred is the equivalent of all three sins combined—idolatry, bloodshed, and immorality."[156]

It is certainly a great blessing to have a marital partner gifted with the trait of *ahavat hinam,* pure love, unmotivated by specific interests. Such a person is likely to be easy and pleasant to live with.

There are many problems with a person who hates others. To hate is implicitly to disavow reverence for God, who commanded that human beings love each other and live in harmony.[157] Hatred also implies a lack of humility, for the hater feels that his personal grudge is more important than God's command. It is the opposite of the trait that most epitomizes the Jew — *hesed,* loving-kindness.

Too Much Talk

It is best to avoid, as a potential marriage partner, one who has a tendency to talk too much and to gossip. The Mishnah quotes R. Simon ben Gamliel: "I have spent all my life among scholars, and have found nothing better for the body than silence; whoever overindulges in talk gives rise to sin."[158]

Just as *sh'tikah,* silence and reticence, are considered great virtues, being loose-tongued is derided. The gossiper may be guilty of one of the most insidious of transgressions, *lashon hara* (belittling or damaging speech against others).[159] Even if the information given is completely true, it can still cause needless pain and damage, ruin friendships and marriages, and result in financial damage. *Lashon hara* is often the result of idleness or lack of careful thought.

Solomon's *aishet hayil,* the valorous woman, is one whose "husband's heart trusts in her."[160] Discreet, and careful with family secrets, she chooses her words carefully to prevent suffering or unpleasantness to her husband. To have a good marriage, husband and wife need to feel that they can talk to each other with perfect confidence in each other's discretion. Solomon declares: "Life and death are in the hands of the tongue."[161]

The tongue is more powerful than the sword, say the Sages. A sword kills only at close range, but a tongue can cause death at great distances.[162]

Speech, the unique gift to human beings, can also be the source of their greatest sorrow.[163] In a marriage, a major fact to be considered is how much control the other person has over his or her speech.

The Quality of Truth

Another major trait to be sought is honesty. Truthfulness is as essential a quality in a spouse as it is to the existence of the world.

According to the Mishnah, truth, justice, and peace are the three pillars supporting the world.[164] Where there is no truth, there can be no trust between the partners, and consequently the marriage cannot be a good one. The Torah teaches: *"Mid'var sheker tir'hak—* Keep your distance from falsehood."[165]

However, with all this, a measure of discretion is required. There are times when telling the whole truth might cause needless pain or anxiety. In this regard, good judgment is necessary.

To please a husband or wife, one sometimes considers covering up flaws, accidents, or errors in judgment. The problem is that in time this will probably lead to more lies, as the original cover-up requires further deception.

If a person lies to protect himself, what happens is that his true character remains hidden from his partner. The only way for a couple to build a relationship based on real communication is for both to be themselves. By presenting each to the other as candidly and honestly as possible, the doors are opened for love and good communication.

Frugality and Indulgence

Thriftiness and frugality are good traits to look for in a marriage partner. Marriages often founder because one partner freely spends money in pursuit of his own interests, but becomes critical when the other partner spends money. Even in good marriages, problems will arise if one partner is extravagant and the family tries to live beyond its means. R. Nahman of Bratzlav taught: "The desire for good eating leads to poverty, contempt, and shame."[166]

If a couple spends unwisely on the little things, they may not be able to save enough for more important needs. R. Nahman further remarks: "He who controls his appetite will have a fine home."[167]

R. Nahman is not merely referring to food here. Controlling an overindulgence in physical needs indicates generally a sense of proportion and balance. A mature adult, in contrast to a child who seeks immediate gratification, will forgo this. To build a home and raise a family takes this kind of maturity. That is why it is important to look for it in a potential marriage partner.

Avoid the Worrier

Although it is pleasing to have a mate who is concerned about the future and makes every effort to protect his family against possible misfortune, someone who worries too much is uncomfortable to live with. The chronic worrier casts a net of anxiety and worry over those around him. It is difficult to function properly in the atmosphere of pervasive gloom and unhappiness which inevitably surrounds someone who is always worried about what troubles the future may bring.

The Talmud interprets the biblical passage, "And you will have no assurance of your life,"[168] as referring to someone who constantly worries about whether he will have sufficient food for the coming year. Even if he has a full supply of wheat, for example, he prepares additional wheat for the coming week, and worries day and night about not having enough.[169] This kind of person will always find something to worry about, and the atmosphere surrounding him and his anxieties will make life difficult for his partner in marriage and for his children.

The Jewish response to such a person is summed up by the nineteenth-century ethical teacher R. Yisrael Salanter: "All worries are forbidden, except when one worries about worrying."[170]

What Kind of Partner Will He/She Make?

One of the reasons for marrying is certainly to establish a family. Indeed, according to the Sages, it may be the principal goal of marriage—since the future of the Jewish people depends on the family. There is a *midrash* that says that there are four major motives for marriage: satisfaction of sensual desire, economic well-being, social status, and raising a family. Of the four, the *Midrash* only considers the family to be a truly valid motive.[171]

It is crucial, therefore, to assess a marital partner's potential as a parent and how he (or she) relates to children. The question to consider is whether the person has the personality traits and character which will provide the children with a good role model. Does the person have the proper combination of firmness and flexibility necessary for effective parenting? Is the person willing and able to impart the traditions and observances of the Jewish way of living so that his or her children will be firmly linked to the chain of Jewish tradition and be able, in turn, to pass it on to their children?

Predicting His/Her Future Behavior

A good way to determine how respectfully prospective mates will act *after* marriage and after many years of living together is to observe how they behave in their home, which is their natural setting, and how they relate to their immediate family. Does the person respect his or her parents? If individuals, in their speech and conduct, show no respect for their parents, this should be taken very seriously, because they are likely to show as little respect for their spouses.

No matter how respectfully people act before marriage, the real key to how respectfully they will act after marriage is their attitude toward their parents, with whom they have been living for a long time, and whom they are duty-bound to respect. Respect needs to be deeply ingrained, for if it is only superficial, it will fall away like a veneer when the marital relationship loses its freshness.

In addition, it is worth looking at the way a prospective mate's parents behave toward one another, because this reveals the level of mutual respect and consideration in the home where the person grew up and the particular attitudes he or she may have absorbed.

It is certainly possible for an adult to learn to behave differently toward a spouse than he did toward his parents. However, this is not usually the case. A deliberate effort of will, as well as a not inconsiderable change of personality is required to overcome natural impulses deriving from long habit. Unless consistent proof is evident that the person has worked on himself to this extent, it is unrealistic to expect it to happen. Few people are equipped with the requisite strength of character or willpower to change themselves in this manner.

In Times of Crisis and Joy

It is important to observe how a potential marriage partner acts in a variety of conditions and situations. It is not too difficult to act well through the security of a daily routine and when life runs smoothly. How well a person acts during crises—and how respectfully he acts toward a spouse—is a different story. People have different ways of reacting; some can become over-excited or overwhelmed with emotion; others, when in despair, become abusive. There are those who recommend testing a potential marriage partner to observe how he reacts under stress, and how his anger is expressed.

To marry someone who is able to enjoy life and make the most of it is a great blessing. Life is made up of joy and sorrow, and how people act in those moments is what makes them what they are. Some three thousand years ago Solomon said: "There is a time to weep and a time to laugh; a time to mourn and a time to dance."[172]

Judaism is a joyous way of life celebrating life's God-given pleasures. In Judaism, joy plays a major role. R. Judah HaLevi, the medieval Spanish poet and philosopher, emphasizes that it is a basic medium through which one can draw closer to God.[173] "Serve the Lord with joy; come before Him with song," King David urges.[174] At one point God became angry when the Jews lacked joy in their service to Him.[175] The Sages explain the verse, "And I praised joy,"[176] as a reference to the joy of performing *mitzvot*, God's commandments.[177] The Talmud teaches: "The Divine Presence does not rest where there is grief . . . but only where there is joy in performing the commandments."[178]

Conversely, Judaism counsels moderation in grief, as in all areas of life, and a measure of control over emotions so that one can continue to function normally. Intemperance in grief can be self-indulgent, and can lead a person to apathy, ignoring the needs of the family.

The ability to feel or to express emotion in a marital relationship is also a big problem. One partner may interpret a restrained emotional expression as coldness or disinterest on the part of the other. Good communication can only be built through the marriage partners' ability to express their feelings. Emotion sustains a relationship; without it, a marriage may starve. For a marriage to be meaningful, it must provide mutual emotional fulfillment.

One trait to watch out for in a potential marriage partner is laziness, because it shows a lack of interest in life. Someone who is indolent does not exert himself, either in study or in work, and just manages to get by in life. Referring to such a person, Solomon wrote: "I passed by the field of a sluggard and the vineyard of a man devoid of understanding, and I noted that it was overgrown with weeds and nettles, and its stone fence was down."[179]

A lazy person is therefore not a good partner for the demanding task of establishing a home based on Jewish values. Such a person is not suited to the challenges of parenthood, and living out one's life with him or her can be a source of great disillusionment.

Self-Esteem — A Desirable Trait

In Judaism, humility is rated very highly. It is beneficial particularly in a marital relationship, for it leads to respect for others, whereas excessive pride leads to arrogance. The Torah's ideal of humility, however, does not mean low self-esteem. It stems from the concept that human beings are created in God's image, and each person has a spark of divinity. Positive feelings about oneself and a realization of one's own worth are important means of attaining satisfaction in life and getting the most out of a marriage. A person needs to recognize and to like the virtues in himself; when a person has healthy, positive feelings about himself, he is more capable of giving of himself in an intimate relationship like marriage. Self-esteem in an individual will guarantee that he will not humble himself beneath human dignity, and his ability to properly fulfill his function as a human being, a spouse, and a parent, will not be impaired.

The way a person feels about himself often affects his abilities. If he believes himself to be incompetent and a failure, he may be laying the groundwork for a self-fulfilling prophecy. Conversely, having good feelings about oneself and one's abilities provides the impetus to achieve desired goals.

A person who lacks self-esteem can end up being overly submissive to others. His feelings of inadequacy and incompetence may translate to indecision where his family's welfare is concerned. Moses, considered the most humble human being who ever lived,[180] was at the same time a dynamic man of action who, when this was required, demonstrated firmness and decisiveness.[181]

How does one learn to cultivate in himself the right measure of pride and humility? The nineteenth-century hasidic Sage R. Simha Bunim of Przysucha says: "Every person should have two slips of paper with him, one bearing the words, 'The world was created for me' and the other with the words, 'I am but dust and ashes.' A person must be wise enough to read each slip at the proper time."[182]

Derech Eretz — A Composite Personality Trait

Finally, we come to the characteristic of *derech eretz,* or proper comportment. This composite personality trait encompasses many attributes which Judaism sees as desirable in a spouse.[183] If a potential husband or wife possesses this characteristic, he or she must possess other favorable attributes as well.

The medieval ethical teacher, R. Y'hiel ben R. Y'kutiel ben R. Benjamin HaRofe, in his *Sefer Ma'alot HaMidot,* the *Book of Good Attributes,* explains *derech eretz* as the ability to think carefully before one does or says anything. One who has this trait is at all times concerned about how he will comport himself. Before he acts or speaks, he always ascertains in his own mind that his deeds or speech will be performed or spoken in a proper manner; one acceptable to God, to human beings, and to himself:

> He should conduct himself piously and with an attitude reflecting reverence of Heaven when he is with people; with modesty, humility and soft speech . . . and he should take care to conduct his affairs in a good manner . . . and praise those with whom he comes in contact . . . and be exceptional in both deed and word, in the manner of his eating and drinking, in his dress and in all of his business affairs; it should even be expressed in the way he walks and the way in which he sits. He will conduct himself in accordance with every good trait in which wise and good people are accustomed, and in this way he will be acceptable to God and to man.[184]

R. Samson Raphael Hirsch summarizes some sterling qualities to seek in a Jewish wife:

> When you choose a wife, remember that she is to be your companion in life, in building up your home, in the performance of your life task, and choose accordingly. It will then not be wealth or physical

beauty or brilliance of mind that will decide you, but you will look for richness of heart, beauty of character, and good sense and intelligence. If, in the end, in order to be able to set up house, you require money, and your wife's family freely offers it to you, you may take it; but woe to you and your future household if you are guided only by considerations of money. If, because the promises made to you are not carried out, you quarrel and insist on your due, and even perhaps cast off your betrothed because she does not bring in the money you expected, do you imagine that the money obtained in such a way would bring in a blessing?

Study well the character of your future wife. However, since character is so often first revealed only by contact with real life [i.e. living together in marriage] . . . look well at the family, which has already established its character in real life. If you see a family in which disputes and quarreling are rife, in which insolence and evil talk are common, in which you behold hard-heartedness, hate, and uncharitableness, do not attach yourself to it. . . . That you should keep aloof from all marriages prohibited by Torah and rabbinic ordinance up to the furthest degree of consanguinity, goes without saying. Our Sages recommend that one should always look for the daughter of a learned man, of a man in whom the public has shown its confidence by entrusting him with communal office; above all, of a man whose daughter can be expected to have learned practical wisdom from the example of her father.[185]

The Traditional Jewish Way to Meet a Mate

Meeting a prospective mate was never a serious problem when tradition was a viable and potent force in the Jewish community. In ancient times and in the biblical world, arranged marriages were the rule.[186] Parents selected potential brides for their sons, and concluded the arrangements with the girl's parents. However, the consent of the young man and woman was a precondition of the match. Especially important was the consent of the bride. Aside from its basic justness, it limited the authority of the bride's father, ensuring that fathers did not abuse their responsibilities. In the words of Maimonides: "A woman cannot be married unless it is of her own free will. If a man should, however, complete a marriage procedure against a woman's will, she is not married."[187]

Although Abraham's servant Eliezer reached an agreement with Rebecca's family regarding the match between Isaac and Rebecca, the matter was not completed until Rebecca was approached and her consent given. As it says in scripture, "Then they said, let us call the maiden and ask her."[188] Only when Rebecca agreed was the match concluded. The principle of mutual consent derived from this passage was incorporated into Jewish law.[189]

Even in ancient times, however, young men and women sometimes arranged their own marriages. The Bible relates that Jacob and Rachel met on their own and decided to marry.[190] Moreover, although it is important for a couple planning to marry to receive the approval of both sets of parents, Jewish law permits a young man and woman to marry despite parental objections[191] from either side.[192] The classic example is that of the talmudic Sage R. Akiva: he and his wife Rachel met on their own and married secretly, in opposition to her parents.[193]

Nevertheless, throughout most of the history of the Jews, young people had their marriages arranged for them by their parents. This system continued through the talmudic and post-talmudic periods, and even through relatively recent times in the ghettos of Eastern Europe, and the *mellahs* (urban Jewish ghettoes) of the Arab world. When Jews migrated to the West and became integrated into Western society, they adopted the dominant Western social mores, customs, and practices. In this new society, young people resented their parents' intervention in the selection of their marriage partners. Parents struggled with futility against the currents of change, and, to avoid friction, acquiesced in their children's wishes, gradually adopting the new customs. Today, the old custom of marital introductions — or modern variations of it — continues primarily among the more traditional Jewish families.

The *Shadchan* as Catalyst

The traditional way to meet a marriage partner was through introductions made by a *shadchan,* an almost legendary figure in Jewish life and lore. A marriage broker, the *shadchan,* performed the valuable service of making a *shiduch,* or marriage match. He came to know Jewish communities far and wide, and the families within them. The *shadchan* was a highly regarded member of the community, often the rabbi of the community, his wife, or a learned Jew well versed in Torah. The *shadchan*'s knowledge, memory, tactfulness, and expertise in psychology, as well as the respect he enjoyed, made him the ideal person to entrust with sensitive marriage arrangements. People felt they could confide appropriate information to him and trusted his discretion. By all accounts, the *shadchan* was immensely successful in a profession that the Sages call difficult even for God.[194]

Today, the *shadchan* functions in much the same manner. When retained by a family, he learns as much as possible about the character, personality, and family of the young man or woman he represents. In a lengthy conversation with the candidate for marriage, he learns about his or her interests and tastes. He then seeks out a prospective candidate whose character, personality, and family background seem suitable. At the same time, he weeds out the unlikely prospects before selecting the most appropriate candidates to introduce to his client. The good *shadchan* is an expert at matching complementary qualities, but with the added human touches of feeling, understanding, and intuition. Often, in a flash of intuition, an ingenious match occurs to him and he follows up with a methodical, well-reasoned procedure.

The *shadchan* often begins his search in the client's home community and among families known to those who have retained his services, along the lines of the popular expression, "It is better to marry someone you know even if he has some deficiencies." It is quite possible that the deficiencies revealed over time in a candidate about whom less is known, but who seemingly lacks deficiencies, will turn out to be far worse than those of a prospect about whom more is known.[195]

When a candidate is recommended for an introduction, each family undertakes a thorough investigation of the proposed individual and his family. Inquiries are made among acquaintances. Rabbis, past teachers, classmates, and friends are discreetly consulted about the person's character, personality, and background. From their combined responses, a composite picture and general character assessment of the individual gradually emerges. It is a thorough process, and many unsuitable prospects are screened out in this manner. If, after the *shadchan*'s recommendation, after the family's thorough investigations, and after inquiries the principals themselves undertake among their acquaintances, the young man and woman decide they wish to get together, a meeting is arranged.

A Jewish Mating System that Works

Contrary to some folklore, even with the services of the most expert of *shadchanim,* traditional young men and women will agree to marry only after meeting several times and deciding themselves. This is an old Jewish tradition.[196]

Jewish law strictly prohibits any physical intimacy before marriage, and even privacy behind closed doors is proscribed for a man and woman lest it lead to compromising the reputations of either party.[197] Thus, traditional men and women avoid being totally alone, and therefore, following their introduction, they usually go out to public places. The meeting is not simply a date; it is not designed for fun, enjoyment, or sexual titillation, and it is not just an evening out. Seduction is not on the agenda. The sole purpose of their meeting is to learn firsthand about each other's qualities and traits in order to assess the other's suitability as a potential marriage partner.

Since neither party is there for any other purpose than marriage, the games and smoke screens that often characterize dates are noticeably absent. Neither party needs to wonder whether and to what extent the other's intentions are honorable. They are both there because they wish to marry — and within a very reasonable period. They are there to learn as much as possible about the other, to examine compatibility, and to determine whether the other is a fitting partner for life, if he or she will be a suitable spouse and a good parent. The several hours they spend together at the meeting are thus devoted exclusively to an in-depth discussion that will be helpful in arriving at a calm, sober, and intelligent decision. They may achieve in several hours what it could take several weeks or months to achieve during conventional dating.

The Sages provide guidelines and advise a young man:

> At the first meeting talk to her about herself, her home, her studies, her work, her leisure activities, hobbies, and interests. Tell her about

yourself in the same manner so that she can get to know you. At future meetings try to learn about her thinking, her attributes, and personality — in particular, try to determine where she is of a stubborn bent. . . . Try to determine her ambitions in life, including the nature of the life she would like to live. . . . It is important, however, that great care should be taken to assure that the meeting is not turned into a kind of interrogation. Every effort should be made to ensure that there not be created an atmosphere of trial or one of criticism. Clarification of the important information required should be done in an easy manner and in an unhurried, flowing conversation.[198]

At the first meeting, both will undoubtedly endeavor to make the best possible impression. Also, many significant personality traits will not be readily obvious and will only emerge after several meetings, or not until after marriage. Therefore, it makes sense for a person not to rely solely on his own impressions. It is best to seek reliable, objective information from people who know the other party well, and to seek the opinions of parents, who are older, more experienced, and who generally have the best interests of their children in mind.

Nurturing Genuine Affection

If either of the two parties decides that they are not suited, they do not meet again. The *shadchan* is notified, and the process begins anew. When a couple meets a second, a third, and a fourth time, their mutual affection begins to develop as they come to know each other better. Emotions play a part, but not to the point where the couple is blinded by them. Ideally, their affection will be based primarily on a deepening knowledge of and respect for each other's qualities. These gradually become revealed during the meetings they devote to mutual discovery and to exploration of one another's personalities. The affection built through these meetings will in time flower into a deep, abiding love, established upon the solid foundation of knowledge and understanding, and not upon ethereal mystery.

If a couple are attracted to each other but, during these meetings, they do not feel that they love each other, this is no reason not to marry if all the positive factors between them are present. Love will follow. In the words of the Sages, "True attraction develops *after* the wedding."[199] When the two arrive at a decision to marry, the families meet.

Not unremarkably, this system of selecting a mate has a very high success rate. While accurate statistics are unavailable, divorces are known to be few, and marriages contracted in this way are, by and large, successful.

R. Samson Raphael Hirsch provides an interesting insight into the traditional Jewish methods of seeking a mate:

> Right up to modern times, Jewish marriages have been brought about not by the winged god of love, but as the result of a careful survey by the parents and relatives on both sides. . . . How decisively are reason and foresight on the side of Jewish custom! Inclination, blind as its own god, concludes marriages in other circles. Passion is the marriage broker, excluding from the outset calm reflection into the place where it seems to be most called for. *Persons of differing disposition blinded by passion do not learn in the least to know one another.* They embark on marriage with quite false ideas and with expectations which are soon falsified by reality, and coolness and estrangement soon follow.
>
> Jewish marriages are preceded by the coolest and most careful investigation to see whether the dispositions, the characters, the personalities, and all other conditions which decide future happiness suit one to the other. The parents, relatives, and friends are much better qualified to make these calculations than the young man and woman themselves, and only when reason has agreed, is inclination also consulted. This is why the percentage of happy marriages among the Jews who follow the traditional Jewish method of finding a mate is so much higher than in other circles.
>
> For Jewish marriages the wedding is not the culmination, but the seedtime of life, with promise for the future that unfolds itself more and more every day. This married life, continued through storm and sunshine, takes ever firmer root and blossoms forth more and more as their hearts come even closer to one another. Their souls in the journey through life become more and more aware of what they are to one another, and the husband finds what a treasure he has in his wife; the wife, in her husband. An Isaac who chooses his Rebecca for himself often chooses wrongly. An Isaac who allows his Rebecca to be brought to him by his Abraham, is seldom disappointed.[200]

A love built on these traditional, Jewish foundations is not shrouded in romantic mystiques. It is not the blind love of poetry and fiction. Rather, it grows from knowledge of each other. The true romance in their relationship begins to flower *after* marriage, as the two grow closer emotionally and physically. Scripture tells us first that Isaac married Rebecca and only then are we informed that he loved her.[201] The affection that abides between a couple before may indeed be genuine, but the deep and lasting love based on knowledge comes only through living and growing together in marriage.

Interestingly enough, an ever-growing number of Jewish university graduates have been opting for various contemporary adaptations of the traditional *shadchan* system. This comes as a result of their rejection of what they see as the indignity of the games they are forced to play in male-female relationships according to contemporary mores. It is also caused by their frustration with society's anachronistic, disorderly procedure for finding a marriage partner and the long, often undignified, process entailed in the search. Egalitarian as contemporary society may appear in some respects, its rules for the game of courtship are particularly unfair to women.

Many Jewish men and women of marriageable age are painfully aware that society's system of matching couples has proven unsuccessful. Most marriages are abysmal failures. Society's accepted procedure for meeting a marriage partner is antithetical to the establishment of a stable marriage and a close nuclear family.

Shadchanim may be found in urban areas with substantial concentrations of traditional Jews. In North America, these are New York and its environs, Toronto, Montreal, Boston, Chicago, Los Angeles, and Miami. There is also Jerusalem, as well as London, and Paris. Good *shadchanim* are located primarily through personal recommendation. A good way to start is to contact a traditional rabbi or his wife.

The Most Important Decision of a Lifetime

In conclusion, although many facets and complexities of a mate's true character usually come to light only after marriage, an alert suitor will be able to discern hints and clues. It is important to keep one's eyes wide open. So much is at stake and so much depends on a keen analysis of character and personality. The price paid for a hasty judgment is far too high.

Before making that crucial decision, therefore, it is important to give it a good deal of cool, objective thought. If a potential partner appears "perfect" in every respect, Jewish wisdom teaches one to reconsider the premises of the decision. Human perfection in all of the desirable traits listed by the Sages is possible, but rare. Realistically, the best one should hope for is to find a person with high marks in the recommended traits and low ones in the undesirable ones.

When a person sees perfection in a would-be mate, it may be cause for concern. It is a signal that one's vision may be blinded by emotion, or that one is not evaluating the other person with enough objectivity. Only by an intelligent, dispassionate analysis of the marriage candidate's strength and weakness in the recommended character traits can an individual come to a proper and sensible resolution of possibly the most important decision he will ever make.

Deciding whom to marry is indeed usually the most important decision of a lifetime. It is a decision that has far-reaching consequences, going far beyond the two people themselves. The Talmud implies that the decision will affect "the entire world."[202] The Sages teach: "Why was Adam created alone? To teach that whoever destroys a single Jewish life is considered as if he has destroyed an entire world, and whoever saves a single Jewish life is considered as if he has saved an entire world."[203]

The late American Jewish thinker, R. Aryeh Kaplan, explains the talmudic passage by pointing to the awesome implications involved in choosing the right mate. Assuming that the couple has at least two children, and that each of their descendants also has a similarly small family averaging only two children, doubling in geometric progression in each generation, after ten generations of twenty-five years each, the couple will have 1,024 descendants. After twenty generations there will be 1,048,576 descendants. After only twenty-four generations (a mere six hundred years) there will be 16,077,216 descendants. This is more than the current world Jewish population.

Thus, when a couple decides to marry, it is more than a personal decision. It is a decision ultimately affecting the entire Jewish people.[204] Every marriage can, in time, produce an entire world population. Creating a marriage, therefore, is like creating an entire world.[205]

II
Love

4

The Jewish
Idea of Love

Judaism may be described as an ethical way of life, governed by God's principles of love and righteousness, as laid out in the Torah. Love is central to the Torah. Its Golden Rule, "Love your fellow as yourself,"[1] is Judaism's gift to humanity.

Christianity delved into the Torah and adopted the Golden Rule for use in the New Testament.[2] As a result, many people, including many scholars all over the world, have erroneously accepted that the precept, "Love your fellow as yourself," originated with Christianity, and are unaware that this great moral maxim is Jewish in origin, was first taught in the Torah, and was practiced by Jews for 1,400 years before the birth of Christianity. No less a moral philosopher than John Stuart Mill expressed his surprise that the Golden Rule came from the Torah.[3] In the words of the English Chief Rabbi Joseph H. Hertz (1872–1946): "It is time that the attempt to rob Judaism of its title to having given the Golden Rule to humanity . . . came to an end."[4]

Concomitantly, the common misconception arose, whereby Christianity was portrayed as a religion of love, while Judaism was seen as the hard and severe religion of justice. This erroneous characterization is easily refuted. R. Akiva (50–135 C.E.), the great talmudic Sage, referred to the Golden Rule as the backbone of Jewish life: " 'Love your fellow as yourself' — this is a fundamental principle of the Torah."[5]

Hillel the Elder (late first century B.C.E.–first century C.E.) urged

Jews to, "Love your fellow creatures."[6] For this renowned Sage, love was the quintessence of the Torah. When a potential proselyte asked him to summarize the Torah briefly, Hillel phrased the Golden Rule as follows: "Do not do to your fellow what is hateful to you. This is the entire Torah. All the rest is commentary. Now go out and learn the commentary."[7]

Maimonides, in the eleventh century, restated Hillel's dictum in this positive formulation: "Whatever you wish others to do for you, you do for them."[8]

Love as the Jewish Formula for Peace

Acting with love toward others is the basis of Judaism. In fact, the Sages declared that anyone who denies the validity of the Torah precept to perform *g'milut hasadim* (acts of love) denies the validity of the essentials of Judaism.[9]

The Sages saw the Golden Rule as the formula for universal peace, as necessarily bringing about peaceful relations between people. But this concern for others has to be expressed not only in words and emotions but in deeds and actions. This is emphasized in scripture and applies even toward enemies: "If you meet your enemy's ox or his ass going astray, you shall surely bring it back to him again; if you see the ass of the one who hates you lying under his burden, you may not allow yourself to pass him, but you must forsake everything and hasten to his aid."[10]

The Jew is not enjoined to speak loving words to his enemy, nor to turn the other cheek to his tormentor. The Torah does, however, command the Jew to perform *acts* of love for the enemy. Also, by specifying "enemy" rather than "friend" or "neighbor," it underscores the universality of the precept to love others, and implies that an act of brotherly love toward one's enemy is the medium for converting him into a friend. Indeed, if both a friend and an enemy require one's aid, the enemy takes precedence over the friend, for in this way a person learns *altruistic* brotherly love. The author of the *Sefer HaHinuch* (thirteenth century) explains why: "As he does for his fellow, so shall his fellow do for him, and resultingly there will be peace among men."[11]

So significant are the precepts concerning deeds of love for one's fellow that they supersede even the sacrifices in the Temple. The *Midrash* teaches:[12] "The Holy One, Blessed Be He, said: More beloved are acts of love than the sacrifices and the burnt offerings which Israel brings upon the altar before Me, as it is said: 'For I desire love and not sacrifices.' "[13]

Since the time when daily prayers replaced the Temple sacrifices as the central medium for the worship of God, *g'milut hasadim* has taken on a greater importance than worship. The Sages even viewed these acts of love toward one's fellow as a method of atoning for sins. They cite an exchange between two first-century talmudic Sages: "Once R. Johanan ben Zakai was leaving Jerusalem with R. Joshua when they saw the Temple in ruins. R. Joshua exclaimed: 'Woe unto us, for the place where Israel could expiate its sins lies in ruin.' Replied R. Johanan: 'Do not grieve, my son, for we have another, equally effective form of atonement. What is it? Acts of love.' "[14]

Love as the Basis of the Torah

The entire Torah is filled with acts of love. The Sages point out that the Torah begins with an act of love — the provision of clothing for Adam and Eve, mentioned in Genesis[15] — and closes with an act of love — God's burial of Moses, mentioned in Deuteronomy[16] — in order to teach man that love should be the guiding principle of his life.[17]

Judaism, therefore, perceives love as more than just a pleasant emotion; it is a vital imperative without which the world cannot exist. As the Psalmist puts it, "The world is built on love."[18] The Sages teach that the entire universe was created on the principle of love; it is one of the three pillars on which the world stands, they declare.[19] R. Samson Raphael Hirsch, the nineteenth-century German spiritual leader, makes this point:

> God . . . created an abundance of forces and caused them to pervade each other, working in accordance with His will . . . uniting them and separating them in such a manner that each should assist in maintaining the other. . . . He, in His infinite wisdom, ordained this mutual interdependence in order that each individual being might contribute . . . to the preservation of the whole. . . . One glorious

chain of love, of giving and receiving, uniting all living things. . . .
Love, say the Sages, which supports and is supported in turn, is the
character of the universe.[20]

R. Hirsch's Italian contemporary, the scholar and exegete R.
Samuel David Luzzatto (1800–1868) writes: "The cornerstone of the
Torah is to strengthen in the human heart the qualities of love and
mercy."[21]

R. Abraham HaKohen Kook (1865–1935), philosopher and first
chief rabbi of the Holy Land, saw the universal implications of the
Golden Rule: "The love of all people must pulsate in one's heart and
soul, the love of every human being individually and of all nations
collectively, expressed by a desire to assist in their spiritual and
material growth."[22]

Different Expressions of Love

Love, in Judaism, comprises a wide spectrum of emotions and
experiences. The Sages point out subtle differences in the various
kinds of love: love between husband and wife, love for one's
children, love of one's fellow man, and the greatest love of all—love
of God.[23]

The Hebrew words *ahavah, rahamim,* and *hesed* are the terms most
frequently used to refer to different types of love. The term *ahavah*
is a comprehensive term which embraces all expressions of love, in
particular God's special love for His people Israel,[24] and a father's
love for a child.[25] It is also commonly used in scripture to express
the love between man and woman,[26] as sensual love or passionate
desire, as, for example, in Judges,[27] 2 Samuel,[28] Jeremiah,[29]
Ezekiel,[30] and Hosea.[31] Parental love for children, to which God's
love for Israel is sometimes compared, is at times expressed in the
liturgy by the word *rahamim.*[32] Literally meaning "compassion" or
"merciful love," the root of *rahamim* is, significantly, *rehem,* or
"womb."

Hesed (or *g'milut hasadim*) refers to loving acts performed selflessly,
solely for the sake of another person. According to the Bible, God
requires of the Jew "but to act justly, to love *hesed,* and to walk
humbly with your God."[33] In this Torah command to love one's
fellow are contained guidelines for translating this concept into
daily, tangible, human activities.

The Supreme Virtue — Love of God

The supreme virtue of the Jew is love of God,[34] and his prime duty is to perform God's will. This love is the foundation of every act the Jew does in his life.[35] Immediately following the *Sh'ma* prayer — which contains the principle of monotheism, "Hear, O Israel, the Lord our God is One"[36] — the Jew recites the scriptural command to love God: "And you shall love the Lord your God with all your heart and with all your soul and with all your might."[37]

Thus, twice daily, the traditional Jew intimately affirms his allegiance to his Creator; it is one of the two major commandments in the Torah on love. To reinforce this command more deeply, Jewish law requires that the words be written on parchment by a specially trained scribe and placed on the exterior and interior doorposts of every Jewish home.[38] The words are also written on parchment and enclosed in the leather *t'filin* cubes, or phylacteries, worn by the observant Jewish man during the weekday morning prayer.[39] One *t'filah* is worn on the head to symbolize intellectual commitment to God, and one is worn on the upper left arm near the heart to symbolize practical and emotional commitment.

This command requires no less than an absolute, freely bestowed submission to God, with heart, soul, mind, and strength — a total commitment of the self to a great transcendent love. Throughout the darkest days of their history, Jews have affirmed that love and devotion to God at the moments of their greatest tests: as they were about to be forcibly "baptized" by drowning at the hands of Christian crusaders in northern France in the twelfth century, as they awaited burning at the stake by order of the papal Inquisition in sixteenth-century Spain, and as they awaited death in the crowded gas chambers at the hands of the Nazis in the twentieth century. With their last words, Jews proclaimed their love for God, saying "Hear, O Israel . . ." — a triumphant assertion that their love had passed the supreme test.

Ancient civilizations were inspired to worship pagan deities out of fear of incurring the wrath of the gods. Later religions persuaded believers to obey religious laws by offering the reward of a place in eternal paradise. Judaism's focus is different. Although *yir'at HaShem,*[40] awe and reverence of God, and *Olam HaBa,*[41] the World to Come, are important concepts in classical Jewish belief, Judaism views the highest level of service to be observance of the precepts of the Torah, not out of fear nor for reward, but out of love of God.[42] Judaism considers *yir'at Shamayim* to be a highly esteemed virtue,[43] the very basis of all knowledge[44] and wisdom,[45] and *Olam HaBa,* the World to Come, a great and desirable reward given to the righteous. However, in Jewish thought it is *ahavat HaShem,* love of God, uncolored by any desire for personal gain, that represents the highest level of service of the Jew for his Creator.

Man Loves God Best When He Loves His Fellow Best

How does the Jew express his love for God? Judaism says that he does so by carrying out the instructions of the Torah. Several times, the Bible uses the phrase "those who love Him and observe His commandments."[47] Furthermore, the Jew manifests his love for God by emulating His attributes.[48] The statement that man was created in God's image[49] is repeated three times in Genesis, underscoring to the Sages the profound symbiosis between the Creator and those whom He has imbued with divine qualities. While Man is not God and cannot become God, he can, by following God's precepts, utilize the divine attributes God has implanted in him to become God-like.

How can man draw close to God? By emulating God's noble attributes — *imitatio Dei.* In accordance with the biblical command to "walk after the Lord your God,"[50] the Jew is required to act in a God-like manner[51] by behaving as God behaves, with love,[52] justice,[53] mercy,[54] and compassion.[55] The Sages teach:

> With reference to the verse "you should walk humbly after the Lord your God,"[56] is it then possible for a man to walk after the Holy Presence? . . . Is it not written that God is a consuming fire?[57] However, what is meant is that one should walk after the attributes of the Holy One, Blessed be He. Just as He clothes the naked[58] . . . so should you do as well; just as God visits the sick[59] . . . so should you do as well; just as He consoles the mourners[60] . . . so should you do as well; just as He buries the dead[61] . . . so should you do as well. . . .[62] His ways are acts of love, truth, and charity,[63] as it is

written, "All the paths of the Lord are mercy and truth"[64] . . . so should you follow after the qualities of God.[65]

According to Maimonides *imitatio Dei* is the goal of all creation: "It is the aim of everything to become, according to its faculties, similar to God in perfection."[66]

If love of God is the Jew's loftiest aim, love of his fellow being is the emulatory medium through which the Jew can achieve love of God. Since love for one's fellow emanates from love for God, one might say that "love your fellow" is another way of saying "love God." In the words of the second-century Roman-Jewish philosopher Philo: "To be pious to God is to be affectionate toward men."[67]

R. Israel, known as the *Ba'al Shem Tov* (1700–1770), founder of the hasidic movement, expresses a similar thought: " 'Love your neighbor as yourself' is both an interpretation and an exposition of 'Love the Lord your God.'[68] He who loves his fellow loves God, for his fellow contains within himself a part of God."[69]

Man, created by God in His divine image, is instructed to love all other beings who are, equally, made in His image. Thus, Judaism exhorts Jews to believe that genuine love for one's fellow both *leads to* and, in fact, *is* love of God. If man does not love his fellow, his claim to love God is a spurious one.

R. Judah Loew (1525–1609) of Prague, the rabbinic leader and kabbalist known as the *MaHaral,* taught: "The love of people is at the same time the love of God. For when we love one we necessarily love his handiwork."[70]

The hasidic teacher, R. Levi Yitzhak of Berditchev (1740–1810), adds: "Whether a man truly loves God can be determined by the love he bears toward his fellow man."[71]

God's Image

Ben Azai, an early second-century talmudist, claims[72] that there is an even more fundamental principle in the Torah than the Golden Rule (in Leviticus) cited by his teacher R. Akiva, and this is the passage in Genesis: "This is the Book of the Generations of Adam; in the day that God created man He made him in the likeness of God."[73]

R. Ben Azai thus expounds the belief that love for one's fellow is ultimately based on man's common origin and universal kinship, and his divine image. *All* people, therefore, are considered to be deserving of brotherly love.

Ben Azai went on to paraphrase another teaching of R. Akiva: "Beloved is man, for he was created in the image of God."[74]

Man is a reflection of the divine; his loving actions both mirror and draw their strength from the divine source, God. The hasidic Sage, R. Nahum of Chernobyl (1730–1798), declares: "It is clear that human love is but an offshoot of the divine love, for without the divine love no real love could be aroused in our hearts."[75]

Similarly, the *Ba'al Shem Tov* says: "It behooves every man to reflect, whence is that source which evokes in me feelings of love, if not the love of God for His creations."[76]

The Jew is commanded not only to love his fellow but also to conduct himself in a proper manner, and act toward others in a genuine, loving manner so that they will be directed toward love of God. The Talmud teaches: " 'You shall love the Lord your God' — You should *cause* the name of the Lord to be loved."[77]

By acting in an authentic, loving manner toward others, they will love the God who has instructed the Jew to behave. The *Midrash* says: " 'You shall love the Lord your God' — This is to say, you should make Him beloved of man as Abraham your father did."[78]

Maimonides comments: "Just as Abraham, being a lover of the Lord . . . by the power of his conception of God and out of his great love for Him, summoned mankind to believe, you too must love God so as to summon mankind to Him."[79]

How does one summon mankind to God? Not through missionary activity. This is not Judaism's way. Once R. Simon ben Shetah (a rabbinic leader of the first century B.C.E.) asked his servant to go to the market and buy a donkey. The servant returned with an animal he had bought from an Arab merchant. Upon examining the beast, they found a precious jewel tied to the donkey's neck. "Praised be God who has sent you this wonderful treasure!" exclaimed the rabbi's disciples. R. Simon thought otherwise. "I bought only the ass and not this precious jewel," he said, and went back to the market and returned the jewel to the merchant. When the Arab realized what R. Simon had done for him, he cried out, "Praised be the God of Simon ben Shetah!"[80]

Once the Jew accepts that all earthly love stems from the

existence of divine love for man, it must follow that neglecting to love others will diminish his capacity to love God. Consequently, if a man does not actively love his fellow man, or if he does not marry and fulfill the divine command to be "fruitful and multiply,"[81] Judaism considers such behavior to reflect outright rejection of the cardinal principle of God's existence.[82]

As Judaism perceives the idea of love, it must be more than just a mental or emotional attitude, that is, having feelings about other people. Just as all the *mitzvot* relating to man and God require not only faith but action,[83] the Torah command to love one's fellow must be fulfilled through concrete *acts,* and not just with belief, emotion, and faith. If these feelings are unaccompanied by deeds, Judaism considers them to be of little value and meaning.

Judaism's insistence upon *deeds* of love as the means to fulfill the Golden Rule, makes it impossible for a person seeking holiness ascetically to withdraw from life. For Judaism understands such a withdrawal, even if motivated by piety, to be an avoidance of one's responsibility toward one's fellows.

As in all matters, Judaism views the responsibility for the fulfillment of this precept as even greater for the scholar and the spiritual leader who must set examples. This is poignantly seen in the story of the talmudic Sage R. Hanina ben Teradion, who was martyred by the Romans during the Hadrianic persecutions in the early second century. He declared that the reason that Heaven ordained his death by immolation, one of the most brutal forms of execution, was that while he had dedicated his life to the study of Torah, he had not devoted enough time during his lifetime to *hesed* — caring for others.[84]

The Talmud emphasizes this point elsewhere. It relates that the great third/fourth-century scholar Rava lived twenty years less than his equally gifted rabbinic contemporary, Abaye, because while Rava devoted himself exclusively to the study of Torah, Abaye also involved himself in acts of love for others.[85]

Love Is More than an Emotion

In order to perform the Torah precepts of love for God and love for one's fellow, the Jew must demonstrate *hesed* — deeds of love and, in fact, base his life on the ethical principles of *hesed*.

If a person says he loves God and expresses this by reciting the *Sh'ma,* that prayer expressing the principle of a personal, mono-theistic God and the scriptural command to love Him, R. Samson Raphael Hirsch asserts that this is not enough:

> Even if you not only recite it, but profoundly and sincerely believe and take it to heart that the Lord your God is One — this belief does not yet make you a Jew. *Only if you seal this belief by deeds, by the devotion of your entire life to the fulfillment of His commands . . . and you raise up your children to obey them . . . only then may you call yourself a Jew.*[86]

In Christianity, man is directed to believe, to have faith. In Judaism, faith is insufficient; it is but a significant prelude to action. This is Judaism's conception of the Golden Rule: belief and acts, faith and deeds, believing in God and His precepts of loving one's fellow and performing acts of love, actually doing *hesed,* living a life centered on selfless giving to others.

The great kabbalist, R. Isaac Luria of Safed (1534–1572), the *Ari HaKadosh,* began his prayers every day with an invocation of faith preparatory to performing *hesed* for others: "Lo! I hold myself ready to fulfill the divine behest 'Love your neighbor as yourself.' "[87]

Putting *Hesed* into Practice

Maimonides and the Jewish ethical teachers list some of the social responsibilities deriving from the obligation of *hesed.* Maimonides rules: "It is a positive commandment to visit the sick, to console the mourners, to attend to the dead, to dower the bride, to welcome one's guests, to perform the rite of burial . . . to cheer the bride and groom and to support them in all their necessities. All these observances are acts of love which one must perform per-sonally. . . ."[88]

Moreover, a Jew is required to lend money without interest, especially to the poor,[89] to establish interest-free loan societies in every community,[90] and to lend his possessions to others.[91]

In addition, the Jew is obliged to open his home to guests,[92] and to establish community facilities for wayfarers.[93] He must give charity to the poor,[94] and do it in a loving manner. The Talmud teaches: "The reward for charity is commensurate with the love in it."[95]

Hesed can also be performed by word, for example, providing advice and counsel to others.[96] The Jew must be concerned about the honor of his fellow man, must only speak of others favorably, never disparagingly.[97] The *Sefer HaHinuch* calls this relationship based on the Golden Rule, *"ahavat hanefesh,"* love of the soul,[98] a relationship manifested by "love, friendship, peace, and rejoicing in his fellow's good fortune."[99]

At the pinnacle of *hesed* stands *hesed shel emet*[100] — "true love." This love, paradoxical as it may sound, is exemplified in kindness to the dead. Such deeds as these, summarized by Maimonides — preparing the body for burial, carrying a casket, and attending a funeral — are considered the epitome of pure love, likened to all of God's acts of love toward men because they involve no expectation of reciprocity.[101] While giving for the sake of receiving does not conform to the Jewish idea of love, in many genuine deeds of love there may exist an underlying motive or expectation.[102] Even if one does not expect but merely *hopes* for the "reward" of another person's gratitude, this is enough to rob the *hesed* of selflessness. Caring for the dead, who can offer nothing in return, is caring in its purest, noblest form. This is the nature of the love a Jew should strive for in all of his relationships.

Love between a parent and a child is considered by Judaism to be the most perfect love.[103] A parent loves his child merely because the child exists, without expecting anything from him. In the Bible, the first reference to love is that of a parent and child, the love between Abraham and Isaac.[104] The second reference is to the love of a man and a woman, Isaac and Rebecca.[105]

The Nature of Romantic Love

It is impossible to grow up in Western society without being influenced by the pervasive exposure to romantic love. It is inevitable that people who grow up in this culture unconsciously absorb this concept without even questioning it. Thus, it becomes the natural expectation of every young person that he or she will inevitably fall in love. For proof of how rooted romantic love has become in society one need only cite the enormous sales of romance novels in America and elsewhere. These romances are prime examples of wish-fulfillment fantasy.

Yet, just as these romances distort the realities of life, there is a distorted perception, especially among young people, regarding the nature of that most profound emotion called love. In this regard, when people talk about "falling in love," it is worth taking a closer look at what they mean. When people talk of love, they refer to it as an ecstatic, turbulent emotion, brought on by a "blind," often irrational attraction of one person for another of the opposite sex, and can at times approach the state of an obsessive fixation. This occurs most commonly in adolescence, but can happen at any period of life. Falling in love always occurs unexpectedly; sometimes it happens at first sight or at first meeting. Definitely then, it is not by conscious choice that one falls in love.

In general, romantic love is described as irrational. In the Middle Ages, the literature connected with it suggests uncontrollable illogicality, sometimes illness (especially mental illness), a "burning fever," and magic. Someone in love is said to have had a "fit," a "seizure," or is simply deemed to be "lovesick." Both philosopher — Plato in the *Phaedrus* — and poet — Shakespeare in *As You Like It* — describe love simply as "madness." Indeed, in *A Midsummer Night's Dream,* Theseus' monologue in the final scenes likens lovers to madmen, and lumps together the lunatic, the lover, and the poet. Shakespeare frequently treats love as a kind of lunacy.

The terminology in the literature closer to our time is not very different. Nietzsche speaks of someone in love as a "happy idiot" who is in the process of some kind of "intestinal fever."[106] Today one is said to fall "madly" in love, or is "moonstruck"; or one falls under a "charm," a "spell," or an "enchantment." Indeed, "witchcraft" is a term used to describe falling in love, with the "bewitched" in a kind of "trance." One falls "helplessly" or "hopelessly" in love, and always "involuntarily" and "passionately."

According to one definition of love by a major dictionary, love is "the sexual instinct and its gratification."[107] This definition of love as an idealized state rooted in lust or sexual attraction, might seem repellant in light of the halo that surrounds the idea of love. Shakespeare, however, had no compunctions in *Troilus and Cressida* to putting in the mouth of Paris the words, "hot blood begets hot thoughts, and hot thoughts begets hot deeds, and hot deeds is love." To which Pandarus responds by questioning whether love is not therefore a "generation of vipers." A close examination will reveal that, unromantic as it may be, the source of romantic love is indeed the libido — physical desire and its satisfaction. In the words of the nineteenth-century German philosopher Arthur Schopenhauer, "all amorousness is rooted in the sexual impulse alone . . . however ethereally it may deport itself."[108] Nietzsche was even more direct, defining love simply as "the spiritualization of sensuality."[109]

No less important in this regard is the philosophy surrounding love that has developed throughout history, especially in the Western medieval world. These ideas have become deeply embedded into people's consciousness as part of their educational process. Indeed, there would be no glorification of romantic love in the world were it not for these ideas.

The Source of Popular Ideas on Love

As much as we might like to think of love as a natural and elemental force in humans, it is not necessarily a universal phenomenon of human nature at all; it may well be a creation of the Western world and Western culture. Such a love was virtually unknown in the ancient world. In the East, it hardly ever existed nor does it today. Anthropologists have shown that love, as it is known in Western society, is unknown in other cultures, even advanced ones.

The popular idea of love in the Western world has its roots in the courtly conventions of the Middle Ages. Courtly love evolved over a period of about five hundred years, from the twelfth to the seventeenth century. Troubadours — medieval singers and balladeers — would travel widely, singing their tales of chivalrous love, which were widely disseminated and became very popular. The poems and ballads of the troubadours survived long after their deaths, and the spirit of romantic love which they introduced influenced all the literature and art of the centuries that followed.

These songs of love by the troubadours are tinged with sadness. This is because the first significant component of the love they celebrated is fatalism — the idea that two people are destined only for each other. Within this literary genre, there occurred democratization of love; love was for everyone, and lovers came from different social strata and from markedly different groups. The democratization in the literature of this period was in sharp contrast to the existing reality of social stratification, since actual marriage unions were almost invariably based on the compatibility of the partners' backgrounds and their particular social stratum and resulted in conflicts between love and society that could not be harmonized.

The second important component of courtly love was idealization, the enhancement of the importance of love and the object of one's love. The troubadours idealized sexual desire and cultivated means of satisfying it, and this resulted in the idealization of the woman, the object of desire, as the man bestowed transcendental significance upon her in a blind, almost mystical manner.

In this literature, the knight placed his beloved on a pedestal, exalted her as the embodiment of the highest ideals, and paid homage to her idealized image through his amorous imagination. His servile relationship was such that the object of his love was at times described as a divinity, and love itself became a kind of religion in which she was the idol he venerated.

In medieval literature, love is almost always unhappy; happy love is virtually unknown. As in *Tristan and Isolde, Romeo and Juliet,* and *The Chatelaine of Vergi,* love begins with an intense, often unbearable pleasure, and almost always ends in pain, sorrow, or disillusionment for the star-crossed lovers. The protagonists in the drama end up as tragic victims of a romantic passion they cannot control.

Andreas Capellanus begins his classical work on courtly love, *Tractatus amoris & de amoris remedio,* written about 1185, with the words, "Love is a certain inborn suffering derived from the sight of and excessive meditation upon the beauty of the opposite sex[110] . . . there can be no torment greater . . . indeed, courtly lovers seem to have a powerful death wish, as if they are in love with death more than of life or each other."[111] Petrarch, the fourteenth-century Italian poet, sees love as a painful calamity, an agony, a "life-in-death" of constant suffering characterized by misery, not joy, and something that constantly destroys those who love.

If love entails torture and usually ends in tragic disillusionment, why is it so exalted, and why do so many people allow themselves to fall in love? This is partly because, as Andreas makes clear, love is related to desire and passion, and both grow in direct relation to suffering. Intense, obsessive passion thrives especially on torment, and it inevitably seeks its own destruction. Without the suffering there is no passion, and without passion there is no love.

Romantic Literature: A Celebration of Illicit Love

In the thirteenth century, Guillaume de Lorris, in his popular French allegorical poem, "The Romance of the Rose," writes, "Love brings a very jolly malady/in the midst of which one laughs and jokes and plays./Lovers by turn feel torment, then joys./Love sickness is a changeable disease;/One hour it bitter is, the next sweet."[112]

Love in medieval literature is, for the most part, neither pain alone nor joy alone; it is both a joy and an affliction. Much of the pleasure undoubtedly lies in the attraction and excitement of doing that which is forbidden. People in the throes of love can give free rein to their passions, permitting themselves to be mastered and consumed by them, the "victims" of and "involuntary slaves" to the very passions they have unleashed by falling in love.

In romantic literature there is a close relationship between love and immoral, illicit passion; love is forbidden, hidden, furtive. A characteristic example of courtly love in medieval literature is a romantic tale by the twelfth-century French author Chretien de Troyes, titled "Le Chevalier de la Charrette," which recounts the adventures of the knight Lancelot and the maid Guinevere. It is a story of knightly adventure and adultery, and of rebellion at conventions that regard marital ties as sacred. It tells of a wor-shipful — almost idolatrous — love at once illicit and ennobling and, because it ran counter to prevailing societal norms, furtive and secret.

C. S. Lewis, in *The Allegory of Love*, describes adultery as one of the principle characteristics of courtly love. Romantic love is actually destructive of the institution of marriage because it rejects marital fidelity, and is usually inextricably linked to adulterous passions and other immoral sexual activity. Furthermore, it is often nourished by jealousy — Andreas says that jealousy increases love, and calls it the "nurse of love" that helps love grow — and is destroyed by exposure.

Looking at the romantic literature of the age—how much of it deals with the happy, requited love of a husband and wife? Happy marital love is seldom, if ever, the subject of this literature. Why? This prosaic, domestic love is attainable and licit, whereas romantic love requires the remoteness and inaccessibility of the unattainable, or the illicit. After all, how much literary interest can be sustained by a love which is licit and unobstructed? If love is lawful and commonplace, it is not magical and ethereal, and, like eating, nobody would write novels about it.

In fact, most medieval writers did not believe that love was possible in marriage. Indeed, while affection in marriage was possible, love was held to be impossible between husband and wife. It had to be sought outside marriage. In the words of one observer, "True, the adored lady was always a wife, but always someone else's wife. This was one of the rules. . . ."[113] Andreas has a woman say, "We declare and hold as firmly established that love cannot exert its powers between two people who are married to each other."[114] Moreover, most writers did not consider adultery and other kinds of illicit love wrong, or at least too wrong. Even Dante, who in *The Divine Comedy* places his protagonists Paolo and Francesca da Rimini in hell because they committed adultery, puts them only in the first, or most moderate, circle of hell, in a region populated by other like sinners, such as Cleopatra and Tristan. Since, in Dante's eyes, their only sin was that they sought love, they are not situated in a region for more serious sinners such as, for example, those guilty of selfishness.

Thus, it is inaccessible and illicit love that is celebrated in romantic literature. Adultery and other moral deviations therefore become the norm. Interest in such love can indeed be sustained in romantic tales. In later, more modern literature, some of the most powerful invocations to romantic love are centered upon incest (Wagner), love for a nymphet (Nabokov), or homosexual love (Proust). It is such love, practiced under the license of a "higher" moral authority of its own, that transcends conventional religious and moral boundaries, that is extolled. It is designed to elicit from the reader empathy and admiration, feelings that become absorbed into his consciousness without his ever being aware of it. The principles of this love ethic can then easily affect his moral views and govern his conduct.

It is this early romantic literature which has, over the centuries, shaped our attitudes toward love. It is one of the tragedies of our time that this medieval concept of romantic love has been adopted by Western culture as the ideal love. For it is this idea of love that threatens the very fabric of marital love and is an obstacle to happy married life. In its attempt to ascribe superior value to love beyond moral conventions, it is destructive of the institution of marriage and has caused inestimable damage to the stability of the family in our modern world.

Furthermore, this medieval concept of love has filled men and women with extravagant expectations of marriage. No relations between two people could possibly measure up to the imagined, idealized relations conjured up by the emotions and dreams of romantic love.

Conveying this view, the popular seventeenth-century French novelist Madame de Lafayette has her protagonist, the widow in *La Princesse de Cleves,* reject marriage to her lover, Monsieur de Nemours, because she says marriage to him would lead only to agony and not to bliss. Their love, she reasons, is as strong as it is only because it is illicit, and marrying would destroy their love. Madame de Lafayette was here expressing the cynical exposition of her acquaintance, the French philosopher Duc de La Rochefoucauld, who said, "There are successful marriages, but no blissful ones."

In actuality, these romantic writers are expressing the idea that romantic love is really a rejection of marital fidelity, and therefore is, in and of itself, destructive to marriage. According to this way of thinking, love and marriage are incompatible. Echoing this thought, Stendhal writes, "When love does exist in marriage, it is a fire which goes out more rapidly than it was lit."[115]

Idealization: Transforming Desire into Love

The Greeks employed terms for different aspects of love: *eros,* which refers to physical desire, and denotes the sensual component in love between man and woman; *philos,* which refers to friendship and affection; *nomos,* which is the idea of love as justice, righteousness; and *agape,* which denotes a feeling that transcends *eros* and *philos,* so that the lover is devoted to the welfare and dignity of the other. *Agape,* which is sometimes translated as charity, is frequently called divine love, because its prototype of selfless love is God's love for man.

As is the case with medieval courtly love, idealization of the object of one's love is central to the Greek concept of romantic love. Romantic love is kindled by desire. *Eros,* which is appetitive and physical, transforms the individual's entire perception. He creates in his imagination a *persona* to suit him, in the process idealizing the object of his desire, and seeing in the "beloved" the embodiment of all virtue. Thus, physical attractiveness is perceived as the highest virtue, and physical attributes of the beloved become imagined merits. The individual may deceive himself into thinking it is not desire that he feels, but something much worthier — love. Desire becomes moralized into love because it is genuine love that person really wants.

In essence, however, no matter how it is described, this love is only a mask for desire. Desire becomes love only by virtue of the fact that the person so describes it. Unwilling to acknowledge his self-deception, this individual creates a romantic idealization around the object of his love, and the feelings and emotions that are kindled become a basis for glorification. The loved one comes to represent the absolute ideal, and his or her shortcomings become nonexistent; he or she embodies perfection.

Romantic love thus involves the transformation of initial erotic desire into a kind of elevated idealized yearning for spiritual perfection. At times the transformation will be so effective that the initial instinctual interest in the other will be totally sublimated as a result of the spiritualization of that person by the other.

Since objective reality could threaten the foundation upon which the infatuation rests, reality is distorted by the lover bestowing greater value on the object of desire than that person may actually possess. Freud views this process as an overvaluation of the object of one's love, whereby that person becomes glorified by bestowing upon her a value that no objective appraisal could possibly justify. His powers of rational judgment disappear, and the person in love becomes infatuated by the achievements or perfections of the object of his love. The character of the beloved is valued more highly than others who are not similarly endowed by the lover. This falsification of judgment is the result of idealization,[116] one characterized by fantasy and an inclination to distort the real nature of the other person. In essence, the lover loves the distortion. Freud describes the phenomenon in this way: "Idealization is a process that concerns the object [of desire]; by it, that object, without any alteration in its nature, is aggrandized and exalted in the subject's mind."[117]

In Santayana's view, love always requires idealization, the idealizing of what would otherwise be an ordinary object of nature. By seeing a woman as personifying some ideal, the lover ignores her shortcomings and elevates and dignifies her in his imagination. The ideal object is imagined, and does not exist. The imagination transforms the natural and imperfect into the unnatural and perfect. As Santayana sees it, the object of one's desire then comes to represent the ideal. In this way the object of one's sensual desire is transmuted into an idealized object of love. Through the amorous imagination, one individual becomes sensually attracted to another.[118]

Stimulated by physical attraction, the powerful, passionate emotions characterizing romantic love embody an overwhelming desire to "possess" the other person. "I love you" becomes synonymous with "I want you." This is reminiscent of Plato's classical definition of love in *The Symposium,* as the "desire for the perpetual possession of the beautiful."[119] Ironically, Casanova, who fell in love frequently, but never "perpetually," explains his behavior by stating that "one does not desire what one possesses."

Such is the intensity of the emotions engendered by passionate desire and the powerful impetus to consummate it, that it is easy for a couple in the throes of passion to conclude that they love one another.

Self-Love: The Basis of Romantic Love

Paradoxically, however, each of the lovers may actually be more in love with himself than with the other. Enamored as they may be with one another, from the very beginning each looks to the other to provide him with pleasure. Despite proclaiming undying, unselfish devotion to one another, the lovers principally seek emotional and physical gratification from each other. Each is interested basically in satisfying his own needs and in quenching his own passions.

Freud explains this phenomenon by understanding narcissism as the primal condition underlying all love. An individual loves another person on the basis of his own needs—basically as a desire to be loved. The lover is essentially attempting to do everything he can to make himself loved by the object of his love. According to Freud, every interest by a lover in another is therefore really a device for narcissism or self-love. Rousseau declares self-love to be a basic motivation for all human behavior, but says that self-love is not all that bad.[120]

This view goes back to Aristotle, who defines one kind of love or friendship as based on utility or pleasure, in which one is basically concerned only with his own welfare and not with the other's. This relationship is governed only by self-interest, with each loving the other only for what he can derive from the other.[121] The Latin poet Ovid expresses a similar idea of love in the myth of Narcissus loving his ephemeral image in the water. In loving himself, he excludes the possibility of genuine reciprocal love. The narcissistic lover uses his beloved as a medium to love himself.

Kant holds that in appetitive love, in which one person treats another as if the other was a thing, and therefore just a means to an end, one is guilty of the greatest immorality. Using people in this fashion in order to derive pleasure, Kant maintains, violates their dignity as autonomous beings, and their basic humanity.[122]

In these circumstances, the object of one's love is important for what he provides, not for what he is. It is like someone saying, "I love this pie." Is it the pie he really loves—or himself? He wants the pie in order to satisfy his need, and to satisfy his need he is prepared to swallow whole the pie that he "loves." Spinoza says it succinctly: "Love is pleasure, accompanied by the idea of an external cause."[123]

The Jewish Sages have a term for this use of a partner as an object to provide gratification—*ahavah ha-t'luyah b'davar,* love that is dependent on an external thing. Romantic love, we have seen, is usually linked to sensual desire. Such a love must necessarily be superficial and transient in nature. Physical attractions eventually fade or passions become sated. The original object of romantic love is then easily replaceable should a more attractive recipient appear. The Mishnah declares: "When love depends on something [sensual], if that [sensual] thing ceases to exist then the love ceases to exist."[124]

The Mishnah cites as an example of *ahavah ha-t'luyah b'davar,* the love of Amnon for Tamar in the Bible. As described in the Book of Samuel,[125] Amnon's love for Tamar, which was based solely on physical desire, culminated in his raping her. His lust satisfied, his love quickly turned to hatred, and then he drove her away.

When a person makes the painful discovery that his love was a romantic illusion that only masked a passionate sensual attraction, his anger at his own disillusionment at having been misled by his emotions may lead him to hate the other, whom he now blames as an enticer. In reality, the object of his desire was not a person, but only a medium to provide physical pleasure.

The Impermanence of Romantic Love

Judaism does not totally denigrate romantic love, as it may at times serve to initiate a deeper, more significant, and lasting relationship. Similarly, Judaism does not denounce physical attraction. It does recognize the importance of the physical relationship in marriage, but teaches that marriage cannot be based upon romantic love alone; this is incompatible with the realities and needs of marriage and family. Such love inevitably involves what Bertrand Russell calls a "glamorous mist" which prevents two people from truly understanding each other's being.[126] The Jewish idea is that marriage must be based primarily on knowledge of one another and on mutual giving.

Romantic love is indeed "blind" because the lover, overcome by the powerful urge to satisfy his desires, is unable to view the situation objectively. Such love is thus subject to serious errors of judgment which the lovers do not recognize until after they have attained gratification. Then their eyes are opened, and they see their love for what it really was, an idealization based upon the libidinous impulse narcissistically directed inward, toward a love of self, what Freud calls "ego libido." Once physical desires are satisfied, the idealization of the other evaporates. According to Schopenhauer, the root of the problem is that when people attain the object of their desire, they quickly lose interest in it. Success leads inevitably to boredom. Therefore, Schopenhauer says, a happy marriage cannot result from passionate, romantic love, because such a love contains within it the ingredients for both short-term happiness and long-term failure. Marriage, which requires long-term happiness in order for it to succeed, must therefore be based not upon love, but upon cool, careful deliberation by two people of the qualities of one another, and consideration of the families, and even of social and economic factors. In brief, declares Schopenhauer, *if one wants to be happy in marriage and have a successful marriage, one must marry for reasons other than love.*[127] Romantic love is incompatible with the idea of marriage.

While most Jews have naturally absorbed the Western approach to love as part of their acculturation, it is not Judaism's idea for the basis of a successful marriage. As experience almost invariably shows, this romantic love is usually no more than an emotional infatuation which, like a flame that flares up brightly, emits a brief, intense light and heat, but has no enduring warmth.

It is understandable, therefore, that a decision to marry, usually the major decision of a person's life, which might be made during an irrational period of romantic intoxication, is bound to fail. Romantic love contains within itself elements that encourage instability in marriage; it is founded on unrealistic idealization of the other and on physical desire, and is devoid both of knowledge of the other and of selfless giving. Thus it is not surprising that marriages based upon romantic love fail.

How to Create an Enduring Love

Agape, the Greek term for a love concerned only with giving to the object of one's affection, is closest to the Jewish idea of love between man and woman. The Jewish concept of genuine love between man and woman is a relationship in which the welfare and happiness of the other is preeminent.

It is based less upon sudden infatuation and self-gratification, and more upon deep knowledge and understanding of one another. A person genuinely in love comes to know his beloved in all his or her moods, acts, and gestures. The person who falls in love "romantically" sees only external features and gestures which awaken his desire. Indeed, "love at first sight" is no more nor less than the experience of *eros,* an intense desire brought on through the physical embodiment of the other.

However, one does not *fall* into genuine love; one *grows* into it. The learning process of understanding the other's personality and becoming aware of the other's interests and needs is slow and difficult. It is far removed from the instant, effortless sensation that "falling in love" implies. Love that is based upon the solid foundations of friendship, affection, empathy, reciprocal giving, knowledge, and understanding is sure to be more enduring.

True love transcends desire. A romantic love rooted in desire and based on libidinal idealization does not involve genuinely benevolent concern for the welfare of the object of such love. George Bernard Shaw refers to romantic love as "an appetite, which, like all other appetites, is destroyed . . . by its gratification."[128] Since romantic love is founded on the appetitive in man, once that desire has been satisfied, there is no longer any need for the object of desire.

People are not things. By using another person to satisfy one's appetite, and taking no interest in his or her humanity, a person turns the other into a thing, and divests the other of dignity; by neglecting the humanity of the other, the other is degraded and dehumanized.

The Components of Ideal Love

Love involves intimacy. It grows from friendship and companionship in which genuine, mutual concern for the well-being of the other is expressed constantly in altruistic, selfless giving, in which each discovers happiness by looking after the other's happiness. This love is nourished by affection, conversation, communion, mutual experiences, sharing, loyalty, mutual dependence and mutual respect. The altruistic feelings develop gradually, as each of the partners comes to understand profoundly and to empathize with the other.

This kind of empathetic love develops, in time, into a condition in which the couple commune with one another and do things together, and results in a virtual integration of their personalities. True love has a tendency to grow with time, while romantic love has a tendency to wither with the attainment of its goal.

Romantic love is an expression of yearning for an ideal goodness represented by the object of one's love. Unfortunately, the love for the ideal will usually be stronger than that for the person, and frustration and disappointment will follow when the loved one fails to fulfill that ideal. According to Santayana, romantic love is always frustrated because "all beauties attract by suggesting the ideal, and then fail to satisfy by not fulfilling it."[129]

The ideal love between a man and a woman, therefore, is love in marriage, the family framework for the nourishment and development of a deep, interpersonal relationship characterized by friendship, altruistic, empathetic concern, and mutual benevolence. Marriage represents the most significant step in man's search for enduring happiness. Since family life is the foundation for a good society, nothing can be more essential for human welfare than the institution of marriage, and love in marriage is the medium for building a successful family and, in a wider sense, a successful society. Marriage is the means for two individuals to merge into a new marital superentity which culminates and receives its fulfillment in the children they produce.

For a marriage to succeed, therefore, it cannot be based upon romantic love. It must rather be based upon the cool, reasoned judgment of two practical, mature people, each of whom first determines to the best of his ability that the other will make a good mate and a fine parent. Key elements in such an assessment must include a sober appraisal of the other's character and personality — whether or not he or she is a moral, compassionate individual or has good personal qualities. The kind of love that grows and develops in marriage through knowledge of one another will continue to grow and flourish as they live together and come to appreciate each other's qualities.

Loving Your Spouse as Yourself

If Judaism requires the individual to love his fellow as himself, how much more powerful is the obligation to love his spouse who, in Judaism, is considered to be as his own flesh?[130] Judaism does not view marriage as incompatible with love. It teaches that a loving relationship is not only possible, but is a state that one can attain by willing it to be, and makes love in marriage *mandatory*. The Talmud teaches: "A man should love his wife as himself and honor her more than himself."[131]

This dictum of the Sages is a required norm of behavior for Jewish husbands.[132] Taking a closer look at the disparity between the degree of love required and that of honor, it becomes clear that respect is more a matter of mind than of emotion. A person can train his mind so that he respects his wife more than himself.

In regard to the requirement that a man love his wife only as much as he loves himself, the Sages express a keen understanding of man, whose nature it is to give more to himself than to anyone else. Since Jewish law never demands more than is humanly possible of an individual,[133] loving someone else as oneself is deemed to be the highest level of love that can reasonably be expected of ordinary mortals.

The Talmud relates that God originally created man and woman simultaneously as a single, androgynous creature, intended to function as one hermaphroditic being. Only later did He separate a part of Adam to create man and woman as separate entities.[134] The purpose of this division into two beings, male and female, may have been to urge man to direct his interest outward and to learn to love and take care of another person in addition to himself, that is, to prevent all of man's efforts from being directed toward benefiting only himself.

Man and woman complement one another, and are drawn to one another by the mutual need for completion. Among animals, however, the male and female are drawn together to copulate but they rarely remain together. Most will fight over food and will not remain together long. (This is why in Jewish thought male and female animals were created separately from dust.) But humans have a strong desire to *be* together. Man and woman, created from a single entity, are impelled, in order to achieve their mutual fulfillment, to revert to their original state of oneness, but to do this they must learn to love each other as each loves his own being. When love is perfect, man and wife become a single entity and can overcome all problems.[135] It is only when they love each other in perfect harmony that together they form the "image of God."[136]

As Judaism understands it, the supreme act of altruistic love is God's creation of the world. A human being can emulate God as Creator when he comes together with a member of the opposite sex.

Then, just as God created life, so too can the pair create life. Indeed, according to Judaism they become partners with God[137] in the creation of life.[138]

The first man, Adam, called his wife "bone of my bone, flesh of my flesh."[139] If someone loves his wife as himself, the Sages say, he will have total empathy with her as if she were truly his own flesh. The story is told of the late R. Aryeh Levin, known as the *Tzadik* (Righteous One) of Jerusalem, that he once took his wife to the doctor when she was in pain, and told him, "Doctor, my wife's foot is hurting us!"[140]

Referring to the verse in Genesis: "Therefore shall a man leave his father and mother and cleave to his wife and shall be as one flesh,"[141] the Italian commentator on the Torah, R. Ovadiah ben Jacob Sforno (c. 1470–1550) provides a meaningful definition of the love which he advises every Jewish husband and wife to seek: "They should endeavor in all their activities to achieve that wholeness that was intended by God with the creation of man as if the two were actually one."[142]

This, then, is the Jewish idea of absolute, selfless love to which a person must strive in all his relations with his life's partner — *oneness* — coalescence into one being. Oneness in body, mind, and soul.

The oneness of genuine love in Jewish thought is alluded to through *g'matria,* the numerical equivalence of Hebrew letters. The numerical equivalent of *ahavah,* love, is thirteen, and the numerical equivalent of *ehad,* one, is also thirteen. The thirteen of *ahavah* and the thirteen of *ehad* fuse into twenty-six, the *g'matria* of God's name, the Tetragrammaton. According to the Sages, when a couple achieves the oneness of genuine love, God comes down and dwells with them.[143] God is the Loving Oneness *par excellence.* The Sages declare: "Neither man without his wife, nor woman without her husband, nor both of them without the Divine Presence."[144]

The *Midrash* says:

> If their love merits it, the *Sh'chinah,* the Divine Presence, dwells with a man and his wife. If not, fire devours them. Adam was called *Ish* and Eve was called *Ishah.* If they go in My ways and keep all My precepts, behold, My name is given to them (referring to the Hebrew letters *yod* and *hay* that form the first half of the *Tetragrammaton*). He

shall be called *Ish* (Man — *Ish* spelled with a *yod*) and she shall be called *Ishah* (Woman — *Ishah* spelled with a *hay*). If they do not walk in My ways I will remove My name (the letters *yod* and *hay*) from them and all that will be left will be *Aish,* a consuming fire. Each will consume the other.[145]

In Jewish thought, if one sees his marital partner as a separate being with needs and wants separate from his own, he will give to his spouse only grudgingly, and with resentment. He must, instead, identify completely with her so that he perceives her good as his good, her needs as his own, "as if the two were actually one." Opposing the other's wishes is then like opposing one's own. When all distinction between one's interests and the other's disappear, and there is reciprocity, love develops in an empathetic, selfless fashion. This is embodied in the rabbinic principle, *ishto k'gufo,* a man's wife is like his very own body.[146]

The Oneness of Love

The hasidic Rabbi Moses Leib of Sassov (1745–1807) said that he learned the real meaning of love from a conversation he overheard between two peasants:

The first peasant asked, "Ivan, do you love me?"
"I love you deeply," answered the second peasant.
The first then asked. "Do you know, my friend, what gives me pain?"
Replied the second, "How can *I* know what gives you pain?"
To which the first peasant retorted: "If you do not know what hurts me, how can you say you love me?"[147]

Empathetic love is based upon a deep understanding of the other person's values, wishes, needs, and fears. According to Jewish thought, to love truly is to have such complete knowledge of the other's character, of his values, needs, and fears as to be able to plumb his or her emotional depths. It involves a virtual symbiosis with the other wherein one identifies completely with the wants and needs of the other.[148] Here, the peasant was disappointed to learn that his friend who claimed to love him was unaware of a most elementary aspect of his character.

The *Midrash* relates a moving tale of the second-century tannaitic Sage, R. Simon ben Yohai:

> A couple who had been married more than ten years without having been blessed with children decided to divorce. The husband told his wife, "Take the most precious object I have in my house and go back to your father's house." They then went to R. Simon, who tried to dissuade them from divorcing. However, the husband persisted. Whereupon R. Simon said to them, "When you wed, you rejoiced and entertained your friends with a feast of food and drink. Now, too, let your separation be like your union. Prepare a feast like your wedding feast, and on the following day come and see me."
>
> The couple did as R. Simon instructed and arranged a "separation feast" which was like a wedding. During the feast, the husband became merry with wine and fell into a deep sleep. Whereupon his wife had him carried to her father's house. Upon awakening, the husband was startled to find himself in a strange place. "Where am I?" he asked. His wife replied that he was in her father's house. "Why should I be in your father's house?" he asked. His wife replied, "Didn't you tell me to take the most precious object in your house and go back to my father's house? I have no object more precious than you, and by our promise I am entitled to keep you."
>
> Her words greatly moved her husband and, overcome with emotion, they went back to R. Simon. He advised them not to part. He said he would pray for them to have children, and he was certain God would reward such a good wife. The couple heeded his advice and returned home together. The following year, R. Simon participated in the circumcision of their son.[149]

How to Have a Happy Marriage

As Judaism perceives it, love between husband and wife, in a happy marriage, is expressed less in words than in deeds—which the two partners constantly extend to each other. The partners constantly work together to build a relationship of loving and giving; their joy in marriage is the natural product of the altruistic love that flows between them. Each senses the other's needs, attends to them, and seeks to satisfy their independent activities. They define themselves in terms of their attachment and devotion to each other. Judaism does not consider love as an option but as an imperative between husband and wife. If love is absent, they must expend every effort to attain it. R. Eliezer Papo, the eighteenth-century ethical teacher, writes in *Pele Yoetz:* "It is *obligatory* for husband and wife to love each other; they *must* have a strong love for one another. . . . Their love should be based fundamentally [not on physical expression but] on a love of the spirit. . . ."[150]

The Sages were aware of the human need to be loved, especially on the part of the woman.[151] They were also aware of the human need to *give* love. The rabbis say in another context: "More than the calf wants to nurse, the cow wants to suckle."[152]

In Jewish thought, if a man loves his wife as himself, her joy will be his own. In a marriage based upon selfless giving, both partners discover that they receive much more than they give. Whereas self-gratification is insatiable, a craving that grows as it is fed, genuine love yields gratification and profound satisfaction specifically to the lover, the giver.

There are two aspects to the Jewish understanding of love as altruistic: the *mitzvah* of the act itself, of giving to another; and the *mitzvah* expressed in the sublimation of the self through the act.[153]

On the other hand, Jewish ethical teachers viewed taking as the epitome of selfishness, the root of evil. "Taking" should be understood as different from receiving. Taking involves the aggressive reaching out into the domain of the other to seize something from the other. God, the source of all good, has created man with the capacity to give, thus enabling him to add to the happiness in the world as God Himself does. The average person might be inclined to adopt the middle way as the ideal mean, that is, to be both a giver and a taker. However, the Sages firmly point out that in this case there is no middle path. The ethical teacher R. Elijah Dessler (1891–1954) stresses this point:

> It is a basic law that there is no middle path in human interest. In every act, in every word, in every thought . . . one is always devoted either to lovingkindness and giving or to grasping and taking. . . . The corrupted world is a world of takers whose aim is to use, despoil and exploit each other as much as they can. This is the social system in which jealousy, greed and competitiveness reign and which inevitably leads to war, murder, robbery, and misery. But the perfected world is one where every person gives to and benefits others

and whose heart overflows with gratitude for what he receives from others. A human society such as this is the perfect and happy society, overflowing with peace and love — the society in which God delights.[154]

The Jewish idea is that the moment one stops giving, the desire for self-gratification begins. Rather than seeing other people as recipients of his love, a person begins to view them as obstacles in his path toward pleasure. If he perceives others as weaker than himself, he will attempt, in order to promote his own well-being, to extract all he can from them. If they appear stronger, he will fear and hate them for possessing what he himself wants. The person who repeatedly succumbs to the habit of taking is likely to end up viewing the entire world as his enemy. The only escape from this mentality, say the Jewish Sages, is concern for others.

Giving, the Key to a Successful Marriage

Nowhere is this point more evident than in marriage. As the Sages see it, marital partners cannot learn to love properly unless they first learn to give freely, selflessly, and unconditionally. For those who lack this ability to give, real love remains elusive. R. Dessler asks: "Is the giving a consequence of the love, or . . . the love a result of the giving? We usually think it is love which causes giving . . . but . . . giving may bring about love for the same reason that a person loves what he himself has created and nurtured . . . for in it he finds himself . . . love flows in the direction of giving."[155]

The Sages teach that this is the essence of God's love for His creations, and this love also characterizes that of a parent for his child. The parents have given the child of their flesh and blood, and continue to give their time, energy, and concern. By giving of himself to another, a person expands, and in gratitude for this, the giver loves the recipient. The act of giving thus forges an emotional bond.

As the Sages perceive it, working to better the life of another person invests the other person's life with importance in the eyes of the giver. Love for that person will grow in proportion to the amount given to him. The other's life eventually appears as important as the giver's own, fulfilling the precept of "love your fellow as yourself." R. Dessler teaches: "By giving of yourself you will find out that you and the receiver are indeed one; you will feel in the clearest possible manner that the other is to you as yourself."[156]

In marriage, neither man nor woman is truly independent — both are mutually interdependent. The Sages declare: "A man is always dependent on his wife and a woman is always dependent on her husband."[157]

The complementary aspect of the union between man and woman lies partly in the structure of their male and female personalities, with each supplying elements that the other lacks. However, their completion of each other is not a passive process. The Jewish ethical teachers insist that each must struggle with all his faculties to give to the other. Only by this "labor of love" is the real union completed.

Why Marriages Fail — And How to Do Something about It

In their daily lives, most people are takers, not givers. The focus of most of their activities, whether for work or for leisure, is on how to glean from them the maximum amount of prestige or pleasure. In marriage, however, the taker aspect has to give way to the giver instinct.

If most marriages turn out to be only temporarily successful, it is because, with the waning biological urge which accompanies gratification of desire, the partners gradually stop being givers and begin to think about taking. Each begins to demand from the other what he deems necessary for his own happiness. In place of the earlier solicitous regard for another's needs comes a more exclusive preoccupation with one's own. Once a source of delight, the familiar words and gestures of the spouse now serve as a source of irritation, and tenderness is swept away by mounting resentment. Each starts demanding things from the other. "When demand begins, love departs," R. Dessler warns.[158] When a couple stop giving and start taking, the marriage begins a downward spiral. Divorce then looms as a real threat.

In the view of the Sages, giving is an important antidote to divorce, as it is a well-tried formula for marital happiness. Moreover, when a person gives to another, there is no diminution of himself. As a single lamp can give flame without diminution of its own light, so can a person give love continuously to another.

Loving by giving is expressed in a variety of ways. Materially, one can offer support and protection to one's partner. Being actively interested and involved in the activities of the other is also a way of giving. The psychological expressions of giving involve a constant awareness of and consideration for the other's feelings, and are therefore much harder to sustain through the marriage.

Judaism teaches that love begins at home. While one is obliged to love all people and to express that love in deeds, one's spouse takes precedence over all others as the recipient of one's love. R. Shlomo Wolbe, a leading contemporary ethical teacher, writes:

> If a man is involved in *g'milut hesed,* acts of love extended to other people — he lends and gives to those in need, he visits the sick, consoles mourners and causes grooms and brides to rejoice — he shall surely receive his just reward, for there are many merits gained by such acts of *hesed.* However, he should certainly know that in heaven they will investigate how he conducted himself *with his wife* — if he did indeed perform acts of love for her all of his days. If so, may he be praised and may it be well with him.
>
> If, however, he forsook her and behaved in his home punctiliously and without mercy and in an angry manner that lacked a semblance of love . . . this will decide his ultimate judgment by Heaven, and none of his deeds of love for others will even be mentioned. . . . May everyone be cautioned lest he conduct himself in a loving and good-hearted manner outside his home but with excessive pedantry at home. . . .[159]

Genuine love, declares R. Judah ben Don Isaac Abarbanel (c. 1460–1523) in *Vikuah al Ahavah (Dialoghi D'Amore),* his philosophical work on love of God, must be bound up with good too, "which is the reason why a reciprocal love does survive the enjoyment of its delight, and not only persists but grows constantly. . . ."[160]

We see that love deepens between married people as they gradually come to understand and to cherish one another. The Bible alludes to love after marriage in the story of Isaac's union with Rebecca.[161] Comments R. Samson Raphael Hirsch (1808–1888), the German rabbi and philosopher:

> The more she became his wife, the more he loved her. Like this marriage of the first Jewish son, [successful] Jewish marriages are

contracted . . . not by passion but by reason and judgment. . . .
Such love grows more and more the more they get to know each
other. But regarding . . . marriages made by what they call "love"
. . . what a gulf usually yawns between the "love" before marriage
and after. How insipid everything then seems. How different from
all the glamour we had imagined. . . . Such "love" is indeed blind.
Every step into the future brings disappointment. But if Jewish
marriage is like that of Isaac and Rebecca, love grows and develops
after marriage. The wedding is not the culmination but the seed, the
root of love.[162]

The nineteenth-century rabbi and exegete R. Meir Loeb Malbim
comments in the same vein:

This was the custom followed by Jews. . . . Their love may be
compared to the growth of a tree, which begins with a tiny seed . . .
and gradually grows and expands from day to day. So too was their
love. At the start, there was but a seed of love sown in their hearts.
But, little by little, the seed of love reached its fullest proportions only
after marriage. . . . This custom of our fathers is only reasonable.
Aware that they lacked total knowledge about each other before
marriage, the expectations were not high. They shared a tacit
agreement that if they were just compatible they would be mutually
acceptable. However, under the contemporary system, people concentrate on enchanting one another. Their imaginations conjure up
a romanticized love which bears no relation to reality. Is there any
surprise, therefore, that when this mutual self-deception becomes
evident, their love gradually cools and eventually disappears, or that
divorce is so much more prevalent today than it has ever been?[163]

The *Malbim,* as R. Meir Loeb is known, was writing about the
greater prevalence of divorce in his day, the mid-nineteenth century. We can but imagine what his reaction would be to the divorce
rate today.

True Love: More Than Yesterday, Less Than Tomorrow

To employ a popular saying, genuine love is "more than yesterday,
less than tomorrow." Jews use the significant phrase *liv'not bayit
ne'eman* — to build a faithful home — to describe the joint efforts of a

couple to express their love and Jewishness in marriage. They painstakingly build their marriage not on emotion alone, but with elements of care, devotion, respect, and consideration. They continually work to preserve and to fortify that marriage. Living together, sharing interests, being concerned for the welfare of the other, they bear good will toward each other, and perform benevolent acts of love for each other. They establish a community of love in which both benefit because they benefit one another. The ideal results and benefits do not come quickly or easily. Like a tree that grows stronger and taller every day under the care of the planter, so too the solid foundation of a happy marriage takes shape only after continuous care. The Torah relates that Jacob toiled for Rachel for fourteen years in order to marry her.[164] But when he stood under the marriage canopy with her, his real work had only begun. The strain and difficulties of physical labor are as nothing compared to the emotional constancy and efforts that a successful marriage requires. You could say that a good marriage is one guided by knowledge, inspired by empathetic love, and fueled by the unceasing dedication of the partners to make it a success.

The best things in love are not free. They call for the most arduous task of all—leaving the comfortable precincts of self-involvement to reach out and care for another as oneself. Indeed, according to Judaism, one knows that he has truly attained love when he is *more* concerned for the other party than he is for himself.

However, it is not that Judaism perceives marriage as a grim task. The husband and wife who live by the tenets of giving discover what all true lovers joyfully discover—that giving to one's beloved—and seeing the joy this brings to the recipient—is its own reward. The more one gives to one's beloved, the greater is the joy of loving. To be loved is wonderful; infinitely more pleasurable is the giving of love.

R. Samson Raphael Hirsch points out that the word *hav,* to give, is half of the word *ahavah, love.*[165] One may say that the two are part of one concept.

The popular notion that marriage should be characterized by a relationship of "give and take" is a dangerous one. In Jewish thought giving is considered a good trait, taking an evil one. Love based upon "give and take" must founder; it is a formula for marital disaster.

The Jewish idea of love is decidedly *not* "give and take": it is *give and give.*

III

The Jewish Approach to Sex

5

Judaism and Sexuality

Harmonizing the Spiritual and the Biological

Sexuality, the difference between male and female, and the physical attraction of one for the other, is that fundamental part of human nature designed by God to ensure that Man and Woman unite in order to propagate.

Sensual desire, the power of procreation, is thus perceived in Judaism as the divinely given creative impulse through which man fulfills God's command to perpetuate the species. This impulse cannot therefore be regarded as either sinful, shameful, or unnatural.[1] This desire, implanted by God in order to fulfill His directive, is a completely normal and natural sensation. The power of procreation, through this drive, which is an integral part of being human, ensures the preservation and continuation of the human race. R. Elijah de Vidas, the sixteenth-century ethical teacher who is the author of *Reshit Hochmah,* cites the view of the talmudic authority and kabbalist R. Isaac D'man Acco (1250–1340), that "he who has not desired a woman is like a pack animal; indeed he is even on a lower level."[2]

According to the Jewish view, sensual desire, therefore, cannot be considered a kind of necessary evil or a compromise with morality, legitimized and tolerated because of the need for procreation. These concepts form an integral part of classical Christian doctrine, but they are foreign to Judaism. Unlike classical Christian belief, the

sexual act is not, in Judaism, understood to be a debasing experience from which holy people abstain. Judaism recognizes that
sensual desire stems from the same divine source as do man's most
ethereal and spiritual components. Bearing God's seal, it is meant,
like everything else with which God endowed man, to be pressed
into His service.

The Jewish view both of sensuality and chastity is thus diametrically opposed to the Christian one. Classical Christian doctrine is
only reluctantly tolerant of sex, even within the framework of
marriage. This attitude reflects a view which splits man into two
separate units, one which is mired in base animal instinct, and the
other which struggles to achieve holiness. Christianity provides no
option for integrating these "lower" instincts into the quest for
holiness. In such a system, man must forever remain hopelessly
divided.

Judaism understands man to have been created with a body and
a soul. The soul is that divine, spiritual element in man that
breathes life into the body, ennobles it, and uplifts man morally and
spiritually into the realm of godliness. However, in Jewish thought,
the body given to man by God is perceived as no less holy than is the
soul.[3] By the holy harmonious fusion of body and soul in the service
of God and the simultaneous application of spiritual principles to *all*
of man's mundane actions on earth, human holiness is attained.

The Jewish Idea — To Sanctify Everyday Life

Judaism teaches that man may succeed in his quest for holiness if he
brings sanctity into his everyday life. There are no fundamental
divisions within man, no parts that are inherently excluded from
holiness. The body is neither bad nor is it the source of evil. The
tenth-century talmudic scholar and sage R. Saadia Gaon declares:
"The body of man contains no impurity . . . it is, to the contrary,
entirely pure."[4]

Maimonides emphasizes this point, explaining that Judaism is
concerned with both body *and* soul: "The general object of the Torah
is the well-being of the soul and the well-being of the body."[5]

In the Jewish view, man has the ability and the divine obligation
to sanctify every part of himself in God's service. In so doing, he

sanctifies God. Commenting on the verse in Leviticus commanding the Jew to sanctify himself, the *Midrash* teaches: " 'You shall be holy . . . because I am holy.'[6] The passage means that if you sanctify yourselves I shall regard it as if you had sanctified Me."[7]

This *k'dushah,* or holiness that God demands of the Jew is considered to be *the* desirable state for man.[8] Judaism defines *k'dushah* as a condition under which one's entire being is permeated by morality to the degree that all evil is excluded.[9]

An individual attains the state of *k'dushah* by fulfilling God's will — observing with the proper intent, the Torah and the *mitzvot.* The very act of so obeying God's commands implies an awareness and acceptance of God's sovereignty. It is a tacit acknowledgment of man's role in the scheme of Creation. Man "sanctifies" God by becoming holy himself — that is, he enhances God's glory in the world through upholding His sacred principles and fulfilling His will by conducting himself properly.

Holiness is demanded of not just a select elite, of a few priests or rabbis, but of the entire Jewish nation: "And the Lord spoke to Moses, saying: 'Speak to the *entire nation* of Israel and say to them, you shall be holy. . . .[10] And you shall be a kingdom of priests and a holy nation.' "[11]

Thus Judaism expects every man, woman, and child in Israel to strive for holiness, to be "priest-like," the laborer as well as the farmer and housewife, not just the religious leader. Indeed, God's special relationship with Israel is considered conditional upon the Jewish people conducting themselves as a holy nation. The Torah declares: "And you shall be holy unto Me, for I the Lord am holy, and I have separated you from the nations to be Mine."[12]

Attaining Holiness through Proper Behavior

The Jewish idea is that to fulfill God's will to become a holy nation, the Jewish people must observe the precepts of the Torah. Sanctity, the desired state for all people, is attained by the proper performance of all *mitzvot,*[13] but especially by those governing sexual behavior. On a number of occasions,[14] the Torah employs the term *k'dushah* and its derivatives in relation to this particular category of regulation, and also to the dietary laws. The Sages ask:

Why is the section in the Torah on forbidden sexual relations juxtaposed to the scriptural readings of *K'doshim,* Holy Ones? To teach you that everywhere you find a fence preventing transgression of the sexual laws, you find holiness. . . .[15] Whoever distances himself from violating the sexual laws is called holy.[16]

Regarding the verse, "For the Lord your God goes amidst your camp to save you and to give over your enemies to you, so let your camps be holy so that He sees no sexual immorality of any kind which would prevent Him from accompanying you,"[17] know that the Holy One does not make Israel His and He cannot be called "your God" unless "your camp is holy." . . . Israel is called holy when they avoid fornication and immoral sexual behavior, as it is written, "And you shall observe My statutes and fulfill them. I am the Lord who sanctifies you."[18] . . . When does the Holy One sanctify Israel? When they observe His statutes. And what are those statutes? These are the forbidden sexual relationships.[19]

The Sages emphasize, however, that it is not sufficient merely passively to avoid doing wrong; one must also actively do right. Scripture exhorts, *Sur mera v'asay tov* — Turn away from evil, and do good.[20] Man attains holiness by participating in a proper manner in that which is allowed; every aspect of sensuality is invested with *k'dushah.* The Sages teach: "Sanctify yourself by that which is *permitted* to you."[21]

Abjuring Illicit Relations: Sanctifying Licit Ones

In Judaism, sex is not wrong, but illicit sex is. Similarly, to be imbued with holiness, such activity must be performed in a manner appropriate to elevated human conduct. The Jewish ideal of holiness is achieved both by renunciation of the illicit and the sanctification of the licit. One becomes holy not merely by avoiding forbidden sexual relations, but also by *participating in sanctioned marital relations,* and by doing so in a decidedly human way. Thus, sanctification means performing the act as a *mitzvah,* in fulfillment of a command of God, with a measure of restraint and sensitivity for one's partner, and with *kavanah,* proper intent.

When regulated by the religious bonds of marriage and when conducted in a human manner and invested with proper intent, the act is viewed in Judaism as the essence of life and an expression of the noblest human creative impulse. Marital relations are a *mitzvah,* a commandment of God. Therefore, notwithstanding the intensely physical nature of the act, the fulfillment of the *mitzvah* (with the proper *kavanah* and a measure of human restraint and sensitivity) provides that spiritual and transcendental experience that leads to *k'dushah;* it is a means of bringing sacredness into life and sanctifying that which would otherwise be an act of physical gratification only.

Yet, the Sages were acutely aware of the allure of forbidden sexual relations. "Man's soul delights in them and lusts for them,"[22] they declare. The precepts which the Jews at Sinai found most difficult to accept were those dealing with the laws of forbidden sexual relations. The Sages teach: "Regarding this passage, 'And Moses heard the people weeping in their families,'[23] they were weeping because they were sorrowful when Moses told them they were required to separate themselves from forbidden and incestuous relations."[24]

Maimonides observes:

There is nothing in the entire Torah from which it is as difficult for the majority of the people to separate themselves as from prohibited sexual relations. Our Sages said: "At the time that Israel was commanded regarding the prohibited incestuous relationships they cried and they accepted these precepts only grudgingly and with much weeping. . . . They wept . . . because of the family relations.[25]

The Reward for Moral Sexual Behavior

The people could not accept with equanimity the laws circumscribing sexual behavior, and they even went so far as to request their nullification.[26] Paradoxically, while residing in Egypt, where sexual immorality and licentiousness were the norm,[27] the Jews adamantly refused to succumb to the allure of debauchery. As lowly slaves, they managed to maintain a moral sexual standard of conduct which was superior to that of the ruling society. Not to have succumbed to their debased surroundings was an extraordinary achievement. Asserting that it was partially because they rose above the level of prevalent sexual behavior that Jews merited redemption from Egyptian bondage,[28] the Sages concluded that anyone who rises above the sexual conduct prevalent in his society will be greatly rewarded. The Talmud teaches: "Regarding the verse, 'And you shall love the Lord your God with all your heart, with all your soul and with all your might'[29] — you should love God with both your impulses."[30]

R. Samson Raphael Hirsch comments that this means God should be loved with "our bodies and our physical desires."[31]

Mastering one's passions is no easy task. The *Dor HaMidbar*, the Generation of the Desert — as the Israelites who made their way from Egypt to the Promised Land were called — demonstrated this by the lack of enthusiasm in their acceptance of the laws regulating moral sexual behavior. Clearly, the strength of sexual desire can be so powerful that even a previous record of exemplary moral living is no guarantee that sexual morality will be maintained.

Yet for one who sincerely seeks to attain holiness, help is forthcoming. The Rabbis make this clear: "Regarding the passage, 'And you shall sanctify yourselves and you shall become holy,'[32] if an individual makes the effort and sanctifies himself only somewhat, heaven does the rest and sanctifies him . . .[33] *Haba litaher, m'say'in oto* — He who comes to be purified, will be helped."[34]

Conjugal Relations — Sacred When Pure

According to the *Igeret HaKodesh*, usually attributed to R. Moses ben Nahman (*Ramban*, Nahmanides) (1194–1270), sexual desire is a holy urge, simultaneously natural and noble, when expressed in loving union between husband and wife and endowed with sacred intent:

> Marital relations are holy and pure when conducted in the proper manner, at the proper time and with the proper attitude and intent, and anyone who says they are shameful and repulsive is in serious error. . . . Marital relations are called "knowledge" . . . and if it did not partake of great holiness it would not be so termed. . . . The Almighty created everything in accordance with His great wisdom, and He did not create anything that is intrinsically shameful.

In creating man and woman and forming all their organs God did
not create anything repulsive or ugly. . . . If we say that marital
relations are intrinsically shameful then we blaspheme, for we
indicate that the private parts of the body are blemished. How could
the Creator fashion something which is blemished? God is pure of
spirit and nothing which comes from Him is intrinsically bad. . . .
Everything created with divine wisdom is exalted, good and pleasant.
Whatever ugliness there is, is derived from man's misuse of what he
was given. . . . Just as the hands that write a Torah scroll are exalted
and praiseworthy and when they steal and murder they are repulsive,
so too is this the case in this area of life.[35]

All organs of the body are neutral, the *Igeret HaKodesh* informs us.
How man *uses* them determines whether they are holy or profane.

Writing in the fourteenth century, R. Isaac Aboab points out in
the *M'norat HaMa'or* that "there is nothing holier or more pure or
more elevated than marital relations conducted with the proper
attitude and intent."[36]

R. Jacob Emden (1699–1776), a noted German talmudist and
halachic authority, expands on this point:

The wise men of the other nations teach that there is shame in the
sense of physical feeling. This is not the opinion of the Torah and of
our Sages. . . . We understand marital relations to be good, elevated
and beneficial for the body and the soul . . . and absolutely holy.
There is nothing impure or shameful about it—only much exalta-
tion. . . . However, because it is an enduring, awesome, and exalted
activity of great sanctity, the act must be conducted in privacy and
with modesty . . . and discretion. . . .

If marital relations were not holy and pure but shameful, how
could the Holy One, Blessed be He, be involved? Undoubtedly,
therefore, when the act is performed with the proper attitude and
intent *there is no human activity which is on a higher level of holiness.*[37]

Human Oneness as the Way to Attain Unity with God

R. Emden's reference to the involvement of God in marital relations
refers to a statement in the *Zohar,* the classic work of the *Kabbalah.*
The *Zohar* perceives the act of physical love between husband and

wife to be of such transcendental sanctity that the Holy Presence of
God Himself joins the couple when they attain that oneness of body
and soul which is the essence of marriage:

> A man is required to gladden his wife . . . that is, to prepare her
> properly for the act so that they should both be of one desire and with
> one intent, so that when they join together they become truly one in
> body and soul. They become one in soul because they cleave to each
> other with one will. They become one in body, for as we learned, a
> man who has not married a woman is like a body divided, for alone
> he is but half a body, and alone she is but half a body. When they
> unite in conjugal relations they become one whole unit, one soul, one
> body — one person. And it is precisely then that the Holy One,
> Blessed be He, dwells among them in that unified oneness, and it is
> then that the *Sh'chinah,* the Divine Presence, is established in that
> oneness.[38]

R. Mordecai Gifter of Cleveland, U.S.A., a noted contemporary
rabbinic authority, adds a meaningful observation:

> True love of God involves absolute nullification of self by the lover
> for the beloved until one attains a state of cleaving oneness. In order
> to achieve this level, one must actually feel this love through the
> physical senses. Concerning the creation of man, the Torah states:
> "Therefore shall a man forsake his father and his mother and cleave
> to his wife and shall be as one flesh."[39] Precisely this kind of cleaving
> is what is meant by total adherence of the lover to the beloved. It is
> only when a man attains this level of cleaving that he is ready to
> elevate himself to the true total cleaving of absolute nullification of
> the lover for the beloved required by love of God.
>
> It is thus possible to understand the passage "It is not good for man
> to be alone."[40] It is impossible for man to achieve the ultimate good —
> the goal of cleaving to God, so long as he is alone — *i.e.,* unmarried.
> For alone he will be unable physically to feel with his senses that love
> which is absolute cohesion. Therefore our Sages taught that every
> man who has no wife lives without good,[41] for it is written "It is not
> good for man to be alone." The good that is the essential good is that
> of cleaving to the Holy One, Blessed be He. If he achieves this good,
> he will merit the good of the blessing of God, which is the true love.
> Anyone who is unmarried cannot possibly attain this.[42]

According to the Sages, sexual relations are given by God to
enable man to become a completely whole being. This cleaving

oneness and wholeness is considered by the Sages to be an indispensable prerequisite to attaining the physical, emotional, and
spiritual sensations required for achieving that sublime cleaving
oneness with God that is love of God. The individual who has never
cleaved deeply to another is thus seen as never having learned to
emerge sufficiently from the confines of self-involvement — the
necessary first step if one is to love another.

To love is to give oneself to the beloved with complete physical
and emotional cohesion. As Judaism perceives it, such cleaving love
between husband and wife is, therefore, an absolute preliminary to
selfless love of God, and is a yearning for that great love. Both loves
are perceived as having been drawn from the same resources of
selfless devotion, of giving of oneself totally to the beloved. Further,
sensual desire, the longing for physical unity with the object of one's
love, is analogous to man's yearning for spiritual unity with the
divine. This yearning is at the core of his love for God.

Use of the Term "Knowledge" in the Torah

In the Torah, the term "knowledge" is applied to that harmonious
unity of body and soul in a transcendental bliss which is the
culmination of the act of commingling of the physical and spiritual
senses into a cleaving oneness. This term is employed on a number
of occasions:

  — "And Adam knew his wife, Eve, and she conceived. . . ."[43]
  — "And Adam knew his wife again, and she bore a son. . . ."[44]
  — "And the maiden was fair to look on, a virgin, and no man had
known her. . . ."[45]
  — ". . . and he knew her again no more."[46]

There are additional examples in the Torah.[47] When the Torah
uses the expression "knowing" for a relationship, it implies a
profound visceral knowledge by one person of the very essence of
the other, the nature of which can be expressed only by a man and
a woman becoming as "one flesh."

R. Jacob Emden points out that the holiness attained through the
physical act of love between a man and his wife derives from the
fusion of the distinctively male and female components which
combine to form "knowledge."

Conjugal relations are called "knowledge." . . . This underscores their holiness. The "knowledge" implied by the act relates to the fact that man represents wisdom and woman represents understanding.[48] Marital relations, when pure, are the means of bringing wisdom and understanding together to form knowledge. This is what the Sages intended when they stated[49] that when a man joins with his wife in holiness the Divine Presence reposes with them. . . .[50]

It is characteristic of Judaism's approach to the whole subject of sensuality that the Sages speak of this "knowledge" (or the intensity of human love) as a pointer to the quality and power of the love that brings man into a union with God. The nature of the "knowledge" attained by the human union is considered to be precisely the same as the knowledge of God required to understand and attain that cleaving oneness with God which is true love of God. Indeed, the Sages say[51] that the proper *kavanah,* or intent, one should have when uniting with one's spouse should include contemplation of the scriptural verse "And you shall love the Lord your God with all your heart, with all your soul and with all your might . . ."[52] and the verse commanding the Jew to "love the Lord . . . and to cleave to Him."[53]

Knowledge as a Metaphor for Understanding God

King David applies the term "knowledge" to a deep awareness and understanding of God. The Psalmist declares: "Because he has desired Me . . . I will set him on high, for he has *known* My name."[54]

"May they have faith in You, those who *know* Your name."[55]

R. Emden comments:[56] "The knowledge referred to in these verses is identical to the kind of knowledge intended in the passage, 'And Adam *knew* his wife.' "[57]

It may be possible in this way to understand more profoundly the prophet Hosea's beautiful metaphor of God's love for Israel: "And I shall betroth you to Me forever; And I shall betroth you to Me in righteousness and in justice and in love and loving compassion: And I shall betroth you to Me in faithfulness and you shall *know* the Lord."[58]

It is not surprising, therefore, that the Jewish Sages used the powerful drive of man for woman as an example of the level of desire that a man must feel for God in order to cleave lovingly to Him. R. Menahem Recanati, the late thirteenth/fourteenth-century Torah commentator and kabbalist, expresses the thought that just as Sh'chem, the son of Hamor, who ravished Jacob's daughter Deena, "adhered with his soul to Deena . . . with cleaving, urgent desire and craving, so should a man cleave to the Holy Spirit."[59]

The fifteenth-century *Orhot Tzadikim,* a classical ethical text, echoes these sentiments:

> A man should be bound up in the ecstasy of his love for God always, as though he was love-sick for a woman[60] and his mind cannot for a moment be free from the love of this woman. He thinks of her constantly with ecstasy, while sitting and when rising, while eating or drinking. . . . As Solomon said metaphorically in the Song of Songs, "For I am lovesick."[61] . . . And indeed, the entire Song of Songs is but a parable of this love for God.[62]

Rabbi Samson Raphael Hirsch writes:

> The highest conception of which this people is capable . . . the conception of its relation to God and God's relation to it, is always visualized by it in the form of wedlock. . . . It is the bride of God . . . and . . . the whole varied story of its inner and outer life is nothing but the picture of a married life, with periods of joy and sorrow, of faithfulness and unfaithfulness, of devotion and estrangement, or quarrel and reconciliation, of rejection and reunion, in an eternal blessed covenant. . . . How pure, how elevated must have been the conception of marriage among this people, what striking example of mutual love and esteem, of mutual devotion and sacrifice must Jewish marriage have offered, how fortunate must the husband have felt in his wife and the wife in her husband, that the covenant between God and His people could have been thought of under such a simile.[63]

Sexual Imagery in the Bible

The Western world has somehow come to identify the Puritanical and Victorian attitudes toward sex with the original biblical treatment of the subject. According to the Jewish perception, nothing could be further from the truth. Neither the prudishness of Puritanical denunciation of sex nor the lack of basic honesty characterized by Victorian squeamishness has any relation whatsoever to the Torah view of these relations. On the contrary, the Torah treatment of the subject is characterized by candor, naturalness, and realistic understanding. Indeed, the biographies of the chief figures in the Torah would be incomplete if the incidents of human love were omitted.

Commenting upon the references to sexual love in the Torah, R. Saadia Gaon writes: "How could there be anything reprehensible about such relations if God's holy men engaged in them with His approval? . . . These men engaged in the act as a natural part of their lives, a part which in no way detracted from their singular relationship to God."[64]

The prophets Hosea,[65] Isaiah,[66] Jeremiah,[67] Ezekiel,[68] and Malachi[69] used vivid sexual imagery in their exhortations to Israel. Depicting the relationship between Israel and God as that between bride and groom, they often deplored Israel's faithlessness in the language of marital infidelity. Terms of sexual jealousy, revulsion, and rage found expression in their impassioned speech. For the Jewish prophets, there was nothing so powerful as the physical bond in marriage, and their writings thus provide a dramatic acknowledgment of the role of sexuality in human life. The *Midrash* relates:[70] "In ten places in scripture Israel is called bride — six times in Song of Songs,[71] three in Isaiah,[72] and once in Jeremiah[73] . . . and for each of these there are ten occasions on which the Holy One clothes Himself in the appropriate groom's garment."[74]

Bride and Groom: Allegorical Symbols for Israel and God

This concept found its grand culmination in one of the most beautiful poetic works of all time, King Solomon's Song of Songs. Though in external form it is a lyrical celebration of human love, Torah tradition reads the Song of Songs as a sublime metaphor of the spiritual marriage between God and Israel, a wedding which took place at the Revelation at Sinai.[75] In Jewish tradition, the Song of Songs is a dialogue of love between Israel, the bride, and God, her beloved.[76] God's divine love for His people is couched in the language of deep human emotion.[77]

R. Akiva, the great Sage of the Mishnah, was emphatic about the transcendent spiritual significance of the Song of Songs. "All of the books of the Torah are holy," said R. Akiva, "but the Song of Songs is the 'Holy of Holies'; indeed, the entire world attained its supreme value on the day the Song of Songs was given to Israel."[78]

It is at its most intense in the Song of Songs, but the imagery of human love recurs often in Jewish tradition. The Talmud relates that a curtain would be open in the Temple in Jerusalem on the festivals, to disclose intertwined *cherubim,* and the festival pilgrims would be told, "Behold, divine love for you is as the love of man and woman."[79]

Guests at weddings were urged to gladden the bride and groom and to cause them to rejoice, for he who acts thus is as though he participated in the nuptial ceremony of the giving of the Torah at Sinai . . . for the day on which the Torah was given is like the day a bride enters the marriage canopy.[80]

The Sabbath, commemorating God's creation of the world, is Judaism's most important institution. Through its observance, the Jew reaffirms each week his bond of commitment to his Creator. In Jewish thought, the Sabbath is referred to allegorically as a bride, who is married each week to the Jewish people.[81] It is a hymn welcoming the Sabbath bride, *L'cha Dodi Lik'rat Kalah, P'nay Shabbat N'kab'lah,* "Come, My Beloved, to Meet the Bride, Let Us Welcome the Sabbath," that serves as the central part of the Sabbath eve synagogue service.

The festive Sabbath eve feast has been likened to the wedding feast. "Come O bride, come O bride," is the way the talmudic sage R. Yanai would greet the approaching Sabbath.[82] For the Jewish people, therefore, the seventh day has served as a weekly "honeymoon" with the Sabbath bride. This symbolism is underscored further by the special *mitzvah* associated with marital relations on Sabbath eve.

The Ten Commandments and the Torah are sometimes allegorically identified as the *ketubah,* the betrothal contract, for the *kidushin* between God and Israel at Sinai.

Israel's Betrothal to the Torah

The Torah itself, Israel's timeless love, is frequently compared to a woman, or to the bride of Israel.[83] The relationship of the Jewish people to the Torah is symbolized as that of husband to wife or of groom to bride. The Torah is betrothed to Israel[84] and to Israel alone.[85]

Thus Shavuot, the festival commemorating the giving of the Torah at Sinai is in many communities traditionally preceded by a Sabbath called *Shabbat Kalah,* "The Sabbath of the Bride." According to this mystical, allegorical Jewish tradition, on her last unmarried Sabbath, the bride, the Torah, awaits Shavuot, when she will be wed to Israel.

Many Sephardic and Italian Jews translate this allegorical relationship into a unique custom. A highlight of their Shavuot observance is a joyous "wedding" celebration of Israel with the Torah. The Torah ark is decorated with bouquets of flowers, and bridal torches stand in front of it. All the Torah scrolls are bedecked in white vestments like a bride. At the climax of the ceremony, the precentor of the congregation takes out a special Shavuot *ketubah,* a marriage contract written on parchment and beautifully illuminated and similar to the *ketubah* between a bride and a groom, and reads it to the congregation in a traditional tune. The text is similar to that of the usual *ketubah* form but is more embellished and includes words of endearment for the "bride," the Torah, by the "groom," Israel. The Torah scrolls are then ceremoniously escorted to the reading desk, preceded by a boy bearing a bouquet of flowers and followed by respected congregants holding the Torah mantle, the "bridal gown."

The Marriage Allegory in Sacred Jewish Institutions

Simhat Torah is the fall festival commemorating the completion of the annual cycle of the reading of the Torah. In synagogues the world over, a leading member of the congregation is honored with the title *Hatan Torah,* Bridegroom of the Torah, and is ceremoniously called to the Torah for the final reading of Deuteronomy. Another leading congregant is likewise honored by being ceremoniously called up to the Torah for the first reading of Genesis, beginning immediately again the annual Torah reading cycle. He is accorded the title *Hatan B'reshit,* Bridegroom of Genesis. In many communities, the custom prevailed on Simhat Torah for the entire congregation to escort the "bridegrooms" to the synagogue through the streets under marriage canopies to the accompaniment of much rejoicing, singing, and dancing.

The holy city of Jerusalem, toward which Jews throughout the world turn in prayer and yearning, is compared to a maiden espoused by her groom, the Jewish people. The prophet Isaiah comforts Jerusalem: "As a young man possesses a virgin, so shall your sons possess you."[86]

The Sages teach that in a future period, with the advent of the Messiah, the relationship between God and the Jewish people will be a matrimonial one. Rabeinu Bahya ben Asher, the thirteenth-century Spanish teacher, writes in the *Kad HaKemah:*

At the time of the Messiah, the world will be in a state of perfection, and Israel's relationship to God will be so to speak matrimonial, although it is presently only in the stage of betrothal. This concept is clarified in the *Midrash:*

"This relationship between God and Israel can be compared to a king who betrothed a woman[87]. . . ." In the days of the Messiah the 'wedding' will occur."[88]

The frequent use throughout scripture and Jewish tradition of the sexual and marital relationships as allegories for the relationship of the Jewish people to God and the institutions He gave Israel which are dearest to the Jewish people, is the clearest indication of the high regard Judaism has for marriage and its physical side.

The Torah as a Guide for Practical Living

The Torah is called *Torat Hayim,* an instruction for living.[89] "The Torah was not given to the serving angels, but to man" is an expression of the Sages.[90] The Torah was seen by the Sages not just as something for theoretical study, nor were its tenets to be practiced in isolation or divorced from everyday life. The Sages view it as a practical blueprint for the Jew for daily living. Jewish tradition regards the Torah as a guidebook to teach people how to live in this mundane world, how to deal with the body's imperatives and the conflicting demands of society, and how to apply the principles of the Torah to all aspects of life in this world.

According to Judaism, therefore, in exercising his own free will and electing to conduct his life in accordance with the Torah, the Jew applies the divine attributes inherent in him as a being created in God's image to achieve the epitome of human potential—a sublime holiness which is equivalent to godliness.

This striving for holiness to which Judaism obligates the Jew does not mean that he should withdraw from everyday life or deny himself that which God has permitted. The Torah does not require self-denial, but self-restraint; the Jewish ideal is the fullest participation in life within a holy framework. The Sages view the biblical command, "You shall be holy," as directing the Jew to be holy while living within the life and on the world that God gave him. The *mitzvot* of the Torah provide concrete guidelines for the way of life that leads to the sanctification of life itself.

The essential criterion for governing and regulating one's mundane biological experiences is the counsel of King Solomon in Proverbs, "Know Him in all your ways."[91] Judaism understands that all of the Jew's actions throughout his life should reflect manifestations of the divine in him as a creature God made in His own image.

Within the framework of knowing Him in all one's ways, Judaism perceives sexuality as the wondrous celestial gift of God to humankind, and holiness as an attainable ideal granted by the Creator to His human creatures. Regulating natural life in accordance with divine disciplines, a Jew may pay the supreme homage to his Creator, *imitatio Dei,* imitation of God. By doing so, he may also attain the lofty level of *k'dushah,* human holiness.

A hasidic interpretation takes the idea somewhat further, "The object of the entire Torah," says the Ba'al Shem Tov, the eighteenth-century founder of modern Hasidism, "is that man *himself* should become a Torah."[92]

6

Jewish Sexual Ethics — From Animalization to Humanization

The Mark of the Master

The Jewish approach to sexuality is characterized simply by humanization. In Jewish tradition, an individual realizes his fullest potential as a being created in God's image,[1] when all of his behavior is human, as distinct from animalistic. People fulfill their obligations to their Creator, to themselves, and to their fellows when they behave decently and with compassion. Sexuality is one sphere of contemporary life where there is a compelling need to set guidelines for behavior.

In Jewish thought, the key to the humanization of the sexual drive is human mastery of it. Through self-discipline in thought and action, Jews are expected to humanize and take responsibility for — but not to suppress — their natural physical urges. Judaism requires that they be channeled in the direction that God desires.

This is considered the basis for the law of circumcision which is mandatory for every Jewish male.[2] Circumcision, a concrete expression of God's covenant with Israel, is an indelible physical stamp on the body of the man. Judaism regards it as a sign of absolute human submission to the will of the Master. In the words of R. Ovadiah Sforno, the Italian fifteenth/sixteenth-century commentator on the Torah: "Its purpose is to serve as a permanent reminder to walk in His ways;[3] it is like the seal of a master on his slave."[4]

Significantly, it is the organ of generation which bears the mark

129

of God's covenant with the Jew. The mark acknowledges the divine
source of sensual desire and serves as a permanent reminder to the
Jew that God has created man as an incomplete being. Man must
strive both mentally and physically to perfect himself.[5] Circumcision is perceived by the Sages as a reminder to the Jew that he has
an unceasing obligation to sanctify — and thereby to complete —
himself as a human being by subordinating all his drives to God's
will.[6]

The mark on the male organ is viewed by the Rabbis as a
mnemonic device to prevent men from establishing a double
standard of morality, one whereby men are privileged over women.
R. Samson Raphael Hirsch writes:

> This [is a] far-reaching deep truth that not only in spiritual matters,
> but also in bodily relations, man and woman are to be equally pure,
> equally moral, equally holy. The human race will never be sound as
> long as the first fundamental virtue of life is not considered with the
> same seriousness by both sexes; as long as youth and men should
> allow themselves things that are not to be permitted to girls and
> women. Not for nothing do Jewish *men* have on their bodies the sign
> of the admonition by God to Abraham, "Conduct yourself before My
> presence and be perfect":[7] keep the presence of God always in mind
> . . . at every step look to Him who has set limits and boundaries for
> everything, who has only granted freedom within the Law — the
> warning that God expects from them the same innocence, the same
> moral chastity as is expected from women.[8]

The Dual Nature of the Sexual Drive

As Judaism perceives it, just as his sexual drive can raise man to the
highest level of holiness, so can it also debase and corrupt him.
Under the wedding canopy, the man tells the woman, "Behold, you
are sanctified to me."[9] The Hebrew word here for sanctification is
m'kudeshet, the root of which is *kadosh,* holy. In the Bible, *k'deshah,*
harlot,[10] has precisely the same root, but its meaning is exactly the
opposite — "one who has perverted her holiness." We find a deep
awareness in Judaism that the very same faculty in man that
produces lofty holiness can also produce degradation.

Judaism requires that in order to differentiate between man and the lower orders of creation, man's sensual drive must be properly channeled. In the words of R. Samson Raphael Hirsch:

> No single one of the powers and natural tendencies which are given to man is either good or bad in itself, from the most spiritual down to the most sensuous. They are all given to him for beneficial purposes to accomplish God's will on earth. The divine Torah gives them a positive aim and a negative limit. In the service of this purpose indicated by God and within these limits set by God everything is good and holy. Separated from these purposes and outside these limits, coarseness and evil begins. Only in exercising one's power of restraint and self-control in things which are permitted but are related to the forbidden is one to gain mastery of one's inclinations and to make all of one's powers and tendencies subservient to the pure fulfillment of the Will of God.[11]
>
> God has given sensuality an appeal to your senses, not that it should master and direct you, but that you should master and direct it; not that you should suppress or kill it, but regulate it, rule over it and direct it. . . . If all good were sweet and all evil bitter, our whole virtue would be no more than the natural unfree following of that which attracted our senses, and the whole nobility of being a human being would be lost. It is just in the correct control and use of our natural tendencies that the loftiest purposes of our life down here are found. So that in truth the relationship between man and his passions should be essentially not unlike that between husband and wife. A man should be freely affianced to his sensuality so as, under his guidance, together with it, he achieves the highest purpose of his life.[12]

The Sages teach that one should feel simultaneously attracted toward and repelled by sexual desire.[13] Aware of the dual nature of the sexual drive, the Sages often termed it the *yetzer hara,* the evil impulse, because used improperly it may easily be diverted into the service of immorality and evil. Otherwise, the sexual urge is good indeed. R. Jacob Emden, the eighteenth-century German rabbi, makes this clear: "There is nothing better than sexual relations in the proper framework: in the wrong framework, there is nothing worse."[14]

The Sages teach: "Regarding the verse in Genesis, 'And God saw all that He created and beheld it was very good,'[15] that which was 'very good' is the *yetzer hara.* And is the *yetzer hara* then 'very good'?

Yes, for without it no man would build a home or marry a woman or bring children into the world or be involved in commerce."[16]

Sexuality is thus seen as a kind of positive, energizing force without which human life would be impossible.

The oft-repeated biblical command to be holy is always an exclusive one directed to the Jew alone. According to the Sages, it is no coincidence that this command refers usually to those laws which regulate man's strongest physical instincts. One is related to man's instinct for self-preservation; the other concerns continuity. These instincts are general ones, granted to all creatures as essential to their existence and propagation. However, only the human being is endowed by the Creator with the ability to become the master over these instincts and desires, and only the Jew is commanded, in order to be holy, to exercise this mastery.

Humanization or Animalization

The compelling goal of the moral individual seeking to attain human holiness is, in Judaism's perception, the exercise of control over the sensuous nature. Failure to exert firm moral direction over the sensory nature, while allowing untrammeled free rein to the dictates of the body's elementary urges, places the human being on the same level as the animals. Indeed, people who are mastered by their desires cannot rise above those components within themselves that make up that lowest common denominator which is shared by humans and animals alike.

In Jewish thought, humans are understood to share certain characteristics with animals, along with the capability of becoming more brutal than any animal. Like animals, humans derive physical pleasure when uniting. However, an animal lacks human consciousness and conscience. Humans are rational beings characterized by free will and a soul. Unlike animals, humans can reason, and can, through the reasoning process of rational beings, both form and amend beliefs and ideas. When they do not act rationally, that is, through reason, when they do not deliberate and weigh alternatives in order to reach decisions, but act impulsively prompted solely by desire — they destroy their humanity.

In the humanly reasonable and rational state, human beings

experience a moral and spiritual imperative unknown to the animal. They desire to elevate themselves above the animal, and as rational beings to exercise finer, more lasting options in order to begin the ascent to holiness.

Jews are directed to utilize their rational, human faculties to rid themselves of dependence upon and submission to their primal urges. However, they are not expected to stifle their God-given inclinations, but to harness them to God's chariot, and to master them. R. Samson Raphael Hirsch teaches:

> The moral and spiritual greatness of human beings demanded by the divine law and God's Torah is based in the very first place on keeping the body holy; that in satisfying all the urges of our senses we keep within the bounds sanctified by God.[17]
>
> The contrast to animals is the touchstone and the rock by which and on which the morality of men proves itself or splits asunder. Sensual enjoyment for man is to be a moral, free-willed act; he is never, and in no way whatever, to be an animal. For that purpose he has both sensuality and godliness within him. . . . Animals have only to develop their sensual nature. . . . Man was not set . . . on the earth to satisfy his sensual nature . . . but rather to serve God and His world.[18]
>
> The Torah ennobles and sanctifies our animal impulses and desires by applying them with prudence to the purposes designated by the Creator. . . . The gratification of physical lust and passion is not, and never has been, its goal. Therefore, man's lower cravings are subordinated to a higher law and limited by the Creator's wisdom for His own infinitely wise purposes. Yet, as means for attaining ends that are proper and necessary, *the Torah recognizes these desires as perfectly moral, pure, and human, and their gratification as just and as legitimate as the fulfillment of any other human task or mission.*[19]

Free Will, a Spiritual Imperative

In the Jewish perception, free will, which distinguishes man from the animal, is both an advantage and a limiting factor, a privilege and a responsibility. Although his will empowers him to conquer worlds, the Jew is commanded to rein in and subordinate his will to the Divine Will. By far the most difficult but rewarding conquest is the mastery of one's own nature.

"Who is strong?" is the rhetorical question posed by the Mishnah. "He who controls his desires."[20] The Jewish yardstick of true strength is neither physical prowess nor animal vigor. Strength is measured by man's ability to exercise his free will and by the tenacity with which he is able to dominate his own natural inclinations.

The disciplined individual, the Mishnah implies, is synonymous with the holy one. The strong person subordinates his desires to God's will. By freely subjugating his powers and inclinations to the higher spiritual imperatives that God has set for him, he is both master of himself and the servant of God. In a paraphrase of the directive of the Mishnah in *Avot,* the Sages declare: "The true leaders are those who rule over their passions."[21]

In a more cryptic vein, the Sages teach that any man who succeeds in mastering his desires can be called a man.[22] Judaism teaches that temperance, restraint, and self-control are attainable human qualities that Jews should practice daily.

Avoiding Confrontations with Temptation

The Talmud relates.[23]

> R. Hanina and R. Jonathan were walking together when their roads diverged into two paths, one of which passed by a house of idolatry and the other past a brothel. One said to the other: "Let us choose the path by the house of idolatry for there no longer exists an inclination to worship idols,[24] and let us avoid passing by the brothel where the evil inclination can take hold of us." Replied the other: "Let us proceed instead on the path which passes the brothel so that we can subdue our evil inclination and be rewarded for it."[25]

It should not be assumed from this story that the Jewish approach in this is a confrontational one, nor even that it is incumbent or even praiseworthy to test one's ability to withstand temptation. The Talmud indicates that they were protected only because the two Sages excelled in Torah learning.[26] Yet, even greatness is not sufficient protection against temptation. A significant talmudic passage relates that King David desired God to test him as He had previously tested the three patriarchs. Concluded the Sages: "A man should never allow himself to be placed in a position where he will be confronted with a test. David, King of Israel, allowed himself to be tested [with Bathsheba] and he stumbled."[27]

If one is neither Sage nor king, how much greater is the difficulty. Thus, human beings are not advised to flex their muscles excessively in this direction. On the contrary, the intrinsic difficulties on this path are so numerous that one may legitimately seek the simplest and smoothest means of travel. Judaism does not believe that holiness is a mountain peak that only a select elite are capable of scaling; rather it visualizes a road, an open highway which should be accessible to all. Judaism believes that the path of holiness may be trodden by every human being.

Why is self-discipline so necessary? We may compare sensuality to a powerful automobile. It is a wonderful mechanism that provides its user with convenience and pleasure. However, the more powerful the automobile, the stronger the framework — the more complex the system of checks and balances necessary to guide its use. What kind of pleasure is there in driving a car when traffic lights or traffic laws are disregarded? Not only is pleasure lost but life or limb are threatened. So too, teaches Judaism, is the situation where paramount emphasis is placed upon sensuality. In the early stage pleasure is lost, and at the later stage life and health are threatened.

The reasons for self-mastery should be understood; educational value is reduced if there is abstention from the right things for the wrong reasons. The *Midrash* teaches: "Say not 'I do not want forbidden food, forbidden clothes or forbidden relations.' Rather say 'I do indeed want these but will not have them, because my Father in Heaven forbade them.' "[28]

The *Midrash* is commenting on the verse in Leviticus, "And you shall be holy to Me, for I, God, am holy, and I have separated you from the nations to be Mine."[29] Expounding on the verse and the *Midrash*, R. Samson Raphael Hirsch declares:

> Keeping the dietary laws and the other laws which make our way of life different from that of other people should not be done out of some inborn aversion and dislike for the food or whatever it is, but just out of our submission to God, and to the obedience we owe Him.

The motive and purpose of our separation from the nations is *lihiyot Li*, "to be Mine," so that every breath which a Jew draws free from sin becomes a homage to God. . . .[30]

Sex before Marriage

Judaism teaches that marriage alone is the only proper framework for sexual relations. To help ensure that this most intensely personal and intimate of all human experiences endures, a binding legal and religious commitment of a publicly recognized nature is required. Only an institution that provides generally accepted requirements obligatory to all who choose to enter into it can provide such a public recognition, because it emphasizes that certain individual actions must be subordinated to society's rules.

Marriage provides such a universally recognized framework powerful enough for the relationship, because the obligations are not merely from a contractual relationship between partners, but are imposed by the institution. It is also the universally recognized framework for bringing children, the product of the sexual relationship, into the world, and for rearing those children.

Judaism does not sanction sexual activity which lacks the long-term covenant of marriage. Sexual relations within the marital structure are desirable and beautiful; unchaste behavior and sexual relations outside marriage are forbidden by Judaism as offenses against God and man.

Judaism thus prohibits both premarital and extramarital promiscuity. To ease the effort involved in withstanding the powerful sensual drive, social relations between unmarried Jewish men and women are governed by rules of conduct designed to minimize those social contacts which might lead to excessive sensory stimulation and to premarital promiscuity.

As we have seen, Jews are encouraged to avoid those situations in which their self-discipline will be tested.[31] Physical contact of any kind between unmarried men and women is, therefore, proscribed by Jewish law. In the traditional Jewish view, the urgency of sexual desire and the ease with which it can be aroused, especially in a man, make necessary the establishment of a set of behavioral guidelines which assert the inviolability of the code of ethical conduct in the face of biological drives.

The Sages understand that, despite the protestations of many young adults, an intense "platonic" friendship between a man and a woman is almost impossible to maintain. The excitement of sexuality and the strength of physical desire are considered to be too powerful. Left to its own devices and lacking restraints, natural instinct will eventually take over and transform friendship and camaraderie between a young man and woman into a physical relationship.

The Sages therefore impose limitations upon a relationship between a single man and woman to ensure that it remains a social one and is not transformed into a physical one. That point of restraint is physical contact (n'gi'ah). While society in general may accept certain acts of physical expression of affection as acts to which no further overtones are attached, Judaism understands that no form of physical contact between a man and a woman, whether it be hand-holding, embracing, or kissing, will necessarily remain casual for long. Physical contact between members of the opposite sex will often eventually progress beyond the casual stage.

The Jewish attitude toward self-control is that for most people it is relatively easy to maintain, provided there is no physical contact. However, the human sense of touch has the power to arouse physical desire and to transform dramatically the nature of a relationship. It is true that no two people, upon exposure to external stimuli, will have the identical threshold of response. Then too, there may be individuals for whom physical contact with members of the opposite sex does not provoke a sexual response; nevertheless, the single gauge of n'gi'ah was established by the Sages as a standard for all Jews.

From a Jewish perspective, biological drives have a dual function. In the first place, two persons who may have been total strangers are enabled, in order to fulfill their basic duty of perpetuating themselves, to cooperate in an act as physical and intimate as the sexual union. Secondly, this union establishes an ardent emotional bond between these two former strangers which allows them to merge their identities into a unified entity—an indispensable condition for the creation of a close-knit family.

Since this intimate act is an expression of love and a vehicle for fulfillment, it is reserved for one's life-partner in marriage. Generally speaking, Judaism considers single men and women to be in a state of preparation for marriage. This preliminary state requires as substantial a measure of restraint, self-discipline, and self-control as does marriage itself, and in this sense an ideal preparation for marriage is provided.

Depersonalization = Dehumanization

The Jewish rules of conduct for single men and women express a keen awareness of the nature of the sensual drive and of the stimuli that activate it. In order to facilitate self-control, Jewish tradition urges young people to avoid confrontations with challenges — that is, unnecessary social contacts between men and women and situations and settings where erotic thoughts and sexual desire are inevitable. Judaism understands that constant exposure of an individual to such situations can easily turn sexuality into an obsession, a preoccupation with the body and a demoralizing factor in the life of an unmarried man or woman. It can also result in the surrender of mind and heart to instinct and passion. In Judaism's view, when people allow instinct rather than reason to determine their behavior, they separate themselves from their *tzelem Elohim,* the God-like image in which both man and woman were created, expressed in part by the purely human attribute of free will.

The individual who does not exercise self-control, and allows himself to become a slave to his passions, thereby subordinates his reason to his instinct; thus there is fundamentally little difference between him and an animal. An animal knows no restraints. It copulates as freely as it eats, whenever it feels impelled to do so. A human being who acts similarly is animal-like in his behavior. Coitus becomes a depersonalized act. That person has relations with an entity, not with a human being. Exclusively concerned with the gratification of his lust, he exploits another in the process. It is not a loving, giving relationship, but a taking one, in which one individual uses another in order to gratify his desires.

Judaism and Homosexuality

Judaism's attitude toward homosexuality typifies the void that separates Jewish sexual ethics from those of contemporary society.

Whereas the attitudes of contemporary society toward homosexuality have become more tolerant, Judaism continues to regard it with abhorrence. The Torah considers homosexuality an "abomination,"[32] a capital offense as serious as incest and relations with animals, punishable by death.[33] The relevant passages read:

> And you shall not lie with mankind as with womankind; it is an abomination. And you shall not lie with any animal to defile yourself thereby; neither shall any woman stand before an animal for copulation; it is the extreme of brutalization. Do not defile yourselves with all of these things, for in all of these things were defiled the nations whom I cast out before you. And the land itself became defiled by these acts, and therefore I visited the iniquity upon it, and the land itself vomited out its inhabitants. . . . And whoever shall commit any of these abominations shall be uprooted from out of the midst of their people. Therefore, keep and guard lest you practice any of the abominable institutions that were practiced by the people before you, and do not become defiled through them: I am the Lord your God.[34]
>
> And a man that lie with mankind as with womankind, both of them have committed an abomination; they shall be put to death, their blood falls upon themselves.[35]

The reasons for Judaism's revulsion toward homosexuality are at least twofold. First, Judaism perceives physical relations between members of the same sex as a perversion of nature and of the divine order. In Judaism procreation is a major — if not *the* major — purpose of the sexual act; the reproductive organs were created for generation. Since homosexual activity cannot result in offspring, it frustrates the natural function of human sexuality. The *Sefer HaHinuch* provides this rationale:

> Among the reasons for the command is the desire of the Holy One to fill the world that He created. . . . [Homosexuality] is a corruptive waste, for there is no fruitful result deriving from this act, nor does it involve fulfillment of the *mitzvah* of conjugal relations. Apart from this, it is an irrational, despicable, scurrilous act in the extreme, in the eyes of God and in the eyes of any intelligent being. For man, who was created to serve his Creator, is too worthy to debase himself ignominiously in such a contemptible fashion.[36]

Homosexuality is also seen as damaging to family life. The Sages take the position that the biblical terminology used to describe the act, *to'evah,* an abomination, indicates that the act is perceived by the Torah as intrinsically repulsive, *prima facie* disgusting. R. Norman Lamm, author of a Judaic analysis of homosexuality,[37] writes: "It is, as it were, a visceral reaction, an intuitive disqualification of the act," which is reason enough for the prohibition, "no matter how much it may be in vogue among advanced and sophisticated cultures."[38]

The attitude is reflected in two biblical stories. In the first, Lot is requested by the population of Sodom to surrender his guests so that they may be known carnally.[39] This episode has given us the term "sodomy" for homosexuality. In the second story, the Benjaminites attempted to defile a guest in Gibeah,[40] but ravished a woman who subsequently died.[41] So horrified was Israel by this act that the tribes joined together to wage war on the Benjaminites to punish them for their immoral behavior[42] and to prohibit intermarriage with them.[43]

Homosexuality was rife among the Canaanite idol worshipers among whom the Jews lived, and in many ancient societies, including those of Greece and Rome. However, the sweeping, uncompromising biblical prohibition against *mishkav zachar* led to its virtual extirpation among the Jews, and resulted in the adoption of moral laws by most civilized societies forbidding such relations. Indeed, the prohibition against homosexuality is considered a fundamental law of humanity which is incorporated in the Noahide Code as one of the seven basic laws applicable to all mankind.[44]

The Rare Incidence of Homosexuality among Jews in the Past

Throughout Jewish history the rarity of homosexuality among Jews was considered a noteworthy phenomenon. In the talmudic period, this was expressed in the statement: "*Lo neh'sh'du Yisrael al mishkav zachar*—Jews are not suspected of practicing homosexuality."[45]

This was confirmed by Maimonides in his day,[46] and was incorporated into the *halachah* permitting two males to be closeted together.[47] So low was the incidence of homosexuality among the Jews, that it was not until the sixteenth century that R. Joseph Caro found it necessary to attach, in his *Code of Jewish Law,* the following caveat to the talmudic statement that Jews are not suspected of practicing homosexuality: "In our generation, lewdness is rampant, and it is best for a man to avoid being alone with another male."[48]

The attitude of Jewish law toward female homosexuality is more lenient than it is toward male homosexuality, since the biblical prohibition is directed specifically at males. However, lesbianism is forbidden[49] on the grounds of its inclusion in the general biblical prohibition against imitating the immoral practices of the Egyptians and the Canaanites.[50]

Traditional Judaism does not excuse homosexuality as a pathological illness, although R. Lamm in his study expresses some sympathy for this approach.[51] Nor does Judaism accept homosexuality as an alternative life-style, even when two members of the same sex may love one another. R. Lamm declares:

> Judaism does not accept the kind of thoroughgoing relativism used to justify the gay life as merely an alternate life-style. And while the question of human autonomy is certainly worthy of consideration in the area of sexuality, one must beware of the consequences of taking the argument to the logical extreme. Judaism clearly cherishes holiness as a greater value than either freedom or health. . . .
>
> "Loving, selfless concern" and "meaningful personal relationships" — the great slogans of the New Morality and the proponents of situation ethics — have become the litany of sodomy in our time. Simple logic should permit us to use the same criteria for excusing adultery or any other act heretofore held to be immoral; and indeed, that is just what has been done, and it has received the sanction not only of liberals and humanists, but of certain religionists as well.
>
> "Love," "fulfillment," "exploitative," "meaningful" — the list sounds like a lexicon of emotionally charged terms drawn at random from the disparate sources of both Christian and psychologically oriented agnostic circles. Logically, one must ask the next question: What moral depravities cannot be excused by the sole criterion of "warm, meaningful human relations" or "fulfillment," the newest semantic heirs to "love"? Love, fulfillment and happiness can also be attained in incestuous contacts — and certainly in polygamous relationships. Is there nothing at all left that is "sinful," "unnatural" or "immoral" if it is practiced "between two consenting adults?"
>
> Judaism . . . cannot abide a wholesale dismissal of its most basic moral principles on the ground that those subject to its judgments find them repressive. All laws are repressing to some extent — they

repress illegal activities — and all morality is concerned with changing Man and improving him and his society. Homosexuality imposes on one an intolerable burden of differences, of absurdity, and of loneliness, but the biblical commandment outlawing pederasty cannot be put aside solely on the basis of sympathy for the victim of these feelings. Morality, too, is an element which each of us, given his sensuality, must take into serious consideration before acting out his impulses. . . . Under no circumstances can Judaism suffer homosexuality to become respectable.[52]

The phenomenon of "gay marriage" is not a new one. Writing about the depravities of ancient Egypt, Maimonides relates, "A man would marry a man and a woman would marry a woman."[53] The phenomenon of homosexual synagogues and temples, while new, is nonetheless considered to be a reflection of the age-old desire of Jews to seek religious sanction for immoral conduct, and to assuage their consciences and avoid feelings of guilt for living their lives in a manner considered by the Torah to be degenerate, abhorrent, and depraved, and in violation of the religious and moral norms of behavior of the Torah. Indeed, the American Reform movement has provided just such religious sanction for these gay synagogues.[54] Comments R. Lamm:

Homosexuals are no less in violation of Jewish norms than Sabbath desecrators or those who disregard the laws of *kashrut*. But to assent to the organization of separate "gay" groups under Jewish auspices makes no more sense, Jewishly, than to suffer the formation of synagogues that cater exclusively to idol worshipers, adulterers, gossipers, tax evaders or Sabbath violators. Indeed, it makes less sense, because it provides, under religious auspices, a ready-made clientele from which the homosexual can more easily choose his partners.[55]

The *Mitzvah* of Marital Relations

Although Judaism perceives the *mitzvah* of procreation as the major purpose of marital relations, it is not the only one. Marital relations are a *mitzvah* in their own right, the *mitzvah* of *onah*. *Onah,* the husband's duty to have marital relations with his wife, is one of his three fundamental biblical obligations toward his partner in marriage, along with providing her sustenance and clothing her properly.[56]

Judaism teaches that, within marital relations, two separate *mitzvot,* each with its appropriate *kavanah,* or proper intention, should be fulfilled. For the *mitzvah* of procreation, the required *kavanah* is that the act should result in "proper, fitting, and pure children . . . who fulfill God's commands."[57] For the *mitzvah* of *onah,* the husband's duty to have marital relations with his wife, the required *kavanah* is that the man, before thinking of his own pleasure, should concentrate on giving his wife pleasure.[58] This is in accordance with the biblical directive, *V'simah et ishto,* "And he shall gladden his wife."[59]

When the act is a selfless, loving, giving one, marital relations attain the highest level. When stripped of these *kavanot,* the act which might have resulted in a loving union becomes instead one whereby each partner uses the other as a vehicle for personal pleasure only. The other partner becomes a depersonalized object to provide the same physical gratification that is obtainable from auto-eroticism, and which is not only unholy but debasing.

Judaism does not view the act as merely a physiological experience or a mechanical-hedonistic exercise; it is perceived as an intensely human activity in which the personal involvement and commitment of the participants are absolute preconditions. Its depersonalization means its dehumanization. Man then becomes debased — a two-legged animal but not a human being.

The Sages employ the term *d'var mitzvah,* an act of kindness extended by one person toward another, to conjugal relations. Through relations conducted in a manner of a *d'var mitzvah,* an act of kindness, and the proper *kavanot,* the physiologically impersonal is transformed into the human and personal. Jewish ethics thus transform the marital union performed with proper intent and in its most humanized and personalized form, into an act of sanctification.[60]

In Jewish thought, man's freedom to rise above the impersonal, elementary, instinctual level of biological impulse expressed in a casting off of restraints, and his control and direction of his biological imperatives so that they are expressed in loving and caring indicate the distinctiveness of humanity. Judaism teaches that the transformation of physical union from an impersonalized act into a personalized one marks man's humanization and his elevation above the animal.

"Sex = Sin" Equals Neurosis

Christianity, since its emergence, has attempted to impress upon human consciousness the relationship between sex and sin. The secular counterpart of this has been to reduce man to an animal. In a significant psychoanalytic study of history, Dr. Norman O. Brown perceives the Christian effort to impress upon man the sinfulness of sex as repressing and as producing a defiant hedonism and neurosis:

> For two thousand years or more Man has been subjected to a systematic effort to transform him into an ascetic animal. He remains a pleasure-seeking animal. Parental discipline, religious denunciation of bodily pleasure and philosophic exaltation of the life of reason have left Man overly docile, but secretly in his unconscious unconvinced, and therefore neurotic.[61]

In fact the main thrust of the sexual revolution, which is really a rebellion against Christian ethics, is that man is indeed a sensual animal. Indeed, the sexual revolution reflects man's acceptance of his animal state as a means of purging himself of his neurosis,[62] by sanctioning pleasure instead of asceticism.

Judaism joyously proclaims that man is not an animal, neither an ascetic nor a pleasure-seeking one. Man, Judaism teaches, is a creature created in God's image.[63] He is equipped with free will and both the ability and the responsibility to conduct himself in his sexual behavior in a manner superior to that of animals. In Judaism, unlike Christianity, there is no grudging submission to sensuality. Sex is not shameful. It is both a *mitzvah,* a joyous, religious act and a natural, physical function, which entails important, human, psychological considerations. These include loving and caring for another, and for a family, a natural outcome of human sensuality.

As Judaism understands it, to humans, in contradiction to

animals, the element of self-control is an indispensable component of the sensual drive. Eating, breathing, and other basic human functions cannot long be put off. Sex can. It is possible to live and function without indulging in sexual activity. By conscious exercise of his free will, a feature in his make-up which distinguishes him from the animal, man can control himself in this respect. Mastering his instincts, he can conduct himself in a *human* fashion. The animal, enslaved to the instincts, is not free to do so — nor is the human who is no less enslaved when in his sexual life he behaves like a "pleasure-seeking animal."

Nahmanides, the thirteenth-century Spanish rabbinic authority and exegete, emphasizes the need for personal involvement and commitment in sexual conduct in order to differentiate, in this area of life, human behavior from that of the animal. In his commentary to the verse in Genesis[64] which is the principal biblical command relating to marriage, the *Ramban* explains:

> Male and female animals do not have this sort of human cleaving to one another. Any male animals can approach any female animal and they will copulate and procreate. . . . There is imbued in humans at an early age a natural yearning of the males and females for greater cleaving and permanence in their relationships. The man leaves his parents and views his wife as if she was truly as one flesh . . . For indeed he perceives his wife as closer to him than his parents are.[65]

Judaism maintains that this intimate bonding that can fuse two people into one should be limited to those who have sanctified the decision to marry by *hupah v'kidushin,* the wedding canopy and the consecration of the marriage ceremony.

Judaism teaches that a love that is not strong enough to commit itself forever is weak indeed. Its lack of a basic element fundamental to the nature of true love, indicates that it is not "love" that motivates the union, but something else. Call it lust masquerading as love or, perhaps, elemental instinct. The impulse of sexuality is a powerful force, and one is not necessarily dishonest with oneself or one's partner in making the basic error of considering as "love" that infatuating sensation which is derived from a fusion of strong biological drives and dizzying emotions.

In the Jewish view, true love between a man and a woman is not attained in a flash of desire; to be lasting it is achieved in a process which may take a long time — and it requires a commitment for life. If the union is not to be rent by some momentary disaffection, the partners require more than a romantic affection fused by heightened desire; they must share an overriding determination to persevere at building a permanent loving relationship that will transcend all threats to the union.

Judaism teaches that it is only within the long-term commitment implicit in the marital framework that there can exist the high level of personalization required for the physical relationship between a man and a woman. This personalization is reflected in that total mutual devotion essential for marriage, which is constantly being honed in the challenges faced in day-to-day living together.

IV

Planning the Nuptials

7

Preparations for the Wedding

It is easier by far to prepare for a wedding than for a marriage. Preparations for a wedding may be involved and at times give rise to anxiety. But when two people feel they have made the proper choice of a life partner and that they are psychologically ready and emotionally mature enough for the marriage, preparation for the wedding itself can be a pleasant experience of happy anticipation.[1]

The Engagement

Once the couple decides to get married, the next step is to arrange a meeting of both sets of parents.

Jewish tradition considers it important to receive parental blessings for the match. However, if parents do object to the choice of a marital partner, Jewish law permits a man or a woman to marry despite these objections. Such an act does not violate the *mitzvah* of honoring one's parents. The Talmud cites the example of Rachel who married R. Akiva against her father's wishes.[2]

Thereafter the couple informs close friends and relatives.

Customarily the man gives the woman an engagement present, and in Western society this is usually a diamond engagement ring. In fact, it is an ancient Jewish custom[3] for a man to present a gift of jewelry to his prospective bride. It is not absolutely necessary, however, and a young man preparing to marry should not get into debt in order to give his fiancée a costly piece of jewelry.

Jewish law deems it preferable to give the ring in private, lest the presentation before witnesses be construed (according to *halachah*) as the principal legal act of marriage which may later possibly require a rabbinic *get,* a letter of divorce.[4]

The *T'na'im* — Conditions of Engagement

In some traditional circles the engagement is legalized by signing the Conditions of Engagement, the *t'na'im* or *t'na'ay shiduchin.* This is done at a festive meal, customarily held at the home of one of the parties, and attended by the immediate family and other close relatives and friends of the couple, as well as by rabbis who are friends of the families. There is a formal ceremony for the signing of a contract that sets the wedding date and specifies other various conditions. These include details as to the venue of the wedding, financial undertakings of the parents, a dowry, if any, the provision of a home for the couple, and monetary support or continuing an education. The contract also contains a penalty clause in case of non-compliance with the specified conditions.

A rabbi in the group usually writes the *t'na'im,* which are signed by the couple and read aloud by the rabbi.[5] Copies are given to both of them.

A *kinyan,* or formal acknowledgement of the agreement, is performed, whereby the officiating rabbi hands over an article of clothing to both of the parties involved, who accordingly accept it.[6]

The festivities are celebrated by the singing of lively wedding songs and the presentation of rabbinic discourses, *divrei Torah,* that make the occasion a *s'udat mitzvah,* a special feast, participation in which is considered a *mitzvah.*[7] Usually the rabbis praise the bride and groom, whom they know, speaking warmly of their personal qualities and characteristics so that all present may learn about the couple.

Among traditional Ashkenazic Jews the event culminates when the two mothers jointly break a porcelain dish wrapped in a cloth,[8] to the shouts of *mazal tov,* good luck. In some circles, pieces of the plate are distributed among the bride's single girl friends, or they may be fashioned into jewelry before distribution. The joint breaking of the plate symbolizes the impossibility of joining a couple together if the agreement to marry is breached.[9] Indeed, a breach of *t'na'im* is considered severe and reprehensible, equivalent to breach of contract. The *Gaon* of Vilna (1720–1797) went so far as to declare that it is better to write a *get* (a letter of divorce) than not to fulfill the *t'na'im*.[10]

Nowadays, most traditional Jews, because of the harsh consequences of a breach, do not write *t'na'im* at the engagement; instead, in order to reduce to a minimum the possibility of the conditions being violated, they draw them up at the reception preceding the marriage ceremony.[11]

Another custom is to write the *t'na'im* at the official engagement celebration, but to leave details of the document intentionally vague and to employ frequently the phrase *kim'dubar,* "as agreed," in the appropriate places. Similarly, *kim'dubar* is used in the penalty clause, without further amplification. Regarding the wedding date, vague terms such as "on, or about" or "before, or after" a particular date are used.

In many traditional circles *t'na'im* are not written at all, for they are regarded as too legally binding an obligation. Instead, at the time of the engagement, a festive ceremony similar in virtually all respects to that of the *t'na'im* ceremony is held, but a much less formal, oral agreement called a *vort* is substituted for the written, contractual *t'na'im.*

Setting the Date

The date of the wedding depends on a number of factors which include:

- Scheduling the date at least seven days following the cessation of the bride's menstrual period so that the marriage may be properly consummated, in accordance with the Jewish regulations of Family Purity.
- Arranging employment leave; or, for students, finding time during a vacation period or waiting for year-end or graduation.
- Allowing sufficient time to set up a proper home.
- Reserving the place where the wedding will be held.

A Jewish wedding cannot take place on the Sabbath or during a major festival, for example, during the High Holy Day period which begins with the New Year, Rosh Hashanah, and ends with the Day of Atonement, Yom Kippur—the ten-day cycle known as the Ten Days of Penitence, Aseret Y'mai T'shuvah.[12] Nor on the Feast of Tabernacles, Sukot; the Eighth Day of Solemn Assembly, Sh'mini Atzeret; the Rejoicing in the Law, Simhat Torah; Passover, Pesah,[13] the Festival of Weeks, Shavuot; nor on Purim. Weddings may not be held during the seven-week period, *S'firah* (counting),[14] between the second day of Passover and the Festival of Weeks, Shavuot, as this is a time of mourning for R. Akiva's students who died in the second century, except for the thirty-third day of the counting, Lag BaOmer, when many weddings usually are held.[15]

Weddings may not be held during the three weeks between the Fast of the Seventeenth of Tammuz and the Ninth of Av, Tish'ah B'Av,[16] a mourning period when Jews mark the invasion of Jerusalem and the destruction of the Temple. These are national, commemorative days of sadness on which celebrations of individual, personal happiness are not held. In like manner, weddings may not take place on religious fast days, including the tenth day of Tevet, Asarah B'Tevet, which marks the start of Nebuchadnezzar's siege of Jerusalem; nor on the Fast of Esther, Ta'anit Esther, which precedes Purim.

According to Jewish law, a wedding may be held on any weekday.[17] Many Jews marry on Tuesday because in the biblical story of creation, in Genesis, the phrase "and it was good" is used twice when referring to the third day.[18]

Nowadays, Saturday evenings are often chosen, since the festivities can continue late into the night as most people do not work on Sunday. If, however, the wedding preparations might lead to Sabbath violation, another day should be chosen.

A wedding should not be held in the late afternoon preceding the Sabbath or a festival because the wedding celebrations might interfere with Sabbath or festival preparations.[19] However, Friday morning or early afternoon is an acceptable time,[20] even a preferable time for a wedding for those of modest means, since the guests would partake of their own Sabbath eve dinners soon after, and the wedding feast would not need to be unduly lavish.[21]

Where to Hold the Wedding

A wedding may be held at any appropriate place — in a synagogue, a hotel, at the kosher caterers, or in a private home. A feast is a significant part of the marriage celebration, and the wedding should take place where kosher facilities and a reputable kosher caterer are available. Often this is in a synagogue. Although there is some objection by rabbinic authorities to holding weddings in a synagogue sanctuary because of its association with a church wedding,[22] other rabbis permit it providing it is conducted in a manner distinctively different from church weddings.[23] Indeed, it was a custom in certain European communities to hold weddings in synagogues,[24] and the custom is still in practice among Sephardic Jews in England and Germany. The Vilna *Gaon* advocated holding weddings in the synagogue.[25]

Whether a wedding will express the proper Jewish spirit — or be merely a less than tasteful display — is often dependent upon the setting and the caterer, so these choices should be made carefully. A couple may find it useful, prior to making a decision, to attend a wedding conducted by the particular caterer they are considering.

Selecting the Rabbi

Probably the single most significant act of wedding planning is selecting a rabbi to officiate. His role is literally arranger of the marriage, that of *m'sader kidushin.* In this capacity, he not only performs the wedding ceremony, but he should be consulted at every stage in the planning, even concerning those details that seem most mundane. A Jewish marriage is a sanctification, *kidushin,* and every aspect of this significant religious rite must be imbued with holiness. All of the many details relating to it, no matter how ordinary, fall within the authority of the rabbi, who should advise the couple as to the proper Jewish procedures.

For a wedding to be truly Jewish, a joyous and meaningful occasion fully in accord with Jewish tradition and in the Jewish spirit, a Jewish *simhah,* details such as selecting the appropriate date, place, and so forth should be discussed with the rabbi as early as possible.

It is important that the rabbi be proper and God-fearing and, if possible, a Torah scholar.[26] The Talmud states: "One who is not expert in the laws of marriage and divorce should not officiate."[27] This is a principle of Jewish law.[28] Many of the rules and regulations relating to this area of personal status are so complex that even rabbis otherwise competent in other functions of their calling might lack the proper qualifications in these matters — even if they have previously performed many weddings. If the wedding will be held in a synagogue, it is a courtesy to ask the rabbi of the synagogue to officiate.[29]

The Marriage Document, the *Ketubah*

The marriage document, the *ketubah,* is the most important part of the wedding and, as such, should be dealt with early in the preparations. Literally "that which is written," "writ," or "her writ," the *ketubah* is an essential prerequisite of Jewish marriage, a written agreement that the groom gives the bride at the wedding, outlining the basic obligations he assumes toward her during their life together, and in the event of their divorce or his death.

Throughout history, where the woman's role was vastly inferior to the man's and when women generally were treated as little more than chattel, the *ketubah* served as an enlightened instrument to commit the husband to certain fundamental responsibilities toward his wife. While most societies relegated a wife to a position devoid of possessions, of utter economic dependence upon the husband, the Jewish *ketubah* ensured that, within a marriage, a woman was guaranteed certain inalienable rights and privileges.

The Husband's Guarantee toward His Wife

The *ketubah* is a unilateral agreement that binds only the husband. It is not a mutual marriage contract obligating the two parties. Judaism recognizes the traditional vulnerability of the woman who, through the ages, bound to the home by social norms and the realities of childbearing and motherhood, has had to depend upon her husband for sustenance and protection. The man has traditionally wielded the real power within the family, if only by his control of the income. The structure of marriage itself might thus lead to a variety of potential evils, to which the wife in her dependent role would be especially vulnerable.

A husband not committed to his wife by an established set of obligations has at his disposal an arsenal of weapons with which he can humiliate or punish her during their marriage and even after divorce. These range from financial deprivation to neglect. By focusing on the husband's legal and economic responsibilities toward his wife, the *ketubah* gives protection to the wife, and raises her status. In addition, it has strengthened the marriage agreement and reinforced its legality.

Equally important are the psychological benefits of the *ketubah;* by endowing the woman with legal and financial rights within the marriage, the *ketubah* allows her to nurture a sense of self-worth. Even when living among societies that traditionally denied women any semblance of privileged status, the Jewish woman has always been able to maintain her dignity and self-respect within the structure of the family. Since she is financially protected by the marriage contract, the husband is not tempted to regard her as a helpless dependent or as his chattel. The *ketubah* corrects these potential imbalances in marriage by forcing the husband to live up to certain basic responsibilities toward his wife.

Such is the importance of the *ketubah* in Jewish law, that the Sages ruled that "it is forbidden for a man to reside with a woman even one hour without a *ketubah*."[30] There is a rabbinic tradition that a marriage without a *ketubah* is not a legal marriage.[31] To safeguard her own interests, therefore, Jewish law requires the woman to make sure not only that she receives a *ketubah,* but that she keeps it in a safe place at all times. If it is lost or misplaced, she must have it replaced.[32]

The Antiquity of the *Ketubah*

The *ketubah* dates back to ancient times. The marriage agreement was referred to as early as the third/second century B.C.E. in the apocryphal Book of Tobit. "And he took paper,[33] wrote a contract and signed it; then they began to eat,"[34] is undoubtedly a *ketubah*. But the *ketubah* predates this reference as well. One of the earliest Jewish manuscripts discovered to date is a *ketubah* from 440–420 B.C.E.,[35] belonging to a woman named Mibtahya, which is part of a remarkable collection of Judaic-Aramaic papyri unearthed early in this century at Elephantine and Aswan in southern Egypt, where a community of Jewish soldiers and their families settled following the Babylonian exile in 586 B.C.E. While the text of the *ketubah* as we know it had not yet become formalized 2,400 years ago, it still bears a striking resemblance in many details to the one used today.

In 1961, Israeli archaeologist Yigael Yadin discovered, high in a cave in the Judaean Desert near the shores of the Dead Sea, a leather pouch containing a bundle of papyri.[36] Carefully opening what turned out to be a woman's purse, Yadin was astounded to find a treasure trove of ancient documents belonging to a much-married woman, Babata. Among them was a document with the words marked on its back, "The *ketubah* of Babata, the daughter of Simon," as well as another *ketubah,* that of Shlomzion, daughter of Judah. Babata's *ketubah* (the date of which is not decipherable, but which Yadin fixes between 128 and 130 C.E.) and that of Shlomzion (dating from 128 C.E.) together with two others, less well preserved (dating from 117 C.E.), discovered in the Wadi Muraba'at in the Judaean Desert by French archaeologist Roland de Vaux, are the oldest existing *ketubot* after that of Mibtahya of the fifth century B.C.E.

Despite the antiquity of these documents, their wording indicates that they followed an accepted format, the general framework of which may have been used by Jews for a considerable period of time even before the fifth century B.C.E. In fact, the *ketubah* is traced by some to the Torah itself,[37] which declares that the woman is entitled, as her minimum requirement from her husband, to the basic provisions of food, clothing, and conjugal rights.[38]

An entire talmudic tract, *Ketubot,* is devoted to the *ketubah* and its contents. A number of clauses in the ancient *ketubot* are similar to those used in contemporary *ketubot*. Babata's *ketubah* is in Aramaic, the vernacular of Eretz Israel in her day, and the language traditionally used in *ketubot,* even today. The custom of writing *ketubot* in Aramaic arose during the lengthy sojourn of large numbers of Jews in Babylon, where Aramaic was spoken.[39] While their dates since talmudic times were usually written in Hebrew, Aramaic was generally preferred to Hebrew for the text, as it was for other legal documents, because of its international character. Subsequently, Hebrew began to be reserved for sacred texts, leaving Aramaic for secular ones.

The Sanhedrin Ordains the Form of the *Ketubah*

In its present form, the *ketubah* probably dates back to the first century B.C.E. when, as indicated in a historic *b'raita*,[40] a tannaic statement not included in the Mishnah, the Sanhedrin (supreme court), under the leadership of its president, R. Simon ben Shetah, formally defines the contents of the *ketubah* and the specific duties to which it obligates the groom. From this we learn of its purpose in relation to the couple's marriage or divorce, and in the event of the husband's demise.

Previously, a man could put aside a sum of money for his wife in the event of his death or of divorce. However, if he lost or hid the money, his wife would be bereft of her rightful *ketubah* sum and could become destitute. The Sanhedrin legislated, therefore, that a husband's entire estate becomes mortgaged through the *ketubah* in order to fulfill his obligations as specified by it. A wife would thus be able to collect the sum due her just as she would any contractual debt.[41] The *ketubah* also provides protection for a woman in the event of her husband's death. A portion of her wealth is returned to her, and she receives the *ketubah* amount as well as an additional sum of money.

Another important function of the *ketubah* is to deter the husband from severing the marital bonds too easily. "So that it should not be considered easy to send her away" is the expression used.[42] According to the Torah, a woman may be divorced willingly or unwillingly, but a man can be divorced only at his will.[43] Since the Jewish idea of marriage is a permanent union, the *ketubah* is a vital instrument circumscribing and making it difficult for the husband to divorce his wife, by placing in her hands a variety of legal means designed to protect her from possible abuse, and to safeguard her rights. Even today, therefore, when by rabbinic ordination since the tenth century a man may not divorce his wife against her will,[44] a *ketubah* is still a required obligation.

The Financial Obligations of the *Ketubah*

One of the most powerful safety mechanisms afforded by the *ketubah* is the husband's commitment, in the event of divorce, to pay his wife an agreed sum of money. The heavy payment itself acts as a deterrent against any impulsive act. A man could divorce his wife, but the Sages wanted to make it a costly procedure so that he would think twice before initiating the process. Thus, a bad marriage could be terminated. However, the man who, in the grip of a towering anger, might be prone to decide hastily on a divorce, is constrained to reconsider his decision coolly in the face of the financial burden such a move might entail. Indeed, the expense might motivate the man to decide to go back and work on the marriage.

The basic sum the Sages decided upon was two hundred *zuzim* — a sum that could provide support for some years, and if properly invested would ensure sustenance for a lifetime[45] — and one hundred *zuzim* for a widow or divorcée. In essence, the *ketubah* sum might therefore be compared to alimony, the difference being that the former has to be paid in a single lump sum.

To ensure the proper fulfillment of his marital pledges, the *ketubah* binds the man to mortgage legally as security all his present and future assets. So essential to the *ketubah* was this financial obligation that the amount itself soon became known as "the *ketubah*," and *ketubah* thus became both a legal and a financial term. In addition to the basic sum of the *ketubah,* the husband is required to provide an additional sum of his own. This amount, representing the bride's dowry and the total value of her personal belongings becomes, in the event of divorce or the death of her husband, her possession.

As a result of the above-mentioned Jewish law forbidding a married couple from living together conjugally without a *ketubah,* a limited number of attractively decorated *ketubot* from various Jewish communities have been preserved. They may be found in several public collections and in notable private ones, primarily in Israel and in the United States.

Commissioning a Personalized *Ketubah*

Ketubot were almost always written by hand. Even after the invention of the printing press, it was rare for printed *ketubah* forms to be used.[46] In almost all Oriental or Sephardic communities, *ketubot* were decorated, often quite lavishly. The calligraphic beauty of the Hebrew letter, the rich and diverse ornamentation to which the *ketubah* lends itself, and the easy adaptability of the paper or parchment used for framing and display, has made the *ketubah* a uniquely fascinating Jewish art form of considerable attraction to museums, collectors, and connoisseurs of art.

The custom of illuminating *ketubot* is an old one, though it is difficult to pinpoint the origin of the practice. A fragment of a *ketubah*, probably Egyptian, discovered in the Cairo *Genizah*,[47] dating back to the tenth/eleventh century and containing the remnant of decorative arches and Hebrew micrography (minuscule script) indicates the existence of illuminated *ketubot* about a thousand years ago. The custom was basically a Sephardic one. Except for one noteworthy exception, a fragment of a *ketubah* from Krems, Austria dated 1392, early decorated Ashkenazic *ketubot* are unknown.

As late as the twentieth century, the custom of decorating *ketubot* was virtually unknown in the Western world. Those marrying were usually supplied by their rabbis with printed *ketubah* forms, with blanks for filling in pertinent details such as names, date, and place. Though not ideal, this form of *ketubah* is acceptable when the marriage is the first for the bride,[48] if it conforms in all respects to the requirements of *halachah*.[49] In the 1950s and 1960s, however, American *yeshivah* students, who became aware of the Sephardic tradition of grooms presenting beautifully decorated *ketubot* to their brides, began commissioning from scribes and graphic artists hand-written, calligraphically lettered and decorated *ketubot* on parchment. Soon these artists and scribes (women as well as men, since Jewish law permits a woman to be a scribe for a *ketubah*) were producing individualized, decorated *ketubot* as well as other Hebrew manuscripts and certificates.

Many young couples marrying today will commission a Hebrew scribe-illuminator to produce on parchment a beautifully designed, hand-written, customized *ketubah* to be displayed in their home as their own distinctive work of Jewish art, and as a cherished memento of their wedding day. In ordering a *ketubah*, to allow sufficient time for its writing and decoration, a couple should ensure that the scribe is absolutely competent, for extreme care is required to ensure that all details conform with established procedure.[50] The cost of the *ketubah* is usually borne by the groom.

If, for various reasons, a hand-written, personalized, decorated *ketubah* cannot be ordered for the wedding, a modest *ketubah* form can be used; and later, when time and means are available, one can be commissioned, perhaps for an anniversary.

The Wedding Ring

An integral part of the marriage ceremony is, under the *hupah,* the handing over of a wedding ring by the bridegroom to the bride; this constitutes the single most vital legal act of validation of the marriage.[51] Its presentation, and not the blessing of the rabbi, makes the couple man and wife according to Jewish law. By ancient custom, possibly dating back to biblical times,[52] the item given is a ring, but it may be anything of value.

Jewish law requires that the ring must belong to the bridegroom; it may not be borrowed.[53] If the ring is a family heirloom, it must first be bought by the groom or given to him as an unconditional gift so that it would be his.[54] And, thereafter, it is unconditionally the bride's. Otherwise, the marriage may not be legal.

In some Italian and certain other Jewish communities in Europe, the custom existed to commission the creation of beautiful communal marriage rings. Such a ring was sold to a groom for a token sum, or presented to him as a gift, and after the wedding the new wife was expected to sell the ring back to the community for a token sum or present it as a gift, so that it would be available to other wedding couples for this purpose.

If a groom does not have a ring which is absolutely his own, it is preferable that the ceremony be performed instead with an object indubitably his—even a coin.[55] Among the Syrian, Baghdadi, and Georgian Jews, a coin is in fact used. There are some halachic authorities who prefer that a coin not be used for *kidushin*.[56] However, what is most crucial is that the groom give the bride an item indisputably his own as a legal consideration, which act effects the transformation of the bride's status from a single woman to a married one.

According to the *Zohar,* the main book of Jewish mysticism, the ring represents the circle of the creative force that surrounded the world at the beginning of Creation. The bride and groom who are created in the image of God, are thus symbolically likened to the Creator when they emulate Him by uniting in the creation of life.[57] In another explanation, the ring is related to a circular link, as in a chain, and symbolizes the new link the couple is adding to the long chain of the generations of the Jewish people. Another popular interpretation is that the ring represents a circle, and just as a circle has neither beginning nor end, so too should the love between the couple be infinite.

The wedding ring should preferably be plain, with no precious stones, in order to avoid possible misrepresentation, that is, the prime legal act of marriage taking place under false pretenses. Thus, the value of the ring should be readily apparent — it may be of gold[58] because of gold's nobility and significance, or of silver.[59] The ring must not be plated,[60] as this would have the effect of disguising its content and thus its true value.[61] The bride must know exactly what the ring is made of, otherwise the marriage is, according to Jewish law, not valid.[62]

Wedding Apparel

The bride and groom are considered king and queen at their wedding, and are expected to dress appropriately; elegantly and modestly, but not ostentatiously. The bride dons a veil as a symbol of modesty.

It is traditional for brides to wear white, not, as in Christian tradition, to indicate virginity, but rather as a symbol of purity. On their wedding day, according to Jewish tradition, all sins of the couple are forgiven[63] and the bride immerses herself in a *mikvah* prior to the wedding as a symbolic act of purification. It is quite in order, therefore, even for a bride at a second marriage to don white wedding apparel.

Similarly, a traditional bridegroom dons a *kittel,* a white linen robe, at the *hupah,* over his clothes. The *kittel* symbolizes purity — in accordance with the passage in Isaiah, "Even though your sins may be as scarlet, they shall be as white as snow"[64] — but is also similar to a death shroud,[65] a poignant reminder to the groom in the midst of his rejoicing that although he may be likened to a king, he is human, and mortal.[66] He should not forget his awe of God, and should repent and be humble.

A bride is expected to look beautiful at her wedding, and to wear beautiful garments. The *Midrash* states that God himself clothed Eve for her wedding with Adam[67] to make sure she was as beautiful as possible. The groom should take pleasure in his wife's beauty.[68] Indeed, it is said that it was Rachel's beauty that first attracted Jacob to her.[69] In ancient times, brides were always dressed and embellished so as to maximize their beauty.[70] The *Midrash* lists no fewer than twenty-four different adornments for the beautification of the bride,[71] paralleling the twenty-four books of the Bible.[72]

The minimum halachic requirements of modesty are that the bride's gown be knee-length or lower, and sleeves should reach at least to the elbows.[73] It should not be decolleté in the front or back,[74] nor should it be revealing and show her body through diaphanous, sheer, or lace filigree material. The concept of Jewish marriage as *kidushin,* sanctification, dictates that a bride should not appear provocative or frivolous.

Others in the wedding party should be similarly guided in their choice of dress for the occasion.

Music

It is an ancient Jewish custom to have music at weddings,[75] and is referred to in the Bible.[76] Music plays a major role in setting the proper mood of a Jewish wedding and is an essential part of it.[77] Care should be taken to ensure that the music chosen is appropriate — a suitable mixture of joy and solemnity for the occasion — and that the musicians can, in their musical presentation, properly interpret the special nature of the occasion.[78] One rabbinic authority states that when wedding music is of a sacred nature, the entire wedding is of a similar nature.[79] In this way, authentically Jewish music plays a vital role in the creation of an authentically Jewish wedding.

The Wedding Attendants

While in contemporary society wedding attendants — best man, maids of honor, ushers, bridesmaids, and flower girls — have no exact parallel in Jewish tradition, there is an old tradition for the Jewish bride and groom to have attendants. Such attendants were traditionally known as *shoshvinin*.[80] *Shoshvin,* possibly from the Greek *syskenos,* friend or companion, means close friend[81] or constant companion.[82] The Bible describes how Samson took thirty young men to be his wedding attendants.[83]

The groom's *shoshvin* would be constantly at his right hand to take care of all his needs;[84] in essence, he was the equivalent of the best man of our times. He acted as the groom's valet, secretary, and general assistant, and looked after details of the wedding for the groom according to his directions. The bride's special attendant was—as she is generally today—her maid of honor, and to some extent she fulfilled similar functions for the bride.[85]

The groom's attendants escort the groom to the *hupah;* the bride's attendants lead her to the groom for the marriage ceremony.[86]

In talmudic times the communal meal for friends at the wedding was known as *shoshvinut*.[87] It may have been prepared by the *shoshvinin,*[88] or it may have been in honor of the *shoshvinin.*[89]

The Week Before

As the wedding date approaches, anticipation builds. To maintain this anticipation at its height, it is customary among some for the bride and groom to remain apart and not to see each other for one week prior to the wedding.[90]

The Sabbath Preceding the Wedding

The Sabbath before the wedding is called the *aufruf*—literally "The Calling Up"—or the Bridegroom's Sabbath, when he is "called up" to the Torah reading in the synagogue. This is a symbolic act representing for the bridegroom a further commitment to the Torah as a married or "completed" individual.[91] Dressed in his finest clothes, he is escorted by his *shoshvinin* to and from the synagogue.

The *aufruf* is a major *simhah,* a festive occasion. Traditionally held on the Sabbath before the wedding, the entire community rejoices with the bridegroom. When Solomon built the Temple in Jerusalem, he wished to encourage Jews to perform *g'milut hasadim* (acts of love for others). He therefore built two special gates to the Temple, one reserved for mourners, and the other for bridegrooms.[92] Every Sabbath, Jews would sit near the "Gate of the Bridegrooms." When grooms entered they would be congratulated and welcomed with the greetings: "May He Who dwells in this abode cause you to rejoice with sons and daughters."[93] When the Temple was destroyed, the Rabbis ordained that bridegrooms be invited to the synagogues and honored by the community by being called up to the Torah. In this way, members of the congregation were encouraged to practice acts of love toward bridegrooms by congratulating them and offering them their best wishes.[94]

It is customary for women in the synagogue, upon the conclusion of the Torah reading for him, to shower the groom with nuts and candies;[95] this is symbolic of the hope that the new union will be a fruitful one,[96] producing offspring as quickly as the almond tree produces its fruit, and that the couple will live a sweet life together. Indeed, Eve, the mother of all mankind, is referred to as a nut tree.[97] The nuts allude[98] to the verse in the Song of Songs, "I went down to the nut garden. . . ."[99] The *g'matria* (numerical value) of the Hebrew word for nut, *egoz,* is seventeen, the same as that for *het,* sin, and *tov,* good, indicating to the bridegroom that all of his sins are forgiven, having been transformed from *het* to *tov.*[100] Children vie with each other to gather the nuts and sweets thrown at the groom,[101] thus participating in the *simhah.* At the end of the services, the groom's family usually provides a festive *kiddush,* or light repast, for the entire congregation following the recitation of the *kiddush* benediction over wine.

The Wedding Day

The theme of the twenty-four-hour period preceding the wedding is that of spiritual purification preparatory to entering into marriage, or *kidushin,* sanctification. Before the wedding—as close to it as possible,[102] usually the night before[103] and preferably after sunset[104]—the bride goes to the *mikvah,* the ritual bath, where she immerses herself. An important requirement of Jewish law, this act is an indispensable prerequisite to the consummation of the marriage and to the wedding ceremony itself.

In Jewish law, a woman has the status of *nidah* (menstruant) from the onset of her menstrual period until she immerses herself in a *mikvah*. *Nidah* (which has its roots in the word *nadod*, to be removed or separated from) means that a woman must be removed from her husband during this period, and must have no physical contact with him. Her designation in Jewish law as *nidah* is a means, through this period of enforced separation, of protecting her from physical intrusion by her husband.

The result is increasingly heightened anticipation as the *mikvah* day draws nearer, continuously imbuing what otherwise might become a routine, mundane physical relationship because of constant availability and overfamiliarity, with freshness and excitement. It provides a refreshing monthly renewal of physical intimacy between a couple and thus serves as a means of drawing them closer together.

The bride's act of immersion in a *mikvah* is analogous with the immersion of the Israelites[105] prior to their symbolic "marriage" with God at Sinai[106] during the giving of the Torah.[107] It is thereby reminiscent of a similar holy preparation undergone by the Jewish people as part of the process of purification and consecration preparatory to a sacred union.*

The Fast

As part of the process of spiritual purification in preparation for the sacred act of *kidushin,* it is customary[108] for the bride and groom to fast on the day of their wedding,[109] an act which underscores for them the solemnity of the occasion for which they are preparing. Both fast and pray fervently that God will bless them and that their marriage will be successful.[110] Marriage is the beginning of a totally new phase of life for the couple. It is therefore like Yom Kippur, the Day of Atonement, at which time a new lease on life is also given, and all previous sins are forgiven.[111]

By fasting, the bride and groom also demonstrate that they can remove themselves from the purely physical, as did Moses who fasted for forty days when he received the Torah.[112] Similarly,

---

*For a discussion of *nidah* and *mikvah,* see Chapter 9, "Family Purity: The Jewish Refinement of Sexuality."

when the Jews stood at Sinai and "betrothed" themselves to God by accepting the Torah, they were oblivious to their physical needs and did not eat. The fast is thus a means for the couple to relate the sacredness of the occasion of their marriage to the sacred act of the giving of the Torah.

In some circles it is customary only for the groom to fast,[113] the bride refraining from it lest the absence of food mar her appearance at the wedding. However, most rabbinic authorities indicate that the bride must fast as well.[114] The fast is broken by the sipping of wine at the *hupah,* followed by their first meal together in private immediately after their *hupah.*

The Bride's Gift to Her Groom: A *Tallit*

On the day of the wedding, it is customary for the bride to send a *tallit* to the groom, the traditional gift for the husband-to-be.[115] Traditional males wear a *tallit katan,* or a small *tallit* under their garments, but upon marrying they don an additional, large *tallit,* which they wear for morning prayer. Except for the German and Sephardic males who don a *tallit* upon attaining Bar Mitzvah and continue wearing it at daily morning prayer thereafter, it is customary for Jewish males to wear the *tallit* in the synagogue only after marriage.[116]

The wearing of the *tallit* derives from the *mitzvah* enjoined in the Torah to wear a four-cornered garment with fringes at the corners.[117] The *tallit* is a full, large, cape-like garment, and not the scarf-like "prayer shawl" in use in some synagogues, which is draped over the neck or over the shoulders. The Torah specifies that the *tallit* be a garment "with which you cover yourself,"[118] and this is understood to mean a full-length garment covering almost the whole length of an individual. It is preferable that the *tallit* be of wool, although one made of silk is also acceptable.

The purpose of the *tallit* is to strengthen a man in his commitment to maintain his marriage vows and his elevated moral calling as a Jew and to help prevent him from succumbing to sexual temptation outside marriage. This conforms with the purpose of the *tzitzit* (fringes on the *tallit*), which is specified in the Torah "so that you may see them and remember all the commandments of God and not go straying after your heart and your eyes,"[119] a reference under-

stood by the Sages to indicate sexual temptation.[120] By wrapping
himself in the *tallit* during his morning prayers each day, a man
thus has a constant mnemonic device to remind him that his
existence as a human being is synonymous with his existence as a
Jew and protect him against the temptation to have relations outside
marriage.

Thus, the bride's gift to her groom of a *tallit* is similar to his
presentation of a wedding ring to her. Just as wearing the ring
symbolizes her fidelity to her husband, so his wearing the *tallit*
represents his fidelity to his wife. Each of the four corners of the
tallit contains eight strings, a total of thirty-two, the *g'matria*
(numerical value) of which is the same as that of *lev,* heart. With the
gift of the *tallit,* therefore, the bride proclaims to her groom on the
eve of her wedding, "I give all my heart to you."[121]

V
The
Wedding

8

The Marriage Ceremony

The Structure of the Marriage Service

The Jewish marriage ceremony has undergone numerous changes over the course of the ages. The marriage customs and traditions of Jews are as many and varied as are the communities from which they originate, and they are principally inherited from their ancestors. Since marriage is a central event in the life of the Jew, it is natural that such a diversity of colorful customs evolved in the widely dispersed areas where Jews resided in the world, reflecting their different cultural experiences and backgrounds.

However, the basic elements of the traditional Jewish marriage ceremony are similar everywhere. The traditional Jewish marriage service consists of two components: *erusin,* usually translated as betrothal, also known as *kidushin* (sanctification), and *nisuin,* literally, "elevation" or nuptials, that is, the marriage itself.

Originally *erusin* and *nisuin* were conducted at different times, sometimes as much as a year apart. Since medieval times, however, the two have been conducted in successive stages within a single marriage ceremony.[1] The ceremonies were combined because of the expense involved in having two feasts. Another reason for combining the two was to minimize the temptation that might result from the long separation between betrothal and marriage. In some communities edicts were enacted in the late medieval period to enforce the joining of the two procedures.

The prime feature in the marriage solemnization is the placing of a ring on the bride's finger by the groom, accompanied by his recitation of the traditional Jewish espousal formula. The public reading of the *ketubah,* the marriage contract, upon the consummation of the *erusin,* serves as an interlude between the ceremonies of *erusin* and *nisuin.*

The recitation of the seven benedictions for the bride and groom, which constitutes the prime element of *nisuin,* terminates the second stage of the marriage ceremony and marks the beginning of their married life together.

The Prenuptial Reception

The traditional Jewish wedding begins with separate simultaneous receptions by the groom and the bride for the wedding guests. The bride's reception is usually the livelier one. It is an old tradition, referred to in the Talmud,[2] for the bride to sit on an attractive throne. Surrounded by her attendants, close family members, and friends, she receives guests and well-wishers. As the musicians play, her friends dance in front of her.

The groom's reception (Yiddish: *hoson's tish*) for men, is held at a table laden with food and drink. Seated adjacent to the groom are his father and the bride's father, surrounded by the rabbis. Around the table are male guests, relatives, and friends of the groom, who toast the groom and sing. Often, the room in which the groom's reception is held is where the late-afternoon *Minhah* prayer service takes place.

It is customary for a groom to deliver (or attempt to deliver) a learned discourse at the *tish* ("table"). But traditionally he is interrupted by his friends shortly after beginning, with lively singing and rhythmic clapping in which all present join to prevent him from continuing. This custom is not intended as an affront or as an act of disrespect to the groom, but is designed to protect the groom who may be less than scholarly, lest he be shamed on what should be his most joyous day.

In many hasidic circles, a *badhan,* or professional wedding jester, would be employed at the *tish* to entertain the assembled guests, by toasting the groom in rhymed couplets sung in traditional tunes.[3]

The most crucial procedure at the groom's reception is the completion and validation of the *ketubah,* the marriage contract (see previous chapter). The *ketubah* is carefully reviewed by the rabbi to determine that all details are correct.

The groom then formally accepts all the unilateral obligations to which he commits himself in the *ketubah* by executing a *kinyan sudar,* a traditional legal consent and agreement process. The officiating rabbi hands him a small article of clothing such as a handkerchief, and the groom, before two witnesses (who may not be close relatives of bride or groom), takes it and lifts it up symbolically to affirm consent, before returning it to the rabbi.

At the conclusion of this procedure, called *kinyan,* a scribe or the rabbi then adds to the end of the *ketubah* text the Aramaic word *v'kanina* (and we have properly concluded the legal act of transference), and the witnesses sign to affirm the groom's acceptance, through the act of *kinyan,* of all the conditions of the *ketubah* document, thereby validating the *ketubah.* In some communities, it is customary for the groom also to sign it.

The Veiling Ceremony

The groom is then escorted by his father and the bride's father, the rabbis, the dignitaries, and the others in his retinue, to the bridal reception area for the veiling ceremony, known in Yiddish as the *badeken* (Hebrew, *hinuma*). Accompanied by his friends, who dance and sing in front of him, the groom leads the procession to the bride. He approaches the bridal throne and covers the bride's face with a veil (Yiddish, *dektich*). He is then escorted back to the groom's reception room by the men, to prepare for the *hupah* ceremony.

The veiling ceremony dates back at least to early medieval times,[4] and some find a reference to the custom in the Talmud.[5] The reason for the ceremony is probably related to modesty; the veil symbolically represents the added level of modesty the bride is expected to adopt with her elevation to the married state. The Torah relates that when Rebecca saw her bridegroom Isaac coming toward her, "she took her veil and covered herself."[6] The *badeken* ceremony thus recalls to all Jewish brides the matriarch's gesture of modesty at seeing her bridegroom, inspiring them to emulate their biblical forebears and conduct themselves with an elevated level of modesty in their married lives.

Some ascribe the custom of the bride's veiling to her position of centrality at the wedding, and the possibility that some men, undisciplined in their thoughts, might cast lustful eyes at her. The veiling accordingly underscores that, from this day on, the beauty of the bride is reserved for her husband alone to appreciate.[7]

Others see in the ritual a symbolic act directing attention away from the physical toward the spiritual at the wedding, constituting a public demonstration by the groom that his interest in the bride lies not in her beauty, but in the deeper, inner qualities of her character which, unlike her physical beauty, will not disappear in time.[8]

There is also a rabbinic opinion that the tradition has a legal basis, as it symbolizes the groom's public obligation to clothe his wife, and is thus a procedure which is an integral part of the legal marriage process.[9]

In some communities it is not the groom, but the rabbi who performs the veiling procedure.[10] When the rabbi veils the bride, he often simultaneously recites[11] to the bride the biblical blessing, "O sister! May you grow into thousands of myriads."[12]

The tradition of Hasidim and some Oriental Jews, and the old Jerusalem community, is for the veil to be opaque, to assure that the bride's entire face is covered for the wedding ceremony, so that she can neither see nor be seen.[13]

Preparing for the *Hupah*

When he returns to his reception room from the *badeken,* the groom is readied for the *hupah* ceremony by his attendants.[14] As the groom, on his wedding day, is compared to a king, he does not don his garments as he does ordinarily, but is dressed by his attendants. The garment worn is usually a *kittel,* a simple white cotton robe.[15]

It is customary for the groom to wear a white garment, a symbol of purity for this ceremony, to emphasize that this day is, for him, like Yom Kippur, when he is to repent,[16] and be forgiven for all his sins.[17] The prophet Isaiah declares, "If your sins are like scarlet, they shall become as white as snow."[18] For the same reason the bride wears white (see previous chapter). The white garments serve as a symbolic reminder to bride and groom that they must henceforth take care to keep clear of sin, thereby fulfilling Solomon's directive in Ecclesiastes, "At all times take care that your garments be white."[19]

The white garments also signify that, apart from the commitment they make to each other on the day of their *kidushin*, they are also making a solemn commitment to God to conduct their lives in an elevated manner.

The *kittel* the groom dons is also reminiscent of the white shroud he will wear when he dies. It thus serves as a poignant reminder on the happiest day of his life of the eventual day of his death. This pointed recollection of his mortality on his wedding day is designed to bring him down to earth, to underscore that henceforth he should pursue a life of meaning, and not one of empty, petty desires.[20]

There are no pockets in the *kittel*. Just as the absence of pockets in a shroud indicates that a person takes nothing material with him when he dies, the groom, wearing a pocketless *kittel* that is compared to a shroud, is reminded of this at his wedding. It also serves as a pointer to the bride that she accepts him for what he is, and not for his possessions. For the same reason it is customary in many circles for the bride not to wear jewelry at the *hupah*.[21]

The Sages also see the *kittel* as a symbol that the bridal couple should view their marital bond as a lasting one, continuing until the day of their death.[22]

In some circles, it is customary for the *kittel* to be worn under the groom's outer garments.

In many areas it is customary for the attendants of the groom to place ashes on the groom's head at this time, in commemoration of the destruction of the Temple in Jerusalem.[23] This is an ancient custom that is referred to in the Talmud.[24] Some leave the ashes on only during the *hupah* ceremony, and remove them immediately thereafter.[25]

The *Hupah*

The marriage ceremony is conducted under a marriage canopy, known in Hebrew as a *hupah* (literally, "covering"). It consists of a square cloth, usually made of silk or velvet, supported by four staves, and ordinarily held by four men.

The *hupah* is mentioned in the Bible in association with marriage: "As a bridegroom goes forth from his *hupah.*"[26] Elsewhere it is stated: "Let the bridegroom proceed from his chamber and let the bride go forth from the *hupah.*"[27]

The *hupah* symbolizes the new home to which the bridegroom will take his bride. In this context, the appearance of the bride and groom together under a *hupah* before an assembly who have come to witness the event is in itself a public proclamation by them that they are now bonded together as man and wife.[28] It is a prelude to intimacy,[29] and thus a significant element in *nisuin.*

The cloth *hupah* was originally draped around the bride and groom[30] but was later spread out over their heads.[31] In some places, a *tallit* was draped over the couple[32] or held above them. The single cloth under which the couple are joined thus symbolizes both the new household they are forming and represents the public recognition of their new status as man and wife.[33]

The canopy is considered an object of Jewish ceremonial art, and in accordance with the Jewish concept of *hidur mitzvah* (embellishing the precept), considerable attention is often lavished on it to create attractive *hupot.*[34]

The Sages find a reference to the *hupah* in the talmudic passage in *Avot*[35] referring to the house which is open on four sides. The Jerusalemite R. Yosi ben Yohanan urges, "Let your house be wide open," and compares the *hupah* to the tent of the patriarch Abraham that, according to Jewish tradition, had entrances on all four sides to welcome wayfarers, so that no traveller, no matter from which direction he came, need be burdened searching for an entrance door.[36] The *hupah,* with four open sides, is thus a symbol of the Jewish home filled with *hesed* (acts of love), an important component of which is *hachnasat orhim* (hospitality to strangers), a mode of conduct that the newly married couple is expected to establish in their home in emulation of their patriarchal forebear, whose hospitality to strangers was legendary.[37]

It is preferable for the *hupah* to be outdoors, under the stars, symbolizing the hopes that the couple will be blessed with a large family[38] in conformity with God's blessing to Abraham:[39] "I will greatly bless you, and I will exceedingly multiply your children as the stars in heaven."[40]

The Sages find an allusion to weddings being held outdoors in biblical times in Jeremiah's reference to "the sound of the bridegroom and the sound of the bride . . . in the cities of Judaea and in the courtyards of Jerusalem."[41]

Strong reservations have been raised in some circles about holding weddings in synagogues because irreverent revelry might result in the profanation of the sanctity of the synagogue. Nevertheless, it was customary in many areas for weddings to be held in the courtyard of synagogues. Indeed, many synagogues in Germany were constructed with a built-in *treustein,* or "marriage stone" at a corner of the structure facing the inner synagogue courtyard, which bore the initial Hebrew letters of the above verse from Jeremiah. In these communities, the culmination of the marriage ceremony was marked by the groom throwing a glass goblet and shattering it at the *treustein.*

Some synagogues and wedding halls have a skylight which opens to allow the *hupah* ceremony to be conducted under the sky.

The Wedding Procession

Following the veiling ceremony, the couple are led to the *hupah* for the marriage ceremony.

The groom arrives at the *hupah* before the bride.[42] Since the *hupah* is considered the symbolic home of the groom, he must be there first to welcome his bride to his home. The tradition is said by some to go back to the very first wedding, when, the Torah says, God took Eve "and brought her to Adam."[43] Eve, since she was created after Adam, is considered in Jewish thought to represent a higher form of life than is Adam, since she was able to carry a fetus in her body.[44] As the first one created, Adam is said to have been waiting under the *hupah* in the Garden of Eden when Eve was brought to him.[45]

In some circles, it is customary for two people[46] to lead the groom to the *hupah* to the accompaniment of appropriate music. In other circles, however, the groom is accompanied by a larger retinue,[47] since the groom is likened to a king.

There are varying customs regarding who accompanies the principals to the *hupah*. Sometimes the groom is accompanied by his parents and the bride by hers. Indeed, this custom is cited by the *Zohar*, which says "the father and mother of the bride bring her to the domain of the groom."[48] However, there is no Jewish tradition of a father "giving away the bride."

Among other groups, it is customary for the groom to be accompanied by the two fathers and the bride to be accompanied by the two mothers. Where the custom is for the principals to be accompanied by their parents, and the parents are divorced, great care should be taken that this should not become a source of aggravation in which one of the parents, out of pettiness or seeking to strike out at a former mate, refuses to accompany his or her child to the *hupah* if the other parent does so. No feelings of hurt or spite designed to hurt the child's other parent can excuse marring the supreme happiness of a son or daughter on a wedding day, and the marrying couple will probably always remember it as an act of supreme selfishness on the part of an immature parent.

It is an old custom for those escorting the bride and groom to the *hupah* to carry candles[49] in order symbolically to light the way of the bride and groom as they begin their future life together. On a number of occasions the Talmud refers to candles or lamps in association with weddings.[50]

Light is associated with joy in Jewish tradition. The Jews are described in the Book of Esther as having "light, joy, happiness and honor."[51] The joyous Sabbath and Jewish festivals are ushered in with lighted candles. At Israel's most joyous occasion, its "wedding" with God at the giving of the Torah at Sinai, the mountain was surrounded by fire and flashes of lightning.[52] So, too, are Jewish brides and grooms accompanied by light and fire at their weddings.[53] Braided *havdalah* candles are used, because their torch-like flickering lights are thought to most resemble the lightning at Sinai.[54]

The Talmud says that the Hebrew words for man, *ish*, and woman, *ishah*, are identical, except for the letter *yod* in *ish*, and the letter *hay* in *ishah*. The two letters, *yod* and *hay*, together make up a name of God. This indicates, says the Talmud, that when there is love and harmony between a man and his wife, God is between them. But when there is dissonance and discord, God's name is removed, and what is left after the removal of the *yod* and *hay* is *aish,* fire.[55] The lighted torches at the wedding are a reminder to the bride and groom, the Sages teach, that if God's name is removed from them as a result of disharmony, their relationship will be as painful as fire. They should make every effort always to maintain a loving and harmonious relationship.[56]

The *g'matria* (numerical value) of the word *ner* (candle) is 250, and since two candles are carried, the sum of the two is 500. The biblical blessing to have children, *p'ru u-r'vu,* "Be fruitful and multiply"[57] also has a *g'matria* of 500. The candles, therefore, symbolize the hope that the couple will have a fruitful marriage.[58]

Among many Jews, it is customary for the bride to be escorted around the groom under the *hupah*[59] three times,[60] or seven times.[61] Many consider the customs to relate to an eschatologic passage in Jeremiah in which the prophet speaks of a time in the future when relationships between men and women will be reversed and "the woman will court the man."[62] The Hebrew term employed in the passage for "will court" is *t'sovev,* literally, "will encircle."

Others see in the custom of the bride circling her groom a symbol of the wife creating a metaphoric wall around her husband to guard against him from outside desires and influences. This is in keeping with a passage in the Song of Songs referring to a woman as a wall,[63] and a talmudic teaching that "whoever lives without a wife lives without a [protective] wall."[64] The Sages comment that a man's wife is like a wall, protecting him from external temptations.[65] After her circling, the bride, by stepping into the symbolic circle she has created, marks the couple's new status in society as a married couple; she has created a community of two, around which there is an intimate wall of privacy, independent and shielded from the rest of society.

Some see in the bride's three encirclements of the groom a symbolic reminder to him of the three primal obligations the Torah requires of him as her husband—to provide her with sustenance, clothing, and conjugal relations. Others find in it an allusion to the threefold expression of God's betrothal to the Jewish people in Hosea, "And I will betroth you to me forever; and I will betroth you to me with a righteousness and justice, and in lovingkindness and compassion."[66]

The prevailing custom of seven circuits probably has kabbalistic origins[67] and may relate to the seven revolutions of the earth during the biblical seven days of Creation. Since every marriage is a reenactment of the process of Creation, the bride's encirclement of the groom is an allusion that the seven cycles of Creation are now being repeated.[68]

The bride stands to the right of the groom under the *hupah,* an allusion to the verse in Psalms, "a queen shall stand at your right side."[69] They stand facing the guests during the marriage ceremony, while the officiating rabbi stands facing the bride and groom and looking in an easterly direction, with his back to the guests.[70]

All those under the *hupah* stand,[71] and in many circles it is traditional for the assembled guests to stand as well, in deference to the bride and groom who are standing. It is customary for the parents of the couple to be present under the *hupah.*[72] Others may also be present.

A *minyan,* or quorum, of at least ten Jewish males over the age of thirteen is required to be present during the ceremony for the legal validation of the marriage in accordance with Jewish law.[73]

Erusin — The Prenuptial Blessing

The ceremony of *erusin* begins with the prenuptial blessing, recited over a cup of wine by the rabbi who performs the service. It is preceded by a benediction over the wine. The rabbi holds the cup, filled to the brim, in his right hand, and recites:

"Blessed are You, O Lord, our God, King of the universe, Creator of the fruit of the vine."

Wine is used for the blessing because it is a prayer of sanctification at a joyous religious occasion, much like the *kiddush* prayer of sanctification which is recited over a cup of wine that introduces the Sabbath and the festivals. Indeed, the relationship of the bridegroom and bride is compared to that of the Jewish people to the Sabbath, who are betrothed and sanctified to each other every Friday evening.

Wine is considered to be a significant beverage that symbolizes joy; it also contributes to the element of joy on religious occasions. "And wine causes the heart of man to rejoice," sings the Psalmist.[74] A wedding is a joyous occasion for God and man, and its celebration in accordance with age-old Jewish traditions; this is highlighted by the presence of the traditional cup of wine raised for the recitation of the prenuptial of sanctification.

The prenuptial blessing is:

"Blessed are You, O Lord our God, King of the universe, who has sanctified us with Your commandments, and commanded us regarding the sexual prohibitions, and has forbidden to us those who are merely betrothed, but permitted us those who are married to us through *hupah* and *kidushin.* Blessed are You, O Lord, our God, who sanctifies His people Israel through *hupah* and *kidushin.*"

Like most of the blessings, it is talmudic in origin[75] and probably dates back to the *Knesset HaG'dolah,* the Great Assembly, about the third century B.C.E.[76] The obligation to recite the blessing is the groom's.[77] So as not to embarrass on such an occasion a groom who might be unable to recite it,[78] and those who may be too nervous at the time to recite it properly,[79] someone other than the groom — often the rabbi — does so.[80] The rabbi and the groom should be aware, during the recitation, that the blessing is really the groom's to make, and it is being recited on his behalf, and the groom's response of *Amen* at its conclusion is the equivalent of his having recited it himself.[81]

Since the rabbi recites the blessings on behalf of the bridal couple, it is they who first drink from the cup[82] without reciting an additional blessing over the wine.[83] Then the rabbi drinks. Some say that the rabbi should sip first since he recites the blessing. However, the rabbi need not drink from the cup at all, as the blessing he recited was for the bridal couple.[84]

Kidushin

Following the prenuptial blessing, the ceremony of *kidushin,* or sanctification, is performed. Since it involves the transformation of the couple's status to that of a married state, it is vital that the legal steps be properly observed. Through the act of the man reciting the traditional Jewish marriage formula while presenting a ring to the woman, which she accepts in the presence of two witnesses, the two are considered married.

From a legal point of view, the rabbi does not make the marriage valid. Indeed, according to Jewish law, he is not even needed at the wedding. The rabbi's function is to ensure that all of the required legal acts validating the marriage are executed and that they are performed in full accordance with all requirements of Jewish law.

Witnesses

There must be two legally proper witnesses to validate the marriage.[85] They should be religiously observant males over thirteen years old,[86] and may not be related to either the bride, the groom,[87] or each other.[88] A rabbi or a cantor may serve as a witness,[89] provided he fulfills all of the conditions listed above.

The witnesses should be specifically designated as such, to differentiate them from all others present,[90] and should preferably stand at the *hupah* to witness the proceedings.

The Recitation of the Marriage Formula

The rabbi takes the ring from the groom or his designates and asks the groom whether it is his.[91] The groom has to respond audibly in the affirmative.

The rabbi then shows the ring to the witnesses and asks them whether it has the minimal value of one *prutah*.[92] (The *prutah* was the coin of the lowest value in ancient times. Its value today is less than one penny.) The witnesses should audibly respond in the affirmative. If the bride's eyes are covered with a veil, she then lifts her veil. The groom turns to the bride and recites the formula for *kidushin: Ha-rey at m'kudeshet li b'taba'at zu k'dat Moshe v'Yisrael*, "Behold! You are consecrated to me with this ring according to the laws of Moses and Israel."

He should say it in Hebrew. If necessary, he should repeat it word for word after the rabbi.[93] The formula may also be repeated in the vernacular,[94] to assure that everything is understood by the couple.[95]

The Presentation of the Ring

With his right hand, the groom places the ring on the index finger[96] — the most prominent finger — of the bride's right hand, in full view of the witnesses. (This is the preferable manner of the ring presentation. However, any manner of presentation and acceptance before witnesses validates the procedure.)[97] The ring should preferably be placed on the finger itself, so that if the bride is wearing gloves she should remove her right glove in readiness.

A double-ring ceremony should be avoided. This may not be a valid *kidushin* according to Jewish law, since the exchange of rings may appear to be a barter. The essence of the procedure involves the giving of a gift by the groom, and its acceptance by the bride.[98] Although the custom of a man wearing a wedding ring is not a Jewish one, if a man wishes to wear a ring he should put it on after the wedding, and not include it as a part of the marriage ceremony.

The Reading and Presentation of the *Ketubah*

With the presentation of the ring completing the ceremony of *kidushin,* it is customary to read the *ketubah,* the marriage contract.[99] The *ketubah* reading is inserted at this point to create a hiatus between the prenuptial ceremony of *erusin* and the concluding marriage ceremony of *nisuin.*[100]

The purpose of the reading of the marriage contract at the *hupah* is to impress upon the groom the gravity of the obligation he has undertaken toward his wife and to emphasize to him its legal import. These are underscored by the solemn nature of the ceremony. The assembled guests, all of whom hear the conditions of the *ketubah* read to them, thus bear communal witness to the groom's agreement to fulfill those obligations.

The *ketubah* is read aloud by the rabbi or by an honored dignitary who is able to read the Aramaic text.[101]

The *ketubah* is then handed to the groom who presents it to the bride. She is expected to keep it in their home, although in some circles it is customary for the *ketubah* to be held by her mother for safe-keeping.[102]

The Seven Blessings

The recitation of the *Sheva B'rachot,* or Seven Blessings, follows the reading of the *ketubah.* This act is the second part of the marriage ceremony, and constitutes *nisuin,* the procedure by which groom and bride fully become husband and wife.

As with the prenuptial blessing, a cup of wine is required for the recitation of the Seven Blessings, although the custom is for two cups of wine to be used,[103] including one not previously employed for the prenuptial blessing. If a cup used for the prenuptial blessing is also used for the *Sheva B'rachot,* any remaining wine must first be emptied before the cup is reused, since the same wine may not be used for two separate rituals.[104] The two cups are reminders that the ceremonies of *erusin* and *nisuin* were originally two separate rituals performed at different periods.[105]

The blessings are recited by the rabbi,[106] or by as many as six designated dignitaries who are accorded the honor of reciting *b'rachot.* Each comes up to the *hupah* and recites the blessing while holding a cup of wine.

The Seven Blessings are:

1. Blessed are You, O Lord, our God, King of the universe, Creator of the fruit of the vine.

2. Blessed are You, O Lord, our God, King of the universe, Who created all things for His glory.

3. Blessed are You, O Lord, our God, King of the universe, Creator of man.

4. Blessed are You, O Lord, our God, King of the universe, Who created man in His own image, after His own likeness, and Who prepared for him a structure to last for all time. Blessed are You, O Lord, Creator of man.

5. May the barren one rejoice and be exceedingly happy when her children are gathered together with her in joy. Blessed are You, O God, Who causes Zion to rejoice in her children.

6. May You grant joy to these beloved companions, just as You granted joy to Your creations in the Garden of Eden of yore. Blessed are You, O Lord, Who grants joy to bridegroom and bride.

7. Blessed are You, O Lord, our God, King of the universe, Creator of joy and happiness, bridegroom and bride, rejoicing and song, delight and good cheer, love and harmony, peace and friendship. Soon, O Lord, our God, may there be heard in the cities of Judaea and in the courtyards of Jerusalem, the sound of joy and the sound of happiness, the sound of a bridegroom and the sound of a bride, the sound of rejoicing from the bridegrooms at their weddings

and youths at their feasts of song. Blessed are You, O God, Who
grants joy to the bridegroom with the bride.

Among all the good wishes showered upon bride and groom on
the occasion of their marriage, none is as important as those
expressed in the Seven Blessings. These are not, as some may think,
the blessings of the rabbi to the marrying couple, and they constitute
more than congratulatory wishes to the couple on their private
bonding. They contain cosmic elements, discussing the creation of
the world and the coming of the Messiah, the Jewish people and the
land of Israel, and they convey the approach of Judaism toward life
and love, marriage and family, and its view of the nature of the
ideal marital relationship.

True happiness, Judaism teaches, is symbolized by the wedding
ceremony. The relationship between God and Israel is constantly
compared in the Bible to that of a bridegroom and bride. In a
similar vein, God says to Israel, "I remember you for the loving
kindness of your youth, the love of your espousal, how you went
after Me in the wilderness, in a land that was not sown."[107] What
married couple cannot reminisce about their early days of marriage
in a similar vein?

The blessings, first and foremost, bring God into the marriage
ceremony. Henceforth the relationship is to be characterized as a
religious one, hallowed by God. To be successful, a marriage needs
God's help. In the Torah's discussion of the destiny of Isaac and
Rebecca, the passage appears, "This thing proceeds from the
Eternal."[108]

All blessings in Judaism provide a momentary pause for contemplation and reflection on a religious act so that it is not performed
in a perfunctory or off-hand manner, but with the proper intent.
The Seven Blessings acknowledge God's place in the marital relationship, praise and thank God for His goodness and bounty, and
pray for His help in granting them marital happiness.

The Meaning of the Blessings

First Blessing: Looking at the blessings, it is readily apparent that
there are not seven but six of them, and it is only when the

benediction over wine is added that there are seven. Indeed, the Talmud lists only six blessings,[109] as does Maimonides in his *Code,*[110] with the wine benediction not mentioned. One reason given for the blessing over wine is that the blessings should total seven,[111] which is considered a very significant number in Jewish tradition.

Judaism considers every marriage to be a human emulation of the divine Creation of the world, which took seven days to complete. Thus each of the six blessings represents one of the six days of Creation, while the seventh, the added blessing on the wine, represents the Sabbath. Rabeinu Bahya ben Asher says:

> Marriage is analogous to the Creation of the world . . . Just as there were seven days — including the Sabbath — at the creation of the world, so the Sages ordained seven blessings, including the blessing over wine. The latter corresponds to the Sabbath, for wine is used in proclaiming the sanctity of the Sabbath both at the commencement and the conclusion of that day.[112]

Second Blessing: This blessing, declaring that everything in the universe was created for the glory of God, is simply praise of God, thanking God for our having survived until this moment and being permitted to partake of this great joy. The blessing places life in clear perspective for the bride and groom; life is neither meaningless nor purposeless, nor is it to be lived selfishly and for one's fame and glory. It tells them that they have a clear purpose in the overall plan — to perpetuate life on this earth and be concerned with others aside from themselves. Thus, they glorify God who created them for this purpose.

The benediction is based upon[113] a verse in Isaiah, "I have created everything for My glory; I have created it and I have made it."[114] The literal translation of the Hebrew, *kol hanikra bishmi v'lichvodi b'rativ, y'tsartiv af asitiv,* is "I have created all which is called in My name; I have created it, I have made it." In the context of the passages around it the verse is seen by the Sages as an eschatological promise to the righteous of Israel. Those who are called in God's name and who recognize God as their creator, and whose task it is to proclaim the glory of God, that is, to spread the knowledge of God's religious and moral teachings in the world, and who have consequently suffered the travails of exile and dispersion — God has prepared all that is necessary for their ultimate redemption.[115]

Third and Fourth Blessings: God, the Creator, has granted His creature, man, intelligence and free choice, and the divine ability to join Him in the continuous process of Creation.

In creating man in His divine image, God has imbued him with attributes of godliness that he is bidden to bring to bear in his life in order to attain godliness. Man has no greater obligation than to strive to behave as a being created in the image of God.

Apart from their sexual differences, both man and woman have been created equally in the image of God. The married couple who rejoice with each other as the one being they once were, prior to their primordial separation, are to behave in an elevated manner as moral beings, and to become partners with each other and with God, in Creation and in helping to bring perfection into the world.

Fifth Blessing: This blessing is for Zion and Jerusalem. It is incumbent upon the Jew to place Jerusalem above his chief joys,[116] and a blessing is included here to express the centrality of Zion in Jewish thought.[117] Indeed, the blessing of Jerusalem is given precedence over the blessing of bride and groom which follows.

Isaiah refers to a depopulated Jerusalem in its sufferings and humiliation as an *akarah,* a barren woman,[118] and this blessing is, in reality, a prayer for the ingathering of the exiles, the return of the Jewish people to Zion, and the rebuilding of Jerusalem. The prophet speaks of Jerusalem's rejoicing at a glorious time in her future, when her children, Israel, will be reunited with her in joy.

The last words of the benediction, which speak of God who causes Zion to rejoice, are based on the passage in Isaiah, "As the bridegroom rejoices over the bride, so shall God rejoice over you,"[119] which is incorporated into the Sabbath eve *L'cha Dodi* hymn celebrating the betrothal of the Jewish people to the Sabbath.

Sixth Blessing: This blessing of bride and groom as beloved friends reflects a deep Jewish understanding of the ideal relationship of husband and wife—that they be beloved and warm friends and companions.[120] *Zeh dodi v'zeh reyi,* "this is my beloved and this is my friend," sings Solomon in the Song of Songs.[121]

This is a blessing of personal joy to the bride and groom that their relationship be idyllic and full of joy, as idyllic as that of the primal couple, Adam and Eve. All of Israel rejoices with them, as God rejoiced with Adam and Eve in the Garden of Eden.

Seventh Blessing: This blessing contains no less than ten expressions of joy for the couple, ending with good wishes for "love and brotherhood, peace and friendship." The Sages[122] find parallels with the ten utterances by means of which the world was created,[123] thus indicating that marriage is analogous to the Creation of the world, which was completed with the marriage of Adam and Eve in the Garden of Eden.

With the conclusion of the seventh blessing, the cup is given to the groom and the bride to sip.

Breaking the Glass

The completion of the Seven Blessings marks the culmination of the marriage ceremony. The custom is for the groom to terminate the proceedings under the *hupah* by smashing a glass.[124] This is usually done by wrapping a thin glass goblet in a cloth napkin and placing it on the floor: the groom shatters the glass with his right foot.[125]

The original custom was for the glass to be shattered by throwing it at a wall.[126] As mentioned earlier, a special stone built into the exterior of the synagogue wall known as a *treustein* (German), and bearing the initial letters of the passage in Jeremiah, "the sound of joy and the sound of happiness, the sound of a groom and the sound of a bride"[127] was used for this purpose throughout much of Europe.

The purpose of the breaking of the glass is to temper excessive, uncontrolled joy at the wedding with a measure of seriousness and sobriety.[128] The Sages were concerned with the dangers involved in people giving free rein to unbridled joy.[129] Commenting on the passage in Psalms, "Serve the Lord in awe, and rejoice with trembling,"[130] the Sages query, "What is meant by 'rejoice with trembling'?" The reply is: "Where there is rejoicing, there should also be trembling."[131] The Sages of the Talmud explain this as meaning that even rejoicing must be tempered with discipline, and restraint.

A wedding is a time for rejoicing, but this does not give license for wild, boorish, or boisterous behavior. Thus, at a time of rejoicing, a person should perform an act to remind him of his duties toward God. The Talmud relates that Mar, son of Ravina, made a wedding for his son, and when he saw that the merriment was exceeding the bounds of propriety, he smashed a precious white goblet[132] worth four hundred *zuz,* whereupon the wedding guests were immediately brought down to earth from their excessive revelry.[133]

A similar experience is related regarding the great biblical and talmudic commentator *Rashi* in the eleventh century who, upon seeing that dignitaries present at his son's wedding had become too boisterous, took a glass goblet and shattered it before his guests, inducing instantaneous propriety.[134] The Sages of the *Tosafot* talmudic commentary take note of such situations and relate that, "As a result of such incidents, it has become customary to break a glass at weddings."[135]

The breaking of the glass is, as indicated above, also a reminder of the destruction of Jerusalem and the Temple,[136] and underscores dramatically that no Jewish joy can be complete since that time.[137] This is one of a number of similar practices, on other occasions, that Jews are required to perform in order to recall the destruction.

Although there has been a Jewish state since 1948, and Jewish sovereignty has been restored to the Temple Mount since 1967, the Temple has not yet been rebuilt and the bulk of the Jewish people is still living in exile. The breaking of the glass thus continues to symbolize the yearning of the Jewish people for the restoration of the Jewish people to its land and for the rebuilding of the Temple.

Among some,[138] it is customary, when the glass is broken, to say "If I forget you, O Jerusalem, may my right hand lose its cunning."[139] In many circles in Israel today, these words are sung to a poignant tune by the assembled guests, along with the following verse, "Let my tongue cleave to the roof of my mouth if I do not remember you; if I do not set Jerusalem above my chiefest joy."[140]

Immediately thereafter, the guests cry out *Mazal Tov!* (good luck), and the orchestra strikes a lively wedding tune.

The Seclusion Room

Amidst singing and dancing, the bride and groom then weave their way through the congratulating guests to the *Yihud* (seclusion) room. It is customary for bride and groom to be alone for a period of time immediately following the marriage ceremony. The complete seclusion of the couple in a closed room is a public act symbolizing their new status as husband and wife. Since this act, more than any other, signifies that they are truly married,[141] a public awareness of their seclusion is required, and it must be attested to by qualified witnesses. The witnesses remain outside the door to ensure that no one enters until the couple have been alone for a reasonable period of time.[142]

Yihud provides a period of respite for the newly married couple, an interval of tranquility for them to enjoy together in total solitude amidst the turmoil of the wedding. It is customary for the two to have their first meal as husband and wife together in the *Yihud* room. Both will have been fasting all day, and this food will be their first of the day.

It is important that the *Yihud* room be prepared before the wedding. It should provide absolute privacy. It should also have food for a light repast for the couple.

The Festive Wedding Meal

The wedding feast is a *s'udat mitzvah,* a festive religious meal integral to a wedding, participation in which is considered to be a *mitzvah.*[143] In many areas, it is customary for a table to be set aside at the wedding feast for the poor and indigent of the community so they can participate fully in the wedding.[144] It is also customary for the poor to be allowed to collect alms from the wedding guests, or for the parents of the new couple to give them a substantial sum.[145]

The wedding meal is a joyous feast, punctuated by lively Jewish wedding tunes and dancing in accordance with Jewish tradition. When bride and groom leave the *Yihud* room to enter the banquet hall during the wedding feast, they are greeted and raised up on chairs by their friends, as the assembled guests dance around them.

It is considered a great *mitzvah,* in the category of *hesed*[146] (obligatory acts of love for others), to cause the bride and groom to rejoice at their wedding.[147] The Talmud declares that whoever gladdens the bridal couple is considered as if he had brought a sacrificial offering at the Temple in Jerusalem, or as if he had rebuilt one of the ruins of Jerusalem.[148]

Accordance to *Midrash,* God and his angels served as exalted exponents of this *mitzvah* when they participated in the wedding celebration of Adam and Eve and caused the couple to rejoice:

> The Holy One, Blessed be He, made ten wedding canopies for them in the Garden of Eden, of precious stones, pearls and gold . . . the angels were playing upon timbrels and dancing with pipes . . . the Holy One, Blessed be He, said to the ministering angels, "Come, let us descend and render acts of love to the first man and his wife, for the world rests upon acts of love . . . And the ministering angels went to and fro, [dancing] before Adam . . ."[149]

Ketsad m'rakdin lifnei hakalah? — "How does one dance before the bride?" — asks the Mishnah.[150] Following the example of the talmudic Sages Hillel and Shammai, Torah scholars usually take the lead in actively participating in the dancing in honor of bride and groom. Friends of the couple vie with one another to enliven the festivities through acts designed to make the bride and groom rejoice at their wedding.

In the words of R. Shlomo Ganzfried, author of the *Kitzur Shulhan Aruch,* the *Condensed Code of Jewish Law,* "It is a *mitzvah* to gladden a groom and bride, and to dance before the bride, and to declare that she is attractive and performs acts of lovingkindness, and indeed we find that [the talmudic Sage] R. Ilai would dance before the bride."[151]

Grace after the Meal

Upon the conclusion of the wedding feast, *Birchat Hamazon,* Grace after Meals, is recited by the assembled guests, concluding with the recitation once again of the *Sheva B'rachot,* the Seven Blessings.

Two cups of wine are required, one of which is held while the grace is recited, and the other for the Seven Blessings.[152] Like the earlier Seven Blessings recited under the *hupah,* these may either be recited by the person who leads the Grace after Meals, or they may be treated as honors which are distributed among different guests.

The person who leads the guests in the grace then recites the blessing over the wine, pours wine from the two cups into a third one, and drinks from the original cup, while the other two cups are given to bride and groom to sip from them.

It is customary in some circles for those closest to the married couple to remain with them after the other guests leave, and have a "*mitzvah* dance" with the bride and groom. Rabbis and other dignitaries take turns dancing with the bride, with the rabbi holding one end of a handkerchief and the bride the other.[153] This custom, which may relate to the *mishnah* that discusses "dancing before the bride,"[154] is ascribed by some as a means by which the rabbis and scholars express to the groom their confidence in his choice of a bride.

The Week after the Wedding

In Jewish tradition, bride and groom do not embark upon a honeymoon immediately after the wedding; they remain for a full week (three days if it is a second marriage for both)[155] to celebrate. These *Shiv'at Y'mei Mishteh,* or Seven Days of Feasting, are said to have been ordained by Moses,[156] and are a custom that is thought to go back to Patriarchal times.[157] These feasting days serve as a focal point for communal rejoicing and for the couple to begin their married life together while in the lap of the community.

During the Seven Days of Feasting, the bride and groom do not work, nor may they be involved in business transactions of any kind.[158] They only eat, drink, and rejoice with each other. Each day, close relatives or friends host the married couple for a festive meal, which is punctuated by singing and rejoicing. It is customary for the groom, if he is learned, to deliver a *d'var Torah,* a learned discourse. Again, in most cases, it is also customary for the groom to be interrupted with singing as he begins, so that he will not be shamed if he is not capable of delivering it.

At the conclusion of the meal, *Sheva B'rachot* are recited. A *minyan,* or quorum, of at least ten adult males is required for each meal,[159] at least one of whom was not present at the wedding and at previous *Sheva B'rachot* for this couple.[160]

VI
The Married State

9

Family Purity: The Jewish Refinement of Sexuality

The *Nidah* Laws

The laws of *Taharat HaMishpahah,* or Family Purity, are central to the Jewish idea of sanctity in marriage. These laws deal with abstention from sexual contact during and after the period of the wife's menstruation.

In brief, Jewish law requires husband and wife to refrain from any kind of physical contact during menstruation and for a period of seven days after its cessation. At the end of this period, the woman, who is referred to as a *nidah,* or menstruant, bathes herself thoroughly and then immerses herself in a *mikvah* (literally, "a gathering of waters"). The *mikvah,* designed according to specific and ancient guidelines, is a specially constructed ritual pool with a natural water source. The wife recites the following blessing: "Blessed are You, O God, King of the Universe, Who has sanctified us with His precepts and has commanded us to observe the *mitzvah* of *t'vilah,* ritual immersion." Thereafter, husband and wife renew their physical relationship.

The laws of Family Purity are considered *gufei Torah,*[1] among the most fundamental directives of the Torah, and their observance distinguishes the practicing Jew from the nonobservant one. The life-style built around the use of the *mikvah* is also one of the significant aspects differentiating a Jew from a non-Jew. It is no coincidence, therefore, that Jewish law regards immersion in a *mikvah* as a vital prerequisite for conversion to Judaism; it is the most important ritual in the halachic process by which a non-Jew becomes a Jew. Over the centuries, the Jewish people, even under the most difficult and dangerous conditions, have adhered rigorously to the rules of *nidah* and *mikvah.*

The word *mikvah* appears in the Bible in the phrase *mikveh mayim* ("a gathering of waters"),[2] and is mentioned once on its own.[3]

Archaeologists have discovered *mikvaot* ("mikvehs") dating back to the period of the Second Temple; these were located on the outside of its southern and western walls. They are close to two of the major ramps that lead to the Temple Mount, and were undoubtedly used for immersion by visitors going up to the Temple. *Mikvaot* dating back to the talmudic period have been unearthed adjacent to a number of ancient synagogues throughout the Land of Israel.

It is only natural that the renowned Judaean Desert mountain redoubt near the Dead Sea, Masada, which was defended by religiously observant Jews, housed *mikvaot,* as the late archaeologist Yigael Yadin discovered during his excavations in the early 1960s.[4] A group of notable Jerusalem rabbis visited the site of the excavations at Masada, and after careful examination excitedly pronounced the *mikvaot* unearthed there to be "in scrupulous conformity with the injunctions of traditional Jewish law."[5]

The law of abstention from sexual contact during the period of *nidah* derives from this scriptural source: "And if a man lies with a woman when she is unwell and uncovers her nakedness, he has exposed the source of her blood and she has exposed the source of her blood, both of them shall be cut off from their people."[6]

Significantly, the following passage in Numbers, in the Torah portion known as *K'doshim* ("Holy Ones") introduces the section on *nidah:* "And the Lord spoke to Moses, saying: Speak to the Congregation of Israel and say to them—'You shall be holy, for I, the Lord your God, am holy.'"[7]

This all-encompassing scriptural passage which introduces the section dealing with *nidah,*[8] is understood to contain the fundamental purpose of Judaism. It provides the Jew with a basic guideline for the conduct of his entire life: to elevate himself to the level of godliness by pursuing a way of life consecrated by the teachings of Torah and the fulfillment of *mitzvot* designed to mold him into a holy, moral, and ethical individual.

Holiness and Sexuality: The Institution of *Mikvah*

In *halachah,* immersion in a *mikvah* prior to her wedding is mandatory for a bride as a spiritual purification preparatory to *kidushin* —
the holy state of marriage. The married woman too, as a precondition for marital relations upon completion of her period of *nidah,*
is also required to undergo immersion.

The *mikvah* is a profoundly symbolic medium of spiritual purification that transforms the nature of sexual relations. Through this
religious ritual, the Jewish husband and wife proclaim that sexual
relations with one's marriage partner are neither sinful nor shameful, but are in fact a positive, holy act performed in the service of
God.

Judaism understands that the ritual, properly observed, elevates
conjugal relations from an act of self-gratification to a meaningful,
blessed *mitzvah* devoted to the service of God — a joyous, sacred
physical-spiritual union of body and soul.

Ritual immersion prior to participation in a religious act denotes
both a rebirth[9] and an elevation of status. The original biblical
consecration of Aaron and his sons as *kohanim* (priests) involved, as
a first step, their immersion in a *mikvah*[10] through which they were
both "reborn" and had their status elevated. Immersion in a *mikvah*
is also used to signify the "rebirth" and change of status of a convert.
The single woman, too, through immersion in the *mikvah* on the eve
of her wedding, undergoes a "rebirth" and her status is raised to that
of a married woman. When the married woman immerses herself in
the *mikvah,* she, too, becomes like a person born anew.

R. Samson Raphael Hirsch compares the married woman's
immersion in the natural waters of the *mikvah* prior to resuming
marital relations to the *kohen's* immersion in the *mikvah* prior to
entering the Sanctuary for the Temple service in Jerusalem. On
Yom Kippur, the climax of the Temple ritual was the entry of the
kohen gadol, the High Priest, into the *Sanctum Sanctorum,* the Holy of
Holies. Five times during this day, before each major service, he
would immerse himself in a *mikvah.* The immersions were symbolic
acts of purification which had the effect of raising his spiritual status
to allow him to enter the Holy of Holies, a place to which entry
ordinarily was strictly forbidden.[11]

Both of these acts are of a consecrated nature and thus require prior *mikvah* immersion: the Jewish woman preparing for marital relations and the *kohen* preparing for participation in the Temple service. In the words of Maimonides: "Purification of the body leads to sanctification of the soul."[12]

A Concern for the Woman and for the Marriage

The Sages teach: "*V'kidashtem bit'vilah* — And you shall sanctify yourselves through immersion in the *mikvah*."[13]

The Jewish rules of ritual purity fall into the category of divine statutes of the Torah for which no reason is given and which the Jew is commanded to observe on faith alone. The most notable other example in this category is *kashrut,* the set of rules governing the foods Jews may eat, and their preparation. These laws, too, are associated in the Torah with the command to be holy. The reasons for these laws are deemed by the Sages to be beyond the human intellect's capacity to understand and are therefore not given. While they are undoubtedly designed to strengthen the bond between God and His people, the manner in which they do so is not obvious. (The traditional interpretation is that their observance is aimed at aiding the Jew in fulfilling God's command to sanctify himself by regulating his two strongest drives — food and sex.)

While one should strive to understand the rationale behind these statutes, the traditional Jew is aware that his conclusions can at best be tentative. Therefore, Jewish law does not permit these rules to be altered should one conclude that the reasons he postulated for their existence are no longer valid, for, while he can speculate about their reasons, he cannot determine with certainty their ultimate rationale. R. Aryeh Kaplan, a twentieth-century scholar, explains:

> We do not observe the commandments because logic demands it, but simply because they were given by God. The required basis is the relationship between the commandments and their Giver. This is higher than any possible human wisdom.[14]

This may be one reason why a convert to Judaism must immerse in the *mikvah*. The convert's first step into Judaism involves a ritual the explanation of which is not apparent and obvious, and therefore, he must reaffirm the initial acceptance of the Torah, declaring [as

did the Jews at Sinai] "I will do and I will hear." To abandon his
gentile identity and to assume Jewish identity, he is required to
participate in a ritual that is inexplicable to one who does not accept
the basis of Judaism. . . .

The fact that we are required to observe certain commandments
without awareness of their reason does not mean that there is no logic
in their observance. The reasons involve deep concepts which are not
immediately obvious. . . .[15]

We can, of course, endeavor to understand as best we can the
significance of these laws.[16] Two of the reasons that come to mind
are concern for a healthy marital relationship and consideration for
the welfare of the woman.

The required abstention from marital relations, and all intimacies
that may lead to them, for twelve to fourteen days each month, can
be explained as providing a medium through which Jewish couples
can develop a strong, healthy relationship rooted in a mutual
attachment other than that of a sexual bond.

The physical element is an essential part of marriage, but there
are many other components in a healthy marital relationship, which
in this period of physical separation hallowed by Jewish law and
tradition are emphasized. It is, therefore, considered especially
important that mutual love and devotion be expressed generously
but in a nonphysical manner, by the couple during the intervals of
physical separation. When physical expressions of love are forbidden, husband and wife have no choice but to devise verbal and other
means of demonstrating affection, which enable the development of
a firm, enduring relationship based on respect and of fellowship of
the spirit. Indeed, it is an ideal preparation for that later period in
married life when physical attraction wanes and potency weakens,
so affection must be expressed in other ways.

Aaron Barth, a mid-twentieth-century Jewish thinker phrased it
this way:

Marriage, according to the Torah, is a true and perfect partnership
requiring love and fellowship of the spirit, not only fellowship of the
flesh. Physical love can find expression according to the laws of the
Torah only during half the life of a married couple. Half of married
life passes without fellowship of the flesh; hence there can be no
marriage according to the Torah unless there is a fellowship of the

spirit. Herein lies the secret of the exemplary family life with which Jewry has been blessed for so many generations.[17]

The Period of "Loving Friends"

One of the blessings for the newly married couple, recited during the nuptials and at the week-long celebrations following the wedding, refers to the bride and groom as *re'im ahuvim,* loving friends. Judaism views warmth, friendship, and companionship as vital ingredients in a successful marriage; these are developed and refined by the traditional Jewish couple during their monthly physical separations. Referring to these periods as those in which husband and wife live together "as brother and sister," R. Samson Raphael Hirsch points out that they do not detract from the intimacy of marriage. On the contrary, they have the effect of "making this intimacy still more intimate and raising it constantly, spiritually and morally."[18]

The Sages declare that the husband actually fulfills his duty of *onah* (marital relations), when he causes his wife to rejoice during the *nidah* separation, through intimacy of a nonphysical nature:[19] "Marital relations are not the only means of performing this *mitzvah:* all kinds of intimacies through which a man gladdens his wife are a *mitzvah,* for all of these intimacies cause her joy."[20]

The Sages teach: "The *mitzvah* of *taharat hamishpahah* and in particular, the laws of separation, train one to understand that the fundamental link between the couple is based on spirit, emotion and mutual understanding — and is not merely a physical tie."[21]

A married couple *needs* the kind of purely emotional interaction which is apt to be neglected when the physical relationship dominates their consciousness. Women, especially, have a need for words of love and admiration from their husbands. For the woman, the pleasure derived from physical relations is often linked to her emotions. Thus, a physical relationship that lacks warmth and tenderness for the woman can render continual relations unfulfilling — if not unendurable. Therefore, the days of enforced physical separation serve as an opportunity for renewal of the couple's emotional intimacy. Thus, when conjugal relations are again permitted, the wife, as well as her husband, can derive full physiological and emotional satisfaction from their resumption.

The period of separation has another vital function. Incidents of marital violence reveal that many who experienced the frustration which brought them to this pass happened to engage in sexual relations with unusual frequency. Apparently, instead of discussing their differences, these couples suppressed their hostility and rage in a desperately compulsive physical relationship. Judaism provides the married couple with a respite — a period of time when sexual activity cannot serve as a replacement for talking to one another. Thus the negative feelings and abrasiveness which crop up almost inevitably in a relationship as intimate as marriage have a chance to be aired; bottled up resentments can be assuaged and differences resolved.

In early talmudic times, R. Akiva objected to the ruling in which women were not allowed to wear cosmetics, nor adorn themselves with jewelry and fine clothes during *nidah*. "Such a rule," he said, "would cause a woman to be unattractive to her husband and resultingly lead to a loss of marital love and divorce."[22]

R. Akiva's amendment of the law was far-reaching. It showed that a woman is not merely a convenient object for the gratification of a husband's sexual desire; her beauty, attractiveness, and companionship can be appreciated at all times without thoughts of sexual relations. It is therefore a halachic obligation for the woman to make an effort to dress attractively and adorn herself during her period of separation from her husband.[23]

The Value to Marriage of Periodic Abstinence

Many marriages suffer because conjugal relations, so exciting at the outset of the couple's life together, gradually become monotonous, a mechanically executed routine. Sensitivities are dulled by repetition and repletion, and the idea of expressing love physically, or in other ways, becomes suddenly boring. The novelty of the experience, the earlier awesome wonder at the pleasure it provides, and finally, the couple's interest in one another, wanes with time, familiarity, and the satiation of physical desire.

The easy and perpetual accessibility of the marital partner in itself lessens the high drama and freshness of the initial emotional bond. The indifference and boredom that result may imperil the marriage itself. Often, as a consequence, couples turn outside of marriage in an attempt to recapture the early thrill of discovery and fulfillment. The eyes that once regarded the wife or the husband with delight may now, in longing for new, illicit adventures to provide renewed excitement, begin to rove.

Here the abstinence required by the rules of Family Purity serves a crucial purpose. Denying the married couple the right of physical access to one another at certain times contributes to a heightened mutual attraction, so that the relationship maintains a continuous enchantment. This was well understood by the Sages. The Talmud provides the following insightful comment:

> Why did the Torah require a period of seven days of separation? Because by becoming overly familiar with his wife [marital relations become routine and] repulsion sets in. The Torah therefore ordained seven days of separation so that she will be as beloved [by her husband on the day of her immersion in the *mikvah*] as she was at the time she entered the bridal canopy.[24]

This enforced separation ensures that the Jewish husband and wife who observe the regulations of Family Purity will not take each other for granted. A book which is readily available may be ignored for years, yet once it is banned it is instantly transformed into an object of desire. Humans have a natural craving for the forbidden. In this context, the Torah, through the rules of Family Purity, places the Jewish wife in a position where she must always remain desirable to her husband. The same desire of the prospective bridegroom for his bride comes to the married man when his wife is inaccessible to him. By forbidding, for a substantial period each month, any marital relations or even the slightest physical contact, the *nidah* interval becomes a built-in means of monthly renewal of the marriage bond. This serves to preserve, between husband and wife, an ever-fresh physical and emotional relationship that is never allowed to remain static.

In addition, usually a husband and wife move in completely different circles during their daily activities. Under these circumstances, a man and wife can easily drift out of touch with each other unless there is a specific area of contact. By inducing fluctuations in the wife's physical availability to her husband, the laws of *nidah* ensure that he is always aware of and interested in her bodily cycles and the changes these entail in their relationship. This fundamental area where their lives overlap constitutes a strong mutual interest and draws the couple together even as other demands upon their time and energy draw them apart.

The Hedge of Roses

There is no temptation so prevalent and insistent as that of an ever-present, beloved spouse. No mutual agreement or voluntary abstinence alone, no matter how well-intentioned, would be sufficient to ensure absolutely that marital relations would not take place during the proscribed period. However, the strict religious sanctions proscribing all physical contact between husband and wife during this period, and the requirement for immersion in the *mikvah* prior to the resumption of marital relations, serve as an absolute and refined deterrent. The *nidah* rules thus effectively preserve the woman's fundamental freedom by protecting her from sexual demands at a time when she requires a measure of solitude and distance.

The Sages termed this refined deterrent "a hedge of roses," in reference to a poetic image in the Song of Songs of a woman's body as a "heap of wheat hedged with roses." The Sages teach:

> When a man marries a woman . . . and he approaches her, and she tells him, "I have seen blood as red as a rose," he separates from her at once. Who held him back and would not allow him to come to her? What kind of an iron wall separates them? What kind of serpent bit him? What scorpion stung him — to prevent him from drawing near to her? — The words of the Torah, that are as soft as a rose.[25]

The image of the "hedge of roses" is particularly apt. In the same way that a hedge of roses, though it is most pleasing to the senses, may not be touched, a woman is forbidden to her husband during this period. The appearance of the hedge is neither hostile nor threatening. Similarly, since it is based on the rules of the Torah, their parting is not angry or resentful. The couple observing these rules recognizes that the act of separation represents simultaneously fealty to Jewish tradition as well as mutual consideration for each other. Thus, rather than isolating them, the separation paradoxically brings them closer both spiritually and emotionally. The interval during which they are physically apart is, like a hedge of roses, perceived as a passing discomfort that is almost a pleasure; it is a loving time, the end of which is, nevertheless, eagerly awaited.

Once the proscribed period is over, it is the wife's responsibility to go to the *mikvah* on the proper night, and the husband's responsibility to join her afterward. Judaism awards no added kudos to those who delay their reunion longer than required by *halachah*. On the contrary, such a delay is indicative of an asceticism upon which Judaism frowns. The Jew is admonished neither to add to nor to detract from the words of the Torah.[26] The Jewish couple abiding by the rules of periodic abstinence may not add even a single day to the proscribed period beyond that required by the letter of the law. The fact that the duties may be pleasurable makes them no less obligatory.

Bride and Groom Once Again

Desire is thus heightened by the pattern of monthly separation and reunion, and simultaneously, the chances of boredom are drastically reduced. Human beings are, in order to alleviate the monotony of routine, naturally restless and eager for change. The Jewish rules relating to *nidah* and *mikvah* effect considerable change, twice each month, in the marital relationship. The onset of his wife's menstrual period brings a sudden halt to the satisfaction of physical desire. The man must now bide his time for nearly two weeks before he may touch his wife. The anticipation that the separation engenders reaches its climax the night of his wife's immersion in the *mikvah*. This symbolic act transforms dramatically the couple's physical relationship from one of heightened anticipation to one of rapturous union and fulfillment.

However, only about two weeks later, just before the first twinge of boredom begins to set in once again, his wife is again plucked away from him by the onset of *nidah,* and is out of reach. These constant periodic changes, however predictable, provide a heightened sense of drama in the intimate relations between a man and his wife, making both the marriage and the marital partner more precious to both.

The periodic abstinence also provides, especially after long years of marriage, psychological benefits for the woman. Though years of familiarity, child-bearing, housework, and child care may lessen her attractiveness in her husband's eyes, this effect is considerably diminished by her periodic unavailability for physical union. On the night of her visit to the *mikvah,* she becomes once again the beloved bride she was when they married. Their union, following her immersion in the *mikvah,* has a freshness reminiscent of her original immersion on the eve of her wedding, and provides the opportunity for a renewed courtship between the two. Workday cares and the daily aggravations of life disappear under the enchantment of their rediscovery of each other and of their romance. On this night, the two relive the original joy and rapture in each other of the early days of marriage.

Not surprisingly, among families observing the Jewish rules of Family Purity, incidence of marital infidelity is rare, and the level of divorce is considerably below the norm.

Preventing the Wife from Becoming a Sex Object

Underlying the concept of *nidah* and *mikvah* is Judaism's concern that the woman should not become a mere sex object; that is, a medium for the gratification of the sexual passions of her husband, who may disregard her emotional and physiological needs.

A man's libido is such that there are no distinct periods of time when he is more or less prone to sexual arousal. A woman's body, however, functions in accordance with an inner feminine rhythm that at different times affects her both psychologically and physiologically, in specific ways. There are certain times, corresponding to her unique biological body clock, when she feels an upsurge of desire and a readiness for physical intimacy. Alternately, there are times when, in response to the monthly physical upheaval in her body, she requires nothing more than rest—physical tranquility accompanied by mental and emotional repose.

The laws of Family Purity are uniquely responsive to these fundamental natural needs of the woman. Following the woman's immersion in the *mikvah* at a time which harmonizes with her body's recovery and readiness both physically and emotionally to resume conjugal relations, her husband is not only permitted to join her, but is *obliged* to do so. In the process, he fulfills not only his own needs, but hers as well.

The laws of *taharah* thus humanize and enrich the physical relationship between husband and wife. The union is thereby prevented from becoming one of autonomous physical satisfaction — which can be considered a form of onanism with a partner. By periodic abstention during the *nidah* period, the husband expresses supreme consideration and concern for his wife as an individual.

The Sanctity of Time

R. Norman Lamm postulates an interesting rationale for the exemption of Jewish women from the observance of many of the time-related *mitzvot,* all of which are required of men.[27] The Sabbath and festivals in Judaism teach that the holiness of time is superior to the holiness of space. The holiness of space refers to places or things that are holy — a synagogue, the Land of Israel, a Torah scroll. The holiness of time refers to the sanctity of many of the *mitzvot,* and in particular those relating to the Sabbath and festivals.

The prime holiness is that of time — "And the Lord blessed the Sabbath day and sanctified it."[28] From the time-related *mitzvot,* a man is taught an awareness of the sanctity of time. However, R. Lamm points out that "women are excused from observing these commandments for the simple reason that *they do not need them.*"

> A woman does not *need* the time-conditioned commandments, because she is already aware of the sanctification of time in a manner far more profound, far more intimate and personal, and far more convincing than that which a man can attain by means of the extraneous observances which he is commanded. For a woman, unlike a man, has a built-in biological clock. The periodicity of her menses implies an inner biological rhythm that forms part and parcel of her life. If this inner rhythm is not sanctified, she never attains the sanctity of time.

But if she observes the laws of Family Purity, then she has, by virtue of observing this one *mitzvah*, geared her inner clock, her essential periodicity, to an act of holiness. By the observance of this single commandment, she is made conscious of the holiness of time to an extent far more comprehensive than that attained by a man. A woman, therefore, does not *need* the time-oriented commandments to remind her of the holiness of time, whereas a man, who does not possess this inner periodicity, must rely upon these many commandments to summon him to the sanctification of time. The laws of Family Purity are, therefore, a divine gift to woman, allowing her to attain this highest of all forms of sanctity.[29]

The Medical Benefits

There exists considerable evidence indicating that the laws of *taharat hamishpahah* benefit women in a very tangible way. Conclusions from many scientific studies reveal salutary medical effects deriving from a life-style shaped by these ancient Jewish laws. Prominent among these findings is the significantly lower incidence of cervical cancer among Jewish women and their consequently lower mortality rate from cancer of the uterus.

Professor David M. Serr, Director of the Department of Obstetrics and Gynecology at the Sheba Medical Center in Israel and Associate Professor of Obstetrics and Gynecology at the Tel Aviv University Medical Center, writes:

> Medically, socially and hygienic-wise, the couple practicing Family Purity ritual is healthier in some important aspects than the couple which does not practice this way of life. . . . It is undisputed statistically that Jewish women suffer less from cancer of the cervix, a rapidly fatal disease, than non-Jewish women. . . . Other possible medical complications of non-observance of Family Purity laws may involve infections of the male and female genito-urinary tracts.[30]

Dr. Moses Tendler, rabbinic scholar and professor of biology, cites a definitive study on the epidemiology of cervical cancer that presents evidence that at certain times in a woman's life her "cervical lining is uniquely sensitive to cancer-producing potential of human sperm."[31]

That it is the laws and way of life associated with Family Purity that are directly responsible for the substantially lower cancer rate among Jewish women can be adduced from the fact that the cancer rate among Jewish women has risen sharply in direct ratio to the general slackening of observance of these rules by Jewish women. Dr. Tendler comments:[32]

> The general pattern of the sex life of the Jew, with its prescribed abstinence after the birth of a child, its abhorrence of sexual promiscuity, and its lesson of moderation, is now considered the key factor in protecting the Jewess against cervical cancer. . . . However, she is fast losing her "superiority." During the last fifty years, the ratio of cervical cancer incidence among non-Jewesses and Jewesses dropped from approximately twenty-to-one to five-to-one. Since the evidence of this disease among the normal population has not changed significantly during this period, the evidence shows that there was a four-fold increase in the incidence of this disease among Jewish women. . . . A leading investigator of this disease summarizes these statistical results as follows:
> "The decreasing difference in incidence of cervical cancer between Jewess and gentile may in some way be due to the liberalization of attitudes toward ancient religious law with associated decline in its observance."[33]

Dr. A. Shechter of Beilinson Hospital in Petah Tikvah, Israel, points out that in modern Israel the rate of cancer of the cervix among the general Jewish population is already not appreciably different from that prevalent among non-Jews. He adds that "among religious Jewish women who observe the rules of *nidah* and have sexual relations with only one man, however, the rate is, of course, quite low."[34]

Nidah and Hygiene

The *nidah* rules provide obvious hygienic benefits to those who observe them, even if it has taken science many centuries to realize the existence of the benefits.[35] Traditional Jewish laws regarding Family Purity should not, however, be confused with regulations regarding health and hygiene. Since the beginning of their existence as a people, there have been Jewish laws relating to hygiene which have been incorporated into the Jews' standard practices and daily lives. Jews are *commanded* to take care of their bodies and to keep themselves clean.

The advantages due to this respect by Jewish law for overall cleanliness and general good hygiene have manifested themselves throughout history. During the periods when disease ravaged plague-infested populations, these rules of cleanliness and hygiene kept the Jews well protected. Traditional Judaism considers such benefits as part of the natural consequences of living a life governed by the Torah and its precepts, a way of life intrinsically designed for human happiness, contentment, and good health, both physical and spiritual.

However, while the *nidah* laws provide obvious hygienic advantages to those who observe them, good health is not the reason that practicing Jews follow the rules of Family Purity, any more than it is the reason they observe the dietary rules of *kashrut*. They observe these laws because the Torah so commands them. Their resulting practical benefits, and the fact that the latest medical findings confirm them as being beneficial, are secondary considerations. Traditional Jews, convinced that the divine plan is a good one, are not surprised when science, medicine, and nature coincide to prove that God, the Creator of the world, knows what He is doing.

The late R. Eliyahu Kitov provides an insightful comment:

If menstrual separation was practiced by the Jewish people because of the many medical authorities who currently recommended such separation, human nature might militate against the constancy of such practice. For human nature is so constituted that the soundest of medical advice often fails to prevail against the temptation of instinct and inconvenience. Such advice is best heeded when reward is immediately tangible and exceeds the inconvenience entailed. Where, however, such reward is intangible and distant, while inconvenience is immediate and pleasure beckons on the other hand, then medical advice often goes unheeded. What cannot be assured in the absence of police and law courts can, however, be assured through the sense of obedience to the divine commandment which attends the observance of the laws of menstrual separation on the part of the Jewish people.[36]

Purification versus Cleanliness

The laws of *nidah,* like those of *kashrut,* therefore, are decidedly religious and not only hygienic; they are intended for purification and sanctification, and not merely for sanitation and cleanliness. However, in Jewish law, a bath and thorough cleaning of all parts of the body are indispensable preliminary preparations for ritual immersion in the *mikvah.* This preparatory physical purification of the body is thus an absolute precondition for its spiritual purification by *t'vilah,* not a substitute for it. Thus, while a *mikvah* is designed for ritual immersion only, and is not at all intended as a bath, the procedures related to *mikvah* provide both spiritual purification and bodily cleansing.[37]

Immersion in a *mikvah,* a ritual hallowed by Jewish law and tradition, is perceived in Judaism as a religious ceremony imbued with profound spiritual symbolism. As such, it requires a benediction thanking God the Purifier "Who sanctified us with His precepts and commanded us regarding *t'vilah.*" In the words of R. Akiva in the Talmud: "May you be praised, O Israel; Before Whom are you purifying yourselves? Who purifies you? Your Father in Heaven . . . Just as the *mikvah* purifies the impure, so does the Holy One, Blessed be He, purify Israel."[38]

R. Samson Raphael Hirsch discusses the nature of natural water in a *mikvah* as a spiritual agent:

> The water must not be contained in a vessel but must still be in its primitive state; for instance, gathered in a natural hollow in the ground. Being underwater was the original condition of the world.[39] Also, water, in contrast to dry land, is that part of the world on which human domain did not establish its realm. So, finally, the world of water is that sphere where no impurity reaches. . . . So that immersion in the element of water expresses a complete departure from the realm of humanity subject to impurity and is a return to original conditions; it completely breaks off connection with the past and introduces a quite fresh, pure future.[40]

According to Jewish law, for a woman's immersion in the *mikvah* to be considered valid, she must have pure and proper intentions during the immersion itself. Body and soul are thus understood to combine in this ritual, since, living in a tangible world, human beings need a physical manifestation of that spiritual service.

The Jew is asked to carry out the symbolic acts of Family Purity with devotion and an awareness that these acts are endowed with profound significance, even if the individual may have but a limited understanding of their logic. He pulls the required strings in this world knowing that they are the correct ones, but he can only guess at how powerful are the tones that reverberate in the spiritual sphere. Maimonides provides a thoughtful comment:[41]

> Immersion in the *mikvah* as a means of freeing oneself from impurities is one of the *hukim,* the statutes of Scripture about which human understanding is not deemed capable of forming a judgment. . . . Impurity, therefore, is not like an adhesion of mud or filth that can be washed off by water; it is a divine Scriptural decree, and is dependent on the intention of the heart. Therefore, the Sages have said, if someone had immersed himself without the proper intention, it is as if he had not immersed himself at all. . . .
>
> Even though nothing outwardly happens to his body, one becomes pure by immersing himself, so long as he sets his heart on purifying himself at the time of immersion. Similarly, he who sets his heart on purifying his soul from impurities such as evil convictions, his proper intent and the washing of his soul with the waters of pure reason, result in application to him of the Scriptural passage "And I will sprinkle clean waters upon you and purify you of all your impurities."[42]

Mikvah and its Priority in Judaism

The lack of knowledge by many Jews of the traditional regulations and procedures relating to *nidah, mikvah,* and Family Purity have resulted in many taking these regulations lightly. However, they are considered in Jewish law as fundamental to Jewish marriage and Jewish family life, and their violation is deemed to be a transgression of major import. Jewish law considers sexual relations between a man and a woman during the period of *nidah* to be a serious sin.

The overriding importance Judaism ascribes to Family Purity can be seen in the severity of the punishment cited in the Torah for violation of the *nidah* laws — *karet,* premature death,[43] one of the severest penalties in the Torah, and the one that is reserved for incest[44] and other major violations[45] of the Torah. Having sexual relations with a woman who is a *nidah* is considered in Jewish law as sexual immorality. We find a biblical passage equating such an act with adultery: "If a man is righteous and would accomplish justice and charity . . . he will not defile his neighbor's wife, nor will he approach a woman who is a *nidah*."[46]

The concept of community in Judaism is often associated with a synagogue. However, according to Jewish law, a *mikvah* is more important than a synagogue. Building a *mikvah* takes precedence over building a synagogue, or even acquiring a Torah scroll.[47] In fact, a community may sell a synagogue or a Torah scroll to provide funds for building a *mikvah*. As long as a group of Jews has no communal *mikvah*, they do not have, according to Jewish law, the status of a community,[48] no matter how many and varied the Jewish institutions they may have. Thus, though ordinarily a synagogue is the very symbol of a community, the assembly place where Jews may pray for their own, their family's, and their community's well-being, if there is no *mikvah*, that synagogue is considered as being an empty symbol of a community.[49]

In establishing the principle that Family Purity takes precedence over such important religious concepts as community prayer and Torah scholarship, the Sages dramatically underscore the *mikvah*'s overriding significance for the spiritual health of the Jewish family and the continued survival of the Jewish nation.

Summarizing the effect of the observance of *taharat hamishpahah*, the late Chief Rabbi of England, J. H. Hertz writes:

> By the reverent guidance in these vital matters which these laws afford, Jewish men have been taught respect for Womanhood, moral discipline and ethical culture. As for Jewish women, they were, on the one hand, given protection from uncurbed passion; and, on the other hand, taught to view married life under the aspect of holiness.[50]

10

Conjugal Relations: Privileges and Duties

"And He Shall Cause His Wife to Rejoice"

Modern Western thought rejects long-prevalent traditions which grant all conjugal rights to the husband while ignoring the needs of the wife. In this regard, Judaism is often erroneously included in a blanket condemnation of that religious framework improperly labelled "Judaeo-Christian heritage." This term is a misnomer for what is, more often than not, the heritage of either Judaism or Christianity and only rarely of both. Indeed, Judaism and Christianity are antithetical in so many respects that one can seldom hyphenate the two terms. However, it is in their differing views on sexuality and marriage in particular, that the contradictions between them are blatantly manifest.

Scripture and the Talmud, in their discussions of sexual matters and marital relations, reveal Judaism's profound and sensitive understanding of female sexuality. The woman, in this area of life, is granted a considerably greater right to fulfillment than is the man; the obligation is placed on the man to give his wife fulfillment.

In traditional Judaism, the newly married man acquires, along with the right of sexual congress with his wife, a strict and definitive responsibility in regard to that relationship. In the *ketubah*, the Jewish marriage contract, the groom, on the basis of a biblical precept, undertakes as a basic duty to provide his wife with *onah*, or marital relations, "according to universal custom."[1] This obligation

213

is separate and apart from his obligation to participate in such relations in order to fulfill the *mitzvah* of *pir'yah v'rivyah*, procreation.[2] This is underscored by the fact that Jewish law requires him to have conjugal relations with his wife during pregnancy and at other times when conception is not possible.[3] In the words of the Sages: "The *mitzvah* of *onah* and the *mitzvah* of *pir'yah v'rivyah* are two separate things, and neither is dependent on the other."[4]

The duty of the husband regarding *onah*[5] is stated quite specifically in the Torah: "*Sh'era, k'sutah v'onatah lo yigra* — He shall not neglect her need for food, clothing, and *onah*."[6]

The Talmud minces no words in condemning the man who does not carry out his conjugal responsibilities: "He who neglects his marital duties to his wife is a sinner."[7]

Applying Courtesy to Privileges

On the other hand, though it is a man's right and obligation to participate in relations with his wife, the scope of his demands is restricted by the simplest laws of human courtesy. Explains the Spanish rabbinical authority R. Abraham ben David (c. 1125–1198), the *Ravad:* "The *onah* specified by the Sages is solely for the purpose of satisfying the desires of the wife. The husband is not free to fulfill his duty to her without her consent. . . ."[8]

Although a man may ostensibly have relations with his wife whenever he desires,[9] his privilege is dependent upon her freely given consent; he may not exact marital relations contrary to his wife's wishes.[10] Sexual compulsion in any form is a violation of Jewish law. A husband may not force conjugal relations on his wife or even approach her in a manner which may cause her to fear him.[11] Certainly the rape of a wife is considered an abomination and is strictly forbidden.[12] Forcing cohabitation upon one's wife is regarded as an abhorrent act that will be reflected in and turned against the man through the character of his children;[13] they will be termed *b'nei anusah*, children of a raped one.[14]

The Jewish idea is that a man's conjugal obligations toward his wife entail far more than merely reasonably decent sexual behavior. Beyond the negative laws forbidding cruel or brutish treatment of the woman, there are also positive obligations. The Torah is explicit in spelling out its directives regarding the husband's duties and in establishing the wife's privileges.[15] Where the Torah does provide specific privileges for the husband, it is only so that he can better serve his wife. This is underscored in the scriptural stipulation that a newly married man is to be given a deferment from military service for one year: "He shall not go out to military service, nor shall he be impressed for any service; he shall be free for his home for one year and he shall cause his wife to rejoice."[16]

The first year of marriage is that critical period when the basic foundations are built. It is a year for establishing mutual trust, learning about commitment and devotion, and allowing the ripening of new love. During this period, the husband obviously benefits from that year of deferment from military duty. Yet, the scriptural command was not designed for his happiness, but for his wife's. This privilege of his is only so that he may "cause his wife to rejoice." How? In the words of the Sages, he must cause her to rejoice with "a matter of a *mitzvah*"[17] — a talmudic euphemism for marital relations.

The Torah recognizes that the success of the marriage and the development of a secure Jewish home depend in large measure on the wife. In obeying the injunction to bring his wife joy, the husband breaks ground for the eventual growth of a cohesive, committed family. And with the family serving as the vital element in the Jewish nation as a whole, it is in the national interest that the husband, in the first year, be excused from military service, in order to build the family foundation based on mutual love. Only when he has laid down that foundation may he be called on to serve his nation in a military capacity.[18]

Preventing Conjugal Neglect

Judaism understands this principle of making the wife rejoice to extend beyond the first year of marriage to all of the couple's married life. The word *onah* literally means season. Thus, "a man may not neglect . . . her season"[19] implies that he may not, through a lack of frequency or regularity in their marital relations, neglect his wife. This is the Jewish legal prohibition against conjugal neglect.

The positive formulation of this law, stressing dutiful physical involvement with one's wife, is derived from the scriptural injunction *V'simah et ishto,* "And he shall cause his wife to rejoice."[20] The two expressions of the law are complementary and, in talmudic terminology, are often combined: *simhat onah,* literally, "seasonal gladness."

R. Isaac of Corbeil, the thirteenth-century codifier of Jewish law and author of *Sefer Mitzvot Katan (S'mak)* teaches: " 'To cause his wife to rejoice' — as it is written, 'And he shall cause his wife to rejoice.'[21] The negative formulation is, 'He shall not neglect her *onah.*'[22] And behold how important is this positive *mitzvah . . .* for even when his wife is pregnant it is a *mitzvah* to cause her to rejoice when she is desirous. . . ."[23]

This statement and others similar to it,[24] reflect an acute awareness by the Sages of a woman's sexuality and her need for physical fulfillment. Morton Hunt, in *The Natural History of Love,* points out that the presence of sexual desire by women was not acknowledged until recently. Until the end of the nineteenth century one would be accused of "casting vile aspersions on womankind" if he suggested that women have sexual desire or, worse, experience sexual pleasure.[25] Comments R. David Feldman: "While this may have been true in the Western world, in Jewish culture and tradition both sexual desire and sexual pleasure of women are not only acknowledged but made into a religious concern for men. 'To fulfill her desire' is one of the two purposes of the . . . *mitzvah* [of marital relations]."[26] This has been the Jewish approach for thousands of years and is reflected in Jewish law.

Moreover, the Rabbis decreed obligations for the husbands to ensure their wives' satisfaction. To clarify the responsibilities of the husband, the Sages prescribed tables of minimal frequencies for cohabitation that have been incorporated into Jewish law. These tables are based on the husband's profession and occupation, the physical labor his occupation may entail, and the amount of time his occupation requires of him to be absent from home.[27] Each situation is to be determined individually, "each man according to his strength and his occupation."[28] The Sages add that the frequency of marital obligations is also determined by the desires of the individual woman.[29]

The husband who denies his wife conjugal relations because of ill health is given six months to regain his health. If, at the end of this period, he is still unable to have satisfactory relations with his wife, she is entitled to a divorce and he is required to pay her *ketubah* sum to her.[30]

The Woman's Conjugal Rights

Jewish law thus provides the woman with options that, in practice, allow her a considerable measure of control over this aspect of her marriage. Indeed, a husband, without his wife's consent, may not even travel on business.[31] This consent must be freely given and not in response to any overt or subtle pressure.[32] Even with his wife's consent, a husband may not absent himself for more than thirty days.[33] Prior to his embarking upon a journey, a man is required to have conjugal relations with his wife.[34]

According to Jewish law, a woman may also prevent her husband from changing his profession if the change will result in a lessening of frequency of their marital relations.[35] However, she may not compel him to change his profession from one which obligates him to have fewer instances of conjugal relations to another which increases the frequency of such relations.[36]

The Jewish legal requirement that a man provide satisfaction to his wife is quite stringent. Lack of virility,[37] or inability to fulfill conjugal obligations, or conscious neglect in these matters toward one's wife, constitute valid grounds for divorce.[38] In addition, a woman is entitled to financial compensation in proportion to the period of neglect which she suffered.[39]

The woman's personal taste is a valid factor in Jewish marriage law. If a woman is so physically repelled by her husband that she cannot bring herself to cohabit with him, she is entitled to a divorce.[40] Maimonides explains: "If a woman says, 'My husband is repugnant and I cannot willingly be intimate with him,' we compel him to divorce her forthwith, for she is in no way like a captive who is compelled to be intimate with the one she hates."[41]

Jewish law does not recognize any mutual agreement between husband and wife to abstain from marital relations, because such an agreement is contrary to biblical requirements.[42] Neither is the husband, in the name of a so-called higher spiritual goal, permitted to deny his wife her conjugal rights. Judaism calls for sanctity within the regimen of a regular daily life; it does not encourage a pursuit of holiness that removes one beyond the realm of human interaction.

Thus, if a man has made a religious vow to abstain from marital relations, and if the period of abstinence exceeds one week, the vow itself is legal grounds for the woman to obtain a divorce.[43] Withholding conjugal relations or using sex to manipulate the other partner is strictly forbidden to either party.[44]

Emotional Commitment

The physical side of marriage is, in Judaism, one facet of a generally harmonious relationship; it is not something to be considered separately. The Torah teaches that husband and wife must strive for a total emotional commitment which finds expression in the physical relationship. Their closeness must be expressed continuously, and not only when they desire physical satisfaction.

R. Shlomo Wolbe, a contemporary teacher of ethics, elaborates, directing his attention to the husband:

> During the first year of marriage, a man is convinced that he has achieved the highest degree of closeness possible with his wife — after all, what can be closer than the physical intimacy of becoming "as one flesh"?
>
> However, while this intimacy is certainly close indeed, a man should not for a moment think that they thus achieved true intimacy. Far from it. Not only may his wife feel otherwise, but to the contrary; it is precisely during their physical relations that she may feel the emptiness and pain if they have not yet attained a true intimacy of the spirit.
>
> Although marital relations do represent the height of intimacy, every height must be preceded by gradual advances in the closeness of relations until that peak is reached. Physical intimacy which is unmatched by emotional intimacy only insults the woman. It is intimacy of the spirit that a fine woman sets her eyes on attaining, and it is a relationship in which attention is paid to her as a person that she loves. If this is the nature of the interpersonal relationship that they achieve, she also desires physical intimacy. However, if her

husband does not properly devote himself to her and does not constantly relate to her in a warm and intimate manner, she recoils from physical intimacy with him. For physical intimacy which does not derive from emotional closeness both demeans and pains her.[45]

Physical intimacy, therefore, must reflect devotion and be matched by emotional intimacy. In a similar vein, the *Shulhan Aruch,* the *Code of Jewish Law,* declares that "a man may not drink of one cup and look at another."[46] This means simply that a man may not think of another woman while having relations with his wife.[47]

Judaism understands that the respect a man owes his wife does not allow for depersonalization or for his using his wife as an object for his personal pleasure. She is first and foremost a sensitive human being with feelings and emotions. For this reason, if a man is even contemplating divorce, he is forbidden by Jewish law to have marital relations with his wife[48] because the requisite devotion is lacking. The same applies to a man who hates his wife.[49] Similarly, a man who during the day has a bitter argument with his wife may not have relations with her before becoming reconciled with her.[50] The Sages summarize this rule succinctly: "A man may not cohabit with his wife unless there is love and peace between them."[51]

Each of the instances cited above is a situation of potential sexual exploitation. Marital relations that lack emotional commitment may provide momentary physical gratification, but will leave a residual taste of shame and loathing. With the depersonalization of the woman, both partners are degraded, and their conjugal relations are compared to acts of prostitution.[52]

Concomitantly, just as a husband is required to cause *his wife* to rejoice, so too must *he* be joyous during the act. The Sages refer to the *mitzvah* of marital relations as *simhat onah,*[53] the "joy" of *onah,* because mutual joy is an indispensable part of the act.[54] The Sages teach that the *Sh'chinah,* the Divine Presence, joins with husband and wife when they unite in love, but they add that if there is no joy between them God will not be there, since the *Sh'chinah* only dwells with a couple when there is joy between them.[55]

Thus, the intangible emotional component, in the Jewish understanding, is not merely incidental to conjugal relations; it plays a central role in the proper fulfillment of the act — as it does in all of the marital relationship. The married couple is expected to achieve emotional unity before their physical relationship is legitimized. Physical oneness must be accompanied by emotional oneness. Thus, Jewish law stipulates that a man may have conjugal relations with his wife only when she is coherent,[56] and not when either partner is drugged or intoxicated,[57] lazy or nervous,[58] or when the woman is asleep.[59]

Besides a man's basic, normative obligation to have regular marital relations with his wife, he is also required, whenever she indicates a desire, to join her on additional occasions.[60] The Talmud declares:[61] "A man is obliged to cause his wife to rejoice with a *d'var mitzvah* (literally, 'a matter of a *mitzvah,*' that is, conjugal relations) [even at other than the usual times for her *onah,* if he perceives that she desires him]."[62]

Maimonides maintains that such a right is not limited to the woman alone, and that the man too can exercise his conjugal rights on occasions other than the regular ones.[63] However, later codifiers do not agree, maintaining that the privilege is one enjoyed by the woman only, since the Torah specifically obliges the man to satisfy his wife with the *mitzvah* of *onah* but no reciprocity is mentioned in the Torah: "She is not obligated to him at every time if she does not wish to . . . for she is not like a captive slave to fulfill his needs every time he so desires."[64]

A Concern for Woman's Sexuality

Judaism understands the woman's conjugal needs to be at least of equal importance to the man's. Indeed, the woman is encouraged to take the initiative.[65] The Sages praise the piety of the woman who intimates her desire for conjugal relations, comparing her to the matriarch Leah.[66] They bless such a woman, proclaiming: "Every woman who requests of her husband to participate in 'a matter of a *mitzvah*' will have children who will be even greater than those who lived in the generation of Moses."[67]

However, Jewish women are advised to be tactful and modest[68] and not brazen[69] in indicating their desire for conjugal relations.[70] Men are instructed to be aware of the woman's sensitivity and greater subtlety in this regard. The Talmud states: "A woman indicates her desire by her heart while a man does so verbally; this is a fine quality among women."[71]

Jewish law teaches that a man must strive to anticipate his wife and endeavor to fulfill her wishes without her having to signal them.[72] This thoughtfulness endears him to her and promotes her happiness.

The obligation in Jewish law for a man to have conjugal relations with his wife involves more than participation in the physical act of coitus. In addition, as stated, a Jewish husband is expected to cater to his wife's emotional, as well as to her physical needs. By going through the motions, and participating perfunctorily in a mechanically executed act, the husband does not satisfy the *mitzvah* of *onah* because he does not thereby cause his wife to rejoice. The Sages emphasize at every turn that the husband's duty to satisfy his wife in this regard extends beyond the basic requirement of participating in cohabitation.[73]

It is in this respect, perhaps more than in any other, that Judaism's consideration for the woman's needs is most apparent. The woman's sexuality, as the Torah understands it, must be cultivated and treated with sensitive care.[74] The Sages manifested an acute awareness of the urgency of the male desire and they were concerned lest a husband's lack of control result in his disregard of his wife's needs and in his maltreatment of her.

The Essential Preliminaries

Out of concern for the woman's sexuality and her emotions, the Sages provide detailed guidelines to the husband on how to treat his wife. The man is obliged to prepare his wife for conjugal relations, for example, by fostering a warm emotional climate between them. Through intimate conversation[75] and appropriate foreplay[76] the husband must prepare his wife with warmth and tenderness and stimulate her psychologically, emotionally, and physically. *Krevut, hibah, ritzui,* and *pius* are some of the terms the Sages use to indicate how the Jewish husband must draw near to his wife through tenderness and endearment in order to establish the proper atmosphere and engage in the appropriate preliminaries. In the words of the Sages: "With coitus alone, he does not fulfill the *mitzvah*. He must, in addition, participate in all of the various forms of *krevut* (literally, 'closeness') with which a man gladdens his wife."[77]

The *Igeret HaKodesh,* the "Epistle of Holiness," dating back to the thirteenth century, which deals with leading a moral family life and in particular with how a Jew should conduct his marital relations, has this guidance for the husband:

> You should first engage her in conversation, beginning with words that will draw her heart to you and put her mind at ease and thus gladden her. In this way your mind and heart will be in harmony with hers. . . . Speak to her charming and seductive words which will arouse in her passion, love, desire, and *eros.* Also, speak of matters that are appropriate and worthy to inspire her intentions for the sake of Heaven . . . words which will elicit reverence for God, piety, and modesty. Tell her of pious women who gave birth to fine, God-fearing children. . . .
>
> Win her over to you with words of love and seduction and with words that inspire reverence of Heaven, modesty, and pure thoughts. . . . Do not compel or force her in anyway, for the *Sh'chinah,* the Divine Presence, cannot abide such a union. Your intents must not be in discord. Quarrel not with your wife, and certainly do not strike her on account of sexual matters. . . . As our Sages taught,[78] just as a lion tramples and devours his prey and has no shame, so a boorish man strikes and copulates and has no shame.[79]

R. Jacob Emden (1697–1776), the German rabbinic scholar and halachic authority, provides additional insights:

> A man should first calm his wife's mind . . . and should begin by bringing his wife into the proper mood by speaking soothing words that attract her heart and soothe her mind and cause her to rejoice, so as to fuse her mind with his and her intent with his.[80] He should speak to her with words that arouse her desire, her love, and her passion. He should also speak to her of reverence for Heaven and of lovingkindness and of modesty, and about righteous Jewish women. . . . He should cause her heart to rejoice so that her desire will be aroused in holiness and in purity. . . . They must embrace and kiss before uniting in love, so that he will inspire the passion in his wife and arouse the desire between them. . . . When her passion becomes evident in her breathing and is reflected in her eyes, then they should make love to one another.[81]

Setting the mood through appropriate conversation and foreplay is considered an indispensable preliminary for marital relations.[82]

The Sages go so far as to declare that he who fails to do this is to be considered as though he had raped his wife.[83]

The Sages use the expression *tashmish v'chol avizerayhu,* "coitus and all its components," to express the total picture of the requirements involved in the obligations relating to marital relations. By fulfilling these requirements, the man is able to turn the act into the highly satisfying physical and emotional experience that will truly gladden the heart of his wife and cause her to rejoice.

The Quality of the Act

The quality of the act is important as well. The Talmud declares that cohabitation is forbidden when either partner or both are fully clothed — "in the manner of the Persians" is the term used — because this demonstrates disrespect and lack of affection for one another,[84] and is therefore considered a diminution of the fulfillment of the marital obligation. Conjugal relations without love and affection are considered to be no different from the relations of a harlot with a client.[85]

Over and over the Sages caution that the very nature and character of the children who will be the issue of the conjugal relations are determined by the manner in which the husband and wife perform the act and by their very thoughts and intent during coitus. The *M'norat HaMa'or* states:

> When a man and his wife love each other and they conduct their marital relations in harmony with one another and with the proper intent, the Holy One fulfills their wishes and the children that result from such a union will be proper ones.
>
> However, if during their union they have foreign thoughts and intent, the act is not conducted in a proper manner and the very nature of their seed is altered.[86]

The woman may also take the initiative in the conduct of the act. The Sages suggest that a woman should properly prepare her husband by enticing him erotically[87] and by engaging him in conversation designed to arouse his desire for her.[88] The Talmud provides explicit guidelines for the woman to arouse her husband skillfully through foreplay so that his passion is progressively heightened and culminates in coitus.[89]

While a woman has the option to take initiatives to increase her husband's satisfaction, it is the man who is duty-bound to "cause his wife to rejoice" and not vice versa. It is the husband who must give his wife physical and emotional satisfaction, and her satisfaction takes precedence over his own. The Talmud teaches that a man is rewarded if he permits his wife to attain satisfaction before he does.[90]

The *Igeret HaKodesh* provides a general guideline for the husband: "When you join with her, do not hasten to arouse her passions. When her mind is completely at ease you may unite with her in the way of love; and arrange it so that you allow her to attain satisfaction first. . . ."[91]

The Talmud praises husbands who are considerate of their wives and of their wives' satisfaction in their marital union, and as a reward assures them of many descendants.[92]

One codifier goes so far as to state that during conjugal relations the man should not seek to derive any pleasure for himself from the act, but be concerned only with giving his wife pleasure.[93]

The Talmud relates that Ima Shalom, the wife of R. Eliezer, said that one of the reasons that her children were so beautiful was that during intercourse her husband was *domeh k'mi shek'fa'o shed,* like a person forced by the devil. (The commentaries explain that he was behaving in a manner "against his own will" so as to avoid satisfying his own desires and concentrate on pleasing his wife.[94]) When Ima Shalom asked her husband why he behaved as he did, he told her that in this way "thoughts of another woman would not arise in me" at the time of the act.[95]

Mutual Pleasure: The Cosmic Plan

The Sages view the physical pleasure as an essential part of the act that is to be *mutually* enjoyed; the Talmud uses the expression *guf neh'neh miguf,* "one body has pleasure from another."[96] The pleasure derived from the marital union is the incentive God provided for man and woman to perform the act of procreation. R. Isaac Aboab, the fourteenth-century Spanish teacher of ethics, stresses the need for mutual pleasure in the act: "At the time of *onah,* one should not intend for his own pleasure alone; he should be concerned with fulfilling his wife's pleasure as well."[97]

R. Judah HeHasid, the twelfth-century German teacher of ethics and piety, in his *Sefer Hasidim,* maintains that the enjoyment from the act is to be mutual, underscoring that a husband may derive pleasure from it so long as he is concerned about providing pleasure to his wife as well. Referring to the scriptural passage, "He who has found a woman has found a great good and has obtained favor from the Lord,"[98] he writes: "All these matters pertaining to conjugal relations must take the wife's desires into consideration as well as his own. If he succeeds in finding a wife whose desires coincide with his own in these matters, then he has indeed 'obtained the favor of the Lord,' and to him the verse 'God has favored your acts' applies."[99]

R. Isaiah di Trani (d. 1270), the Italian talmudic commentator and author of the *Tosafot Rid,* says that when a pregnancy constitutes a physical hazard to the woman, the pursuit of pleasure is in itself a legitimate reason for conjugal relations.[100]

R. Jacob Emden maintains that the pleasure involved in conjugal relations is the inducement to participate in an act which might otherwise seem too physical and therefore might cause people to recoil.[101]

Cohabitation in moderation is also seen in Judaism as an eminently healthy expression of a physical need, and a medium to provide relief of physical pressure.[102] R. Emden expresses the conviction that such activity also provides relief from psychological tension, "dissipates melancholy, soothes nervousness and temper, and gladdens the soul."[103]

Advocating Moderation

Maimonides reminds us that while the conjugal relations should be enjoyed, the act has another goal beyond that of physical pleasure:

> The purpose of marital relations is the perpetuation of the species and not only for the pleasure of the act. The enjoyment of the act was given to living beings in order to induce them to participate in coitus so as to inseminate. This is proven from the fact that following

semination passion subsides, while all physical pleasure from the act
ceases. . . . If pleasure was the entire purpose, it is obvious that the
enjoyment of the act would continue after semination for as long as
one desired.[104]

However, Maimonides, who apart from being a major codifier of
Jewish law was also a renowned physician, was concerned about
possible physical debilitation resulting from sexual overindulgence,
and he counsels moderation.[105] The Sages point out that in certain
respects, the two great physical needs of human beings, food and
sex, are similar. Just as hunger often becomes intensified with
eating, so too is the desire for sexual activity intensified by frequent
indulgence. The Talmud states: "Man possesses a small member
which becomes more ravenous the more its hunger is appeased, and
which is satiated when its appetite is denied."[106]

In the same way as gluttonous eating increases one's craving for
food, so too does overindulgence in sexual activity increase the
sexual appetite, whereas nonindulgence or moderate indulgence
tempers it.[107] Maimonides[108] and the other codifiers[109] advise
against sexual excess, noting that even though his wife is accessible
to him, "a man should . . . not be constantly with her [conjugally]
like a rooster. . . ."[110] In other words, a person should at all times
be master of his desires, and never a slave to them.

Marital relations are also forbidden during periods of famine.[111]
However, according to Maimonides, this is only if one has already
fulfilled his obligation of bringing children into the world.[112] The
Sages derive their prohibition from the principle that at a time when
the community suffers, one should share that pain in a personal
way.[113]

The Imbalance in Favor of the Woman

Clearly there is a considerable imbalance in Jewish law between the
conjugal rights of the woman and those of the man, the scales being
tilted in favor of the woman. Yet the very nature of the sexual
relationship often intrinsically places the initiative in the hands of
the man. Thus, the woman's preferred status in this regard may be
seen as a means of establishing equity.

In the area of conjugal rights in marriage, Judaism contrasts sharply with the tradition that has for centuries dominated the Christian world. In the words of researchers Masters and Johnson: "The concept bolstered by ancient laws that sex is a husband's right and a wife's duty has made and continues to make for marriages in which sexuality is exploited and dishonored."[114] As we have shown, Judaism's conception of the marital relationship is a far cry from this attitude toward marriage. If anything, one might make a strong case for the view that Jewish law has always expressed the opposite principle: sex is a wife's right and a husband's duty.

Taken as a whole, however, Judaism views marital relations in terms of mutual privileges and duties, with particular concern for the woman's needs. The burden of responsibility is upon the husband, who must be sensitive to his wife's needs and must constantly strive to satisfy them, even before his own. Thus, far from being sexually exploited, the Jewish wife is to be treated tenderly and affectionately, and her needs are to be satisfied as fully as possible.

Communicating Love and Peace

The Sages perceive marital relations themselves as a medium for peace in the home. A sage is quoted in the Talmud as lamenting his old age and the cessation of one means by which he could achieve domestic harmony.[115] The *Midrash* also points out that the physical relationship is a significant contributing factor to peace in the home and love between husband and wife.[116]

In Judaism marriage is perceived as an important milestone in the path of human sanctification of life. The urgency of the sexual drive, therefore, is neither denied nor condemned, but is accepted as a gift of God, to be properly channeled through marital relations. Central to the marriage relationship, conjugal relations are understood to be a unique medium through which the partners in marriage communicate love for one another.

Perhaps the most vital factor in understanding the way Judaism perceives marital relations is that they are considered a *mitzvah*, a divine command, and cohabitation between husband and wife, when correctly conducted, with proper intent, restraint and concern for one's partner, constitutes a holy act which sanctifies the name of God.[117] In this way, a purely physical human function, also common to animals, is imbued with a lofty spiritual dimension which influences the way the participants perceive the act and the manner in which they conduct their physical relations.

Judaism's requirement that husband and wife provide each other with physical and emotional gratification through their marital relations, is in order to help them strengthen the matrimonial bond between them.[118] There is also a higher purpose for it: "Proper physical union can be a means of spiritual elevation," declares the author of the *Igeret HaKodesh*.[119] Judaism transforms and elevates the act of coitus between a man and his wife from the primal level of physical gratification to the exalted planes of sanctity and purity, a level which attains its most sublime peak when it is a joyous affirmation of the noblest of human emotions — love, devotion, and mutual respect and consideration.

11

The Woman's Rights in Marriage

Marriage: A Legal Contract

The rights that Judaism accords to a woman in the marital relationship are based upon three principles: divine decrees, human duties and privileges, and ethical and moral proprieties. Cognizant of the fact that a marital agreement requires legal acts and instruments to contract the relationship and to terminate it, Judaism has embodied these principles in Jewish law.

The contractual arrangement of traditional Jewish marriage with accompanying legal technology is similar to that used in effecting any mundane commercial transaction. Unlike American law, however, where a contract is bilateral, in Jewish law a contract is unilaterally executed. A person "takes" or "acquires" a spouse.[1] *Kinyan* ("taking" or "acquiring") is the legal ceremony marking the change in title or status, and provides the marital relationship with a solid legal foundation. In Judaism, the difference between a marital transaction and a commercial one in which legal title is transferred, is that the former includes mutual legal responsibilities. Because the husband is recognized as the outgoing one, he is the one who takes the initiative and "acquires" a wife. Therefore, it is he who must write a *ketubah*, which places obligations upon him in her favor. Concomitantly, the wife "acquires" a husband who is obligated to her, while she simultaneously places herself under obligation to him.

In fact, in the Bible and in rabbinical writings, the term *kinyan* is also used metaphorically to indicate the establishment of a close and intimate relationship. Thus the Bible states, *am zu kanita*—"This people that you have acquired,"[2] indicating God's establishment of a special relationship with the Jewish people. The Talmud teaches: "The Holy One, Blessed be He, has five *kinyanim* in this world: Torah, Heaven and Earth, Abraham, the Jewish people, and the Temple."[3]

Here again, the term *kinyan* is used to express a deep and intimate bond. *Kinyan* in marriage is thus both an expression for the warmth that the marriage relationship offers, as well as the term for the legal contract which results in a change of status.

It is a principle of Jewish marriage law, enunciated in the Talmud[4] and the law codes, that the freely given consent of the woman is an absolute precondition to the marriage; a woman may not be married against her will.[5] By the same token, according to Jewish law, a father may not arrange a marriage for his daughter while she is still a child.[6] As the Talmud says: "A man is forbidden to arrange a marriage for his daughter while she is a minor; she must first be mature and say: He is the one I want."[7]

Jewish marriage is thus a legal contract that is validated when the following requirements have been met: the consent of both parties has been obtained, the contract has been properly executed by one partner, accepted by the other, and attested to by two witnesses.

The Husband's Ten Obligations

The marriage relationship in Judaism includes extra-legal responsibilities as well. When the groom recites the traditional marriage formula referring to marriage as "sanctification," and ends with the words: "according to the laws of Moses and Israel," the couple is considered to have acknowledged their acceptance of all Jewish laws and traditions relating to the relationship between husband and wife.[8]

The fundamental principles governing the relationship between a man and his wife are delineated by Maimonides:

> When a man marries a woman . . . he assumes ten obligations toward her and acquires four obligations from her.[9] The husband's

obligations are:[10] (a) to supply sustenance and maintenance; (b) to supply clothing and lodgings; (c) to provide conjugal relations; (d) to provide the *ketubah* sum (an amount to be paid out in the event of death or divorce); (e) to procure her medical care; (f) to ransom her if she is taken captive; (g) to provide her suitable burial; (h) to provide for her sustenance after his death from his estate, and to ensure her right to live in his house; (i) to provide for the maintenance of her daughters after his death; (j) to provide that her sons shall inherit her *ketubah* sum.[11]

The woman, in turn, in return for her sustenance[12] (a) relinquishes the earnings from her labor and (b) any objects she may happen to find, and (c) her husband is entitled, during her lifetime, to the profits from her property, but not the property itself, for the benefit of the household as a whole,[13] and (d) he is entitled to inherit her estate.[14]

It should be emphasized that the husband's ten obligations are designed to provide his wife with security. The wife's four obligations are, on the other hand, designed only for the establishment of good will, and to compensate for some of the husband's obligations toward her. If the woman wishes to be financially independent, however, she has the option of unilaterally abrogating her obligation to supply her husband with her earnings and sustaining herself.[15]

However, while Jewish law permits the woman to enforce such an exchange, her husband does not have, in the same circumstances, a similar option to abrogate his responsibility for her sustenance. Maimonides rules: "If a woman decides, 'I do not wish to be sustained by you and I do not wish to give over my earnings,' we accede to her wishes and she is not to be compelled otherwise. However, if the husband says, 'I shall not support you and I shall take none of your earnings,' he is not to be heeded."[16]

Interestingly, according to the Torah, a woman has the legal right to retain all her earnings and still receive full support from her husband.[17] This basic inequity in her favor, however, was seen as a potential cause for marital discord, with the woman enjoying all of the benefits but not contributing to the household. Therefore, the Sages introduced an option of a trade-off, whereby the woman is granted the choice between financial dependence and financial independence. If she opts for independence, she reimburses her husband for her food, but still receives his support for such expenses as clothing, cosmetics, and personal needs. Even when the woman decides not to retain her own earnings and elects instead to contribute them to the family finances, the Sages still frown on the husband making use of his wife's earnings. "He who looks to his wife's wages will not find blessing," they declare.[18]

The *Ketubah*, a Charter of Women's Rights

The concern of Judaism for the married woman is reflected in the *ketubah,* the legal document that, under the marriage canopy, the Jewish groom hands the bride. It is a basic precondition for a valid Jewish marriage, embodying the essential obligations that the husband assumes toward his wife for the course of their life together and in the event of the dissolution of the marriage.[*]

The husband's obligations, outlined in the *ketubah,* are publicly proclaimed when the *ketubah* is read aloud to the assembled guests at the wedding. This emphasizes to him that they are not only a matter of private concern between the two of them, but are a matter of public record and accountability. A traditional Jewish husband thus becomes bound by Jewish law, morality, and community pressure to act correctly toward his wife.

The *ketubah* plays an essential role in Jewish marriage in its function as a protector of the woman's rights,[19] and is thus an indispensable prerequisite to a Jewish marriage.[20] In clear, succinct legal prose, the *ketubah* spells out the husband's obligations toward his wife for the duration of their life together — and beyond. In the event of divorce, the *ketubah* obligates the man to provide for the woman; in the event of his death, his estate is to be used for her maintenance. The financial arrangements outlined in this legal document serve, in the event of her becoming widowed or divorced, to protect the woman from undue economic hardship.[21]

The *ketubah* sum has been compared to alimony. The difference is that the *ketubah* amount, on the dissolution of marriage through either death or divorce, is paid in a single sum and is not, as is the case in divorce alimony, paid out over a period of time. In ancient

---

[*]For a full discussion of the *ketubah,* see Chapter 7, "Preparations for the Wedding."

times, the sum of money, if conservatively invested, was intended to be sufficient to provide a steady income to sustain a woman for life and enable her to support and properly raise her children.[22]

Historically, societies dominated by men have delegated the overriding position of strength within marriage to the husband, permitting him to control the destinies of his wife and children by controlling the family's finances. In Jewish marriage, the woman has never been helpless, nor has she been completely dependent on her husband's good will. Her own strength has derived in large measure from the terms granted her in the *ketubah*. According to its terms, the property she brings to the marriage legally remains her own as long as the union lasts. In the event of divorce, she continues to maintain ownership of her property and her former husband is obligated also to pay her certain compensatory sums. The *ketubah* is her financial buttress within the marriage. Should the man fail to live up to the obligations outlined in it, she can request that the rabbinical court either compel him to carry out his obligations, or force him to grant her a divorce. If the husband should be tempted to initiate divorce proceedings that are contrary to her interest, he cannot easily do so. Dissolving the union requires his fulfillment of a number of legal obligations outlined in the *ketubah* in addition to the outlay of substantial sums of money.

The *ketubah* thus raised the status of the woman within marriage, placing a substantial measure of control in her hands. While in many other traditions and among many peoples, the married woman held a generally degraded position, the Jewish woman has maintained her dignity within the family. Her position and, accordingly, her self-worth, have been bolstered by the *ketubah,* which was given to her to offset the power of her stronger husband. As Judaism perceives it, the man did not require his position to be further strengthened by laws and legal instruments; the woman did. By committing a husband to a strict set of responsibilities toward his wife, the *ketubah* thus balances the potentially uneven structure of marriage. The Jewish wife is not subject to either abuse or to marital neglect by an all-powerful husband.

Historically, the *ketubah* also provided assurance to the woman that her husband would not treat her as a mistress or servant girl to be sent away according to his whim, and that he would not leave her

when her attractiveness began to wane.[23] Since the biblical requirement for divorce is a comparatively simple act on the part of the
husband, the financial, economic, and legal provisions of the *ketubah*
are specifically designed to complicate the divorce procedure and
protect the woman.[24] The difficulty of discharging all the legal
provisions, and the time required to study and settle numerous
financial adjustments required by the *ketubah* often made divorce a
time-consuming and involved affair, serving to some extent as a
deterrent to the potentially exploitative husband.

The significant legal and psychological benefits the *ketubah* brings
to the Jewish marriage have contributed substantially to the stability
of the Jewish family. The obligations to which the contract commits
the husband with respect to the wife serve to cultivate in him a sense
of responsibility and respect that is the cornerstone of a healthy,
enduring relationship.

The contrasting approach between Jewish tradition and other
religious traditions regarding the ideal relationship between husband and wife is underscored at the very beginning of married
life — at the wedding itself. The traditional marriage vows of the
Church, in accordance with the New Testament's obligations of
wifely obedience and subjection to her husband,[25] call on the
woman to pledge to "honor" and "obey" her husband. The Torah
obligates the husband to give his wife a *ketubah* at the Jewish
wedding, a solemn written obligation to protect her rights in
marriage as delineated in the Bible.[26]

Long before a conception of women's rights existed in the world,
Judaism, through the *ketubah* and a series of laws designed for her
protection, established for the woman a check and balance system of
human rights.

Divorce

Behind the Jewish laws of divorce lies the interest of Judaism in
discouraging divorce and keeping the family together. Divorce, like
marriage, is a contract in Jewish law, and thus is unilateral; for the
divorce to be acceptable, however, both parties must consent to its
execution. A variety of means are employed to convince a man and
woman contemplating divorce to reconsider a decision which might

have been hastily reached, and to remain together for their own greater good and for the benefit of their family. Rabbinical courts will often recommend marriage counseling. The courts may intentionally procrastinate; they might insist on frequent visits by the couple to the court. The *get* (divorce contract) itself must be written by a scribe especially for the parties concerned—it may not be a printed or a filled-in form—and it has to meet many detailed and exacting criteria. The slightest deviation in form renders it invalid. All of this is designed to provide additional time for a couple to reconsider the decision to divorce, to encourage reconciliation—and especially to protect the woman.

In actual practice, among Jewish communities everywhere, there were always strong motivating factors including economic, social, and communal pressures, that militated against divorce; these, under ordinary circumstances, ensured the permanence of marriage.

There are times, however, when the greatest efforts are of no avail; there are couples who should never have married, whose personalities are just deeply, intrinsically incompatible. The community of spirit that they may once have shared has long ceased to exist. When all efforts to achieve compatibility and reconciliation have failed, Judaism regards divorce as a legitimate, realistic possibility.

The following discussion takes place in the Mishnah on the question of divorce.[27] The School of Shammai claims that the only grounds for divorce should be adultery. The School of Hillel argues that divorce should be easy—"even if he has nothing more against her than that she has spoiled the soup."[28] R. Akiva goes further, and contends that a man may divorce his wife "for the sole reason that he has found a woman more attractive than she."[29]

Judaism adopted the lenient position, that is, that divorce should be granted on the grounds of incompatibility,[30] and not limited to that extreme of marital dissatisfaction—adultery. This is not to imply that Judaism regards divorce lightly. On the contrary, divorce is considered to be the painful disintegration of that which was once so hopefully built. Says the Talmud: "He who divorces the wife of his youth—even the Temple sheds tears for him."[31]

The idea of marriage as a basically permanent union is evident in scripture.[32] There are no instances in the Bible where divorce is undertaken lightly. Ezra's ruling, in the pre-Second Temple era, that men must give up their non-Jewish wives met with significant opposition.[33] In the fifth century B.C.E. the prophet Malachi denounced the frequency of divorce in Judaea with a cry of moral anguish.[34]

The basic liberality of the Jewish divorce laws reflects an insight into family dynamics: it was evident to the Sages that two people may harm, by their destructive proximity, more than just one another. The children's lives and well-being are involved. The children's suffering grows progressively more acute as their awareness develops and as the marriage hobbles along, progressively deteriorating. It is, in certain cases, in the children's best interest that a poor marriage be terminated early.

Divorce by Mutual Consent

In most systems of law, the court decides whether a divorce is in order. In Jewish law, divorce is decided not by the courts but by the parties concerned. Mutual consent, the agreement of both parties, is, in Jewish law, sufficient for divorce.[35] The function of the courts under Jewish jurisprudence is to intervene when the parties are unable to agree on the terms of the divorce, to decide the conditions of the divorce agreement, and to determine that the legalities of the divorce procedure are punctiliously met.

There are other legal systems where divorce is conditional upon establishing a "guilty party," that is, one of the marital partners who is at fault and bears the blame for the marriage break-up. Even in English law, the commission of matrimonial offense was, until recently, a prerequisite and *sine qua non* for divorce.[36] Under Jewish law, divorce is not dependent upon the establishment of legal responsibility. If both parties are agreed, a divorce is granted with no specific cause required, a situation that under certain legal systems might be termed collusion and could be a bar to the dissolution of the marriage.[37]

In the absence of an agreement between the parties to a divorce, the rabbinic courts are empowered to decide if there is a legal basis to compel a husband to give a *get p'turin,* a writ of divorce, or for a wife to receive one. Under certain conditions the courts, in the event of one of the parties demanding a divorce and the other being unwilling, have the right to use methods of compulsion to terminate a marriage. These powers of compulsion have been particularly useful in protecting wives when their welfare was at stake.

In the event that a recalcitrant husband refuses to grant a divorce where circumstances require it, Jewish law has empowered its courts to force the husband to do so. Thus, if a woman has valid grounds for divorce — and Jewish law provides the woman with considerably more grounds for divorce than it does the man — she can petition the *Bet Din,* the rabbinical court, which will then direct the husband to give his wife the *get.* This court then has the jurisdiction to implement its decision. Maimonides rules: "If one is obliged by law to divorce his wife and he refuses to do so, a Jewish court in every place and in every period may even cause him to be beaten until he declares 'I am willing.' He then writes the *get* and it is a valid divorce contract."[38]

The use of force to compel a recalcitrant husband to issue a divorce is obviously limited to countries in which Jewish courts have such power. In modern Israel, for example, where the rabbinic courts hold jurisdiction in the areas of marriage and divorce, imprisonment has been a powerful threat that the courts have used to force men to grant divorces to their wives.

As for countries in which Jewish courts have no power to enforce their decision, Maimonides rules that non-Jewish courts may enforce the decisions of the Jewish court: "If the non-Jewish court beat him and said to him, 'Do what the Jewish court told you,' and they applied pressure on the Jew until he had no choice but to initiate divorce, the divorce is nevertheless valid."[39]

However, Maimonides rules that dissolution of a marriage enforced by non-Jewish courts where the Jewish courts had not previously ruled on the matter, is invalid, even if the woman's claims for divorce are valid, since she must first approach Jewish courts.[40]

When the Husband May Compel Divorce

In the instance where the wife refuses her consent to a divorce, a husband, under the following conditions, can unilaterally compel it:

1. The wife changes her religion or knowingly transgresses "the laws of Moses and Judaism," or knowingly misleads him into doing so — for example, causes him to transgress the dietary laws or having conjugal relations when she is a menstruant or during her *nidah* period.[41]

2. The wife commits adultery, or the husband produces two witnesses who provide evidence that indicates strong probability that she has committed adultery.[42]

3. The wife is guilty of habitual indecent behavior or dresses immodestly in public,[43] or so loudly demands conjugal relations of her husband that outsiders hear her discussing the matter with her husband,[44] and he is shamed.[45]

4. The wife grossly and publicly insults her husband or her father-in-law by cursing or assaulting either of them.[46]

5. The wife refuses conjugal relations for the course of a whole year.[47]

6. The wife suffers from a disability or illness that precludes marital relations.[48]

7. The wife is barren, after ten years of marriage.[49]

8. The wife unjustifiably refuses to move with him to another domicile in the same country where the standard of living is not lower.[50]

9. The wife refuses to settle with him in Eretz Israel — this applies even if the move will result in a reduction in their standard of living.[51]

When the Wife May Compel Divorce

Similarly, a wife can compel her husband to give her a divorce under any of the following circumstances:

1. The husband changes his religion[52] or forces her to violate the laws of Judaism knowing that she observes them.[53]

2. The husband is morally dissolute or commits adultery.[54]

3. The husband suffers from a major physical defect.[55]

4. The wife finds him repugnant and cannot bear marital relations with him.[56]

5. The husband refuses marital relations with her.[57]

6. The husband insists on having marital relations while clothed.[58]

7. The husband becomes weakened or debilitated to the extent that, for a period of more than six months, marital relations are not feasible.[59]

8. The wife claims her husband is impotent.[60]

9. The wife wants children, and her husband is incapable of begetting children.[61]

10. The husband is malodorous.[62]

11. The husband is engaged in a disgusting trade.[63]

12. The husband is chronically angry and quarrelsome, and habitually turns her out of the house.[64]

13. The husband habitually beats his wife.[65]

14. The husband refuses to support his wife.[66]

15. The husband unreasonably prevents her from visiting her parents at reasonable intervals.[67]

16. The husband prevents her from attending a wedding or paying a consolation visit to mourners.[68]

17. The husband insists that they live with his parents, when she claims they are unpleasant toward her.[69]

18. The husband prevents her from adorning herself.[70]

19. The wife wishes to leave a neighborhood which has undesirable elements, and to move to another domicile, and her husband unreasonably refuses.[71]

20. The wife wishes to leave the diaspora and move to Eretz Israel, and her husband refuses.[72]

12

Making a Marriage Work

Sh'lom Bayit — A Vital Goal

The Jewish family is a social unit created, enveloped, and sustained by love. The warm and intimate nature of Jewish family life throughout every age and in every place has its roots in the Jewish concept of *sh'lom bayit,* "peace in the home." For the Jew, domestic harmony is not a matter of luck, nor, in its absence, is it a wistful dream. It is a vital, impelling goal incumbent upon husband and wife to strive for as heads of the household and as the family's nucleus.

Creating *sh'lom bayit* is considered a worthy, even a holy task. The Sages teach that where there is harmony, God Himself dwells there.[1] Where *sh'lom bayit* is nonexistent, so too is the presence of God, with the home subsequently disintegrating. As the Sages express it, "A home in which there is dissension will not stand."[2]

Sh'lom bayit is therefore more than merely an asset to family living; it is basic to the survival of the family. Obviously, however, attaining it is no easy task. Husband and wife each bring to the marital unit a complex spectrum of physical and emotional attributes. This unit may be powered by the best of intentions and fueled by genuine love. Yet the course it steers is a difficult one, and the dangers are multifarious.

A cynic once remarked: "All marriages are happy ones. It's the living together afterward that is the problem." There once was a time when marriage was a permanent union. This is no longer so.

The statistics are well known. Some fifty percent of American marriages end in divorce. The average marriage in America lasts six-and-a-half to seven-and-a-half years. Moreover, the majority of those who remain married are said to be unhappy with their marriages. What is causing this?

Marital dissonance begins early. The first marital quarrels are often brought on simply by the disillusionment of failed expectations. Most people go into marriage mistakenly expecting the other to provide them with fulfillment and contentment. Most of us, since childhood, have been reared on the romance of love and concomitant expectations that marriage precedes living happily ever after. These thoughts are only strengthened when couples date, when each tries to make the best impression on the other, and each fantasizes about the other. Both imagine that marriage will bring a kind of heavenly bliss, that their marriage will be a happy one, and that it will last that way forever.

At the very beginning most marital relationships are indeed reasonably good and happy because of the newness of the relationship, doing interesting things together, having fascinating conversations, sharing great mutual affection — simply enjoying one another's company.

After the initial idyllic romantic phase following marriage and the breaking-in period, each comes down to earth and discovers the reality of the other. At this point, however, the first reaction is often one of shock. The new spouse is not the faultless human being he or she was thought to be. The other's true personality and character traits differ substantially from previously held romantic expectations of perfection, and the two turn out to have serious differences of opinion on important matters. Disappointment and dismay may follow, then bitterness and anger. Both partners may express or act out their feelings of resentment toward each other, suffering pain and disillusionment at the sober reality of married life together. Many quarrels may result from this, and all too often the arguments become more bitter and abrasive, leading to a more or less permanent state of mutual disrespect. At best the marriage will be miserable; at worst it may end in divorce.

Often at the root of the problem between couples is their initial expectation that marriage itself will bring them happiness and bliss.

Such happiness is attainable, but it does not automatically accompany marriage. It takes conscious and continuous effort on the part of both partners to achieve it. Their relationship cannot be static. It may be compared to an airborne craft — as long as the engines are working properly it stays in the air on course; the moment they stop working, it plummets to the ground.

If both partners do not make a conscious effort to draw closer by constantly working on their marriage, that marriage, originally flying smoothly, ceases to function in the manner that it should and crashes to earth. Even marriages that have great potential and begin well often, simply because of laziness, fall apart. The partners do not give much thought to working at their marriage and vaguely expect that the initial idyllic period will continue indefinitely. However, the essence of what makes a marital relationship deep, strong, lasting, and fulfilling is how a husband and wife treat each other every day. If they are not constantly aware of the need for a continuous effort to work at their marriage and to always treat each other well, gradually, and often without being aware of it, they will begin taking their spouses for granted.

There is no dearth of potential problems that could trip them up as the marriage progresses, as a husband and wife strive to keep up with busy careers, professions or businesses, work around the home, the advent of children and the attention and responsibilities involved, and community commitment. The years of familiarity and the demands of day-to-day living — a concentration on completing the tasks required to be done each day — combined with a lack of attention to the fundamentals of their relationship take their toll, and the marriage often deteriorates. The husband and wife often simply lose sight of one another, and their individual needs for warmth, affection, communication, and shared experiences, and they neglect one another. The effect of continuous neglect is a cumulative one that contributes to a constant and increasing erosion of the marital relationship. A result of such neglect is that a couple stops respecting one another.

The Peaceful Home and the Peaceful Nation

The Sages teach: "Whoever manages to establish peace in his home is regarded by scripture as if he [were a king who] establishes peace in Israel. . . . And whoever permits jealousy and dissension to reign in his household is regarded as if he [were a king who] establishes jealousy and dissension among all Israel."[3]

The comparison of the inner working of a family to that of the larger national sphere is an appropriate one, for the mechanisms governing each differ only in their scope. A stable, peaceful society must be based, at least in part, on a solid, good family life. Peace is the major goal, and attaining domestic peace is a significant responsibility of the head of the household, just as peace in any nation is the duty of its head of state. The guidelines provided by the Sages for acquiring harmony in the Jewish home parallel the criteria for achieving peace in the nation. For the nation to be content, the leader must show respect both for his ministers and for the citizens of his realm. This respect derives in part from a just delegation of responsibility and labor as well as a fair and equitable system of reward; the citizens provide the monarch with taxes in return for his protection and vital civil services. The governing body, in addition to fostering a national feeling of security, must present a solid and united front. History has shown that great nations are weakened by internal dissension to the point of extinction. Finally, a true leader is devoted to his people, placing their well-being above his own pleasures and needs.

Each of the above factors finds its echo in the search for domestic tranquility. To the Jewish husband is given the task of establishing peace in his small domain. To do this, his highest priorities must be respect for the needs, feelings, and opinions of his wife, together with a compassionate concern for her. Implicit here is also a fair and mutually satisfactory division of duties, a system of mutual giving and particular acts manifesting genuine devotion.

Hatred and dissension are abhorrent to God. The Sages teach that the reason the Second Temple in Jerusalem was destroyed and the Jewish people subsequently exiled from their land, was because of widespread *sin'at hinam* — needless hatred of Jews among themselves.[4]

Conversely, peace and harmony are most beloved by God. The *Midrash* teaches that God found no greater blessing for His people than peace:[5] "Great is peace, for all blessings are encompassed by it. As it is written, 'May the Lord grant His people strength; may the Lord bless His people with peace.'"[6]

Ultimately, the peace of the nation of Israel itself depends on the existence of peace in its smallest social unit, the family. By the comparison of peace in the nation to that in the home, the Sages underscore both the latter's importance and the need for a detailed course of action in order to attain it. They provide behavioral specifications that serve as a practical guide to establishing and maintaining a happy, harmonious home.

A Division of Roles

For a marriage to be successful, a central principle, according to the Sages, is that a woman should both complement and constructively aid her husband. An interesting commentary in Genesis, in the section on the creation of Woman, illustrates this. The passage reads: *E'eseh lo ezer k'negdo,* "I shall make him a helpmate opposite him."[7] The Sages comment: "If he is worthy, she is *ezer,* a helpmate; if he is not worthy, she is *k'negdo,* opposite him."[8]

Underlying this is the understanding that man and woman are two very different beings who, although "opposite" in many respects, are so complementary that they can give each other completion when, through marriage, they form a single cohesive unit. Their distinctiveness can be expressed in a positive manner through complementary interaction and reciprocity. Or, it can serve as a source of abrasive friction. Where there is no clear mutual understanding by the marriage partners of the overall divisions of responsibility and of the duties devolving upon each partner, a marital relationship can easily deteriorate.

Maimonides provides some broad guidelines for the Jewish husband and wife:

> The woman is commanded to honor her husband exceedingly and to revere him and to abide by his wishes, considering him as a prince or king, fulfilling that which he wishes and rejecting what he despises. . . . The Sages commanded that a man should honor his wife more than himself and love her as he loves himself. If he has the means, he is obligated to increase her portion accordingly. He is forbidden to cause her to fear him; indeed, he must speak to her softly. And he may not be too melancholy, nor may he be quick to anger.[9]

To men and women in modern society, Maimonides' view may seem outdated and antiquated. "Who is he (or she) for me to honor him (or her)?" might well be their indignant reaction. However, such a response is inimical to the traditional Jewish understanding of how to create good, lasting relations between husband and wife.

Judaism understands that for a marriage to be built on solid foundations, it must be based upon mutual concern and interest and reciprocal giving. There must be a keen awareness by both partners of the distinct complementary role each must play in the family if it is to function smoothly as a well-oiled, efficiently functioning unit. When a Jewish couple enters the married state unaware of the role of each partner in their marriage and of their responsibilities to the family, the marriage is built on precarious foundations and is in danger of collapse.

Judaism assigns specific duties to husband and wife in relation to their separate roles in the marital partnership and to their distinctive roles in life in general. These clear role divisions, which have been hallowed by Jewish practice over the years, have contributed immeasurably to the sustenance of the cohesive Jewish family.

When Jewish traditional attitudes toward marriage are replaced by those in vogue in a particular milieu, this specifically Jewish approach of mutual respect based on an awareness of their role divisions is simultaneously rejected. Marriages founder, and divorce becomes rife. The extraordinarily high divorce rate, in recent times, among Jews distant from their heritage and traditions, bears witness to this abandonment by many Jews of the traditional Jewish approach to the marital relationship.

The Jewish idea is that a wife should honor her husband, for by so doing she proclaims her respect for that new marital superentity they have created together through marriage. It also reflects her awareness of Judaism's recognition of the husband's position as head of the household. This honoring of her husband entails neither servility nor degradation.

Conversely, a man must respect his wife in recognition of her indispensable role in the home as his partner in marriage, the mother and educator of their children, and as administrator of the household. His obligation to love her as he loves himself and to respect her more than he respects himself means that he must treat her at least as well as he treats himself. Since people are innately selfish and self-centered, it is no easy task to relate to another's needs as one's own. However, the success of the marriage depends in large measure on the man's ability to do this. It involves his working to fulfill his wife's emotional as well as her physical needs. Maimonides' idea is for each partner to place the other partner on a pedestal. Each should place the needs and concerns of his partner on a *higher* priority than his own.

Maimonides emphasizes that the Jewish guidelines for mutual honor and respect on the part of marital partners will produce tranquil and happy marriages, and he recommends that they be followed. He concludes: "This, then, is the way Jewish daughters and Jewish sons . . . behave in marriage. In this way, their lives together will be beautiful and exalted."[10]

When a man subordinates his own honor to that of his wife, this does not imply that he is inferior to her — any more than her respect for him implies her inferiority. Their mutual respect is an expression of their deference to the newly synthesized superentity they have formed by their fusion through marriage into a single cohesive unit. This marital superentity, which supersedes and transcends the power of the two as individuals, is superimposed on their own individual personalities and is represented, for each of them, in the person of the marital partner.

In order for this marital superentity to properly work, both of the partners must think in terms of "we" rather than "I." Individualism may be wonderful for establishing a business; it can wreak havoc in a marriage.

The attainment of the vital goal of domestic peace and tranquility is not left to vaguely formulated generalities. Judaism expects husband and wife to conduct themselves in a manner respectful to each other and, in this way, to create the best possible environment for the marriage.

The Jewish Wife — The Source of All Good in the Home

As wife and mother, the woman occupies a pivotal position in the Jewish home. The Sages direct their attention to her, emphasizing her importance to husband and home and their dependence upon

her. In fact, they equate her with the home itself. In The Book of
Esther, we are told that Mordecai took Esther *l'bat* — as a daughter.[11]
The *Midrash* interprets this to mean that he actually took her *l'bayit,*
literally, "as a home" — that is, he took her for his wife.[12]

In the Talmud, R. Yossi accords a similar tribute to the Jewish
woman's role in the home. R. Yossi said: "In all my days I have
never referred to my wife as *ishti,* 'my wife.' Rather, I refer to my
wife as *beyti,* 'my home.' "[13]

Wife and home, R. Yossi says, are synonymous. A man's home
is his wife, and his wife is his home. When he "comes home," he
comes to his wife. This is the way a traditional Jewish husband is
taught to relate to his wife. The Sages emphasize this idea elsewhere: "The home is not called after the man, but only after the
woman, as it is said: 'My home — that is my wife.' "[14]

The Sages acknowledge the wife as the source of all the good in
the home and caution the husband, therefore, to be ever mindful of
his obligation to honor his wife. The Talmud declares:[15] "A man
should always show the respect due to his wife, for whatever
blessings rest on a home are only on account of his wife. As it is
written, 'And because of her [Sarah], Abraham was well treated.' "[16]

R. Nahman of Bratzlav, the eighteenth-century hasidic teacher,
moralist, and mystic, says that treating one's wife well has its very
tangible rewards in this world. He says: "Honor your wife, and you
will become wealthy."[17]

The blessings of which R. Nahman speaks are material. Yet,
according to the Sages, a good wife bestows blessings upon her
household far beyond the physical; they are spiritual as well,
extending to the wife's successful intercession with heaven on behalf
of her family. The Sages teach: "A pious wife, living modestly
within her domestic circle, is like the holy altar, an atoning power
for the household."[18]

Throughout the ages, Jewish poets and philosophers have continued in this vein, waxing lyrical about the wife. They have called
her the touchstone of the Jewish family and its anchor. A source of
love, compassion, and understanding for her husband and children,
she is the one to whom they turn, to whom they confide and
unburden themselves, and by whom they are guided, soothed, and
comforted. The embodiment of feminine piety and modesty, she
occupies the epicenter of the domestic circle. Whatever other

activities involve her outside the home, within it she is serene and
secure in her role — and her family is secure in her. This relationship
is at the very core of the Jewish concept of *sh'lom bayit.* The
sixteenth/seventeenth-century ethical teacher, R. Isaiah HaLevi
Horowitz (c. 1565–1630), known as the *Sh'lah HaKadosh,* has some
hints for the Jewish wife in this connection:

> A wife should soothe her husband when he is angry, and calm him
> when he has problems. And she should console him when evil has
> befallen him. When she is worried, she should hide the worry from
> her husband so that he should not be saddened.
>
> She should dress attractively for him at all times, but she should do
> so with charm and modesty. Her clothes should always be immacu-
> lately clean. She should honor his father and his family, even should
> they be unworthy. She should rejoice in his gifts, and even if they
> should be modest she should react as if they were significant.
>
> She should pray daily for her husband to succeed in his activities.
> And she should pray for children who will attain success in Torah
> and properly observe the *mitzvot.* [19]

The advice of the *Sh'lah HaKadosh* demonstrates an acute awareness of the distinct attributes of men and women and the way in
which they complement each other. The husband is usually the
physically stronger of the two and the one who provides material
support, while the wife is perceived as the psychological pillar of
strength and support. In traditional Jewish thinking, when husband
and wife act out these roles assigned to them by their own natures,
they inevitably complement one another perfectly. Like two
matching pieces of a puzzle, they combine to form a solid, stable
unit around which a peaceful family may revolve and grow strong.

R. Samson Raphael Hirsch understands that to be the builder of
the home is a complex task requiring considerable dexterity:

> The guidance of domestic life entrusted to her hands comprises an
> abundance of seemingly minor relationships, but the wise and unwise
> handling of these can be so decisive for the comfort, prosperity, and
> happiness of the home that simple wisdom is not sufficient. Rather,
> a whole combination of knowledge, insight, abilities, and skills as
> well as moral virtue and spiritual excellence make up the art of the
> home builder. [20]

It is fashionable nowadays to denigrate the woman who stays at home as "just a housewife." A contemporary poster provides another view. Headed "The Most Creative Job in the World," it reads:

> It involves taste, fashion, decorating, recreation, education, transportation, psychology, cuisine, designing, literature, medicine, handicraft, art, horticulture, economics, government, community relations, pediatrics, geriatrics, entertainment, maintenance, purchasing, direct mail, law, accounting, religion, energy, and management. Anyone who can handle all those has to be somebody special. She is. She's a homemaker.

If marital responsibilities seem heavy today, one has only to turn to a Mishnah which lists the tasks that the wife performed in ancient times. She "ground the wheat, baked, washed the clothes, cooked, nursed the children, made the beds, and weaved wool."[21] A man was urged to provide his wife with household help if this was feasible and he could afford it, and to relieve her of most of the tasks,[22] excepting her personal obligations to her husband.[23]

The *Shevet Musar* updates the Jewish wife's responsibilities:

> She should always try to be personally spotlessly clean in her dress [when she is not working]. . . . She should maintain her home in a meticulous fashion. . . . The vessels and garments should be clean and mended. For if her husband should come home and constantly see the house untidy and the dishes and vessels unclean, etc., he will come to envy his neighbor's home and his neighbor's wife . . . And this will lead to arguments.[24]

However, in order to accomplish best her complex tasks in the home, a woman needs to be given love and appreciation. Everyone has a need to be loved and to feel appreciated, no less the wife and mother who does so much for the home and the family. A husband should, therefore, go to great lengths to compliment his wife, express his appreciation, and demonstrate his love and affection for her at every occasion and in every way he can. One must show love if one hopes to receive it.

It is often the little words of appreciation and acts of intention that are important in creating a continuous atmosphere of love and harmony in the home. A man should therefore get used to complimenting his wife for things she does: for a special dish she has prepared, for example, or when she endeavors to look particularly attractive for him. If he finds the home neat and clean, or if his wife has rearranged furniture or hung a painting or placed flowers on a table, he should be sure to remark on it.[25] An especially appropriate time to express appreciation for a wife's efforts is on the Sabbath, for it is she, as a result of her preparatory work, who is in large measure responsible for the festive Sabbath meals and the special Sabbath atmosphere in the home.

A man should take care that his compliments are sincere. However, there is indeed a place for praise of one's wife even when the praise is not completely justified by the circumstances, as a fascinating discussion in the Talmud indicates.[26]

> What does one say when dancing before the bride? The School of Shammai maintains that one should proclaim the bride's true qualities only.[27] The School of Hillel maintains that one should proclaim: "The bride is beautiful and she is graceful."
>
> Whereupon the School of Shammai said to the School of Hillel: "Do you imply that if the bride is lame or blind one should proclaim that she is beautiful and graceful? Doesn't the Torah declare 'Remove yourself from falsehood'?"[28] The School of Hillel replied: "If one made a poor purchase in the market, should he praise it or should he denounce it? Clearly he should praise it!"
>
> The Sages derive from this that a person should ever be sociable with others—tell each person what he wishes to hear.[29]

The Sages explain that one should say something that the recipient wishes to hear, even if he knowingly tells a lie.[30] The rationale is that it is really not a lie, for in the eyes of the groom, the bride is indeed beautiful and gracious.[31] The conclusion is that one may not only avoid telling the truth when it may insult or hurt someone; one is *obliged* to speak falsehood in praising one's wife if the praise is designed to create harmony and *sh'lom bayit*.[32]

It is important that a man should never leave the slightest doubt in his wife about how he feels about her. If there is one attitude in marriage that should never change, it is a husband's expression to his wife of praise and affection. It is difficult to overdo this. Through verbalizing his praise and appreciation for his wife—for example, saying things like "how happy I am to be married to someone like you" — the husband's love for her will grow and will be reflected in all his behavior toward her. In this way, their bonds of mutual love and devotion will grow ever more intense.

The Jewish Husband — His Responsibility to Provide

The husband's responsibility to support his family is regarded in Judaism as his prime obligation. This is spelled out in a significant talmudic passage which Maimonides has interpreted as legally binding:[33] "A man should always eat and drink in a manner that is less than he can afford, and he may dress and clothe himself only in accordance with his means. However, he must honor his wife and children by providing for their needs in a manner that is more than he can afford."[34]

The Sages were acutely aware of the part that money and the way it is allocated play in *sh'lom bayit.* Miserliness, they emphasize, is incompatible with a man's responsibilities to his family. While a man is directed to be conservative in spending and not to be wasteful, the Sages oblige the Jewish husband to be generous with his wife and children, even spending on them "more than he can afford." Why do the Sages demand this extra effort on his part? The goal of *sh'lom bayit,* they maintain, will be achieved by these means. The Sages teach: "A man should be most careful to properly provide food for his household, for discord in a home is often based on the [lack of] proper provision of food."[35]

The Sages are concerned that a husband be aware of his wife's sensitivity in this regard, since the daily care of the household, including the preparation and serving of meals, ultimately devolves upon the wife. The Talmud declares: "A wife, when there is no wheat in the house, begins to shout."[36]

A husband who ignores the needs of his family will make his wife feel desperate. Withholding funds for the support of his family verges on cruelty and expresses the fact that money is more important to him than is the welfare of his family. Food is an elementary need of human beings; it is also a symbol of love and security. Its absence is disturbing and is frightening to those who depend on it. When the man who can afford it fails to provide enough food and other necessities for his family, the wife, propelled by insecurity and resentment over the implicit disrespect to her and the children, will be angry and upset, and will be likely to express those feelings. Children may begin to argue over food allotments. Exasperation and indignation will mount, and *sh'lom bayit* will evaporate.

R. Isaac Aboab, writing in the *M'norat HaMo'ar* in the fourteenth century, instructs a man to be particularly sensitive to his obligations as the family provider: "Since his wife brings him both completion and blessing, it is his duty to acknowledge them. He must be particularly careful to provide for the needs of the home, for lack of provision is often the beginning of strife."[37]

A man's respect for his loved ones is reflected, in part, in the extent of his generosity toward them. Consequently, the Sages advise the husband not to be overly exacting in his supervision of the household expenses.[38] For example, he should not demand from his wife an accounting of her financial management of the home,[39] but should allow her considerable independence in this area.[40] This applies even to a husband who is punctilious in providing for household expenditures. The Sages add that if a woman is given this freedom to manage her household, she will do it in a thrifty manner.[41]

The Sages teach that a man should also provide his wife with her own discretionary funds, in accordance with her husband's means and social standing,[42] to spend as she wishes.

The Sages advise that a married couple's possessions should be jointly owned,[43] and bank accounts jointly controlled.[44] A man's relationship with his wife is governed by the principle, incorporated into Jewish law, of *ishto k'gufo,* she is like his own body.[45]

Making a Wife Happy

Many injunctions to the Jewish husband by the Sages on how to behave toward his wife are based on a talmudic passage in Tractate *Y'vamot:* "He who loves his wife as himself and honors her more than himself . . . of him scripture says, 'And you shall know that your tent shall be a peaceful one.' "[46]

The Polish rabbinic scholar, R. Shlomo Eger (1786–1852), the

MaHarsha comments: " 'And honors her more than himself'—that is to say that he dresses her with clothes more honorable than his own."[47]

The *MaHarsha* bases his comment upon another talmudic statement: "Women take priority over men in dress."[48] Therefore, even if a man dresses shabbily, he is still required to provide fine clothing for his wife.[49]

Generally speaking, women are more concerned about their appearance and dress than are men. Since a woman's wardrobe is more elaborate than a man's, a woman requires a considerable number of garments in a variety of style and colors. A man's need for clothing is considerably less than his wife's. A man should, therefore, be sensitive to the fact that his wife's need for attractive clothing is greater than his, and requires a greater expenditure.

The Talmud declares: *Ishah baalah m'samhah*—A husband must give his wife joy.[50] *Rashi* and *Tosafot* comment that the joy to which the Talmud refers includes buying her colorful (that is, attractive) clothes. It is incumbent upon the husband to satisfy his wife's need for beautiful clothes.[51] The Sages specify the minimum quantities for the fulfillment of this obligation.[52] In addition to these minimums, the husband is required to buy his wife new clothes in honor of each festival and at the beginning of every winter and summer.[53] If he can afford it, and her situation warrants it, he is even obliged to dress her in "fine silks and costly embroidered dresses."[54] Jewish law stipulates that if a husband does not willingly provide his wife with the clothing due her, the Jewish court may compel him to do so.

The evidence suggests, however, that compulsion in this respect rarely had to be resorted to among traditional Jews. The philosopher-historian Will Durant, writing about the medieval period, relates:

> When the King of Castile banned finery in raiment, the Jewish males obeyed, but continued to array their wives in splendor. When the king demanded an explanation, they assured him that the royal gallantry could never have meant the restriction to apply to women. And the Jews continued throughout the Middle Ages to robe their ladies well.[55]

Some of the Sages add to the husband's requirement to provide his wife with "fine raiment," also food and drink, "since they are a joy to the body and are for her honor. . . ."[56] Indeed, Jewish law obliges the husband to provide wine for his wife at meals if this is customary or if she has been accustomed to this before her marriage, as this is included in the category of "a joy to the body and for her honor."[57]

The Sages also express an acute awareness of a woman's inner need to surround herself with objects that are aesthetically satisfying to her. The *Midrash* declares that the woman enjoys a fine home "decorated with pictures."[58] "She longs for these,"[59] say the Sages. The Sages thus express a keen understanding of some of the significant features and fundamental components of the psychological structure of the woman. They add: "Depriving a woman of the decorative is an embarrassment for her."[60]

In addition, women generally enjoy decorative jewelry. Although some men may consider jewelry as superfluous and even an unnecessary extravagance, the need women have for it is intrinsic.[61] R. Jacob Mollin (c. 1365–1427) of Germany, known as the *MaHaril*, writes, "It is virtually impossible for a woman to do without jewelry."[62]

The Sages explain that a woman requires jewelry in order to enhance her feminine nature: "A woman is drawn after jewelry.[63] Indeed, a woman is not a woman without jewelry."[64]

R. Elijah, the *Gaon* of Vilna (1720–1797), comments: "Jewelry brings out the beauty of a woman."[65] According to the *Gaon*, Jewish men, in the past, would choose jewelry for their wives designed to correspond symbolically to their inner qualities. In reference to the passage in Proverbs, "For they shall be a graceful garland about your head and a chain around your neck,"[66] the Vilna *Gaon* writes:

> In those days men would have jewelry fashioned for their wives to correspond to their deeds . . . and they would design and create primarily two kinds of jewelry, a tiara for the head and a necklace pendant to hang from the neck. The tiara would be [on the head] for the woman who was wise, and the pendant [falling above the heart] would be for the woman who would perform deeds of loving kindness. The tiara would be made of a single piece, corresponding to the wisdom, which is a single unit, and the pendant would be made up of many pieces, corresponding to her many good deeds, each of which is a *mitzvah* by itself.[67]

Far from merely idly speculating on the subject, the Sages' discussions actually determine the degree of a man's legal responsibility toward his wife. Their conclusions were incorporated into Jewish law. Maimonides, for example, in his code, obligates a man to provide his wife with jewelry.[68]

Commenting on the husband's requirements to love his wife as himself and to honor her more than himself.[69] *Rashi* explains this additional "honor" as referring to adorning his wife with "beautiful jewelry."[70] The Sages teach:

> For it is indeed difficult to understand how it is possible to honor his wife more than his own self when he is only required to love her as himself. However, if the desire of a woman and her great need for jewelry and to display it is understood by her husband, he will obligate himself to fulfill his wife's heart's desire to the utmost, even if his love for her is only as for his own self . . . for that which is a natural need to a person is like bread and butter to that individual . . . [Fulfilling her need] is not optional [for the husband], but is mandatory.[71]

Adorning Herself — A Woman's Obligation

Not only is a man required by Jewish law to provide his wife with jewelry and cosmetics, but it is obligatory for a woman to look attractive[72] — although she is cautioned not to wear flamboyant jewelry that draws excessive attention to herself.[73]

A woman who did not take care of her appearance was admonished.[74] The medieval German halachic authority R. Meir ben Baruch, the *MaHaram* of Rothenburg (c. 1215–1293), severely condemns women who, after they are married, neglect themselves: "Let a curse descend upon a woman who has a husband and does not strive to look attractive."[75]

The severity of this invective undoubtedly stems from the *MaHaram*'s opinion that such neglect on the woman's part can lead to marital discord. The Talmud mentions that Ezra the Scribe, who helped rebuild the Temple following the Babylonian Exile, convened a special rabbinical court to pass a law requiring clothing shop owners to visit populated areas to ensure that Jewish women had access to their products.[76]

Scripture tells of the construction of the copper basin for the Tabernacle, smelted from the copper handmirrors of Jewish women.[77] *Rashi's* commentary quotes a fascinating *midrash:*

> The daughters of Israel had, in their hands, mirrors which they would use when they were decorating themselves, and even these they did not hold back [and brought them to the Tent of Meeting to contribute to the construction of the Tabernacle and its vessels]. These mirrors were distasteful to Moses because their use was intended as a means for a woman to excite sexual desire.
>
> The Holy One, Blessed be He, said to Moses: "Accept them, for these mirrors are dearer to Me than everything. For through them the women caused the multiplication of many hosts of Jews in Egypt." When their husbands would return home at night weary from the back-breaking slave work, the women would bring them food and drink and feed them. Then they would take out their mirrors, and standing by their husbands would gaze into them. Seeing their images, each woman would say to her husband "See, I am prettier than you!" In this way they would excite their husbands who would desire them; they would have relations, and the women would conceive and bear children.[78]

R. Samson Raphael Hirsch comments that the use of these mirrors for the Tabernacle vessels emphasizes that human sensuality, too, was included in the sphere of sanctification provided by the Tabernacle. Indeed, says R. Hirsch, "It is the first and most essential object of this sanctification."[79]

Even if a husband has simple tastes, he must still be sensitive to his wife's taste and to her need for a pleasant home and attractive clothing and jewelry. Although these may be far removed from his own interests, her wishes in this area take precedence over his.

In which areas do the husband's wishes prevail? In matters of Jewish law and custom; he is to guide the spiritual life and religious conduct of his wife. The Bulgarian rabbi and scholar R. Eliezer Papo (c. 1760–1824) writes in the *Pele Yo'etz:*

> A man is obliged to guide his wife in a pleasant manner in the proper ways of modesty [in dress and behavior] and in the laws relating to gossip, slander, and anger . . . and to caution her regarding the details of the *mitzvot,* and especially the prayers and the benedictions,

as well as the proper observance of the Sabbath laws. It is especially
praiseworthy for the husband to convey to his wife the Jewish ethical
and moral teachings of the Sages in all matters which might relate to
her.[80]

By awakening her religious awareness, the husband is perceived
as benefitting not only his wife, but his children and the whole
atmosphere in the home. Her spirit and attitude toward home-
making and childraising depend upon her religious and moral
orientation, and husbands and wives are advised to set aside time
for Torah study together.[81]

Take a Wife's Counsel

When a woman speaks to her husband, he should endeavor to give
her his full attention, even if it means putting everything else aside.
Since he lives with her, it is easy to neglect this. He should bear in
mind that he owes her at least the same respect he gives others when
they speak, and just as he would not affront others by not listening
attentively, he should not affront her. If a man's attitude to his wife,
who devotes her time and energies to home and family, is in essence:
"What does she have to talk about with me—dirty diapers, the price
of eggs in the market?" he must know that if those are the things that
are part of her life and are important to her, he should indeed listen
attentively to her when she discusses them—as should she listen
when her husband speaks to her of his activities. Couples who have
close, warm relationships talk to each other constantly about the
other's interests and continue to find each other interesting.
    A frequent problem busy married couples encounter is the virtual
cessation of meaningful communication between them. Discussing
important issues while one is deep in a newspaper or the other is
concentrating on a household activity results in a lack of genuine
communication and reflects rudeness, disrespect, and a totally
uncaring attitude.
    Regularly taking time out to simply talk with one another, about
anything and everything, is a rewarding experience and is a
distinguishing characteristic of a good marriage. Discussions need
not be limited to the usual, i.e., work, the household, children,—

indeed, too much attention to these might only exacerbate a communications problem. Conversations should encompass a wide range of topics, similar to their discussions early in married life. A good idea is, where feasible, for husband and wife to go out for a walk by themselves for such discussions.

A husband is expected, as an expression of his respect for her, to consult constantly with his wife and to seek her advice and counsel.[82] Even should he be spiritually and intellectually superior, he must still strive to find a common language with his wife so that they might arrive jointly at decisions. The Talmud makes this clear in a succinct directive written in Aramaic: "*It'cha gutza g'hin v'tilhosh lah* — Even if your wife is short, bend down and whisper to her" [that is, consult with her].[83]

The Sages point to a *midrash* relating that Abraham, who was wealthy, was successful in his affairs only because he followed his wife's advice.[84]

The talmudic Sage, R. Elazar ben Azarya (first/second century C.E.), when offered the exalted position of *nasi*, ethnarch of Israel, did not immediately accept the high honor. He requested permission to consult with his wife first.[85]

The reason Judaism insists that a man consult with his wife even if she is less knowledgeable than he, is that, as the Talmud tells us, a woman possesses superior discernment and intuitive powers exceeding the objective extent of her knowledge.[86]

R. M'nahem HaM'iri, the thirteenth-century French commentator on the Talmud, emphasizes the obligation of the husband to acquiesce in his wife's decisions concerning the home: "Every man is required to follow his wife's advice regarding the needs of the household and the maintenance of the children. If this is done, there will be *sh'lom bayit*."[87]

R. M'iri takes it for granted that a husband will *consult* his wife regarding decisions on these matters. His directive to the husband here is that he *follow* his wife's advice when she gives it.

However, a man is not expected to consult with his wife merely on household matters; his obligation extends to other areas as well. The contemporary scholar and ethical teacher, R. Joseph Epstein, points out that, to fulfill his obligations to honor his wife more than himself, a man must confer with her in all matters of significance: "To be listened to on matters relating to the household is not much of an honor; he manifests proper respect for her if he consults her on general matters."[88]

Moreover, a husband is told to go out of his way to solicit his wife's opinion, even if he is certain that her counsel will contradict his own thinking on the matter.[89] Even if he sees no need for her advice, he is still required to consult with her as a sign of his courtesy and honor for her.[90]

The earliest precedent for this type of consultation is in Genesis where we learn that God consulted with his angels before creating man.[91] Obviously, the Creator had no need of their help; the consultation was all for their honor and benefit. In the case of the married couple, however, the husband may benefit much more than he anticipates. As R. Epstein puts it: "In truth . . . it is not because of the honor he owes her, and not even because of *sh'lom bayit* [that a man is obligated to consult with his wife on all matters]. Rather, it is simply excellent advice for a man to take if he truly wishes to succeed."[92]

If a man is successful because of his wife's counsel, she may bask in the success and enjoy its gains. However, if he fails, the Talmud says that he fails alone, following the halachic principle that a wife rises with her husband's success but does not descend with his failure.[93]

Economic Problems in a Marriage

If a man finds himself in straitened circumstances and fears that he will be unable to provide for his wife, he is cautioned to be discreet with her. He has to consider whether an open discussion of his affairs will embarrass him and cause her to look down on him.[94]

Domestic peace and harmony are, under certain circumstances, elevated even above truth. The Talmud teaches: "Great is peace — for in its cause even the Holy One, Blessed be He, deviated from the truth."[95]

In this case, the peace of mind of a loved one and *sh'lom bayit* take precedence over a free exchange of information. R. Elijah Ha-Cohen Itamari (d. 1729) offers guidance to the woman when her husband is having financial difficulties. He writes in *Shevet Musar:*

> If it should appear that he is under considerable financial pressure, she should refrain from excessive probing, even if it relates to the

household. . . . Rather, she should pray for divine compassion for her husband. . . . She should make the effort to constantly display a pleasant demeanor and strengthen him with optimistic hopes. And she should proclaim to him, "My love for you is [not dependent upon your financial condition; it is] an eternal love." And when a husband perceives his wife's love even during a period when he lacks everything, joy will enter his heart and cause his worry to leave him. This will provide the impetus he needs to propel him forward to find the solution to his problems.[96]

Aware of the problems that could arise, the Sages were concerned with the economic factor in a marriage. When a wife desires greater material wealth than her husband is able to provide, they say the marriage can be seriously undermined. The *Pele Yo'etz* counsels:

A woman must be sensitive to the possibility that her husband is not quite as economically well-off as she may have believed, and he is embarrassed to inform her of his true financial condition lest her esteem of him be lowered. . . . She should, therefore, refrain from pressuring him to undertake expenditures which may be beyond his means. And if at times he appears to be unreasonably vexed, she should consider the possibility that he is reacting in this manner because things went badly for him in the market . . . and she should be patient with him and try not to upset him.[97]

If a woman is disappointed over her husband's financial situation, it is best for her to control her feelings, to avoid interrogating him excessively about financial affairs, and criticizing his ability to provide adequately. For the sake of *sh'lom bayit,* love, and compassion, she should come to the fore to sustain her husband, even if it means her temporarily putting aside her own needs.

Friendship — The Core of a Good Marriage

A couple who have a happy, successful marriage generally have established a relationship of genuine friendship with each other. Each is the other's best friend. The prophet Malachi refers to a wife as "your friend (companion) and the wife of your covenant."[98] Just as friends enjoy sharing interests and experiences together, so too should married couples make every effort to do things together so as to build a close friendship. A marriage where husband and wife are good friends is a happy marriage.

Since a good friendship has to be based on honesty and openness, a husband and wife should be honest with one another and have no secrets from each other. However, it is unwise to burden one another with unnecessary negative emotions and worries. It is best, when conveying adverse information, to employ discretion.

To achieve a true and lasting *sh'lom bayit* requires a delicate balance between sharing and withholding. Husband and wife are encouraged to discuss their feelings freely in order to grow closer, but they are warned about losing all restraint and causing unnecessary pain or worry to one another. When one partner senses that the other is unhappy, it is his or her task discreetly to guess at or gently probe the other's feelings.

The Danger of Anger in a Marriage

Solomon declares in Ecclesiastes: "Be not hasty in spirit to anger, for anger rests in the bosom of fools."[99]

The Sages add that the angry person is not only foolish, but disrespectful to God: "An angry man is indifferent to the Divine Presence. . . . He forgets Torah and becomes exceedingly foolish."[100]

The *Mishnah* speaks of various types of anger:

If a person is easily provoked but is easy to pacify, his loss is counterbalanced by his gain. If one is not provoked to anger easily but is difficult to pacify when he does become angry, his gain is counterbalanced by his loss. If an individual is not easily provoked to anger, but when he occasionally does become angry he is easily pacified, he is a saint. If a person is provoked to anger easily and is not easily pacified, he is wicked.[101]

The Talmud remarks: "Anger in the home is like a worm among sesame seeds."[102]

Anyone who has ever lived in close proximity to a bellicose personality knows its destructive potential. Anger pervades the environment, bringing distress to one's spouse and discord to the household. R. Isaac Magriso (c. 1700-1760), the Turkish scholar, speaks of its harmful ramifications:

> When a person loses his temper . . . he hates himself and is hated by those around him. The members of his household are strangers to him . . . He does not recognize his father or mother and can actually dishonor and mistreat them. . . . He dishonors all who are around him. He must beg them to pardon him; and when he is pardoned he remains ashamed of what he did.[103]

The angry man forgets the Torah, loses control of his faculties, and is no longer influenced by reason, the Sages declare: "Whoever is enraged is under the control of the hellish forces."[104] "Anger is tantamount to idol worship because it is evidence of the Satanic force."[105]

The Talmud states: "Whoever rends his garment or breaks his vessel in wrath, or whoever throws away money in anger should be viewed as an idol worshipper."[106]

In Judaism, the stifling of anger is highly revered. The Sages find that a person is forgiven his transgressions if he overcomes his inclination to anger and acts magnanimously. On the other hand, the Talmud teaches that anger clouds one's judgment and results in serious errors.[107] The Sages point to major errors in judgment made by Moses on several occasions when he acted while he was angry.[108]

At times, even ordinarily calm people may find themselves driven to anger by someone else's behavior. The ethical teachers point out that the true test of a person's character is if he can consistently control his words and behavior even in such a difficult situation.[109] They add that one can learn what a person is really like by how he reacts when he is angry.[110] *Orhot Tzadikim*, the fifteenth-century German ethical work, carries this thought a step further and advises anyone about to marry or to establish some other close relationship with a person, to observe that individual when he or she becomes angry.[111] Indeed, it may be advisable for a person contemplating marriage to put his potential partner to the test in this respect.

The Sages consider a person who is easily angered to be insensitive to others and not compassionate, and to be highly vulnerable to violations of numerous Torah commandments.[112]

Such a person, when someone acts against his wishes, can easily lose control over his emotions and commit all sorts of transgressions. Unable to use reason, he is considered to have descended to the level of a wild beast. Since he cannot restrain himself, his anger is regarded by the Sages as akin to idolatry.[113]

Although a husband is regarded as the prime authority in the Jewish home, he may never abuse that right by autocratic bullying or tyrannical behavior. The passage in Maimonides about a wife regarding her husband as a prince or king is followed by the directive to the husband to love his wife and honor her. The Talmud teaches that one who imposes fear, disregarding the moral boundaries of emotional interaction, will be led to cross other moral boundaries as well. "He who causes excessive fear to fall upon his household will eventually violate three transgressions: that of the biblically prohibited incest laws, the spilling of blood, and the desecration of the Sabbath."[114]

A husband who is angered is at times driven by disillusionment that his wife is not the perfect, faultless woman he had originally imagined. Such a man should be aware that he too is not perfect, and yet his wife bears his faults and is committed to him. His commitment to her should be no less strong, and he should respect her all the more when he realizes what she does for him despite his shortcomings.

The Sages warn against being unreasonably jealous of one's spouse.[115] Such jealousy will cause the marriage to deteriorate and must be taken very seriously. If necessary, a rabbi or a marriage counselor should be called upon. Every couple needs to grow to accept that what each possesses belongs to the other as well, be it wealth, attainments, or social standing, and it is in the other's interest to promote his spouse's well-being and to take pride in his or her accomplishments.

The Sages counsel a man to refrain from expressing anger toward his wife: "Never become angry with your wife. If you put her off with your left hand, hurry and draw her back with your right."[116]

A man who refrains from becoming angry with his wife is substantially rewarded. The Talmud relates that R. Ada bar Ahavah attributed his long life to his never having allowed himself to be provoked by his wife.[117]

Handling Anger through Self-Restraint

Every effort should be made to avoid dissension, since each quarrel contributes to the erosion of the marriage. It takes two to quarrel. If one responds to harsh words with silence, aggressiveness will be warded off. The flame of discord that is ignited will not develop into a conflagration without the fuel needed to keep it alight; thus the fire soon burns out. The Talmud teaches:[118]

> Those who allow themselves to be insulted but do not reply in kind, and those who allow others to shame them and do not respond — they act as they do out of love [for God and for his command to love one's fellow] and [because they thereby fulfill God's command] they rejoice in their plight. Of them scripture says: "And let those who love Him be as the sun when it comes out in its might."[119]

Excessive pride and lack of humility are often the cause of anger; indeed, the Sages consider haughtiness and anger related traits.[120] When a person feels his ego threatened by another, he will often turn upon that individual and unleash his anger upon him. To learn humility requires overcoming the urge to respond to real or imagined affronts and keeping silent when provoked. The Sages emphasize frequently the transcendent value of stoic silence in the face of provocation.

The qualities required to channel one's anger are, in essence, the same as those required to maintain domestic peace: mutual respect and understanding, patience, compassion, and self-control.

Modern marriage counseling often advocates a free expression of angry feelings on the grounds that keeping feelings locked in is bad for the marriage. Deciding that it is unhealthy to practice self-control and restraint, or that they are unattainable, marriage counselors often teach the popular system that is known as "fair fighting." However, angry words, while temporarily making one feel better, have a tendency to feed upon themselves and to grow out of proportion.

Judaism aims higher. Rather than learning how to fight and express anger in a minimally destructive manner, husband and wife are directed instead to control and constructively channel their anger. They are always to be aware of the necessity for mutual respect and restraint, and to utilize that awareness to develop and improve the communication lines between them.

Judaism prescribes patience and thoughtfulness as preventative measures. Those who are patient in the face of provocation, says the *Zohar*, "are the emissaries of righteousness."[121]

Maimonides obliges a man to speak to his wife softly and to be slow to anger.[122] Even if he is strongly tempted to raise his voice in response to stubbornness, he should make the extra effort and refrain from doing so. Scripture teaches: "A soft tongue breaks the bond."[123] An angry response, however, will only provoke further anger. "A grievous word stirs up wrath," explains Solomon.[124] The way to deflect anger, however, is to reply softly. As Solomon teaches in Proverbs, "A soft answer turns away wrath."[125]

The Sages advise practicing silence as a means of stifling the anger within oneself. *Orhot Tzadikim* teaches:

> Silence nullifies anger. Speaking softly also nullifies anger. When a man perceives that he is becoming angry, he should therefore be silent or speak softly; under no circumstances should he raise his voice in anger, for if he does so he will only arouse further anger. He should also not look directly while speaking to someone who is angry with him, but rather speak to him without looking directly at him. If he does so, the other will cease being angry.[126]

A frequent cause of marital discord is the husband's criticism of his wife. Whether or not the criticism is justified—a lapse of one kind, a task not performed or improperly executed, or forgetfulness—if the incident is not kept in proportion, but is exaggerated or becomes a means to score points in a competition over who errs more frequently, a serious disagreement may ensue. A critical comment, even when justified, can provoke a defensive response or a reference to previous lapses on the husband's part. Other incidents or criticisms, no matter how trivial, may then be added to the scoreboard, the arguments may become more and more exacerbated and abrasive, and the situation may eventually lead to a major crisis.

The way to defuse, from the start, such potentially explosive situations is to accentuate the positive and to minimize the negative.

On his arrival home, a husband should consider complimenting his wife on something she has done or on the way she looks, or on something she says. If he wants to raise an issue with her that entails criticism, he should first reflect on how he might do so in a way that most spares her feelings. His wife may have had a difficult day dealing with the children, the household, or her own work, and therefore a reproof, even if justified but improperly delivered, might trigger an adverse reaction.

If criticism must be conveyed, therefore, it should be done in a positive, constructive way, and in as subtle a manner as possible. It is best for him to address the particular situation that requires attention rather than to attack his wife or her character. Showing sensitivity to his wife's feelings is more likely to produce a positive response than will a direct frontal attack. Most importantly, the criticism should be voiced calmly, quietly, and in a gentle manner, to avoid hurting his wife's feelings and to make it clear to her that his love for her is uppermost.

By the same token, it is equally true that a woman can cause a quarrel by criticizing her husband, either through doing so in an insensitive way or at an inappropriate time.

Anger, as mentioned earlier, is frequently the result of injured pride. It is often a reaction to what the person who is reproved perceives as an insult. Strange as it may seem, most people like to see themselves as faultless. Intellectually, they realize that no one is perfect, and they are not perfect, but when criticized for personal shortcomings they react as if they have received a slap in the face. It is as if acceptance of criticism is an acknowledgment that they are less than perfect. Their reaction is therefore impelled by a desire to save face at all costs. Consequently, someone who is criticized may immediately move into an offensive position and charge the other person with worse faults and mistakes made on previous occasions, beside which the situation at hand pales in comparison. A quarrel results.

This situation need not happen. If the criticism is unjustified, the best approach is to sit down quietly and calmly point out why it is not justified. One might add that since the other person feels it is justified, perhaps something might be done in the future to prevent such a misunderstanding from recurring. If the reproof is warranted, all that is required is to respond: "I'm sorry — it won't happen again." This formula, which is simple, almost always prevents a quarrel from developing. However, it requires a certain maturity to acknowledge error, to accept responsibility, and to understand that such an admission need not entail a simultaneous loss of pride. God set the example. The prophet Jeremiah quotes God as saying: "I will forgive their iniquity, and I will no longer remember their sin."[127] Forgive and forget — that is the divine example. Apologizing and asking for forgiveness is the way to assure the satisfactory termination of the situation. Forgiving is the ultimate healer.

The Art of Avoiding Quarrels

One of the hallmarks of a good marital relationship is not constant agreement, or the absence of disagreement, but rather the ability to calmly discuss and work out disagreements in ways that are reasonably satisfactory to both parties. The way to avoid quarrels is to discuss difficulties and problems freely and openly and try to work them out. This is the best way to stop anger and resentment from building up. The Sages urge couples to make every effort to ensure, when they tackle a problem, that an exchange of views does not deteriorate into an angry quarrel. Husband and wife should practice the art of peaceful, calm discussion — allowing the other to have his say, responding calmly, and avoiding angry, abusive tones.

The couple should try to limit themselves to the specific issue under discussion and not to range widely. No matter what one partner says, the other should stay with the issue at hand. They should not turn to other problematic issues. Moreover, they should not go to past problems. They should confine themselves to the present and not dredge up ancient history, with one partner seeking to gain the upper hand by referring to previous, unrelated incidents. In this way, every argument neither becomes a continuation of the one before nor a prelude to the next one.

Both partners should assiduously avoid insulting remarks about the other that could arouse the other's anger. Each spouse knows the pressure points and weaknesses of the other, the references that are sure to hurt the partner, and is aware that their use is sure to elicit an intemperate response. The prudent spouse will refrain from doing what the other partner is sure to interpret as a deliberate invitation to escalate the level of the quarrel.

Similarly, while arguing, the threat of divorce should never be used. On the contrary: both should be constantly aware that they have a mutual commitment to making their marriage work and to staying married. The threat of divorce — even the implied threat — is proof positive of insufficient commitment. Although divorce certainly exists as an avenue of escape from an impossible marriage, it should be considered only as the very last resort — a step that should be avoided and seriously contemplated only when there is absolutely no alternative. The threat of divorce by a marital partner during quarrels will only facilitate the possibility that the situation will deteriorate to the point where pride may make it appear to be the only viable alternative.

In a tense situation, the chief priority is often to soothe ruffled feelings. This involves replying calmly, tactfully, and with sensitivity, and not assuming a defensive stance. A momentary distraction or a light joke in the midst of a difficult discussion can ease the tension and convert a charged atmosphere into a more relaxed one, more conducive to calm discussion. In fact, a sense of humor is an important factor in preventing arguments from getting out of hand. Those couples who can look at the subject of their disagreement and laugh at it will surely be reconciled.

However, humor should be gentle and should not be at the expense of one's partner. When a husband or wife teases the other about an area in which the other is sensitive, or the spouse is put down under the guise of being funny, this can only exacerbate matters. Such "joking" is a reflection of underlying hostility or even a desire to punish the other. A marital partner should not be diminished in any way, through humor or otherwise.

The tendency of some marital partners to belittle their spouses often comes to the fore at social gatherings. When a husband and a wife are with others, the spouses sometimes vie with each other for attention, each trying to tell a particular story or joke better than the other, with the result being the diminution of the other before others. With patience and respect for a marital partner, the spouse can *reinforce* the partner by selective comments. Where one partner is left out of a group discussion, a spouse can bring the partner in by asking a question that will allow the partner to make a comment of interest to the group.

A couple who must argue should always do so privately, never in public. They should also take pains to avoid quarreling in front of their children. Numerous psychological studies have shown that children, when their parents quarrel, experience bewilderment, frustration, and deep guilt. These become psychic scars that are difficult to heal. Children are great imitators, and in a home where husband and wife quarrel frequently, fights between siblings, as well as parent-child conflicts, are likely to be rife.

Probably the best way to terminate a quarrel is to apologize. The adage that "love means never having to say you're sorry" sounds like a nice ideal. However, it is simply untrue, and it does not work.

No one is perfect, yet many people have a false pride and find it difficult, or even impossible, to admit that they err, and they never do so. It is a sign of personal strength to recognize and acknowledge error or, when aware of having hurt another's feelings, to sincerely say "I'm sorry."

Indeed, a spouse, in order to put an end to a quarrel, can even apologize when he knows he is not at fault. In any event, for the apology to achieve its purpose, it has to be conveyed wholeheartedly and not in a perfunctory or sullen manner. The idea is to make peace as soon as possible, and not to allow the dissonance to fester. It is preferable, for an apology to be effective, that it be given in specific, not general, terms.

Giving in, even when one is right, is sometimes the best method to defuse tension. In fact, a good practice for couples to consider is for them to agree that the spouse who knows he is right always should be the first to give in. In an effort to assure *sh'lom bayit* in a new household, one Sage advised a bridegroom to give in to his wife the first ten times after their marriage. "From then on," he told the groom, "you will never have to give in to her again; she will always give in to you."[128] In a similar vein, a wise woman counseled her daughter on the day of her wedding, "Act toward him as his servant, and he will behave toward you as a slave."[129]

The Obligation of Mutual Courtesy

Judaism teaches that husband and wife should be polite to each other at all times, never forgetting to use with each other those elementary social courtesies that they use with all their other acquaintances and that they used with each other when they were courting. It is extremely difficult to have a good relationship with anyone, *especially* with a spouse, without good manners and basic courtesies. Between husband and wife, small courtesies, such as saying "please" and "thank you" or opening a door for the other, and the use of all terms of politeness associated with proper civil behavior, should not be dispensed with as being unnecessarily formal. On the contrary, their use indicates respect, consideration, sensitivity, and appreciation for the other. They are all ways of saying, "I'm always aware of you and I care. I do not take you for granted."

Courtesy and good manners convey sensitivity to another's needs and concerns, as well as an awareness of the impact of decent personal behavior on others. A good rule to follow is for a person to treat his spouse like a stranger — in the positive sense. It means simply that one should be as polite to his partner in life as he is to the total stranger. Politeness is no less a virtue in marriage than in life in general.

Maimonides teaches that a man must go to great lengths to relate to his wife with courtesy and gentleness.[130] The Talmud expresses a keen awareness of a woman's sensitivity: "A man should always be careful not to hurt his wife's feelings, because a woman cries easily and is quick to hurt."[131]

The Mishnah states that on the Sabbath eve a man is required to remind his wife of the three duties she is required to do prior to the onset of the Sabbath.[132] The Talmud declares: "Even though the Sages teach that a man should say those three things, he should be sure to state them softly, so that she should be receptive to his reminder."[133]

In fact, this is an excellent rule for any husband or wife to follow in relation to any reminders one may wish to make to the other.

Even when a man is justifiably upset, Judaism obliges him to behave toward his wife at all times in a kind and patient manner. When R. Israel Meir Kagan, the nineteenth/early twentieth-century Sage known as the *Hafetz Hayim,* remarried in his old age, for Sukot he built his *sukah* in the place he had done so in previous years. When he had completed it, his wife commented: "I don't think this place is suitable for a *sukah.*" Whereupon the elderly — and very busy — rabbi quickly took down the *sukah* and rebuilt it. When she saw the rebuilt *sukah* in its new location, his wife decided that the original location was more suitable after all. Whereupon the *Hafetz Hayim* patiently took the *sukah* down again and put it up for the third time, this time in its original place.[134]

When a man asks his wife to give him something, he is required to address her in a pleasant manner, never in an arrogant, demanding or demeaning fashion.

The Little Things that Count

In an earlier chapter, the importance of *hesed,* acts of love that a man must perform throughout his life to fulfill the Golden Rule, was mentioned, and the idea that *hesed* begins at home was conveyed. First and foremost, a man must perform *hesed* for his wife.

We have said that Judaism views the married state as a means provided by God to remove man from his selfish, self-centered state and become concerned with another person's welfare. Every time a person gives to his spouse, he demonstrates this in a concrete manner. Everyone likes to receive gifts. Furthermore, the giver becomes endeared to the recipient for being so thoughtful, for taking the time and making the effort to express love and appreciation. The giver takes pleasure, as well, in the joy his gift has brought.

It is important, therefore, for a spouse to remember dates significant to the two of them, such as birthdays and anniversaries, and to commemorate them in ways that will please the other. A man should remember to give gifts to his wife. They need not be costly, because the gifts themselves represent love and attention. Gifts or flowers are tangible expressions of a man's love for his wife and reflect his appreciation for all that she is to him and all that she does for him. The Talmud relates that when R. Hiya was asked why he always brought his wife presents even though she was constantly tormenting him, he replied: "It is enough that they rear our children and deliver us from sin!"[135]

When his affairs take him away from home, a Jewish man is advised to be especially thoughtful to his wife, sending her gifts and returning home with a gift. When he is traveling, he should, by telephoning and writing, keep in frequent touch with his wife. Jewish law considers this of such great importance that it provides a special dispensation, allowing a person to write to his wife during *Hol HaMoed,* the intermediate days of Passover and Sukot, when writing is normally avoided.[136]

A gift need not be limited to such occasions. Surprise gifts add an element of unexpected excitement to what might ordinarily be dull routine. A thoughtful husband or wife will pick up little gifts for the spouse from time to time, simply to indicate love and caring.

In addition, a man must invest all that he does for his wife with *hesed;* that is, when he performs an act for her or presents her with a gift, he must do so in the manner of *hesed,* in a kindly, affectionate way. *How* one does something in marriage is therefore often as important as what one does. The gifts are not, in and of themselves, a goal; they are material symbols of altruistic love and devotion for which a wife yearns.

A man may, therefore, provide his wife with generous support, maintenance, and all kinds of beautiful things, but if he does so grudgingly and in an unpleasant manner, he has not fulfilled his obligation toward her. The Sages determine this from a talmudic saying: "A man may give his father the finest foods to eat, but at the same time drive him from this world because of the manner in which he does so."[137]

A couple should eat together. The dinner table should be devoted to regular intimate family gatherings. It is no place for a newspaper, books, or television. The dinner table is not just for eating. It is both a symbol of and the practical center of the togetherness of husband and wife and the other members of the family. It should not be used by husband and wife for arguing, or for amplifying disagreements, or for disciplining children.

A Woman's Need for Outside Interests

A man should encourage his wife to have interests outside the home. While traditional Judaism perceives the ideal of the woman as centered in the home, it also recognizes that a woman can become too involved in the home to the exclusion of other abilities, talents, and interests; this is detrimental to her well-being and to that of her household. The husband is advised of the danger of denigrating his wife by associating her only with home activities. The ethical teacher R. Shlomo Wolbe admonishes: "*Oi v'avoi*—Woe to the woman—and to her husband!—to whom such less significant things [as housework] serves as the total contents of her life!"[138]

A husband should also show an interest and involvement in his wife's outside interests, equal at least to what he shows toward her home activities.

The Dual Obligation of *Sh'lom Bayit*

The husband is obliged to strive for *sh'lom bayit.* The wife has fewer formal requirements but, obviously, it is equally in her interest to work toward this goal. The perceptive wife, though she might be tireless, is nevertheless more subtle in the task of establishing *sh'lom bayit* in her home. R. Isaac Aboab relates, in the *M'norat HaMa'or.*[139]

> A wise woman said to her bride-daughter as she accompanied her to her groom: "My daughter, if you will respect him as you would a king and act toward him as a servant-girl, he will behave toward you as a slave and honor you as a queen. However, if you will be over-proud, he will assert his mastery by force, and he will consider you as a maid-servant."
>
> If your husband will visit his friends, ascertain that he be properly attired in fine raiment. And if his relatives come to visit, receive them well and set more food before them than they require so your husband will be respected by them. And watch well over the household and all of your husband's possessions.
>
> Resultingly, he will be delighted with you, and you will be the crown of your husband, in accordance with the passage in Proverbs, "A meritorious woman is the crown of her husband."[140]

The interest of *sh'lom bayit* dictates that each partner concentrate specifically on *his own obligations* toward the other and not on the other's obligations toward him. If a husband frequently reminds his wife that "a good wife fulfills her husband's will," and a wife perpetually informs her husband that he must "honor her more than himself," it becomes difficult to create a harmonious household. *Sh'lom bayit* comes when each is mindful of his own obligations toward the other.

The Sages recognize the unfortunate possibility of a man being married to a shrew or a woman to a tyrant. Nevertheless, they caution the husband to accept his lot graciously and to mobilize every strategem of patience. They urge him to try to assuage his wife's anger and to mollify her in order to maintain a tranquil home.[141]

Likewise, the Sages console the woman who falls into the hands of a difficult husband and urge her, for the sake of peace and the fulfillment of the family destiny, to be tolerant. All this the Sages say while expressing acute awareness of the woman's weaker physical constitution, her keener sensitivity, and her "propensity to tears."

In the words of one wise sage, "Surely, bearing insults and not returning them involves enormously greater challenge within one's home than in public; yet, it is fundamental to the discipline of marriage."[142]

The Rules for a Successful Marriage

R. Zelig Pliskin, Jerusalem scholar and ethical teacher, offers ten rules for a successful marriage, based on the teachings of the Sages and on his own counseling experience:

1. Keep your main focus on "giving" rather than "taking." When your goal is to give your partner pleasure you will always find opportunities to meet your goal. You too will gain by doing this since people tend to reciprocate positive behavior.

2. Be careful to remain silent if your spouse insults you. By ignoring slights and insults, you will prevent many needless quarrels. The momentary unpleasantness will quickly pass.

3. Give up unrealistic expectations. People come into marriage with many expectations which are not consciously expressed. By giving up unrealistic expectations, you will prevent frustration and anger. Don't expect your spouse to be perfect and don't make comparisons.

4. Avoid labeling those things which are not to your liking as "awful." Try for a more positive perspective.

5. Think of how to motivate your spouse to want to do what you want him or her to do. If your first strategy is not effective, keep trying different strategies. Remember that tactful praise is a powerful motivator.

6. In communicating with your spouse, never lose sight of your main goal—to have a happy marriage. If the response to your communication is a negative one, rethink your method of communication—i.e., change or modify your approach.

7. Be prepared to compromise. Be willing to do something you would rather not do in return for similar behavior from your spouse.

8. Don't blame or condemn your spouse for mistakes. Plan on the best method to prevent the mistakes from recurring without arousing resentment or hurting your spouse's feelings.

9. Live in the present. Whatever went wrong in the past is over. Focus on improving the current situation.

10. Keep asking yourself: "What can *I* do to create a pleasant atmosphere in my home?"[143]

The Value of Peace

Even if making peace with one's spouse involves sacrifice, the goal is a worthwhile one. The Sages declare: "Great is peace, for no sacrifice is too great in the interest of preserving peace."[144]

The *Midrash* teaches:[145]

Great is peace, for with regard to other commandments it is written: "*If* you meet your enemy's ox or ass going astray. . . ."[146] "*If* you see the ass of your enemy lying under its burden. . . ."[147] "*If* a bird's nest be before you. . . ."[148] That is, *if perchance* the opportunity arises for you to perform the *mitzvah,* you must perform it, but *if not* you are free from performing it. However, in the instance of peace you are *obligated* to seek out ways of performing the *mitzvah,* as it is written: "Seek peace and pursue it."[149]

The Sages went to some lengths to elaborate on the importance of peace. God Himself, they point out, is called by the name of *Shalom.*[150] The Sages emphasize, however, that domestic harmony is more important even than the ineffable name of God. They teach: "So important is peace that the Great Name, written in holiness, may be erased in water if necessary to bring peace between a man and his wife."[151]

According to R. David Abudarham, the fourteenth-century Spanish liturgical commentator, *sh'lom bayit* is the reason that a woman is exempt from Judaism's many time-related *mitzvot.* Her performance of these percepts may conflict with her obligations to husband and household, and so, in the best interest of *sh'lom bayit*, she is excused from them.[152]

Reconciling Couples

Today, with the forces of a fast-moving secular society eroding the traditional stability of the Jewish home, marital counseling is an especially serious challenge. If willingness is there, timely and insightful counseling by someone who understands what it takes to build *sh'lom bayit* may be the missing ingredient needed to improve or save a modern marriage.

R. Jonah Gerondi, *Rabeinu Yonah,* the thirteenth-century Spanish scholar and teacher of ethics, urged Jewish communities to select skilled marriage counselors for the purpose of bringing couples back together.[153] The tradition of counseling married couples and restoring peace dates back to Aaron the High Priest who was renowned for his patient and wise methods of repairing marital rifts.[154]

The Talmud tells a story of the lengths to which the great Sage R. Meir went to reconcile a couple. It relates that he would lecture in the synagogue at Hamat near Tiberias every Friday evening. Once R. Meir concluded his discourse later than usual. A woman who had attended his lecture returned home late. Her husband asked her where she had been. When she replied that she had been at R. Meir's discourse, her husband angrily banished her from the house telling her she could not return until she spat in the lecturer's eye.

At the next lecture, R. Meir, having learned of the husband's demand, asked that the woman come forward. Before the assembled onlookers, he told her that his eye was troubling him. He asked her if she would spit in his eye to relieve it. When she hesitated, R. Meir insisted, saying that if she spat in his eye seven times it would be fully healed. The woman finally did as he asked, after which he told her to tell her husband that she had done even more than he had asked. He had asked that she spit once, and she had done so seven times.

R. Meir's students reproached their teacher, saying, "Rabbi, this way the dignity of Torah is shamed! If you had informed us of what the husband had done we would have had him brought to the synagogue and forced him to apologize to his wife."

Replied R. Meir: "And is my honor greater than that of the Creator? If the Holy Name of God, written in holiness, may be erased to bring peace between man and wife, surely R. Meir's honor may be diminished for the sake of this important task."[155]

The point the Talmud emphasizes is relevant to everyone, though especially to rabbis and those charged with communal responsibility: no one should consider himself too dignified to intervene to preserve *sh'lom bayit* between husband and wife.

The Home as a Temple

The advice of the Sages on how to create *sh'lom bayit* spans the entire constellation of good *midot* (character traits). They include respectfulness, self-restraint, patience, cheerfulness, self-respect, forbearance, compassion, modesty, and responsibility. These are but a few of the traits that are necessarily brought into play in the process of building a peaceful household. Thus, the effort toward *sh'lom bayit* aids each of the partners in realizing his or her own personal potential as a human being and as a meaningful member of society.

Dissension in the home is often the result of pointless and causeless hatred arising from petty disagreements. The Talmud states: "Because of the sin of needless hatred, there is great conflict within the home."[156]

Needless hatred, the Sages teach, is worse than idol worship.[157] Indeed, they declare it to be the equivalent of the three central sins of Judaism combined—idol worship, murder, and incest.[158] The destruction of Jerusalem's First Temple was caused, the Talmud teaches, by idolatry, murder, and incest[159]; however, the destruction of the Second Temple was ascribed, as mentioned, to *sin'at hinam,* personal, groundless hatred.[160] Just as *sin'at hinam* caused the Temple's destruction, so *ahavat hinam,* genuine love without the prospect of personal gain, is considered to be the indispensable ingredient required for the ultimate reconstruction of the Temple.

The Jewish home is called a *mikdash m'at,* a Temple in miniature. Its invisible bricks are eroded by the corrosiveness of hatred, and its rafters are ignited through the heat of anger. Only unconditional love can be its binding mortar and keep it standing. According to Judaism, when there is *sh'lom bayit* in the home and love between husband and wife, they have created a miniature and holy Temple.

VII

The Jewish Family

13

The Jewish Home and Raising Children

Family: The Medium for Jewish Survival

Great civilizations have had their days of radiance, and then their glories have faded and died. Yet the tiny Jewish nation clings to life against all odds, tenaciously guarding its unique heritage. The theory has been postulated that the larger national survival is linked to the survival of the smaller, nuclear family unit. Thucydides (c. 455–400 B.C.E.), the ancient historian who chronicled the Peloponnesian War, has written that Greece fell not because of wars and battles, but because of the disintegration of its home life. It was a similar cause that weakened the Roman Empire, leading to its military downfall.

Yet the Jewish nation, despite all odds, including its near decimation by the Holocaust, survives. The current intensive scholarly and intellectual activity in Jewish studies and the increasing production of works in all areas of Jewish knowledge are indications that the Jewish people, notwithstanding a declining population, may be on the threshold of a new epoch of cultural and intellectual renaissance.

What is the secret of the social and national cohesion of the Jews? Nearly everywhere we witness the deterioration of marriage and the erosion of the family unit, that institution representing all of the positive social values. Yet, among those Jews who observe the

Jewish traditions, marriage and the nuclear family continue to be strong, and divorce remains remarkably uncommon.

Central to Jewish life, the family serves as the significant social unit for the maintenance and propagation of Judaism and Jewish culture. The Jewish family is the instrument for the transmission of Torah values from one generation to the next. It is the sturdy vessel in which the Jew is forged into a living bridge connecting the Jewish past and the Jewish future. As it is the family that is the prime factor in Jewish continuity and dynamism, Jewish existence is therefore dependent on the strength of the Jewish family and its spiritual vitality.

Marriage and Family: Primary Torah Commands

For the Jewish man, marriage is mandatory in order to "be fruitful and multiply,"[1] that is, to fulfill the *mitzvah* of bringing at least one male and one female child into the world.[2]

The duty of building a home and of rearing a family usually appears as the first of the rabbinic enumerations of the six hundred and thirteen Torah commandments. R. Joseph H. Hertz, the English rabbinic scholar, comments:

> To this commandment is due the sacredness and centrality of the child in Judaism. "O Lord God, what will you give me, seeing that I go childless?"[3] was Abraham's agonizing cry. Of what value were earthly possessions to him, if he was denied a worthy child who would continue his work after him? This attitude of the father of the Jewish people toward the child has remained that of his descendants to the present day. A childless marriage was deemed to have failed in one of its main purposes.
>
> Among even the most enlightened nations of antiquity, the child had no rights, no protection, no dignity. In Greece, for example, weak children were generally exposed on a lonely mountain to perish. The Roman historian Tacitus decreed it a contemptible prejudice among the Jews that "it is a crime among them to kill any child." What Roman society! It is in such a society that Judaism proclaimed the biblical view that the child was the highest of human treasures.[4]

Indeed, childlessness has always been considered a cause of deep grief[5] and soul-searching among the Jewish people.[6] Fecundity, on the other hand, is viewed as the greatest of blessings,[7] and parenthood as the most significant of all rewards in marriage.[8] The Psalmist sings: "Children are the inheritance of the Lord. . . . Happy is the man who has filled his quiver with them."[9]

The *Zohar* teaches: "A man without children is like a piece of wood which, although kindled, does not burn or give out light. . . . No children, no bliss, here or hereafter."[10]

Children provide parents with personal fulfillment representing, as well, the indispensable link for the perpetuation of the living Jewish tradition. They serve as a visible guarantee of the nation's continued existence. Parents are the trustees and guardians during their children's educational apprenticeship. When Jewish parents provide their children with an intensive Jewish education and a home environment of dynamic, living Judaism, they are preparing their children to observe and spread a knowledgeable, effective Judaism.

A Child-Centered Judaism

The traditional Jewish approach to children contrasts dramatically with that of many societies. Not just in ancient Greece and Rome, but also in such "advanced" societies as Egypt, Mesopotamia, China, and India, it was not uncommon for children to be killed, maimed, abandoned, sacrificed, drowned, or eaten. According to one specialist, such maltreatment of children was not limited to prehistoric times or early civilizations. It occurred in "enlightened" European nations as late as the nineteenth century and is the bane of most modern societies.[11]

Regarding children as a divine trust, Jews have expressed a deep commitment to children and child rearing; this is highlighted by the fact that children, during the major events in the Jewish calendar, especially the Sabbaths and festivals, usually occupy the central position. This may be seen on Passover when the entire ceremony, the *Seder* and the reading of the *Hagadah* guidebook, are focused upon the children's involvement, education, and enjoyment. In fact, one of the commandments of the Torah is that Passover should be geared to the interests of the children.[12]

Although traditional Judaism obliges Jews to live their lives according to the Torah, parents are given the obligation of handing over the principles of Judaism and Jewish living to their children, so that they have the proper training to go on to live full Jewish lives. The *Midrash* illustrates the full extent of this duty when it says that it was for the sake of the children alone that God gave the Torah.[13]

R. Samson Raphael Hirsch has this to say to Jewish parents concerning their responsibility:

> These new human beings, created in spiritual and physical resemblance to their parents, are to carry in themselves all that is noblest and best, both divine and human, that is inherent in the parents. . . . Nurse and fashion the offspring you have produced in your own likeness so that you may reproduce yourselves in them and multiply yourselves through them. . . . It is not enough that they should simply be born. The birth must, so to speak, be continued; the father and mother must further unite their labors to bend, train, and fashion the child, and this is practically nothing else than the continued transmission of what is best and noblest both of the divine and human in the parents to the children so that they may grow up in their image both spiritually and physically. . . . The nursery of human culture is the house, the family.[14]

The Home as the Prime Educator

"Train the child in his way," says Solomon in Proverbs, "and when he grows old he will not depart from it."[15] This passage is interpreted by the Sages to mean that it is the responsibility of parents to train their children in their tasks as Jews. Becoming aware of the heavy responsibility of molding the ethical and spiritual character of the children is the first premise of being a Jewish parent. Throughout the course of childhood, values and ideals are absorbed from parents and home. Socially, children develop a view of the world and of their place in it. Spiritually, children with the right training learn to recognize the divine character of the universe. The Jewish family shapes the emerging character of the child, his relationships with God and with his fellow man, his ethical and moral development, and the quality of his life as a human being and as a Jew. The parents' behavior toward one another, toward others, and in their relationship with God, will strongly influence the child's attitudes and actions.

In traditional Jewish schools the children receive an intensive education consisting of day-long formal courses in Jewish as well as secular subjects, but these schools were never meant to take away from parents their primary responsibility for the children's Jewish education.[16] The schools are designed to provide a *formal* education, including a grounding in Torah literature and in the traditional Jewish texts, not to substitute for Jewish education in the home. The Torah command "And you shall teach them diligently to your children"[17] is followed by the phrase, "when you sit in your home."[18]

The home is the child's first school, and in Jewish tradition it continues to play, for the growing child, a primary role as his most vital educational environment. The home, in Jewish tradition, is not a supplementary educational medium; it is the significant, primary medium for the rearing of Jewish children. While teachers instruct and transmit information to children, they can never be as effective as can loving parents in imbuing the child, through personal example and affectionate guidance, with the principles of Jewish life.

The family's role in shaping the character of the Jewish child goes back to earliest Jewish history. God promised Abraham, the Torah relates, that his descendants would become "a great nation through which all of the nations on earth will be blessed, for I have given him the knowledge *so that he will instruct his children and his household after him* that they will keep the way of the Lord, to do benevolence and to act justly."[19]

Thus, Judaism has always taught that the Jews' fate as a nation depends on adhering to Judaism's teachings and on instructing their children to do likewise. Abraham is told not only to "instruct his children," but also "his household after him." The scriptural requirements, therefore, include both living in accordance with God's rules and in actively transmitting, from generation to generation, the Jewish heritage of benevolence and justice. These are the means for accomplishing the Jewish mission to the world: to be a people through which the nations of the world will be blessed.

The *Midrash* teaches:

> When Israel stood at Mount Sinai to receive the Torah, the Holy One, Blessed be He, said: "If you want Me to give you the Torah, bring Me good guarantors that you will keep it."

They replied: "King of the Universe, our ancestors will be our guarantors."

God responded: "Your guarantors require guarantors. I have found fault with them."

They replied: "Our prophets will serve as our guarantors."

Replied God: "I have found fault with them as well."

Finally they said: "Our children will be our guarantors."

And God replied: "In truth, these are excellent guarantors. For their sake I will give you the Torah."[21]

When to Begin Jewish Education

For a Jewish child his parents are the most important teachers. His father, his *aba,* is also referred to as *avi-mori,* my father-teacher. His mother, *ima,* is *ima-morati,* my mother-teacher.

When should parents begin to teach their children Torah? As early as possible, according to Jewish tradition. The mother of the talmudic Sage, R. Joshua ben Hananya, would carry her infant son to the *yeshivah* in his cradle to accustom the child to the words of Torah.[22]

Jewish tradition says it is never too soon to begin teaching a child how to be a Jew. For example, even before a child has any understanding, he is to be fed only kosher food.[23] He is to be taught right from wrong as soon as he can grasp the difference. Before a child can speak, he is taught to revere holy books by kissing Bibles and prayer books. And when the child is able to talk, his parents begin their roles as active teachers of the tradition.[24]

The Sages teach:[25]

When a child learns to speak, his father is required to teach him Torah and to read the *Sh'ma* with him. To what does teaching him "Torah" refer? R. Hamnuna said: To the verse, "Moses commanded us the Torah; it is a legacy of the Congregation of Jacob."[26] To what does reading the *Sh'ma* refer? To the first verse, *Sh'ma Yisrael HaShem Elokainu HaShem Ehad*—"Hear O Israel, the Lord Our God is One."[27]

It is with these two scriptural verses that the child's Jewish education traditionally begins. Immediately afterwards he is taught the passage *Reshit hochmah yir'at HaShem* — "The beginning of wisdom is reverence of the Lord."[28] The Sages say these are the first words a Jewish child needs to know, because they are designed to accompany him through life.

Thereafter, Judaism obligates the father to continue teaching his child Jewishly until he is of school age,[29] and then to provide him with the necessary formal education.[30]

Honoring Parents: The Child's Primary Duty

The exceptional dignity which Jewish tradition accords children is paralleled by a fundamental requirement of the Torah: that a child honor[31] and revere[32] his parents. This is a duty and value that parents are instructed to inculcate in the child at an early age. R. Aaron HaLevi of Barcelona, the medieval Spanish Sage, discusses in *Sefer HaHinuch* the significance of the laws of filial respect in their wider application to man's relations with his fellow man:

> The reason for this *mitzvah* is that it is proper for man to acknowledge and repay acts of love to one who has treated him well. One should not be ungrateful, for this is an evil trait and contemptible before God and man. One should take to heart that his father and mother are the cause of his existence; it is therefore proper for him to accord them all honor and help in any way he can. For they not only brought him into the world, but they also endured so much for his sake during his childhood.[33]

The dual lesson of the command to honor one's parents is that of elementary human gratitude and of human interdependence. The gratitude is first of all for being brought into the world,[34] then for being taken care of. The debt is spiritual as well as physical. Jewish parents are the transmitters to the child of the Jewish heritage. They serve as the medium for the child's connection to God, the Torah, and the Jewish people. A child needs to express his appreciation for all that his parents have done for him — all the love, care, and concern they manifest for him — by honoring and revering them. By being aware of what he owes them and then acting on this awareness, the child's character develops so he is able to concern himself with the welfare of others beyond the family circle. In the words of Philo (c. 20 B.C.E.–50 C.E.): ". . . Who could be more truly called benefactors than parents in relation to their children? First, they have brought them out of non-existence; . . . they have held them . . . to nurture and later to educate, body and soul, so that they may have not only life, but a good life."[35]

Honoring one's parents is one of the Ten Commandments, and is therefore a major tenet of Judaism. The Talmud teaches that honor is due to parents because father and mother are equal partners with God in the creation of a child;[36] resultingly, "the honor due to parents is like the honor due to God."[37] As the Sages teach:

> There are three partners in a human being[38] — the Holy One, his father, and his mother[39]. . . . When a man honors his father and mother, the Lord says: I consider it as though I abided with them and they honored Me.[40] It is written, "Honor your father and your mother,"[41] and it is written, "Honor the Lord with your substance."[42] The Torah thus likened the honor of parents to the honor of the Holy One. It is written, "A person should revere his mother and his father,"[43] and it is written, "You shall revere the Lord your God and serve Him."[44] The Torah thus likened reverence of parents to reverence of the Lord.[45]

In addition, God's special relationship to Israel is compared to that of a parent to a child. Scripture states, "You are the children of the Lord your God."[46]

A Mishnah in *Avot* declares: "Beloved are Israel for they were called the children of God; it is because of a special abundance of divine love for them that they were called children."[47]

Philo states that "what God is to the world, parents are to their children."[48] The philosopher adds: "Just as He achieved existence for the non-existent, so they, in imitation of His power . . . immortalize the race. . . . How can reverence be rendered to the invisible God by those who show irreverence to the gods who are near at hand and are seen by the eye?"[49]

The talmudic Sage R. Simon bar Yohai maintains that the obligation to honor one's father and mother even *exceeds* that of the duty to honor God:

Great is the honor one must accord his father and mother, for the Holy One made it preferable to honor parents than to honor even Himself. It is written, "Honor your father and mother," and it is written, "Honor the Lord with your substance." How do you honor God with your substance? You separate gleanings for the poor and tithes and sheaf-offerings and *halah* and special tithes for the poor . . . you build a *sukah* and make a *lulav,* take a *shofar,* make *t'filin* and *tzitzit,* and feed the hungry. If you have the means, you must do so; however, if you do not have the means, you are free from these obligations.

When it comes to honoring parents, however, whether you have the means or not, you are *obliged* to honor your father and mother. You are duty-bound to do so even if you must become a beggar going from door to door.[50]

The Required Extent of Filial Reverence

How can we know how far filial reverence extends? The Talmud does not give definitive rules. Rather, it contains a set of brief, insightful tales conveying a sense of the degree of filial honor that mature, sensitive people can attain. The guiding principle is that children should see their parents as having great importance for them, and should constantly express reverence for their parents through actions. Nothing should be done that might diminish the dignity, worth, and status of one's parents. The Talmud teaches:

In what does reverence for a father consist and in what does honor for him consist? Reverence means that the son must neither stand nor sit in his father's place, not contradict his words, nor judge him harshly. Honor consists of providing parents with food and drink and clothing and covering them, and in aiding them to enter and to leave the house.[51]

The *Code of Jewish Law* provides guidelines for filial reverence based on talmudic sources: "A child must not stand in his father's place . . . nor sit in it [at home or in the synagogue], and not contradict him in his presence . . . nor even may he address him by his first name . . . nor endorse his father's opinions as being correct."[52]

A child is also forbidden to wake his parents from their sleep, unless they request that he do so or he knows they would want to be awakened.[53] The Talmud relates the example of Dama ben Netina:

> [The Sages] asked R. Eliezer how far one must go in honoring one's father and mother. He told them: go and learn from the behavior of a gentile from Ashkelon, Dama ben Netina, toward his father. The Sages wished to buy jewels from him for the [priestly] *ephod* for the sum of sixty thousand—according to R. Kahana, the figure was eighty thousand—but the key to the jewel box was under the head of his father [who was sleeping], so he did not disturb him.
>
> The next year, the Holy One rewarded him for his deed by causing a red heifer (an extremely rare animal, and one required for the Temple service) to be born to his flock. When the Sages came to buy the red heifer, he told them: I know that even were I to demand all the money in the world you would pay it. However, I ask only the amount that I lost in honoring my father.[54]
>
> [The Sages] asked R. Eliezer: How far must one go to properly honor one's father and mother? He replied: Until the father takes his son's wallet and throws it into the sea—and his son does not shame his father for his deed.[55]

How should a child honor his mother? The Talmud cites the example of R. Tarfon:

> R. Tarfon's mother was walking one Sabbath day when her shoe tore and came off. R. Tarfon placed his hands under her feet, and walked with her in this way until she reached her own seat. Once when R. Tarfon was ill and the Sages came to visit him, she told them: Pray for R. Tarfon, for he serves me with undue respect. They asked: What did he do for you? She told them of the incident. They replied: Were he to do that a thousand times over he would not have bestowed even half of the honor that the Torah requires of a child to his parents.[56]

The Talmud relates that when R. Joseph heard his mother's footsteps he would say: "Let me rise before the approach of the *Sh'chinah,* the Divine Presence."[57]

How should a child honor his father? The Talmud brings the story of R. Abahu in this regard:

> R. Abahu said: An example of one who properly fulfills the requirement of filial respect is that of my son, Abimi. . . . When R.

Abahu would come to his son's house, Abimi would run rapidly to the door to open it, while saying "yes, yes" [I'm coming, I'm coming] until he reached the door.[58] Once R. Abahu asked for a glass of water. By the time Abimi brought the water, his father had dozed off. Abimi waited with the water nearby until his father woke up.[59]

The Jewish approach to filial respect is that a child should cater to his parents' needs and desires, even if they seem unreasonable. Included in the idea of honor and respect is obedience to their wishes.

In his code, Maimonides refers to the talmudic examples cited, and he sums up the *halachah:*

How far must one go in honoring one's father and mother? Even if they take his wallet full of gold coins and cast it before him into the sea, he must not shame them nor even show pain before them, nor be angered at them — but should accept the decree of the Torah with equanimity and remain silent.

And how far must one go in their reverence? Even if he is dressed in precious garments and is sitting in a place of honor before a large assemblage, and his parents come and rip off his clothing and hit him on the head and spit in his face, he must not embarrass them, but must remain silent, in fear before the King of Kings who commanded him to act in this way. If a king of flesh and blood decreed that he had to do something even more painful than this, he would not omit even one aspect of it. How much more so when he is commanded by the Creator of the world?[60]

How to Teach Children to Honor Parents

For their part, parents also need to respect their children; this respect will give back great dividends to parents who thereby demonstrate to their children how to behave toward them.

The way parents behave and interact in the home not only provides the children with role models — but it teaches them how to conduct themselves toward others outside the home. It is important that filial honor be inculcated in the child early on, so that respect for parents and people in general becomes an integral part of his normal behavior as he grows older.

However, Judaism does not intend parents to place too heavy a burden on children. It is unwise for parents constantly to insist on the reverence due them, using this as a kind of cudgel with which to admonish the child. It is far better for parents to work on creating an environment where such filial reverence comes naturally. Too frequent reminders to the child of his duty in this regard will cause resentment. The Sages teach: "It is forbidden for a person to place too difficult a yoke on his children and be too exacting with them regarding his honor, lest he bring them thereby to stumble. Rather he should be forgiving and close his eyes to their acts."[61]

The best method is to use positive reinforcement. Parents engender respect best when they instill in the child a desire to honor them, by complimenting him and expressing love and appreciation whenever he performs an appropriately respectful act.

Parents should go out of their way, especially in front of others, to praise, and thus encourage, a child for good behavior, or achievements of any kind. Children thrive on parental approval. For praise to be effective, it must be honest and deserved and as specific as possible, relating to a particular act, or a successful achievement.

When to Disobey Parents

Although the child's obligation to honor his parents is primary, according to Judaism he is obligated to disobey them if they direct him to violate the Sabbath or to transgress any teaching of the Torah.[62] The Sages derive this from the verse in Leviticus, "Every person shall revere his mother and his father; and you shall observe my Sabbath; I am the Lord your God."[63] Comments *Rashi:* "Observance of the Sabbath is juxtaposed to filial reverence to teach that although you are cautioned to revere your father, nevertheless, should he tell you to desecrate the Sabbath you must not obey him. And this is the case regarding all other *mitzvot* as well."[64]

God, as the source of the Torah and the *mitzvot,* emphasizes that obedience to parents is fundamental. However, if parents order a child to act against the teachings of the Torah, they forfeit their special role, since obedience to them is a consequence of obedience to God.[65]

R. Samson Raphael Hirsch explains:

[The commandment to honor our parents] demands of us that we demonstrate in every way how thoroughly we are permeated by the great importance that God has given to our parents with regard to ourselves. This comprises complete obedience to them and courteous anticipatory carrying out of all their wishes. The only limit to this is, if these wishes should be contradictory to the wishes of God. Parents are meant to be the heralds of God's wishes, and it is the transmission of these that gives them great importance.[66] [Parents are] not only the medium of the physical existence of the child, but the medium through which the mission and calling of Jewry, its history and the Torah is to be transmitted from God's hands to every coming generation.[67] It is this mission of parents, and not the greater or lesser amount of self-sacrifice and care that they give to their children, which lies at the root of honoring and revering one's father and mother.[68]

Good Parenting and Eternity

Because of the crucial role of a teacher in implanting the Jewish heritage in a child, traditional Judaism instructs a person to honor his teachers of Torah even more than his parents.[69] This scale of priority is derived from the Mishnah:

If one's father's lost object and one's teacher's lost object require attention, his teacher takes precedence, because his father brought him into this world, but his teacher, who instructed him in wisdom, brings him into the future world. However, if his father is a sage, his father's object takes precedence. If both his father and his teacher were carrying burdens, he must first assist his teacher, and then his father. If his father and his teacher are both in captivity, he must first redeem his teacher and then his father. However, if his father is a sage, he must first redeem his father and then his teacher.[70]

Rama elaborates: "A teacher takes precedence only when the father has not hired the teacher. However, if the father hires the teacher, then it is the father who takes precedence."[71]

Halachah makes it clear that when parents make it possible for a child to study, they are to be accorded greater honor than a child's teacher.[72] However, the supreme honor is accorded to those who fill the dual roles of being both parents and teacher. In fact, the Hebrew word for parents, *horim,* is related to *hora'ah,* teaching, which, in turn, is related to the word Torah. "He who teaches Torah to his children," the Sages declare, "abides with the *Sh'chinah.*"[73]

To parents who succeed in educating their children in Torah and good *midot,* character traits, the highest reward is promised — immortality. The Talmud declares that one of the three categories of individuals who will inherit the world-to-come are "parents who raise their children in the study of Torah."[74] The Sages teach: "He who is survived by a son who toils in Torah study is regarded as though he had not died."[75]

Elsewhere the Sages declare that he who teaches his son Torah is considered as if he had taught not his son alone, "but also his grandson, his great-grandson, and even unto the end of generations."[76] Concludes *Rashi:* "Whoever trains his child to be righteous is compared to an immortal."[77]

There exists in every human being a powerful urge to perpetuate himself and thereby to touch the fringes of eternity. The most direct means of achieving this is through bringing children into the world. However, as we have said, giving birth to children is not enough. It is only the beginning of the arduous task of raising children to respect, embrace, and live the Jewish life for their own benefit, and to strengthen the Jewish heritage.

Jewish parents who do not convey Judaism to their children and who, although they are aware of their responsibility in this regard, do not transmit to their young their Jewish spiritual heritage, do not perpetuate themselves, because they weaken the link in the chain of generations of the Jewish heritage. There is no *Jewish* stamp of the parent upon the child.

What Makes a Happy Home?

Happy parents are likely to raise happy children. The hasidic Sage R. Nahman of Bratzlav teaches: "If husband and wife quarrel, they cannot raise good children."[78]

Love and respect between parents are essential to the security of the family. Caring behavior and speech between parents generate respect among children, and strengthen family unity.

When parents set rules and regulations for their children to follow, the children have to know that the parents themselves set the example. The responsibility of being a parent is so great that parents should be constantly aware that their children are watching them, and that children imitate their parents' behavior.

A child's development is influenced to an incredible extent by the attitudes and conduct of his parents. It is vital, therefore, that parents behave in an ethical and moral way, and that they be consistent in their attitudes.

Children are highly sensitive to hypocrisy in their parents, therefore they cannot afford to have two sets of standards, demonstrating the social niceties outside, while behaving rudely in the home. Whatever the parents do or say, their children emulate. The Sages say: "What a child says in the market he has heard either from his father or his mother."[79]

How to Discipline a Child

Judaism obliges a parent to reprove his child if he acts wrongly. A child is born socially unformed, and seeks only to satisfy his physical and emotional desires. It is essential for parents to instill discipline in a child in order to mold him into a social, caring human being interested in others and not just in himself. Not only is it the parent's duty to discipline his child, but it is a child's *right* to receive such discipline from his parents. As King Solomon said, "Whoever spares the rod spoils the child."[80]

The rod thus referred to may be physical, or it may be metaphorical—a frown, verbal chastisement, or, perhaps, withholding a desired privilege. However, to be effective, it must be employed in the manner of a rod, in a firm and authoritative way, without hesitation or vacillation. When a parent feels guilty about it, a child quickly senses it. Moreover, it is important for a parent not to let a child talk him out of a punishment if the parent knows it is required.

Very few parents find difficulty in expressing love for a child. But many have difficulty in expressing authority. Many parents tend to view expressions of love as positive, but view authority or discipline as negative. Finding it difficult to discipline their children, they do so hesitantly or apologetically, feeling guilty about it.

They see the withholding of discipline as somehow synonymous with the expression of love. In fact, authority and discipline are viewed in Judaism as significant expressions of genuine love. Parents who find it too painful to punish their children might think of the punishment as being like a bad-tasting medicine that it is necessary to take to heal a physical disorder. Sparing a child punishment out of misguided compassion is a serious error that will ultimately be detrimental to both parent and child. The Sages say that Absalom's rebellion against, and attempt to kill, his father, King David, was caused by David's failure properly to discipline his son when this was required.[81] Likewise, the Sages blame Esau's turn to wickedness on Isaac's failure to discipline his son.[82]

Rules for Maintaining Discipline

To be effective, especially with very young children, it is important that punishment be meted out as soon as possible after a misdeed. It should then be quite clear to the child that the punishment was inflicted because of his misbehavior. A mother shouldn't say, for example, "When your father comes home, he will punish you." Not only does this show her to be weak, but it places a difficult burden upon a father, and will cause the child to dread his father's homecoming.

However, especially in the case of older children, if a short postponement would result in the punishment being administered calmly and without anger, it is preferable to summary justice.

The Sages teach that a parent should always try to be even-tempered, even when meting out punishment. He must try not to do so unlovingly or in anger. A parent should try to make it clear that he is acting out of love and the desire that his child learn to behave properly. It is also important to a child to know why he is being punished, and that the punishment is directed at his misbehavior, and not at him. He should be told that parental discipline is an expression of genuine parental love and affection. The next step is for a parent to follow up the punishment with calm words of love, so that the child will see that the punishment derives from love. Without the tempering expressions of love, discipline will be felt only as parental tyranny.

The way to begin discipline is to set a few simple, easily understandable rules of behavior and clear guidelines, and then to adhere to them. The child needs to have a clear picture of the rules, and they should not be changed from day to day. Otherwise, he will not have a strong sense of security in his environment. Whenever possible, a parent needs to explain the reasons for the directions and rules. The young child should be told, for example, that playing with matches or fire will burn him, that touching electrical wires could hurt him, that climbing on a window sill is dangerous, as is running out onto a street, because he could be hurt by a car. As he grows older, the child will understand why certain behavior is right or wrong.

Nevertheless, at times, good discipline requires telling a child to do something just because his parent tells him to do so. However, if a child comes up with a reasoned argument in response, it is important to try to understand the child and, whenever possible, to meet him part of the way. This will result in a closer relationship.

R. Samson Raphael Hirsch says: "Do not ask a child to do something trivial and unnecessary, and do not unreasonably refuse his harmless request."[83]

Good parenting requires flexibility. Allowances should be made for unintentional disobedience or forgetfulness. It is a good idea when a parent is about to discipline a child for being forgetful, to check on his own lapses in this regard, and not to expect a child to have a higher standard than his own.

On occasion, rules may be bent to accommodate a particular situation. R. Hirsch says: "Allow your child to do whatever you can permit him, provided that it is not physically or morally harmful."[84] Because each child is so different, what may work for one may not be effective for another.

Proper discipline is an essential preparation for helping a child to adjust to the world, and it will enable him to be happier and better able to cope with life.

Being Positive and Consistent

When training a child, it is best to use a positive approach, giving the child directions on what to do rather than telling him what not to do. In this way unnecessary conflict will be avoided, and the young child will be skillfully guided toward the proper way of behaving.

To be most effective, parents need to present a consistent and united approach, helping each other whenever possible, and cooperating at all times in the rearing of the children. It is vital that one parent not criticize the other's handling of a discipline problem in the child's presence. Disagreements between them regarding discipline should only be discussed privately.

In addition, punishment should never be administered in front of anyone, so the child is not shamed.[85] A child's desire to save face in front of others may impel him to continue or worsen his improper behavior.

Regarding the nature of the punishment for a young child, isolating him from family activities by sending him to his room or depriving him of a treat or privilege often works well. If a child hurts another, it is best to make him apologize; if he causes damage to property, he should apologize and make restitution from his own funds.

It is best as far as possible to avoid physical punishment. Nevertheless, when it is necessary, the Sages do permit corporal punishment to be administered to a child. To be effective, however, physical punishment must be used sparingly, and should not be resorted to frequently.[86]

It goes without saying that a child should never be beaten or hit on the head. The Sages teach that when punishing a child physically, a parent should administer "a light stroke which will not harm."[87]

The Sages also teach that a parent should never punish in anger, or hit to assuage his own anger. The placid, even-tempered parent, tries to remain so even when punishing his child; otherwise, if the parent is prone to lose his temper, he will provoke the same reaction in his child. If a parent needs to hit, he should first be sure to rid himself of his inner anger.

Tempering Discipline with Love

Most importantly, parental discipline only works when parental love is present. Discipline must be seen as a true expression of love, and never as a withholding of love. Therefore, discipline must always be tempered with compassion. Love and affection must govern a parent's relationship with his child, *especially* when punishing a child. In this way, the child feels that he is loved and will more readily accept his punishment. The message to be conveyed is that it is the child's action that is unacceptable, not the child.

The Talmud teaches: "While the left hand pushes away (disciplines), the right hand draws close (loves)."[88]

The right hand is the stronger one; thus it is the loving hand that dominates. R. Samson Raphael Hirsch emphasizes that the right hand drawing the child close must be the controlling one, adding that excessive strictness is counterproductive and will result in rebellious disobedience.[89]

The Sages continually emphasize that love must go hand in hand with discipline. The Vilna *Gaon* says that one should admonish a child with soft words and with reproofs that he is likely to accept.[90] One method to use is to sit down with a child, hold his hand and speak quietly and calmly to him while at the same time reproving him, thus demonstrating parental love while chastising.

Love isn't what you feel, it's what you do. It is a vital task of parents to express their love for their children always: verbally — through loving words — and physically — through loving actions. To be real, parental love has to be constant and unconditional, and be present even when a child is behaving in a very unlovable manner. Children need to be told verbally of their parents' love, and to be shown it, so that they may never doubt its presence. Parents should hug their children frequently, and praise them at every opportunity. Such love gives children a sense of security, and smoothes out the rough edges of childhood.

How to Build a Close Relationship with Children

To build a good relationship with their children, parents need to spend constructive time with them, to play with them frequently, and to participate jointly with them in activities — such as family outings and social events — so that the bonds of familial love may grow as they experience life together.

Another way to deepen the bond with their children is for parents to take time to talk with them, with both sides listening to, understanding, and responding to the other. This is an excellent habit to build, even from the child's earliest years. It means putting aside other activities and paying full attention; it means encouraging the child to express himself, his feelings and emotions — and even to express anger knowing he will not thereby lose parental affection.

A parent should try to understand and genuinely respect a child's opinions. A child should be made to feel that his opinions count no less than those of an adult. Children should not be interrupted or contradicted when they speak, nor be dismissed with disdain. This will encourage the child to think for himself, to build up his self-esteem, and will help him grow. A parent should offer his own opinions when conversing with a child, but should clearly specify which are the opinions and which are the directives.

For all this, there is a fine line between building a good relationship with one's children and becoming "buddies" or equals with them. Traditional Judaism excludes any egalitarian parent--child relationship. It is an unnatural, contrived distortion of the family structure, and profoundly bewilders children — even though they may appear to enjoy it. Parents must exercise parental authority and children should never be allowed to forget their obligations to revere and respect their parents.

Parents as Role Models

Parents should, in a clear manner, teach their children right from wrong. They should also teach them the value of truthfulness. However, if parents want children who control their tempers, and are not impatient, jealous, or selfish, and who are always truthful, they have no choice but to provide personal examples. Parents must set personal examples in their speech and behavior, in their attitude toward others and in their overall conduct as Jews, in the home and outside it.

All family members should treat each other with respect. Parents set the proper example when they act respectfully toward their children. They should be polite to their children in conversation, for example, by making ample use of such social graces as "please" and "thank you." Parents, when in the wrong, should certainly apologize to a child. When a parent admits to a child that he has erred and apologizes, the child will learn that it is quite right to admit wrongdoing and to apologize for his mistakes.

The firmest punishment, the strictest authority, can never substitute for proper parental example. Deviations in their own personal behavior from those rules that parents lay down for their children are quickly spotted by the children, who proceed to do as their parents do — and not as they say.[91]

R. Shlomo Ganzfried (1804–1886), the compiler of the widely read *Condensed Code of Jewish Law,* lays down the rule as follows: "The father who wishes to be genuinely compassionate to his children will live according to the Torah and perform good deeds and will be pleasant toward God and toward people, and thus his children will be honored through him. However, he who does not act properly, his children too will be disgraced by him."[92]

Teaching Children Good Manners

The term *derech eretz* refers, in general, to proper behavior and demeanor. The Sages underscore the connection between Torah and *derech eretz:* "The Torah teaches us *derech eretz,*"[93] "*derech eretz* precedes the Torah,"[94] and "if there is no *derech eretz,* there is no Torah."[95] With these bywords, the Sages emphasize the importance of a wide and varied range of desirable behavior. These include personal refinement, courtesy,[96] good manners,[97] polite speech,[98] personal cleanliness,[99] neat dress,[100] etiquette[101] and table manners,[102] good behavior,[103] honor of elders,[104] and respect and consideration for others.[105]

So important is *derech eretz* considered that two talmudic tractates — *Derech Eretz Rabah* and *Derech Eretz Zutah* — are devoted to the subject.

Judaism instructs parents to inculcate *derech eretz* in the home and to train their children to practice it outside the home as well. In the words of the Sages: "Improper behavior in the home can destroy it."[106] Parents are expected to teach their children basic values and manners in order to get along well with their siblings and parents at home, and in society at large.

It is best to start teaching children *derech eretz* at an early age. This involves, for example, teaching them not to take things from others, not to interrupt others, not to use improper language, not to shout, and to use social niceties in speech, such as saying "please" and "thank you." It also involves teaching table manners, how to behave while eating, and how to use cutlery properly. Parents need to insist that their children greet friends and adults in a decent manner, speak pleasantly to others, answer the telephone properly, and generally to treat all people with kindness, respect, honesty, and integrity. And, of course, first and foremost, parents have to set the example themselves.

The Influence of the Sabbath

Traditionally, the Sabbath has been at the center of the Jewish home and Jewish family living. The Sages teach that the Sabbath candles symbolize *sh'lom bayit,* the peace of the Jewish home; the twin Sabbath lights also represent husband and wife. Since Judaism's customs, traditions, and values are so intertwined with Jewish family life, the Sabbath serves actually as an opportunity to transmit Judaism's teachings to a younger generation. A day of peace of mind and soul, the Sabbath is intended as a day for parents and children to be together.

On the Sabbath, the workday pressures and vicissitudes of everyday life are absent. Father and mother are free to devote their full attention to each child and to convey to them in a relaxed fashion Jewish ideas and values. They have the time to give attention to their children, to their interests, and their individual problems. In the warm atmosphere engendered by the Sabbath and with their parents' attention and encouragement, children have the opportunity to blossom intellectually and emotionally. The weekly opportunities for relaxed Torah study with their parents can also become a much-anticipated pleasure for the children.

The Sabbath has therefore had an inestimable influence in shaping the character of the traditional Jewish family. The feeling of family togetherness is a significant element that the Sabbath brings. Every week, for one day, all members of the household forsake their separate activities and join together as a single family entity. The warmth and companionship of loved ones combine with the spiritual atmosphere of the Sabbath, making it a day of pleasure and tranquility to be shared by the family as a unit.

The family gathers together on the Sabbath day as a cohesive entity because it is the acceptable Jewish "thing" to participate in Jewish activities together on the Jewish Sabbath. All celebrations of the Sabbath are centered around the family. Children are encouraged to help prepare for, and to take part in, all activities associated with the Sabbath. Daughters participate with their mothers in the ceremony of ushering in the Sabbath by kindling the Sabbath candles late Friday afternoon. Members of the family walk to and from synagogue together. The family gathers for the festive Sabbath eve and Sabbath day meals. In short, the Sabbath is designed to bring the family closer.

The Weekly Sabbath Meals

Sabbath meals take on a special significance; they are at once religious feasts and warm family occasions. During the festive meals, religious observance and family togetherness intertwine and they become joyous weekly occasions for physical and spiritual replenishment and family bliss.

A central idea in Judaism is the sanctification of the mundane, to raise ordinary activities to a higher moral and spiritual plane by performing them in an elevated manner. Eating, for example, becomes a holy activity when the meal is punctuated with Torah discussion. The Sages teach: "If three eat at the table and speak words of Torah, it is as if they eat at the table of the All-Present. To this table is applied the scriptural passage, 'This is the table before the Lord.' "[107]

The "table before the Lord" referred to here is the altar of the Temple in Jerusalem where sacrifices were offered up. In Jewish tradition, the table in the home is compared to the altar and the food to the sacrifice.[108] When a Jew eats in the prescribed traditional Jewish manner — he observes the dietary laws, and he recites benedictions before and after eating — he thereby thanks God for the good. By acknowledging that his sustenance is dependent on God, he transforms an ordinary act into one of transcendental holiness.

The act of eating becomes no longer a mere physical act to satiate hunger; it becomes a significant, elevated spiritual activity.

The Sabbath feasts are therefore weekly occasions for the Jew to acquire spiritual enrichment and intellectual development. They also provide an exceptional opportunity each week for all members of the family to come closer to one another and to develop intimate family ties — parents to children and children to parents, grandparents, and siblings. These relations become cemented over the many hundreds of Sabbaths and festivals that over the years are shared and experienced together by the family. The Sabbath is undoubtedly the most important source of that unique solidarity of the traditional Jewish family which is so often envied by outsiders.

The Golden Rule in the Home

In Jewish tradition, the Sabbath guest is an almost indispensable presence on the holy days. Whenever the traditional Jew celebrates a holy day and enjoys a festive meal at his table, he looks about him for others with whom to share his bounty. *Hachnasat orhim* ("bringing in guests") is a significant expression of *g'milut hasadim,* "loving acts," that the Jew, in fulfillment of the Golden Rule, is obliged to extend toward his fellow.[109]

The Talmud teaches that hospitality to guests is more than a kindly act; it is a *mitzvah* greater than that of welcoming the *Sh'chinah,* the Divine Presence.[110] The Sabbath is an especially appropriate time to perform this *mitzvah,* since travelers and those without family feel all the more on this day the absence of a home, and they welcome the opportunity to enjoy the Sabbath in a Jewish home atmosphere. In traditional Jewish homes on the Sabbath, therefore, there is hardly a home without wayfarers, school friends, students, singles, or acquaintances of various family members. Traditionally, a traveling Jew would enter the local synagogue for Sabbath eve services, and would leave later as a guest of one of the congregants. At times, he might find himself regretfully declining many other invitations extended to him in the synagogue, so eager were people to welcome guests into their home on the Sabbath.

The presence of guests at the Sabbath table provides an especially profound lesson for Jewish children. They grow up with the idea that loving one's fellow man is not an empty slogan, a distant ideal, or a mere recitation of a pleasant sounding biblical quotation. In Judaism, brotherly love is a *mitzvah* that is fulfilled only through the performance of deeds. Helpfulness and consideration for others, therefore, become ingrained in the child at a young age. "Love your fellow as yourself"[111] is more than a nice adage; it is a fundamental Torah command which is fulfilled by deeds of love, performed regularly as part of the normal routine of Jewish life.

Weekly Sabbath guests provide one means by which Jewish parents teach their children helpfulness and consideration for others. When the children see their parents' hospitality on the Sabbath, they learn to be compassionate and to reach out to others. When parents go out of their way to inculcate these principles in their children at every opportunity, they will become integral parts of their children and second nature to them. As in all matters, parents must demonstrate *hesed* to their children by being considerate toward them, toward one another, and toward others, and thus serve as living behavior models for their children. By encouraging children to be helpful in the home, to their parents, to their siblings, and to their guests, they also teach them to behave likewise to all people outside the home.

Opportunities for Family Discussion

The long, unhurried Sabbath meals in traditional Jewish homes are punctuated by traditional, melodious Sabbath songs, lyrical poems expressing the Jew's love for this day. Time is devoted to *divrei Torah* — Torah discussions. All members of the household, as well as the Sabbath guests, contribute to these discussions, usually centering on the scriptural readings of the week, or on ethical teachings of the Sages. At times, *divrei Torah* evolve into keen exercises in theology, exegesis, and logic, but the moral message is always emphasized. The young children are expected to tell of their experiences during the past week and to share with other members of the family some of the Torah learning they have accumulated during the week. The Sages consider these discussions essential: "A home where Torah is not heard will not endure."[112]

At the beginning of the Sabbath eve feast, the father blesses his children. He glances at the Sabbath lights — representing *sh'lom bayit* — and then places his hands on the head of each child in turn. To the boys he says: "May God make you like Ephraim and Menashe";[113] and to the girls: "May God make you like Sarah, Rebecca, Rachel, and Leah."[114] He ends with the threefold priestly blessing: "May the Lord bless you and protect you; May the Lord cause His countenance to shine upon you and may He be gracious to you; May the Lord turn to you and may He grant you peace."[115]

The children, in turn, bless their parents in the grace they recite following the meals.

R. Joseph Hertz, the late English chief rabbi, wrote of the Jewish home on the Sabbath:

> In modern times, friend and foe of the Jew alike speak with admiration of this home, and echo the praise of the heathen seer: "How beautiful are thy tents, O Jacob, thy dwelling places, O Israel."[116] The following description of the Sabbath eve . . . in the London ghetto [and the turn of the century] may well be quoted:
> The roaring Sambatyon of life was at rest in the ghetto; on thousands of squalid homes the light of Sinai shone. The ghetto welcomed the Sabbath bride with proud song and humble feast, and sped her parting with optimistic symbols of fire and wine, of spice and light and shadow. All around, their neighbors sought distraction in the blazing public houses (pubs), and their tipsy bellowings resounded through the streets and mingled with the Hebrew hymns. Here and there the voice of a beaten woman rose on the air. But no son of the covenant was among the revellers and the wife-beaters. The Jews remained a chosen race, a peculiar people . . . a little human islet won from the waters of animalism. . . .[117]

Jews have long appreciated the Sabbath as God's precious gift to the Jewish family, and they are aware of its evolution into the unique, vital institution of inestimable value that it has become in Jewish life. The Jewish home on the Sabbath, in its utter removal from the strife and discord of the world outside, has served many generations of Jews as a refuge, a palace in time or, as the Sages put it, *me'en olam haba,* a taste of paradise.[118]

Sabbath as the Climax of Family Living

For the traditional family, the Sabbath is the climax of living. It is the family's most important day of the week and of the year, a family occasion that comes not one, but fifty-two times each year. The days of the week become as a mere interim leading to this most beloved day. For Jews throughout the ages, the Sabbath, with its atmosphere of sacred tranquility and its beautiful customs and observances, has immeasurably strengthened the Jewish family unit.

It is no coincidence, therefore, that in homes where traditional observance of the Sabbath has been discontinued, its positive influence on the Jewish family has disappeared. Neglect and desecration of the Sabbath and ignorance of those traditions that give the Sabbath its peculiarly Jewish flavor, have invariably been accompanied by erosion of the closeness of the Jewish family structure. In homes where individual family members go their separate ways on the Sabbath as they do the rest of the week, the family ceases to function as a close, integrated unit. Without this special time each week when the family gathers around the table to be with each other, they soon find that their separate activities, interests, and acquaintances assume greater importance in their lives than does their family; consequently, as they are drawn further and further apart, the family unit is weakened.

Among Jews in many areas of the world, it was not infidelity or drunkenness that led to the dissolution of the family. The first step toward the breakdown of the traditional Jewish family was the desecration of the Sabbath. Many Jewish parents who turned the Sabbath into an ordinary day, for work, shopping, or recreation, often discovered — usually too late — that this was the beginning of the end of their close family ties. Even when they provided formal Jewish education for their children, it could not combat their own parental example of disregard for a fundamental institution of Jewish life. Many who in their own youth had experienced authentic Jewish Sabbaths decided that the Sabbath was inconvenient, and they eventually reduced it to an insignificant feature in their lives. As a result, they often found that their children, who knew little of Jewish tradition and what an authentic Jewish Sabbath experience was like, found it easy to absent themselves from the home on those occasions when their parents wanted the family together for an occasional Sabbath or festival meal.

Following six days of active involvement in the affairs of the week — business, school, and different forms of recreation — the Sabbath has traditionally been a time when the Jew simultaneously reaffirms his Jewish identity as a committed member of his family. It is the day in the life of every member of the Jewish family that is set aside for God and for family. To the traditional Jew, the Sabbath is perceived as a reward from God, a blessing eagerly anticipated following six days of toil — a day to visit the synagogue, but mostly to be celebrated at home with those closest to him.

"And You Shall Teach Them Diligently to Your Children"

The Sages teach: "Who is an ignorant man? He who has children but does not raise them properly by teaching them Torah."[119]

The Torah command "and you shall teach them diligently to your children"[120] represents both a fundamental charge and a challenge to Jewish parents. In addition to giving their children love and affection and a set of goals, proper motivation, and preparation to earn a livelihood, parents are called upon to implant in their children an awareness of their Jewish heritage together with a functioning set of Jewish values based on Torah morality and reverence for God. Generally speaking, the goal is to prepare children so that they can live full Jewish lives and be properly equipped with a system of ethics and values based upon Judaism's teachings to guide them in all their actions. Ideally, such children will be equipped and ready to transmit their Jewish heritage to the coming generation.

The *mitzvah* of parents to teach their children, therefore, encompasses several essential elements:

1. Reverence for God and love of God; love, respect, and gratitude toward parents; knowledge and observance of the *mitzvot* — the laws of the Torah and the *Code of Jewish Law* — and the rich traditions and customs of Judaism that serve as guidelines for the Jewish way of life.

2. Torah values, represented by the teachings of the Torah and the Jewish Sages and the ethical teachers, designed to mold the character of the child into an ethical, moral personality characterized by acts of love and kindness, humility, respect and consideration for others, honesty, charity, and mercy.

3. Intensive study of the Torah, the Talmud, and the primary and secondary Jewish texts in school and at home. Here the child absorbs the wisdom of Judaism and learns how to live as a Jew.

4. Concern, personal interest in, and close identification with *Klal Yisrael,* the Jewish community and the Jewish people all over the world, and *Eretz Israel,* the Jewish ancestral homeland, and their ancient capital, Jerusalem.

Education in Jewish Schools

The most fundamental learning a Jewish child must acquire is that of the ethical and moral values of Judaism. The Torah and teachings of the Jewish Sages will comprise the essential foundation upon which everything the child does later in life will stand. It will give an ethical and moral dimension to his world so that his life will have direction and purpose.

A religious education for Jewish children, therefore, cannot be a "secondary" education, the kind of educational afterthought that can be satisfied with several afternoons of Hebrew school or several hours of Sunday school classes. A good Jewish education is of prime importance in the priorities Jewish parents set for their children because it provides vital training that the Jewish child requires for living.

In light of the overriding importance of Jewish education, Jewish law considers a school where Torah is taught more significant than a synagogue; indeed, it permits the conversion of a synagogue into a school, but not *vice versa.*[121]

As mentioned, traditionally Judaism is imparted to Jewish children in two places: the school, where the primacy of the Jewish religio-ethical system is emphasized, but where the child also receives a general education; and in the home, where parents foster the child's development as a Jew and as a human being, while transmitting to him the principles of his Jewish heritage. The idea is for the two institutions together to promote the spiritual growth of the child, his development as a moral, ethical individual, and his intellectual evolution. This combined training is intended to give the child an awareness of his place among his people and of his responsibilities, and to provide a value system that will serve as his blueprint for life.

Art, Music, and Sports for the Child

Besides the religious subjects, the child's education may include
many other useful activities. A child might study and become skilled
in the arts. The Torah praises Bezalel and Oholiav, the master
artists and craftsmen who fashioned the Tabernacle and the Jewish
ceremonial art for it.[122] A child could learn to play musical
instruments. Music has always played an important role in Jewish
tradition, from the Levites in biblical times, who played the musical
instruments in the Temple, and King David the Psalmist, who
played the harp, to the hasidic rabbis of the last two centuries who
composed music and led their followers in song. Also, there is
definitely a place for sports in a healthy regimen. Indeed, Jewish
law obligates the father to teach his child to swim.[123]

Once the child is given an intensive Jewish education and
becomes firmly grounded in Judaism, then — and only then — is it
incumbent upon parents to attend to the question of how he is to
earn a living. In fact, helping their children to learn a trade or
profession is a duty, incumbent upon parents, which is spelled out
in *halachah*. The Sages teach: "A person is obligated to teach his child
a respectable trade."[124]

According to one talmudic view, it is so important for a parent to
arrange for his child's career or professional education that one may
even do so on the Sabbath.[125]

However, it is far easier to prepare a child to earn a good
livelihood than it is to prepare him to be a good individual capable
of living a proper moral life. The order of priorities chosen by most
parents is usually the reverse. Parents are concerned that their
children should succeed in the world, and stress earning a livelihood
and becoming established economically. R. Nahman of Bratzlav
points to the error in this: "When your children grow up, their
ability to earn a livelihood gains accordingly. Have no anxiety
regarding them."[126]

Common Mistakes Jewish Parents Make

Jewish parents who emphasize the general education of the child at
the expense of his training as a Jew through the study of Torah and

his Jewish heritage will pay a heavy price. The Sages teach: "He who denies a child Torah study robs him of his heritage."[127]

Relegating Jewish religious and moral teaching to the secondary or tertiary role of some afternoon classes or of a weekly Sunday school program where the child is provided with a smattering of superficial, elementary instruction, is a mistake of lasting consequence. These forms of instruction for Jewish children have proven to be ineffective instruments for transmitting the Jewish heritage to children. Graduates of this system have emerged from it, for the most part, ignorant of Judaism — of Jewish law, ethics, history, literature, thought, values — and the Jewish way of living.

When this system of education was instituted in America, its failure could have been foreseen. In Germany, in the middle of the nineteenth century, at a time when the Reform movement had made inroads into Jewish life and large numbers of Jews were assimilating into the majority culture and disappearing as Jews, R. Samson Raphael Hirsch expressed deep concern about a similar educational phenomenon then current. In retrospect, his words were prophetic. This German Jewish innovation was adopted in America and helped turn America into a veritable wasteland of Jewish knowledge. In a country populated by millions of Jews, the overwhelming majority are ignorant of even the rudiments of their faith, their heritage, and the Jewish contribution to civilization. That innovation was the afternoon Hebrew school. R. Hirsch writes:

If your children receive their education proper in [public] non-Jewish . . . institutions where the instruction ignores the Jewish element and . . . where, moreover, your children spend the greater and best part of the day; and if they then, having completed their homework and envying their colleagues their leisure, have to attend the lesson of a "Hebrew" teacher — who himself may be greatly inferior to the child's other teachers in general education and knowledge, or who has in his heart no enthusiasm for the Judaism with which he is supposed to inspire his students — if thus general education is imparted by the best and most appropriate methods, while "Hebrew" has to be content with such time, energy and teaching as can be found for it after other subjects have taken off the cream, you will frequently learn to your distress that your children are interested in everything but Hebrew; that all their teachers are satisfied with your children except the

"Hebrew" teacher; that instruction in all subjects bears fruit in your children while Hebrew instruction cannot even take root, and your children, being eternally and painfully tied down to elementary studies, learn to know Judaism and its study only as a nuisance.[128]

"Where Did We Go Wrong?"

Children are highly perceptive. They are especially quick to recognize insincerity, indifference, and negative attitudes. For all the enthusiasm parents might generate and exhibit for the after-hours Hebrew school or the one-morning-a-week religious school to which they send their children, children correctly gauge the value that the parents place on a Jewish education. They are well aware of it being relegated to an inferior position, in terms of scheduling and importance, relative to their secular education.

Judaism cannot be departmentalized in the way that music, dance, or sports activities can be; it is a way of life. When a child receives a proper, comprehensive training in Judaism and Jewish living, his entire life is affected. He applies Judaism and Jewish ethics and principles to every aspect of his life. A child can attend some courses in Hebrew for a few hours a week, and can perhaps even learn a few Hebrew words and a few Bible stories and ideas which are quickly forgotten; however, he will not thereby learn to live as a Jew, nor will he be equipped with an ethical system of living based upon Judaism and Jewish values.

As a result, Jewish parents discover the loss to themselves and to their people that they incur for neglecting the proper Jewish education of their children. Jewish youngsters grow up ignorant of Judaism and of their Jewish heritage, with no understanding of Jewish ethics and the Jewish way of life, and they see no reason to pay continued allegiance to the Jewish faith and the Jewish people.

The resultant rampant assimilation, intermarriage, and broken Jewish homes comprise a veritable spiritual holocaust that is eroding Jewish continuity and existence. This holocaust is not externally imposed, engendered by anti-Semites bent on extirpating Judaism or the Jewish people; rather, it is caused by well-meaning, loving Jewish parents and grandparents, who want "only the best" for their children, but who err seriously in determining what is "best." By so doing, Jewish parents and grandparents violate a sacred trust placed in their hands: to maintain the Jewish heritage and to transmit it to the next generation.

A Jewish parent who does *not*

- Practice the basic laws and traditions of Judaism,
- Observe the Sabbath and festivals,
- Observe the Jewish dietary laws,
- Practice *hesed,* acts of lovingkindness toward others on a regular basis,
- Maintain the various customs of Jewish life

paves a natural path for his child's next steps: assimilation and intermarriage. In answer to the pained, often bewildered cry of parents, "How did this happen?" the only reply is, "How could it *not* have happened?" Who can blame the child? He was simply not given any powerful persuasion that his heritage was fundamentally different from that of non-Jews; he had no rich set of Jewish values, and was not shown what a meaningful Jewish way of life was like and that the effort required not to assimilate and intermarry was worthwhile.

Intermarriage — The Ultimate Break

There are many Jewish parents who themselves have only a nebulous grasp of Judaism. If any one of these parents were slowly to grope his way back to his own recent history he would probably find a grandparent or great-grandparent to whom none of this was foreign, but who, pressured by war, by the move to a new land, by social upheaval, or by financial stress, abandoned the practices and traditions of Judaism and did not teach them to his children. And, such is the irony of Jewish history, that his grandparent before that one might have been a talmudist, a famous learned rabbi and scholar, and a righteous and pious Jew.

To the parents who were not given the chance to know Judaism, and to the grandparents who fell victim to outside pressures, we address ourselves here: there is no way to rationalize intermarriage.

Intermarriage is the ultimate Jewish catastrophe. In the words of R. J. H. Hertz:

> The training of every Jewish child should be such that he remains part of Israel, that he continues the work of the Jewish people and that he makes the building of a Jewish home [imbued with Judaism and Jewish values] the ambition of his youth and manhood. Intermarriage would then be out of the question for any son or daughter of Israel . . . Judaism expects that its sons and daughters should feel themselves duty bound . . . to refrain from courses of conduct that undermine the stability of the Jewish people. Every Jew who contemplates marriage outside the pale must regard himself as paving the way to a disruption which would be the final, as it would be the culminating, disaster in the history of his people.[129]

Deciding Where to Live

A major decision facing all married couples concerns their place of residence. For Jews interested in Jewish continuity and in their children living full Jewish lives in a positive Jewish environment, the area upon which they decide should be selected with great care and planning. Because it will so greatly affect the children, it should be chosen not only because it is demographically a Jewish neighborhood, but because of the nature of its Jewish community, and the nature of the friends the children will have.

It is important to make every effort to choose a community where children will be exposed to influences of others who are striving to live fully Jewish lives and to maintain their Jewish identity — where they will have a positive Jewish environment consistent with the Jewish training being provided in the home. Parents who live in a Jewish community where Jews live Jewishly, observing Jewish values and teachings, provide for their children an environment conducive to normative Jewish living. By living among Jews unconcerned with their Judaism, parents may cause their children to feel isolated on the Sabbaths and festivals.

Integral to a proper Jewish environment is a synagogue within easy walking distance of the home.

In Judaism, the end does not justify the means. Jewish law forbids *mitzvah haba'ah b'averah*, performing one precept by transgressing another.[130] Praying in a synagogue on the Sabbath, while desecrating the Sabbath by driving to the synagogue, is a serious transgression, not at all modified because the person is violating the Sabbath in order to go to a synagogue to pray.

The synagogue is considerably below the Sabbath on the scale of Jewish priorities. Although it is preferable to pray in a synagogue, it is permissible to pray at home. Faced with the choice, therefore, of praying at home or violating the Sabbath by driving to the synagogue, Jewish law *obligates* a person to stay at home. Therefore, a rabbi who sanctions violation of the Sabbath by allowing his congregants to drive to the synagogue on the holy day seriously violates Jewish law; he is considered a transgressor who causes others to transgress. No rationalization can justify a rabbi's advocating desecration of the sanctity of the Sabbath in order to give his congregants a spiritual experience or to fill the synagogue.

Jewish law permits one to drive on the Sabbath only in order to save a life; indeed, such an act is considered a *mitzvah,* a holy obligation which may not be put off.

The hallmark of a true Jewish community is the easy accessibility of its synagogue, which should be within walking distance of one's home. Those living far from the synagogue should move closer to it; or, small branch synagogues should be set up in private homes distant from the main synagogue. Another possibility is for houses or apartments to be purchased or rented close to the synagogue to house families over the Sabbath.

A Jewish school, providing an intensive Jewish education, is also central to a proper Jewish community. Such a school should preferably also provide a good general, secular education. It is important to seek a community that possesses such an institution or, alternately, to consider sending children away from home to such a school, a far less desirable option. Living close to his school gives the child the warmth, the reinforcement, and the positive Jewish environment he requires for his total education, in which Torah study forms an integral part of his home life. The Sages teach: "A home in which there are heard the sounds of Torah study will never be destroyed."[131]

The Jewish Home: Role Model to the World

The family is the protective armor of the Jewish nation. The continued vitality and dynamism of the Jewish national body has its source in the home, where the teachings of Judaism are practiced, and where the sacred duty of transmitting the Jewish heritage from generation to generation is enacted.

The Sages perceived the Jewish home as a *mikdash m'at*, a miniature sanctuary, which derives its sacred character from the conduct of the family and the nature of the Jewish life lived in the home. By his behavior as a religious, ethical individual the Jew sanctifies his home so that it becomes a dwelling place for God and thus the best place in which to discover God. In Jewish thought, the home is considerably more important than is the synagogue. Indeed, Judaism may be able to survive without the synagogue; it cannot without the home. The synagogue is holy in the influence it can have on the Jew and his home. It is the home that is the supreme Jewish sanctuary where the highest ideals of life can find fulfillment. Therefore it is the home that has primacy.

R. Samson Raphael Hirsch writes:

> Holiness is to flow out of [the synagogue] and penetrate all human conditions and places. However, *God is to be sought above all in the home* . . . the sphere in which human souls are planted and blossom, to which people take everything they accomplish and in which all their activity in building up their lives takes place, *that is the greatest and nearest place for finding the revelation of God.* [The idea is to create] a home in which such a life shall be lived that God will enter therein. Thereby, and thereby only, by making God [at home] ourselves, can a place on earth become a house of God. Not to realize this is the mistake that ages which pride themselves more than anything else in building beautiful cathedrals and "houses of God" so often make . . . They visit God in His house but forbid His entry into theirs, where His presence with His demands might certainly be inconvenient . . . The sanctity of the home is the necessary condition for the sanctity of God.[132]

The Jewish concepts of ethical and moral living, of brotherly love, compassion, and charity are perfectly incubated in the warmth of the Jewish home. There are those who leave their homes and go out to seek God in nature. The Jew finds God best in his own home. By living a proper Jewish life, the Jew invites God into his home and consecrates it as a temple. It is in the happiness of a good Jewish home that the Jew experiences his closeness to God.

There are many non-Jews who have marveled at the special

nature of Jewish family life. Francis Bacon, in *New Atlantis,* his novel about a utopian community, included a single Jewish family. The Jewish family had been invited to the community in order to teach the inhabitants the nature of Jewish family life and the qualities for which the Jewish people had been renowned.

Commenting on the moral impact of Jewish living in general and on the Jewish family in medieval times in particular, the historian and philosopher Will Durant writes:

> No Jew is known to have died from hunger while living in a Jewish community . . . Each Jew, however poor . . . contributed to the community chest which took care of the old, poor or sick, and the education and marriage of orphans . . . Hospitality was accorded freely . . . Jewish philanthropic societies [were] in great number . . . There were hospitals, orphanages, poorhouses, homes for the aged . . . organizations providing ransoms for prisoners, dowries for poor brides, visits to the sick, care for destitute widows and free burials for the dead. Christians complained of Jewish greed, [but] tried to stir Christians to charity by citing the exemplary generosity of the Jews . . .
>
> Discriminated against at every turn, pillaged and massacred, humiliated and condemned for crimes not [their] own . . . [nevertheless] of violent crimes . . . the Jews were seldom guilty . . . Their sex life was remarkably wholesome . . . Their women were modest maidens, industrious wives, prolific and conscientious mothers . . . Even hostile witnesses testify to the warmth and dignity . . . thoughtfulness, consideration, parental and fraternal affection that marked and mark the Jewish family. The young husband merged with his wife in work, joy and tribulation, developed a profound affection for her as part of his larger self; he became a father, and the children growing up around him stimulated his reserve energies and engaged his deepest loyalties . . . the parental relation was even more nearly perfect than the marital . . . The child was reverenced as a visitor from heaven, a very angel become flesh. The father was reverenced almost as a vicar of God . . . [Judaism] cast its awe and sanctity over every stage of development, and eased the tasks of parentage . . .
>
> The family was the saving center of Jewish life.[133]

Afterword

Through the centuries, many different ways of life, with their various charms and seductive allure, have competed for the loyalty of the Jew. Every culture to which the Jew has been exposed has had its "with-it" society — from the societies of ancient Egypt and Canaan to those of classical Greece and Rome, to that of contemporary America.

Invariably, whenever Jews substituted their elevated system of living and Judaism's social mores for those of the society in which they lived, they succumbed to the social ills endemic to those cultures. It is no different today.

There are those who have tried to make Judaism "meaningful" to a young generation by altering Judaism's character so as to reflect society's norms of behavior, stating that in this way Judaism will meet the needs of young Jews today. Arguing that the rules and regulations of the Torah related to a specific *milieu* and are now obsolete, they have tried to make Judaism "relevant" to the changing times.

Unfortunately, they make it relevant by mirroring as closely as possible the current practices of Jews who have forsaken their tradition and the elevated way of Jewish living for the values of a civilization suffering from moral disintegration and spiritual exhaustion. Inevitably, instead of preventing assimilation, such movements have had the opposite effect: they have encouraged assimilation and intermarriage, and they have made both of them appear to be viable alternatives for many Jews.

319

The error these Jews make is that historically Judaism has *never* been in step with the times and has *never* aped contemporary mores and practices. On the contrary, from its very inception, in the days of Abraham and Moses and throughout history, Judaism and its adherents have always been *in opposition* to the age and to the contemporary mores.

Judaism's perpetual strength is that it has never been timely; it has always been timeless. Judaism has always transcended the times and has never reflected them; as a result, it influenced the times. Judaism has always demanded of the Jew that by his behavior he, too, transcend the times and influence others, and thus serve as a moral example. Had Judaism been in the habit of succumbing and allowing itself to descend to the level of contemporary "needs" to harmonize with the age, it would have long ago disappeared. In the words of the nineteenth-century German rabbinic leader R. Samson Raphael Hirsch, "If the Jew was permitted to bring his Judaism up to date at any time, he would no longer need it anywhere."

Judaism is never perpetuated by those who bring Judaism down to the level of the age; if past experience is any guide, they or their descendants inevitably disappear as Jews. Judaism is perpetuated by Jews who are loyal to their heritage and its principles; they marry young and have sizeable families, and they provide their children with homes suffused with Jewish values, Jewish experiences, and intensive Jewish education.

When Jews are taught the elevated system of Jewish living, which involves faithful adherence to Jewish tradition and a life governed by rules requiring service to God and concern for one's fellow, there is personal happiness and communal strength. Throughout history, when the Jewish way of living has been practiced by Jews, they have succeeded in making the Jewish family the envy of the entire world. When it has not, Jewish life has been subject to the same destructive influences as those of society at large.

The Torah, as the wise King Solomon said, is "the tree of life for those who hold on to it, and those who uphold it are rendered happy" (Proverbs 3:18). Living the Jewish life has been for Jews its own best reward. It is a system designed to make the most of the life God gave to Man. When the Jewish people view the Torah as the *Or LaY'hudim,* "light to the Jews," they merit the attainment of their destiny of being a role model to the world, *Or LaGoyim,* "a light to the nations."

Notes

Notes to Chapter 1

1. Genesis 2:18.
2. Genesis 2:24.
3. *Ketubot* 8a; *Eruvin* 18a.
4. Genesis 1:27; see *Rashi* to Genesis 5:2.
5. Genesis 5:2; *Rashi* to Genesis 5:2.
6. See S. R. Hirsch, *Commentary to the Pentateuch*, trans. Isaac Levy (Gateshead and New York: Judaica Press, 1976), Genesis 2:24.
7. *Tiferet Tzion*, quoted in Moshe Weissman, *The Midrash Says* (Brooklyn, NY: Benei Ya'akov Publications, 1980), 38; see *Sanhedrin* 58a.
8. Genesis 2:24.
9. Genesis 9:17. The earlier version of the command *P'ru ur'vu* in Genesis 1:28 is considered to be a blessing, not a command; see *Rashi* to Genesis 9:7.
10. *Yvamot* 61b; Maimonides, *Yad, Ishut* 15:14; *Shulhan Aruch, Even HaEzer* 1:5.
11. Isaiah 45:18.
12. *Sefer HaHinuch, Mitzvah* 1.
13. See *Genesis Rabbah* 11:6.
14. Genesis 1:27.
15. *Shabbat* 133b.
16. *Shulhan Aruch, Even HaEzer* 1:1.
17. *Abarbanel* to 1 Samuel 1:1.
18. *Shulhan Aruch, Even HaEzer* 1:1.
19. *Genesis Rabbah* 68:4.
20. *Gittin* 90b.

21. *M'gillah* 27a; Maimonides, *Yad, Sefer Torah* 10:2; *Shulhan Aruch, Even HaEzer* 1:2.

22. *Responsa Hatam Sofer* 9:11. The halachic decision is based on the scriptural directive, "Therefore shall a person forsake his father and his mother and cleave to his wife," in Genesis 2:24.

23. *Yvamot* 61b; Maimonides, *Yad, Sefer Torah* 10:2; *Shulhan Aruch, Even HaEzer* 1:5.

24. *Yvamot* 61b; Maimonides, *Yad, Sefer Torah* 15:16; *Shulhan Aruch, Even HaEzer* 1:3.

25. *Yvamot* 62a.

26. Maimonides, *Yad, Sefer Torah* 15:16; see *Magid Mishne* commentary.

27. *Shulhan Aruch, Even HaEzer* 1:3.

28. *Rama, Shulhan Aruch, Even HaEzer* 1:3.

29. S. Baron, *The Jewish Community: Its History and Structure to the American Revolution*, 3 vols. (1942), vol. 2, 38.

30. *Yvamot* 63a.

31. Genesis 5:2.

32. *Zohar,* Genesis 5:2.

33. *Avot* 2:6.

34. *Genesis Rabbah* 68:4.

35. *Zohar, Kedoshim.*

36. *Zohar, Kedoshim* 24.

37. *Zohar, Mishpatim.*

38. *Shevet Musar,* chap. 24.

39. *Igeret HaKodesh.*

40. *Ruth Rabbah* 2:15.

41. Ruth 3:1.

42. *Sanhedrin* 22b; *Yvamot* 65b; see *Shabbat* 111a; *Gittin* 43b; *Kidushin* 35a; Maimonides, *Yad, Sefer Torah* 15:2.

43. *Shulhan Aruch, Even HaEzer* 1:13.

44. Genesis 2:24.

45. Deuteronomy 22:13.

46. *Kidushin* 2b.

47. Proverbs 3:17.

48. R. Meir Simha HaKohen, *Meshech Hochmah* to Genesis 9:7.

49. See *Shabbat* 111a.

50. Genesis 1:27.

51. Genesis 1:28.

52. *Gittin* 41b.

53. Isaiah 45:18.

54. *JT Yvamot,* end of chap. 6.

55. *Tosafot* to *Gittin* 41b.

56. Maimonides, *Yad, Isurei Bi'ah* 21:26; *Ishut* 15:2.

57. *Shulhan Aruch, Even HaEzer* 1:13.

58. Maimonides, *Yad, Isurei Bi'ah* 21:25; see *Rama* to *Shulhan Aruch, Even HaEzer* 1:13.

59. *Yvamot* 113a.

60. Genesis 30:1.

61. *Yvamot* 65b; Maimonides, *Yad, Ishut* 15:10.

62. Maimonides, *Yad, Ishut* 15:10.

63. D. S. Shapiro, "Be Fruitful and Multiply," in *Studies in Jewish Thought* (New York: Yeshiva University Press, 1975), 384.

64. *Bava Batra* 9a.

65. *Hidushei HaRan, Kidushin* 41a; see *T'shuvot HaRan* 32.

66. *Ecclesiastes Rabbah* 4.

67. Leviticus 19:18.

68. *Avot* 1:2.

69. Leviticus 19:18.

70. S. Wolbe, *Alei Shor,* 255, quoted in *Binyan Adei Ad* (Jerusalem: D'var Y'rushalayim, 1979), 46.

71. Genesis 2:18.

72. M. Meiselman, *Jewish Woman in Jewish Law* (New York: Ktav, 1978), 23.

73. *Shabbat* 25b.

74. *Genesis Rabbah* 17:1–2.

75. Genesis 2:18.

76. Ibid.

77. Ibid.

78. Deuteronomy 14:26.

79. Ezekiel 44:30.

80. Leviticus 17:11.

81. Isaiah 25:6.

82. Ecclesiastes 9:9.

83. Genesis 5:2.

84. Genesis 9:6.

85. Genesis 9:7.

86. *Sanhedrin* 22a.

87. *Sanhedrin* 22a; *Gittin* 90b.

88. *Ruth Rabbah* 1.

89. *Hagigah* 22b.

90. *N'darim* 64b; *Genesis Rabbah* 20.

91. *Shabbat* 31a.

92. *Yvamot* 61b, 62a; Maimonides, *Yad, Ishut* 15:4; *Shulhan Aruch, Even HaEzer* 1:5.

93. *Yvamot* 62b, 63a.

94. *Zohar* III, 7a.

95. *Tana D'bei Eliyahu Zuta* 14.
96. Ibid.

Notes to Chapter 2

1. *Shulhan Aruch, Even HaEzer* 15:1.
2. Deuteronomy 7:4.
3. N. Goldberg, W. J. Fried (editors), *Jews and Divorce,* quoted in *Encyclopaedia Judaica* 6:136.
4. Maimonides, *Yad, Isurei Bi'ah* 19:17.
5. *Bet Yosef, Even HaEzer* 4, end; *Darkei Moshe, Even HaEzer* 4:14; *Rama, Shulhan Aruch, Even HaEzer* 4:37; *Ba'er Hetev, Even HaEzer* 4:49.
6. Roland B. Gittelsohn, *Love, Sex and Marriage* (New York: Union of American Hebrew Congregations, 1980), 278.
7. Associated Press report in *Ma'ariv,* Tel Aviv, March 17, 1983, 7.
8. See *Jerusalem Post,* July 18, 1983, 15.
9. *Halachah* requires that the mother be Jewish in order that the child be Jewish.
10. See *Kidushin* 6a, 13a; *Shulhan Aruch, Even HaEzer* 44:93.
11. *Sotah* 27b; *Shulhan Aruch, Even HaEzer* 11:1, 178:17.
12. Maimonides, *Yad, Isurei Bi'ah* 15:1; *Shulhan Aruch, Even HaEzer* 4:13.
13. *Yvamot* 78b; Maimonides, *Yad, Isurei Bi'ah* 15:1; *Shulhan Aruch, Even HaEzer* 4:1.
14. Deuteronomy 23:3.
15. *Yvamot* 45b; *Kidushin* 69a, 74a; Maimonides, *Yad, Isurei Bi'ah* 15:33; *Shulhan Aruch, Even HaEzer* 4:24.
16. *Yvamot* 79b; *Kidushin* 67a and *Rashi, Kidushin* 67a, 72b, 73a; Maimonides, *Yad, Isurei Bi'ah* 15:7, 33; *Shulhan Aruch, Even HaEzer* 4:22.
17. Maimonides, *Yad, Isurei Bi'ah* 12:17; *Shulhan Aruch, Even HaEzer* 4:9. The exception is a *kohen,* who may not marry a convert. See list at end of chapter.
18. Deuteronomy 23:3; *Yevamot* 78a; *Shulhan Aruch, Even HaEzer* 4:1.
19. *JT Kidushin* 3:12; see *Yevamot* 76b.
20. *Sefer HaHinuch, Mitzvah* 576.
21. See *Targum Jonathan Ben Uziel* to Deuteronomy 23:3.
22. *Ramban,* Commentary to Deuteronomy 23:3.
23. S. R. Hirsch, *Commentary,* Deuteronomy 23:3.
24. Maimonides: "In order to create a horror of illicit marriages, a *mamzer* was not allowed to marry an Israelite woman; the adulterer and the adulteress were thus taught that by their act they bring upon their seed irreparable injury." *Moreh Nevuchim* 3:49; C. Chavel, *The Commandments* (New York: Soncino, 1967); *Lo Ta'aseh* 554.

25. *Shulhan Aruch, Even HaEzer* 49:3.

26. See Maimonides, *Yad, Isurei Bi'ah* 13:1-8.

27. Maimonides, *Yad, Isurei Bi'ah* 12:1,2; *Shulhan Aruch, Even HaEzer* 16:1, 44:5.

28. Maimonides, *Yad, Isurei Bi'ah* 12:1,2, also 12:7, 13:1-8, 14:1-8; *Shulhan Aruch, Even HaEzer* 16:1, 44:5.

29. *Bet Yosef, Even HaEzer* 4, end; *Darkei Moshe, Even HaEzer* 4:14; *Rama, Shulhan Aruch, Even HaEzer* 4:37; *Turei Zahav, Even HaEzer* 4:24; *Ba'er Hetev, Even HaEzer* 4:49.

30. *Shulhan Aruch, Even HaEzer* 17:1-2, 49:3.

31. Maimonides, *Yad, Isurei Bi'ah* 15:1, 10, 21, 22.

32. *Sotah* 27b; *Shulhan Aruch, Even HaEzer* 11:1, 178:17.

33. Maimonides, *Yad, Gerushin* 10:22, 11:14.

34. A ritual which obviates the necessity for levirate marriage (see Deuteronomy 25:5-6) between the brother of a man who died childless and his widow, if either of the two do not wish to marry one another.

35. Maimonides, *Yad, Yibum* 1:1-2; *Shulhan Aruch, Even HaEzer* 156:1.

36. Maimonides, *Yad, Gerushin* 11:12.

37. Maimonides, *Yad, Gerushin* 10:12, 11:14.

38. *Shulhan Aruch, Even HaEzer* 15:1.

39. Ibid.

40. Ibid., 15:12.

41. Ibid., 15:10.

42. Ibid., 15:17.

43. Ibid., 15:15.

44. Ibid., 15:13-4.

45. Ibid., 15:14.

46. Ibid., 15:26.

47. Ibid., 15:22.

48. Ibid., 15:8-9, 18.

49. Ibid., 15:19.

50. Ibid., 15:19.

51. Maimonides, *Yad, Isurei Bi'ah* 17:1; *Shulhan Aruch, Even HaEzer* 6:1.

52. Maimonides, *Yad, Isurei Bi'ah* 12:12, 17, 13:1-18, 14:1-8; *Shulhan Aruch, Even HaEzer* 16:1, 44:5.

53. Ibid.

54. See note 23.

55. *Otzar HaPoskim, Even HaEzer* 1:61; *Takanat Rabeinu Gershom; Shulhan Aruch, Even HaEzer* 1:10.

56. See note 25.

57. *Y'vamot* 24b and *Rashi ad loc.; Shulhan Aruch, Even HaEzer* 11:1.

58. Maimonides, *Yad, Gerushin* 11:12.

59. *Shulhan Aruch, Even HaEzer* 15:12.

60. Ibid., 10:12, 11:14.
61. Ibid., 15:13–14, 19.
62. Ibid., 15:10, 17, 22.
63. Ibid.
64. Ibid.; Maimonides, *Yad, Isurei Bi'ah* 17:1.
65. *Shulhan Aruch, Even HaEzer* 15:11.
66. Ibid., 15:24.
67. Ibid., 15:25; see *Rama, Shulhan Aruch, Even HaEzer* 15:25.
68. Ibid.
69. Ibid., 15:17.
70. Ibid., 15:21.
71. Ibid., 15:26.
72. Ibid., 15:11.
73. Ibid., 15:24.
74. Ibid., 15:17.
75. Ibid., 15:26.
76. Ibid., 15:25.

Notes to Chapter 3

1. Exodus 31:14.
2. *Genesis Rabbah* 68:4; *Numbers Rabbah* 3:6; see also *Midrash Tanhuma* to Numbers 16:18.
3. Proverbs 30:18–19.
4. Genesis 2:24.
5. Proverbs 24:32.
6. *Avot* 3:17.
7. *Zohar Hadash,* Genesis 5.
8. *JT Yvamot* 15:3.
9. Maimonides, *Yad, De'ot* 5:11.
10. See *Kidushin* 29b.
11. Maimonides, *Yad, Ishut* 15:2; *Shulhan Aruch, Even HaEzer* 1:3,4 and *Rama.*
12. Maimonides, *Yad, Ishut* 15:2.
13. *Kidushin* 29b.
14. *M'norat HaMa'or, Ner* III, Rule 6, part 2, chap. 4.
15. *Yvamot* 63a.
16. *Rashi, Yvamot* 63a.
17. See Chapter 4, "The Jewish Idea of Love," this volume.
18. Ben Sira 26:1; see *Yvamot* 63b, where a similar statement is applied to "a beautiful wife."

19. *Rashi, Y'vamot* 63a, b.
20. Proverbs 31.
21. See Psalms 34:10, 86, 110, 111:10, 112:1; Proverbs 1:7, 9:10; Job 28:28.
22. *Orhot Tzadikim, Sha'ar Yir'at Shamayim.*
23. See *Ma'alot HaMidot, Ma'alat Yir'at Shamayim.*
24. Deuteronomy 13:5.
25. See Maimonides, *The Guide for the Perplexed,* trans. M. Friedlander (London: Dover, 1956), Part I, chap. 69, p. 104.
26. See *Sotah* 14a; *Midrash Tanhuma, Vayishlah* 10: *Midrash* Song of Songs *Zuta* 1:15.
27. Psalms 19:10.
28. See Deuteronomy 21:11; Samuel 13:1, 14:27.
29. See S. Wolbe, *Binyan Adei Ad* (Jerusalem: D'var Y'rushalayim, 1979), 29.
30. Genesis 12:11, 14.
31. Genesis 23:16.
32. Genesis 29:17.
33. 1 Samuel 25:3; 2 Samuel 13:1, 14:27; 1 Kings 1:3–4; Songs of Songs 1:8, 15, 2:10, 13, 4:17, 5:9, 6:1, 4, 10; Esther 2:7.
34. *Eruvin* 21b.
35. *Kidushin* 21a.
36. *Sanhedrin* 107a.
37. 2 Samuel, chap. 18.
38. 2 Samuel, chap. 11.
39. *Sefer Hasidim* 378.
40. See *Binyan Adei Ad,* 18.
41. *Pele Yo'etz, Yofi.*
42. Psalms 111:10.
43. *Ta'anit* 26b.
44. Proverbs 31:30.
45. *Kidushin* 70b.
46. Genesis 24:23.
47. *Bava Batra* 109b.
48. See *Binyan Adei Ad,* 24.
49. Ibid., 24–25.
50. See *Eduyot* 2:9; *JT Kidushin* 1:7.
51. *Bava Batra* 110a.
52. *Sefer Hasidim* 378.
53. Ibid.
54. *Rashi, Kidushin* 71a.
55. See *Shulhan Aruch, Even HaEzer* 2:2.
56. Based on the principle, *Haposel, b'mumo posel.* He who invalidates

others, does so on the basis of his own defect. See *Shulhan Aruch, Even HaEzer* 21:2.

57. Maimonides, *Yad, Isurei Bi'ah* 19:17; see also *Kidushin* 70a; *Tur, Even HaEzer* 2:5.
58. *Y'vamot* 79a.
59. See *Betzah* 32b.
60. *JT Kidushin* 3:1.
61. *Sefer Hasidim* 156.
62. Proverbs 4:12.
63. *Y'vamot* 79a.
64. *Sefer Hasidim* 377.
65. See *Horayot* 13a.
66. See *Yoma* 71b.
67. Genesis 24:3-4.
68. *Sefer Hasidim* 1015.
69. Genesis 24.
70. S. R. Hirsch, *Judaism Eternal*, trans. I. Grunfeld (London: Soncino, 1959), vol. II, 67-68. Excerpts reprinted by permission of Judaica Press.
71. *Yalkut Shim'oni* 95.
72. *Ketubot* 17a.
73. R. Ezekiel Levenstein, quoted in *Binyan Adei Ad*, 24.
74. Genesis 24:67.
75. *Rashi*, Genesis 24:67.
76. *Onkelos*, Genesis 24:67.
77. *Shabbat* 25b.
78. Song of Songs 1:15.
79. *Song of Songs Rabbah* 1.
80. *Sefer Ma'alot HaMidot*, chap. 10.
81. *B'rachot* 12b.
82. *Sefer Hasidim* 41.
83. *M'norat HaMa'or, Ner* III, Rule 6, part 2, chap. 3.
84. *Yoma* 47a; see *Shulhan Aruch, Even HaEzer* 21:2.
85. Psalms 128:3.
86. *Midrash Tanhuma*.
87. *Tana D'bei Eliyahu Rabbah* 18.
88. *Sefer Ma'alot HaMidot*, chap. 1.
89. *Shabbat* 119b.
90. *Sefer Ma'alot HaMidot*, chap. 1.
91. *Ta'anit* 7b; *Yalkut Shim'oni* II, 268.
92. *Avot* 5:20.
93. *Avodah Zarah* 20b.
94. *Mishnah, Pe'ah* 1:1; *Shabbat* 127a.

95. *B'rachot* 7b.

96. *Ketubot* 17a; Maimonides, *Yad, Evel* 14:9; *Sefer Mitzvot Gadol, Asin D'Rabanan,* 2; *Tur, Yoreh De'ah* 360; *Tur, Even HaEzer* 65:4; see *Tosafot* to *Ketubot* 17a, *"M'vatlin."*

97. *Avodah Zarah* 17b.

98. Ibid.

99. *Rosh Hashanah* 18a.

100. *Avot* 1:17.

101. *Pe'ah* 1:1; *Shabbat* 127a.

102. *Kidushin* 40b; *Bava Kama* 17a.

103. From the *Daily Prayer Book.*

104. *Yoma* 72b, and *Rashi, "Tarti Gehinom."*

105. *Siddur Bet Ya'akov, "Sulam Bet El,"* Introduction.

106. S. R. Hirsch, *The Hirsch Siddur* (New York: Feldheim, 1969), 95.

107. S. R. Hirsch, *The Nineteen Letters* (New York: Feldheim, 1969), Fifteenth Letter, 95.

108. *JT Horayot* 3:5.

109. Maimonides, *Commentary* to the Mishnah, *Horayot* 3 (end).

110. *JT Horayot* 3:5.

111. Deuteronomy 6:13.

112. *P'sahim* 22b; see *Tosefta, M'chiltin,* chap. 2.

113. *Avot* 4:1.

114. *Ketubot* 111b.

115. *B'rachot* 34b.

116. *Yoma* 72b, Rashi *(v'tir'ah l'dartei avid).*

117. Psalms 111:10.

118. *P'sahim* 49a.

119. *Yalkut, Yitro* 268.

120. Ibid.

121. *P'sahim* 49b.

122. Ibid.; Maimonides, *Yad, Isurei Bi'ah* 21:32.

123. *P'sahim* 49a; *Yalkut, Yitro* 268.

124. Maimonides, *Yad, Isurei Bi'ah* 21:32.

125. *Igeret Hazon Ish,* quoted in *Binyan Adei Ad,* 146.

126. *Kidushin* 70a.

127. Hosea 5:7.

128. *Rama, Shulhan Aruch, Even HaEzer* 2:5.

129. *Ba'er Hetev, Shulhan Aruch, Even HaEzer* 2:5.

130. *HaM'iri* to Proverbs 14:1.

131. *Sefer Hasidim* 341.

132. *Sotah* 47a.

133. *Rashi, Sotah* 47a.

134. *Sefer Hasidim* 385 cites an example to show that it is a pious trait of *hasidut* for a single woman to refrain from the use of cosmetic artifice to attract a man.
135. See *Piskei Tosafot, Ta'anit* 34.
136. *Ketubot* 17a.
137. *Sukah* 49b.
138. *Zohar, Vayikra* 52.
139. *Avot D'Rabbi Nathan,* chap. 26.
140. *Kidushin* 70a.
141. Ibid. See also 70b.
142. Ibid.
143. *Yalkut,* Ruth 606.
144. *Sanhedrin* 76a.
145. *Sefer Hasidim* 379.
146. *Y'vamot* 63a.
147. *Kidushin* 49a.
148. See *Binyan Adei Ad,* 23–24.
149. See Exodus 20:56, 34:6–7; Deuteronomy 5:9–10.
150. Deuteronomy 16:20.
151. *Bava Batra* 9b.
152. *Avot* 2:5.
153. Leviticus 19:17.
154. *Yoma* 9b; *Gittin* 57b, and *Rashi.*
155. Ibid.
156. Ibid.
157. *Sifra,* Leviticus 19:18; *Genesis Rabbah* 24:7.
158. *Avot* 1:17.
159. See *Hafetz Hayim, Sh'mirat HaLashon,* English adaptation by Zelig Pliskin, *Guard Your Tongue* (New York: Feldheim, 1975), 13ff.
160. Proverbs 31:11.
161. Ibid., 18:21.
162. *Arachin* 15b.
163. Ibid.
164. *Avot* 1:18.
165. Exodus 23:7.
166. *Likutei Etzot HaShalom* (Warsaw, 1913), 55–56.
167. *Sefer HaMidot* (Warsaw, 1912), 96.
168. Deuteronomy 28:66.
169. *M'nahot* 103b.
170. Dov Katz, *T'nuat HaMusar* (Tel Aviv: *Baitan HaSefer,* 1952–1963), vol. I, 303.
171. *Seder Eliyahu Zuta,* chap. 3.
172. Ecclesiastes 3:4.

173. *Kuzari* 2:50.

174. Psalms 100:2.

175. Deuteronomy 28:47.

176. Ecclesiastes 8:17.

177. *Shabbat* 30b.

178. Ibid.

179. Proverbs 24:30–31.

180. Numbers 12:13.

181. Exodus 2:11.

182. I. Berger, *Simhat Yisrael* (Piotrkov, 1910).

183. See *Sefer Ma'alot HaMidot,* chap. 23.

184. Ibid.

185. *Horeb: A Philosophy of Jewish Laws and Observances*, II, trans. I. Grunfeld (London: Soncino, 1962), 394–395.

186. See Genesis 28:2, 34:4, 16, 38:6; Jeremiah 29:6.

187. Maimonides, *Yad, Ishut* 4:1.

188. Genesis 24:57.

189. Maimonides, *Yad, Ishut* 13:19.

190. Genesis 29:10–11.

191. *Shulhan Aruch, Yoreh De'ah* 240:25; *T'shuvot MaHarik* 166:3; *T'shuvot Rashdam, Yoreh De'ah* 95; *Sefer Hasidim* 561.

192. *T'shuvot Tashbetz* 3:130; *T'shuvot R. Akiva Eiger, P'sahim* 68; *T'shuvot Giv'at Pinhas* 3 (L'vov, 1838); *T'shuvot Mahaneh Hayim* 1:32 (Munkacz, 1872).

193. *Ketubot* 62b.

194. See *Genesis Rabbah* 68:4; *Numbers Rabbah* 3:6; *Midrash Tanhuma* to Numbers 16:18.

195. See *Binyan Adei Ad,* 20–21.

196. *Kidushin* 41a.

197. See Maimonides, *Yad, Isurei Bi'ah* 22:23.

198. *Binyan Adei Ad,* 32.

199. Ibid.

200. *Judaism Eternal,* 70–71.

201. Genesis 24:67.

202. See *Sanhedrin* 37a.

203. Ibid.

204. Aryeh Kaplan, *Made in Heaven* (New York: Moznaim Publishing Corp., 1983), 4–5.

205. See *Zohar* I, 89A.

Notes to Chapter 4

1. Leviticus 19:18.

2. Mark 12:37.

3. J. H. Hertz, *The Pentateuch and Haftorahs* (London: Soncino, 1981), 563.

4. Ibid.

5. *Sifra*, Leviticus 19:18; *Genesis Rabbah* 24:7.

6. *Avot* 1:12.

7. *Shabbat* 30b.

8. Maimonides, *Yad, Avel* 14:1.

9. *Ecclesiastes Rabbah* 7.

10. Exodus 23:4–5.

11. *Sefer HaHinuch, Mitzvah* 219.

12. *Pirkei D'Rabbi Eliezer,* chap. 12.

13. Hosea 6:6.

14. *Avot D'Rabbi Nathan,* chap. 4; see *Bava Batra* 20b.

15. Genesis 3:21.

16. Deuteronomy 34:6.

17. *Midrash Tanhuma, Vayikra* 10.

18. Psalms 89:3.

19. *Avot* 1:2.

20. S. R. Hirsch, *The Nineteen Letters* (New York: Feldheim, 1969), 36.

21. *Y'sodei HaTorah,* 1880, 9.

22. *Musar Avikha Umidot* (Jerusalem: Mossad Harav Kook, 1973), 125–126.

23. See *Orhot Tzadikim* (The Ways of the Righteous) (New York: Feldheim, 1974), 98–128.

24. Deuteronomy 7:8, 23:6; Malachi 1:2.

25. Genesis 22:2, 25:28, 37:3–4.

26. Genesis 24:6, 29:18, 30; Isaiah 18:20; Esther 2:17; Song of Songs 2:4–5, 3:10, 5:8, 8:6.

27. Judges 16:4.

28. 2 Samuel 13:1, 4, 15.

29. Jeremiah 2:33.

30. Ezekiel 23:5, 9.

31. Hosea 2:9, 12, 3:1.

32. See Psalms 103:13.

33. Micah 6:8.

34. *Orhot Tzadikim,* 98–99.

35. *Sotah* 31a; Maimonides, *Yad, T'shuvah* 10:1, 2, 4; Deuteronomy 3:2.

36. Deuteronomy 6:4.

37. Deuteronomy 6:5.

38. Deuteronomy 6:9, 11:20.

39. Deuteronomy 6:8, 11:18.

40. See Leviticus 19:14, 32, 25:17, 36, 45; Deuteronomy 6:2, 24, 8:6, 10:12, 14:23, 17:19, 25:18, 28:58, 31:12.

41. *B'rachot* 17a; *Pe'ah* 1:1; *Megillah* 28b; *Mo'ed Katan* 9a; *Y'vamot* 47a; *N'darim* 8b; *Sotah* 3b; *Sanhedrin* 90a; *Avodah Zarah* 4a.

42. *Sotah* 31a; Maimonides, *Yad, T'shuvah* 10:1, 2, 4.

43. See Psalms 34:10, 86:11, 112:1.

44. Proverbs 1:7.

45. Psalms 111:10; Proverbs 9:10; see Job 28:28.

46. *Sotah* 31a; Maimonides, *Yad, T'shuvah* 10:1, 2, 4.

47. Deuteronomy 7:9; Daniel 9:14; Nehemiah 1:5.

48. *Shabbat* 133b.

49. Genesis 1:27, 5:1, 9:6.

50. Deuteronomy 13:5; see *Rashi*.

51. See Yisrael Meir Kagan, *Hafetz Hayim, Ahavath Hesed,* trans. Leonard Oschry (New York: Feldheim, 1976), 82–84.

52. See Deuteronomy 10:18–19; see *Ramban* to Genesis 18:18.

53. Genesis 18:25; see Isaiah 61:8.

54. See Jeremiah 9:23.

55. See Exodus 22:26.

56. Deuteronomy 13:5.

57. See Deuteronomy 4:24.

58. See Genesis 3:21.

59. See Genesis 18:1.

60. See Genesis 25:11 and *Rashi*.

61. See Genesis 18:1.

62. *Sotah* 14a.

63. *Midrash Tanhuma, Vayishlah* 10.

64. Psalms 25:10.

65. *Song of Songs Zuta* 1:25.

66. Maimonides, *The Guide for the Perplexed,* trans. M. Friedlander (London: Dover, 1956), 104.

67. Philo, *Abraham,* 37.

68. Deuteronomy 6:4.

69. See *Ahavas Yisroel* (Brooklyn, NY: Kehot Publication Society, 1977), 10.

70. Quoted in B. D. Bokser, *From the World of the Cabbalah* (New York: Philosophical Library, 1954), 79.

71. Quoted in Martin Buber, *Tales of the Hasidim* (New York: Schocken, 1947), 227.

72. *Sifra,* Leviticus 4:12; see *Sifra,* Leviticus 19:18; *Genesis Rabbah* 24:7.

73. Genesis 5:11.

74. *Avot* 3:18.

75. *M'or Enayim* to *Parashat Pinhas,* quoted by I. Epstein, *The Faith of Judaism* (London: Soncino, 1968), 216.

76. *Tzava'at Ribash,* quoted by Epstein, ibid.

77. *Yoma* 86a.

78. *Sifri,* Deuteronomy 6:5.

79. Maimonides, *Sefer HaMitzvot,* Positive Commandment 3.

80. *Deuteronomy Rabbah 3.*

81. Genesis 1:28.

82. See *Ecclesiastes Rabbah* 7:4; *Tosefta, Pe'ah* 4:20; *Sifri,* Deuteronomy 116; *Yalkut Shimoni* 11:64.

83. See Maimonides, *Yad, De'ot* 6:3.

84. *Avodah Zarah* 17b.

85. *Rosh Hashanah* 18a.

86. S. R. Hirsch, *Commentary* to the *Sh'ma.*

87. Quoted by J. H. Hertz, *The Authorized Daily Prayer Book* (London: Soncino, 1976), 2.

88. Maimonides, *Yad, Avel* 14:1.

89. See *Ahavath Hesed,* 131–136.

90. Ibid., 148–152.

91. Ibid., 176–179.

92. *Shulhan Aruch, Yoreh De'ah* 256:1.

93. *Ahavath Hesed,* 189–193.

94. Ibid., 153–166.

95. *Sukah* 49b.

96. See *Ahavath Hesed,* 224–228.

97. See *Sefer HaHinuch, Mitzvah* 219; *Sh'mirat HaLashon.*

98. Ibid.

99. Ibid.

100. See *Ahavath Hesed,* 212.

101. Ibid.

102. Simon Shkop, *Sha'arei Yosher,* Introduction.

103. See Aryeh Kaplan, *Made in Heaven* (New York: Moznaim Publishing Corp., 1983), 11.

104. Genesis 22:2.

105. Genesis 24:67.

106. Friedrich Nietsche, *The Will to Power,* trans. Walter Kaufmann and R. J. Hollingdale, ed. Walter Kaufmann (New York: Vintage, 1968), 427.

107. *The Shorter Oxford English Dictionary,* third edition (London: 1972), 1171.

108. Arthur Schopenhauer, *The World as Will and Representation* (New York: Dover, 1966), vol. 2, 533.

109. "The Twilight of the Idols," in *A Nietzsche Reader* (Harmondsworth: Penguin), 26.

110. Andreas Capellanus, *The Art of Courtly Love* (New York: W.W. Norton, 1959), 28.

111. Ibid., 29.

112. Guillaume de Lorris and Jean de Meun, *The Romance of the Rose* (New York: Dutton, 1962), 47. Translated by Harry W. Robbins.

Translation copyright © 1962 by Florence L. Robbins. Introduction by Charles W. Dunn copyright © 1962 by E. P. Dutton. Used by permission of the publisher, Dutton, an imprint of New American Library, a division of Penguin Books USA, Inc.

113. Eileen Power, *Medieval Women*, ed. M. M. Postan (Cambridge: Cambridge University Press, 1975), 24.

114. Andreas Capellanus, *The Art of Courtly Love*, 107.

115. Quoted in Emmet Kennedy, "Destut de Tracy and the Origins of Ideology," in *A Philosopher in the Age of Revolution* (Philadelphia: American Philosophical Society, 1978), 260.

116. Sigmund Freud, *On Narcissism: An Introduction*, in *The Standard Edition of The Complete Psychological Works of Sigmund Freud* (London: Hogarth Press and The Institute of Psycho-Analysis, 1957), vol. 14, 94.

117. Freud, "Three Essays on Sexuality," in *The Complete Works of Sigmund Freud*, vol. 7, 150.

118. George Santayana, "Platonic Love in Some Italian Poets," in *Essays in Literary Criticism by George Santayana*, ed. Irving Singer (New York: Scribner's, 1956), 99.

119. *Marsilio Ficino's Commentary on Plato's Symposium* (Columbia, MO: University of Missouri Press, 1944), 140.

120. Jean-Jacques Rousseau, *Emile, or On Education*, trans. Allan Bloom (New York: Basic, 1979), 48, 214.

121. See "Ethica Nichomachea," in *The Student's Oxford Aristotle*, vol. 5, 1156a.

122. Immanuel Kant, *Lectures on Ethics*, trans. Louis Infield (New York: Harper and Row, 1963), 163.

123. "The Ethics," in *The Chief Works of Benedict de Spinoza*, trans. R. M. Elwes (New York: Dover, 1955), vol. 2, 175.

124. *Avot* 5:19-20.

125. See 2 Samuel, chap. 13.

126. Bertrand Russell, *Marriage and Morals* (New York: Horace and Liveright, 1929), 74.

127. Arthur Schopenhauer, *The World as Will and Representation*, vol. 2, 535-558.

128. Bernard Shaw, Preface to *Getting Married*.

129. Santayana, "Platonic Love," 99.

130. See Genesis 2:24.

131. *Yvamot* 62b; *Sanhedrin* 76b.

132. Maimonides, *Yad, Ishut* 15:19.

133. The principle is derived from the passage in Leviticus 18:5: "And you shall live by them" (the *mitzvot*), which is interpreted as "And you shall live by them, but not die by them" (*Sanhedrin* 74a).

134. *Ketubot* 8a; *Eruvin* 18a.

135. See *Bava M'tzia* 84a.
136. *Sotah* 17a.
137. *Nidah* 31a.
138. Kaplan, *Made in Heaven*, 13.
139. Genesis 2:23.
140. Simha Raz, *A Tzaddik in Our Time* (New York: Feldheim, 1978), 150.
141. Genesis 2:24.
142. *Sforno,* Genesis 2:24.
143. *Sotah* 17a.
144. *Genesis Rabbah* 20; See *JT B'rachot* 9.
145. *Pirkei D'Rabbi Eliezer,* chap. 12.
146. *M'nahot* 93b.
147. Quoted by L. I. Newman, *The Hasidic Anthology* (New York: Schocken, 1963), 221.
148. R. Judah ben Isaac Abarbanel, *Viku'ah al Ahavah* (Lyck, 1871), 6a, 13a.
149. *Song of Songs Rabbah* 1:31; *P'sikta d'Rav Kahana* 22.
150. *Pele Yo'etz, Ahavat Ish V'Ishto.*
151. See *Sotah* 20a.
152. *P'sahim* 112a.
153. See J. I. Schochet, *Gemiluth Chassadim* (Brooklyn, NY: Kehot Publication Society, 1967), 15.
154. Elijah Dessler, *Michtav MeEliyahu,* "Strive for Truth" (NY: Feldheim, 1978), 121, 150–155.
155. Ibid., 126–127.
156. Ibid., 130–131.
157. *Midrash Tanhuma, Vayishlah,* 18.
158. *Michtav MeEliyahu,* 132.
159. S. Wolbe, *Hoveret Hadrachah L'Hatanim,* 10, quoted in *Binyan Adei Ad,* 106.
160. Judah ben Isaac Abarbanel, *Viku'ah al Ahavah.*
161. Genesis 24:67.
162. S. R. Hirsch, *Commentary,* Genesis 24:67.
163. *Malbim,* Deuteronomy 24:1.
164. Genesis 29:18–20.
165. S. R. Hirsch, *Commentary,* Leviticus 19:18.

Notes to Chapter 5

1. See *Ketubot* 8a, 48a; *Genesis Rabbah* 49:7.
2. *Reshit Hochmah, Sha'ar Ha'Ahavah,* chap. 4.
3. See S. R. Hirsch, *Commentary,* Genesis 2:25.

4. Saadia Gaon, *HaEmunot V'haDe'ot*, vi.
5. Maimonides, *Moreh N'vuchim* III, 27.
6. Leviticus 19:2.
7. *Sifra*, Leviticus 19:2.
8. See S. R. Hirsch, *Commentary*, Genesis 2:25.
9. See S. R. Hirsch, *Commentary*, Leviticus 19:2.
10. Leviticus 19:1, 2.
11. Exodus 19:6.
12. Leviticus 20:26.
13. *Megillah* 27b.
14. Leviticus 11:44, 45; 19:2; 20:7, 26.
15. *Leviticus Rabbah* 24:6.
16. *B'rachot* 57b.
17. Deuteronomy 23:15.
18. Leviticus 20:8.
19. *Numbers Rabbah* 9:7.
20. Psalms 34:15.
21. *Y'vamot* 20a.
22. *Hagigah* 11b; see *Makot* 23b.
23. Numbers 11:10.
24. *Sifri, B'ha'alot'cha* 90; see *Yoma* 75a; see *Shabbat* 130a.
25. Maimonides, *Yad, Isurei Bi'ah* 22:18.
26. *Midrash Tanhuma* 58:13.
27. *Torat Kohanim, Aharei Mot* 18.
28. *Song of Songs Rabbah* 4:24.
29. Deuteronomy 6:5.
30. *B'rachot* 54a.
31. See S. R. Hirsch, *The Hirsch Siddur* (Jerusalem: Feldheim, 1978), 115.
32. Leviticus 11:44.
33. *Yoma* 39a.
34. Ibid., 38b.
35. *Igeret HaKodesh*, chap. 3.
36. *M'norat HaMa'or, Ner* III, Rule 6, part 6, chap. 1.
37. Jacob Emden, *Siddur Bet Yaakov, "Hanhagat Leyl Shabbat," Hadar HaMitot, Mitot Kesef* (Lemberg: David Balaban, 1904), 158–160.
38. *Zohar, K'doshim* 22–23.
39. Genesis 2:24.
40. Genesis 2:18.
41. *Y'vamot* 62b.
42. Mordechai Gifter, Foreword to *Song of Songs* (New York: Artscroll, 1977), xix.
43. Genesis 4:1.

44. Genesis 4:25.
45. Genesis 24:16.
46. Genesis 38:26.
47. See Genesis 4:17, 9:18; Numbers 31:17; 1 Samuel 1:19; 1 Kings 1:4.
48. See *Nidah* 45b.
49. *Sotah* 17a.
50. *Siddur Bet Yaakov, "Sulam Bet El."*
51. *Pele Yo'etz* 7.
52. Deuteronomy 6:5.
53. Deuteronomy 11:22, 30:20.
54. Psalms 91:14.
55. Psalms 9:11.
56. Jacob Emden, *Siddur Bet Yaakov,* 158–160.
57. Genesis 4:25.
58. Hosea 2:21, 22.
59. Cited in *Reshit Hochmah,* Hosea 2:21, 22.
60. See Maimonides, *Yad, T'shuvah* 10:3.
61. Song of Songs 2:5.
62. *Orhot Tzadikim, "Sha'ar Ha'Ahavah."*
63. S. R. Hirsch, *Judaism Eternal* (London: Soncino, 1959), vol. 2, 82–84.
64. Saadia Gaon, *Ha'Emunot V'haDe'ot* 10:6.
65. Hosea 2:4, 18, 21.
66. Isaiah 62:5.
67. Jeremiah 2:2.
68. Ezekiel 15:8.
69. Malachi 2:11.
70. *P'sikta d'Rav Kahana,* 22.
71. Song of Songs 4:8, 9, 10, 11, 12, 5:1.
72. Isaiah 49:18, 61:10, 62:25.
73. Jeremiah 33:11.
74. Psalms 93:1, 104:1; Daniel 79; Isaiah 59:17, 63:12.
75. *Deuteronomy Rabbah* 3:12; see also *M'chilta* to Exodus 19:17.
76. See *Agadat Shir HaShirim* to Song of Songs 8:5; *Seder Eliyahu Rabbah* 6:7, 9, 10.
77. See *Orhot Tzadikim, "Sha'ar Ha'Ahavah."*
78. *Yadayim* 3:5; see also introductions of *Rashi* and *Ibn Ezra* to Song of Songs.
79. *Yoma* 54a.
80. *Orhot Hayim L'HaRav Eliezer HaGadol,* attributed to R. Eliezer ben Isaac of Worms of the eleventh century, cited by Israel Abrahams, *Hebrew Ethical Wills* (Philadelphia: Jewish Publication Society of America, 1926 and 1976), 41.
81. *Genesis Rabbah* 11:8.

82. *Shabbat* 119a.

83. *Exodus Rabbah* 41:5.

84. *P'sahim* 49b.

85. *Sanhedrin* 59a; *Exodus Rabbah* 33:7.

86. Isaiah 62:5.

87. *Exodus Rabbah* 15:3.

88. *Kad HaKemah*, English ed., trans. C. Chavel (New York: Shilo, 1980), 259.

89. From the *Amidah* in the Prayer Book.

90. *B'rachot* 25b.

91. Proverbs 3:6.

92. Cited in *Studies in Judaism* (Philadelphia: Jewish Publication Society of America, 1924), vol. 1, 29.

Notes to Chapter 6

1. Genesis 1:27.

2. Genesis 17:10-13.

3. Deuteronomy 8:6, 19:9, 26:17, 28:9, 30:16; 1 Kings 2:3; Psalms 128:1.

4. *Sforno*, Genesis 17:11.

5. *Sefer HaHinuch, Mitzvah* 2.

6. *Sifra*, Leviticus 19:2.

7. Genesis 17:1.

8. S. R. Hirsch, *The Pentateuch — Commentary,* trans. Isaac Levy (Gateshead and New York: Judaica Press, 1976), Genesis 2:25. Excerpts reprinted by permission of Judaica Press.

9. *Kidushin* 2b.

10. Genesis 38:21-22; Deuteronomy 23:18; Hosea 4:14.

11. S. R. Hirsch, *Commentary,* Leviticus 19:2.

12. Ibid., Genesis 4:7.

13. See *Sotah* 47a.

14. Jacob Emden, *Siddur Bet Yaakov, "Hanhagat Leyl Shabbat," Mitot Kesef* (Lemberg: David Balaban, 1904).

15. Genesis 1:31.

16. *Genesis Rabbah* 9:7.

17. S. R. Hirsch, *Commentary,* Genesis 2:25.

18. Ibid., Genesis 3:1.

19. S. R. Hirsch, *The Nineteen Letters* (Jerusalem: Feldheim, 1969), 94-95.

20. *Avot* 4:1.

21. *Bava Batra* 78b.

22. *Zohar* to Exodus 1:28.

23. *Avodah Zarah* 17a, b.
24. See *Sanhedrin* 64a; *Yoma* 69b.
25. See *Rashi* to *Avodah Zarah* 17b.
26. *Avodah Zarah* 17a,b.
27. *Sanhedrin* 107a.
28. *Sifra*, Leviticus 20:26.
29. Leviticus 20:26.
30. S. R. Hirsch, *Commentary*, Leviticus 20:26.
31. See *Sanhedrin* 107a.
32. Leviticus 18:22.
33. Leviticus 20:13.
34. Leviticus 18:22–30.
35. Leviticus 20:13.
36. *Sefer HaHinuch, Mitzvah* 209.
37. Norman Lamm, "Judaism and the Modern Attitude to Homosexuality," in Fred Rosner and J. David Bleich, *Jewish Bioethics* (New York: Sanhedrin Press, 1979), 197–218. Excerpts reprinted by permission of the publishers, Hebrew Publishing Company, P.O. Box 157, Rockaway, NY 11693. Copyright © 1979. All rights reserved.
38. Ibid., 204.
39. Genesis 19:5.
40. Judges 19:22.
41. Judges 19:25–26.
42. Judges, chap. 20.
43. Judges 21:1.
44. *Sanhedrin* 57b, 58a.
45. *Kidushin* 82a.
46. Maimonides, *Yad, Isurei Bi'ah* 22:2.
47. Ibid.
48. *Shulhan Aruch, Even HaEzer* 24:1.
49. *Sifra* 19:18; Maimonides, *Yad, Isurei Bi'ah* 21:8.
50. Leviticus 18:3.
51. Lamm, "Judaism and Homosexuality," 210 ff.
52. Ibid., 208–214.
53. Maimonides, *Yad, Isurei Bi'ah* 21:8.
54. See Lamm, "Judaism and Homosexuality," 217.
55. Ibid., 217–218.
56. Exodus 21:10; see *Ketubot* 47b, 48a, 59b, 61a, 66b; *Bava M'tzia* 59a; *Hulin* 84a; *Y'vamot* 62b; *Shabbat* 25b; *N'darim* 15b; *Sefer HaMitzvot, Lo Ta'aseh* 262; *Sefer Mitzvot Gadol* 81; *Sefer Mitzvot Katan* 277–278; *Sefer HaHinuch* 46; Maimonides, *Yad, Ishut* 12:25; *Shulhan Aruch, Even HaEzer* 70, 73, 76.
57. *Igeret HaKodesh.*
58. *Shulhan Aruch, Orah Hayim* 240:1.

59. Deuteronomy 24:5.

60. See Eliezer Berkovitz, *Crisis and Faith* (New York: Sanhedrin Press, 1978), 62.

61. Norman O. Brown, *Life Against Death, The Psychoanalytical Meaning of History* (New York: Random House, 1959), 31.

62. Berkovitz, *Crisis and Faith,* 76.

63. Genesis 1:27.

64. Genesis 2:24.

65. *Ramban, Commentary,* Genesis 2:24.

Notes to Chapter 7

1. I am indebted to R. Aryeh Kaplan's *Made in Heaven* (New York: Moznaim Publishing Corp., 1983) for much of the information in this and the following chapter.

2. *Rama, Shulhan Aruch, Yoreh De'ah* 240:25, *Sefer Hasidim* 561; *Ketubot* 62b.

3. *Rashbam, Bava Batra* 145a.

4. See *Shulhan Aruch, Even HaEzer* 45:1.

5. *Shulhan Aruch, Even HaEzer* 68; *Shulhan HaEzer* 2:2:19.

6. See *Bava M'tzia* 7b.

7. *Shulhan HaEzer* 2:1:21.

8. *Eliyahu Rabah* 560:7; *Pri M'gadim, Mishb'tzot Zahav, Orah Hayim* 560:4; see *Darkei Moshe* 560:2; *Likutei Moharan* 60:8.

9. *Toldot Aharon,* quoted in *Ta'amei HaMinhagim,* note to 970.

10. *Sha'arei Rahamim* (Vilna, 1871); see *Genesis Rabbah* 14:7.

11. See *Shulhan HaEzer* 2:2:1.

12. *Mateh Ephraim* 602:5; *Shulhan HaEzer* 4:6:13.

13. *Shulhan Aruch, Orah Hayim* 546:1; *Even HaEzer* 64:6.

14. *Shulhan Aruch, Orah Hayim* 493:1.

15. See *Igrot Moshe, Even HaEzer* 97.

16. *Shulhan Aruch, Orah Hayim* 551:2.

17. *Shulhan Aruch, Yoreh De'ah* 192:6.

18. Genesis 1:10, 12.

19. *Magen Avraham* to *Orah Hayim* 546:4.

20. *Rokeah* 353.

21. See *Mordechai, Ketubot* 129.

22. *Shulhan HaEzer* 7:2:3.

23. *Igrot Moshe, Even HaEzer* 93.

24. *Nahlat Shiv'ah* 12:9.

25. *HaGra* to *Even HaEzer* 55:1.

26. *Rama, Shulhan Aruch, Yoreh De'ah* 242:14.

27. *Kidushin* 6a, 13a.

28. *Shulhan Aruch, Even HaEzer* 49:3.

29. *Shulhan HaEzer* 6:7; *Keter Shem Tov*, note 702.

30. *Bava Kama* 89a; see *Ketubot* 57a.

31. See *Ketubot* 56b, 57a; Maimonides, *Yad, Ishut* 10:7; *Shulhan Aruch, Even HaEzer* 66:1.

32. *Shulhan Aruch, Even HaEzer* 66:3; *Helkat M'hokek* 66:14.

33. In the Greek form of Tobit — only several fragments of the original Hebrew or Aramaic were found among the Dead Sea Scrolls in Qumran — the word for "paper" is *biblion,* which also means scroll or letter, and the word for "contract" is *syggraphon,* or "that which is written," a literal translation of *ketubah.*

34. Tobit 7:13–15.

35. Known as Aswan Papyrus G.

36. See Yigael Yadin, *Bar Kokhba* (New York: Random House, 1971), 222-223.

37. R. Simon ben Gamliel, *Ketubot* 10a; R. Meir, *Ketubot* 56b; see *Ketubot* 110b; *Rashi, Ketubot* 10a, *"Hachamim"*; Tosafot, Ketubot 10a, *"Amar"*; *Yvamot* 89a, *"Ta'ameh"*; *Sefer Mitzvot Gadol,* Positive Precept 48.

The predominant view, however, is that the *ketubah* is ordained by rabbinic legislation. This is the opinion of R. Naham, R. Samuel, R. Simon ben Elazar, and others. *Ketubot* 10a, 56b; see *Hidushei HaRan, Sanhedrin* 31b; *Rosh, Ketubot* 1:19; Maimonides, *Yad, Ishut* 10:7; *Helkat M'hokek* 66:26.

38. Exodus 21:10.

39. See Isaiah 36:11; 2 Kings 18:26.

40. *Ketubot* 82b.

41. *Shabbat* 14b; *Ketubot* 82b.

42. *Ketubot* 1a, 39b, 54a; *Yvamot* 89a.

43. See Deuteronomy 24:1; see Hillel's view, *Gittin* 90a.

44. *Rama, Even HaEzer* 119:6.

45. See Mishnah, *Pe'ah* 8:8, and S. R. Hirsch, *Commentary,* Exodus 15-16.

46. In Germany and Holland, some communities used printed *ketubah* forms in the eighteenth and nineteenth centuries.

47. In the Bodleian Library, Oxford No. 2807.

48. If the bride has been previously married, it is not halachically permissible to cross out and change any of the words in the printed *ketubah* form; if a form for a divorcee or a widow is not available, a specially written *ketubah* is required. See *Ta'amei HaMinhagim* 964, *Kuntres Aharon.*

49. *Shulhan HaEzer* 6:9; *Nahlat Shiv'ah* 12:72.

50. See *Hoshen Mishpat* 48:1; see *Hagahot Maimoniot, Yad, Ishut* 10:7, no. 4; *Shulhan HaEzer* 6:8.

51. *Bava Batra* 167b; *Shulhan Aruch, Even HaEzer* 66:1.

52. *Da'at Z'kenim Miba'alei Tosafot* to Genesis 38:18.

53. See *T'shuvot Ramban* 144; see *T'shuvot Rashba* 1241; see *Shulhan Aruch, Even HaEzer* 28:19. A groom may use someone else's ring only when it is given to him as an unconditional gift.

54. *Even HaEzer* 28:1.

55. *Shulhan Aruch, Shulhan HaEzer* 8:1:18; see *Hochmat Adam* 129:16.

56. *Bet Sh'muel* 227:1; *Avnei Miluim* 27:2; *Aruch HaShulhan* 27:3.

57. *Tikunei Zohar* 5 (19a); see *Zohar* 3:256b.

58. *Mordechai, Kidushin* 488; *Hagahot Maimoniot, Yad, Ishut* 7:8 No. 5; *Shulhan HaEzer* 8:1:22, 8:21:1.

59. See *Edut L'Yisrael* 45; However, some rabbinic authorities maintain that silver should not be used; see *Bet Yosef, Even HaEzer* 30.

60. *T'shuvot Radbaz* 467.

61. *Hagahot Maimoniot, Yad, Ishut* 8:1 No. 2.

62. *Kidushin* 48b; Maimonides, *Yad, Ishut* 8:1.

63. *JT Bikkurim* 3:3; *Genesis Rabbah* 67:13; *Rashi* to Genesis 36:3; *Ramban* to Genesis 36:3; *Magen Avraham* 573:1; *HaGra* 61:9; see *Y'vamot* 63b.

64. Isaiah 1:18.

65. *Siddur Bet Yaakov*, 124; see *Rama, Orah Hayim* 610:4.

66. See *B'rachot* 31a.

67. *Genesis Rabbah* 18:1, 13; see *B'rachot* 61a.

68. See *Ta'anit* 31a; *Ketubot* 59b; *B'rachot* 57b; *Y'vamot* 63b.

69. Genesis 29:17; see *Radak.*

70. See *Exodus Rabbah* 23:5; see Isaiah 3:24; see *Y'vamot* 34b; see *Yoma* 38a, 39b.

71. *Genesis Rabbah* 18:1; see Isaiah 3:18-24.

72. *Exodus Rabbah* 41:5; *Song of Songs Rabbah* 4:22; *Midrash Tanhuma, Ki Tisa,* 16; *Rashi* to Exodus 31:18; see *Zohar* 1:48b; see Isaiah 41:18, 61:10.

73. *Ketubot* 72b; Maimonides, *Yad, Ishut* 24:12; *Shulhan Aruch, Even HaEzer* 15:4; *Zohar* 1:142a; *Rokeah* 324.

74. *B'rachot* 24a; *Shulhan Aruch, Orah Hayim* 75:1.

75. See Genesis 31:27.

76. See Psalms 78:63 and *Radak.*

77. See *MaHaril, Eruvei Hatzerot* 31b.

78. See *Darkei HaHayim V'HaShalom* 1051; *Igrot Moshe, Even HaEzer* 96.

79. *Mordechai, P'sahim* 604; see *Magen Avraham* 670:4.

80. *Sanhedrin* 27b; see *Tosefta, Shabbat* 17:4.

81. See *Targum Onkelos* to 2 Samuel 13:3, 15:37, 16:16, 18:37; 1 Kings 4:5; 1 Chronicles 27:33 and *Rashi.*

82. See *Radak* to 2 Samuel 15:37, 1 Kings 4:5.

83. Judges 14:11.

84. *Mahzor Vitri* 488.

85. See *Kidushin* 81a, and *Rashi (Shosvintey).*

86. See *B'rachot* 61a; *Eruvin* 18a; *Genesis Rabbah* 18:3.

87. *Bava Batra* 144b; see *Eruvin* 18b, 145a, b.

88. Maimonides, *Yad, Z'chuyah u'Matanah* 7:1; see also Maimonides to *Sanhedrin* 3:5.

89. *Rashbam, "HaAchin"* to *Bava Batra* 144b; *Eruvin* 18b; *Tur Even HaEzer* 60; *Tosafot* to *Bava Batra, "HaAchin"* 144b; Maimonides to *Bava Batra* 10:4.

90. See *Yoreh De'ah* 192:1.

91. See *Yvamot* 62b.

92. *Masechet Sofrim* 11; *Pirkei D'Rabbi Eliezer* 17.

93. Ibid.

94. Ibid.

95. *Shulhan HaEzer* 6:1:15.

96. See *Rashi (Mamshichin), B'rachot* 50b; *Rokeah* 352.

97. *Rokeah* 353; *Rosh, Ketubot* 1:15; *Shulhan Aruch, Even HaEzer* 63:2; *Mahzor Vitri* 586; see *Rama, Even HaEzer* 63:2.

98. *Shulhan HaEzer* 6:1:5.

99. Song of Songs 6:11.

100. *Ta'amei HaMinhagim* 940.

101. See *JT Ketubot* 2:10; *JT Kidushin* 1:5; *Ruth Rabbah* 7:9; see *JT Bava M'tzia* 4:12; *P'sahim* 109a.

102. *Rama, Yoreh De'ah* 192:2.

103. *Shulhan HaEzer* 8:5:5.

104. *Dagul Mer'vava* to *Yoreh De'ah* 197:3.

105. *K'ritot* 9a.

106. See Ezekiel 16:8, 9.

107. *Radak, M'tzudat David,* Ezekiel 16:8, 9; see *Abarbanel,* Ezekiel 16:8, 9.

108. See *Rokeah* 353; *Rama, Shulhan Aruch, Even HaEzer* 6:1:1; *Rama, Shulhan Aruch, Orah Hayim* 573:1; *Kitzur Shulhan Aruch* 146:1; *Shulhan HaEzer* 6:3; *Edut L'Yisrael* 2.

109. Most Sephardic Jews do not have this tradition; *Magen Avraham* 559:11; *Rama, Shulhan Aruch, Even HaEzer* 61:1; *L'vush, Even HaEzer* 60:1; *Birkei Yosef, Orah Hayim* 470:2.

110. See *Shabbat* 130a.

111. *JT Bikurim* 3:3; *Genesis Rabbah* 67:13; *Rashi* to Genesis 36:3; *Ramban* to Genesis 36:3; *Magen Avraham* 573:1; *HaGra* 61:9; see *Yvamot* 63b.

112. See S. R. Hirsch, *Commentary,* Genesis 3:19.

113. *Mateh Moshe* 3:2; *Likutei MaHarich* 3:13a; *Pri M'gadim, Eshel Avraham* 571; *MaHaril* 65b.

114. *Rama, Shulhan Aruch, Even HaEzer* 61:1; *Nahlat Shiv'ah* 12:15; *L'vush, Even HaEzer* 60:1; *Shulhan HaEzer* 6:3; *Edut L'Yisrael* 2:2.

115. See *Likutei Moharan* 49:7; *S'dei Hemed, Hatan V'Kalah* 11; *Shulhan HaEzer* 9:9.

116. See *Magen Avraham* 8:3; see *Likutei MaHarich* 1:13b; *S'dei Hemed, Hatan V'Kalah* 85.

117. Numbers 15:37-41.

118. Deuteronomy 22:12.

119. Numbers 15:39.

120. *B'rachot* 12b.

121. *Ta'amei HaMinhagim* 947.

Notes to Chapter 8

1. *Mahzor Vitri* 469; *Tur, Even HaEzer* 63; *Hagahot Maimoniot, Ishut* 10:3; *Rama, Shulhan Aruch, Even HaEzer* 55:1.

2. *Kelim* 22:4; *Eduyot* 1:11; see *Yvamot* 110a; *Genesis Rabbah* 20.

3. See *Shulhan Aruch, Even HaEzer* 6:6.

4. See *MaHaril* 64b; *Rashi, Ketubot* 17b, "*Karite.*"

5. *Ketubot* 17b, "*Hinuma*"; see *Rashi*, ibid.

6. Genesis 24:6.

7. See *Likutei MaHarich, Vayaged Moshe*, based on *Sukah* 49.

8. *Mat'amim* 55.

9. See *Kidushin* 18b; *Tosafot, Yoma* 13b, "*L'hada*"; *Rama, Shulhan Aruch, Even HaEzer* 55:1; *Helkat M'hokek* 55:9.

10. See *Turei Zahav* 65:2; *Kitzur Shulhan Aruch* 147:3; *Ta'amei HaMinhagim, Kuntres Aharon* 950.

11. *Kitzur Shulhan Aruch*, 147:3; *Shulhan HaEzer* 7:16.

12. Genesis 24:10.

13. See *T'shuvot Rashba* 1186; *Rama, Even HaEzer* 31:2; *Edut L'Yisrael* 9:7.

14. See *Ta'amei HaMinhagim* 958, quoting *Ya'avetz*.

15. *Kitzur Shulhan Aruch* 147:3; *Shulhan HaEzer* 7:1:10; *Likutei* 147:3; *MaHarich* 3:31b.

16. *Kitzur Shulhan Aruch* 147:4.

17. *Mateh Moshe*, quoted by *Ta'amei HaMinhagim* 957.

18. Isaiah 1:18.

19. Ecclesiastes 9:8.

20. See *Kol Bo* 75.

21. See *Ta'amei HaMinhagim* 951.

22. See *T'shuvot MaHaram Schick, Even HaEzer* 88.

23. Maimonides, *Yad, Taanit* 5:13; *Shulhan Aruch, Even HaEzer* 65:3; *Shulhan HaEzer* 7:1:11.

24. *Bava Batra* 60b.

25. *Shulhan HaEzer* 7:1:11.

26. Psalms 19:6.

27. Joel 2:15.

28. *Aruch HaShulhan* 55:17.

29. See *Shabbat* 33a; *Aruch HaShulhan* 55:15.

30. *JT Sotah* 9:15, 46a; *Rashi, Sotah* 49a; *Tosafot, Gittin* 7a; *"Atarot";* *HaGra, Shulhan Aruch, Even HaEzer* 55:9; see *Tosefta, Sotah* 15:19; *Midrash Psalms* 79:3.

31. *Shulhan Aruch, Even HaEzer* 61.

32. *Shulhan HaEzer* 7:3:1; *Ta'amei HaMinhagim* 963.

33. See *Shulhan HaEzer* 7:3:4.

34. See *Ta'amei HaMinhagim* 963, quoting *Tolaat Yaakov.*

35. *Avot* 1:5.

36. See *Rabenu Yonah* to *Avot* 1:5; Bertinoro to *Avot* 1:5; *HaGra* to *Avot* 1:5.

37. *Ezer M'kudash, Even HaEzer* 55:1.

38. *Knesset HaG'dolah* 61:2.

39. Genesis 22:17.

40. *Kitzur Shulhan Aruch* 147:1.

41. Jeremiah 7:34.

42. *MaHaril* 64b, 65a, *Mateh Moshe* 1; *Shulhan HaEzer* 7:4:3; *Edut L'Yisrael.*

43. Genesis 2:22.

44. See *B'rachot* 61a; *Rashi* to Genesis 2:22.

45. *Zohar,* Genesis 49a.

46. *Rama, Shulhan Aruch, Yoreh De'ah* 391:3.

47. *Mat'amim* 140; *Likutei MaHarich* 3:131a.

48. *Zohar,* Genesis 49a.

49. *MaHaril* 64b; *Shulhan HaEzer* 7:4:4.

50. *Gittin* 89a; See *JT Ketubot* 1:5, 5b, *Rabeinu Hananel, Sanhedrin* 32b.

51. Esther 8:16.

52. Exodus 19:16.

53. *Sefer Rokeah* 353; *Ta'amei HaMinhagim* 960; *Likutei MaHarich* 3:131b.

54. *Likutei MaHarich* 3:131b.

55. *Sotah* 17a.

56. *Mat'amim HeHadash* 16; *Otzar Kol Minhagei Y'shurun* 16:4; *Shulhan HaEzer* 7:4:4.

57. Genesis 1:28.

58. *Ta'amei HaMinhagim* 958.

59. *Shulhan HaEzer* 7:4:8.

60. Ibid.; *Mat'amim* 79; *Ta'amei HaMinhagim* 961; *M'kor HaMinhagim* 74; *Siddur Bet Yaakov,* 124b.

61. *Tikunei Zohar* 6, 23a.

62. Jeremiah 31:21-22; see *Rashi, Radak, M'tzudat David* to Jeremiah 31:21-22; see also *Targum Jonathan* to Jeremiah 31:21-22, who understands the "woman" to refer to the Jewish people, and the "man" who will be courted in those future days to refer to the Torah.

63. Song of Songs 8:9, 10, see *Sforno*.

64. *Y'vamot* 62b.

65. *MaHarsha,* Song of Songs 8:9,10.

66. Hosea 2:21–22.

67. See *Tikunei Zohar* 6:23a.

68. Aryeh Kaplan, *Made in Heaven* (New York: Moznaim Publishing Corp., 1983), 161.

69. Psalms 45:10.

70. See *Aruch HaShulhan* 62:9; *Mahzor Vitri* 475; *MaHaril* 64b; *Siddur Bet Yaakov,* 124; *Kitzur Shulhan Aruch* 147:5; *Kerem Shlomo, Even HaEzer* 62.

71. *Ba'er Hetev* to *Even HaEzer* 62:1.

72. *MaHaril* 64b.

73. See *Shulhan Aruch, Even HaEzer* 34:4; *Helkat M'hokek* 34:8; *Bet Sh'muel* 34:7; *Ba'er Hetev* 34:10; *Shulhan HaEzer* 8:6:4.

74. Psalms 104:15.

75. *Ketubot* 7b.

76. *B'rachot* 33a.

77. Maimonides, *Yad, Ishut* 3:24; *Shulhan Aruch, Even HaEzer* 34:1.

78. *Aruch HaShulhan, Even HaEzer* 34:8; *Shulhan Aruch, Orah Hayim* 2:64; *Hagahot Sefer Mitzvot Katan* 183:19; *Ba'er Hetev* 34:2.

79. *Mat'amim* 65.

80. *Rama, Shulhan Aruch, Even HaEzer* 34:1, *Hagahot Maimoniot* 3:23, 60; *Darkei Moshe* 34:1; *Sefer Mitzvot Gadol, Asin* 48.

81. *Kol Bo* 75.

82. *Mahzor Vitri* 476; *Rokeah* 351; see *Shulhan HaEzer* 8:1:10.

83. See *Edut L'Yisrael* 45.

84. *Aruch HaShulhan* 34:9; *Shulhan HaEzer* 8:1:9.

85. *Sotah* 3b; *Kidushin* 64a.

86. *Shulhan Aruch, Hoshen Mishpat* 34:2.

87. *Shulhan Aruch, Hoshen Mishpat* 33:2.

88. *Shulhan Aruch, Hoshen Mishpat* 33:17.

89. *Aruch HaShulhan* 42:40; *Sh'arim M'tsuyanim B'Halachah* 147:7.

90. *Hagahot Sefer Mitzvot Katan* 183:7; *K'tzot HaHoshen* 36:1; *Shulhan HaEzer* 8:1:20; *Edut L'Yisrael* 6:6; *Aruch HaShulhan* 27:2.

91. *Shulhan HaEzer* 8:1:14.

92. *Rama, Shulhan Aruch, Even HaEzer* 31:12; *MaHaril* 64b; *Ba'er Hetev* 37:1 *Shulhan HaEzer* 8:1:22; *Edut L'Yisrael* 6:6.

93. *Keter Shem Tov* 16; *Shulhan HaEzer* 8:2:12.

94. Maimonides, *Yad, Ishut* 3:8.

95. See *Ba'er Hetev* 27:5.

96. *MaHaril* 64b; *Shulhan HaEzer* 8:2:2; *Edut L'Yisrael* 6:7.

97. *Aruch HaShulhan* 27:4.

98. See *Igrot Moshe, Even HaEzer* 3:18.

99. *Rama, Shulhan Aruch, Even HaEzer* 62:9; *Shulhan HaEzer* 8:3:1.

100. See *Mordecai, Ketubot* 132; *Aruch HaShulhan* 62:8; *Edut L'Yisrael* 3:6.

101. *Shulhan HaEzer* 8:3:2; *Edut L'Yisrael* 3:6.

102. *Shulhan HaEzer* 8:3:5.

103. *MaHaril* 64b; see *Rama, Shulhan Aruch, Even HaEzer* 62:9; *Shulhan HaEzer* 8:3:6.

104. *P'sahim* 102b and *Tosafot, "She-ain"*; *Shulhan Aruch, Even HaEzer* 62:9.

105. See *Mahzor Vitri* 469; *Shulhan Aruch, Even HaEzer* 62:9; *Kol Bo* 75; *Rokeah* 351.

106. *Shulhan HaEzer* 8:3:18.

107. Jeremiah 2:1.

108. Genesis 24:40.

109. *Ketubot* 7b, 8a.

110. Maimonides, *Yad, Ishut* 10:3; *B'rachot* 2:11.

111. Maimonides, *Yad, Ishut* 10:4; *Mahzor Vitri* 469.

112. *Kad HaKemah, Hatan B'Bet HaK'nesset.*

113. See *Shitah M'kubetzet* 41a; *Mateh Moshe* 12.

114. Isaiah 43:7.

115. See *Rashi, Radak,* and *M'tzudat David* and *Targum Jonathan* to Isaiah 43:7.

116. Psalms 137:6.

117. *Rashi, Ketubot* 8a, *"Sos Tasis."*

118. Isaiah 54:1; see *Rashi* and *M'tzudat David* to Isaiah.

119. Isaiah 62:4.

120. See *Rashi, Ketubot* 8a, *"Reyim HaAhuvim."*

121. Song of Songs 5:16.

122. *Zohar,* Genesis 265; Exodus 169.

123. Genesis, chap. 1, in which the Creation of the world is described, contains the expression "and God said" nine times, while the verse "In the beginning God created" is understood as being the tenth utterance, in accordance with Psalms 33:6.

124. *Mahzor Vitri* 476; *Rokeah* 353; *MaHaril* 64b; *Rama, Shulhan Aruch, Even HaEzer* 65:3; *Rama, Shulhan Aruch, Orah Hayim* 560:2; *Edut L'Yisrael* 5:2.

125. *Shulhan HaEzer* 87:3:23, 24; *Edut L'Yisrael* 5:2.

126. *Mahzor Vitri* 470; *MaHaril* 64b.

127. Jeremiah 7:34; 16:9; 25:10; 33:11.

128. *Ta'amei HaMinhagim* 976, based upon *Rokeah* 353.

129. *B'rachot* 30b.

130. Psalms 2:11.

131. *B'rachot* 30b.

132. See *Rashi, B'rachot,* 31b, *"Kasa D'mukra."*

133. *B'rachot* 30b, 31a.

134. *Rashi, B'rachot* 31b.

135. *Tosafot, B'rachot* 31b, *"Aity Kasa D'zugaita Hiverta."*

136. See *Rama, Orah Hayim* 560:2.

137. *Mat'amim* 36.

138. *Turei Zahav, Orah Hayim* 560:4.

139. Psalms 137:5.

140. Psalms, chap. 6.

141. See *Turei Zahav, Even HaEzer* 57:1; *Aruch HaShulhan* 55:11, *Kitzur Shulhan Aruch* 148:1.

142. *Kitzur Shulhan Aruch* 148:1.

143. Maimonides, *Yad, De'ot* 5:2; *Eruvin* 6:6; *Shulhan HaEzer* 9:1:3; *Edut L'Yisrael* 7:1.

144. *Shulhan HaEzer* 9:1:12; *Edut L'Yisrael* 7:1.

145. *Shulhan HaEzer* 7:5:3.

146. See *Pirkei D'Rabbi Eliezer.*

147. See *Hafetz Hayim, Ahavath Hesed* (New York: Feldheim, 1976), 216–217.

148. *B'rachot* 6b.

149. *Pirkei D'Rabbi Eliezer.*

150. *Ketubot* 16b.

151. *Kitzur Shulhan Aruch* 149:9.

152. *Tosafot, P'sahim* 102b; *Shulhan Aruch, Orah Hayim* 182:1; *Mishnah B'rurah, Orah Hayim* 182:1.

153. See *Shulhan HaEzer* 9:8:5.

154. *Ketubot* 16b.

155. See *Shulhan Aruch, Even HaEzer* 64:2; *Kitzur Shulhan Aruch* 149:12.

156. *JT Ketubot* 1:1; *Shulhan Aruch, Yoreh De'ah* 342:1; see *Tosafot B'rachot* 47b, *"Mitzvah"*; Maimonides, *Yad, Ishut* 10:12.

157. See Genesis 29:27; *Pirkei D'Rabbi Eliezer* 16.

158. *Kitzur Shulhan Aruch* 149:12.

159. *Ketubot* 7b; *Shulhan Aruch, Even HaEzer* 62:4.

160. *Ketubot* 8a; *Shulhan Aruch, Even HaEzer* 62:7.

Notes to Chapter 9

1. *Avot d'Rabbi Nathan* 27; see *Hagigah* 10a.

2. Genesis 1:10; Exodus 7:10.

3. Isaiah 22:11.

4. See Y. Yadin, *Masada* (New York: Random House, 1966).

5. Ibid., 164–167.

6. Leviticus 20:18.

7. Leviticus 19:1, 2.

8. Leviticus 20:7.

9. See *Reshit Hochmah, Sha'ar Ha'Ahavah* 11. For discussion of the concept of immersion in the *mikvah* as a spiritual rebirth, see R. Aryeh Kaplan, *Waters of Eden* (New York: NCSY/Orthodox Union, 1976).

10. Exodus 29:4; *Targum Jonathan, ad loc., Rashi, ad loc.;* S. R. Hirsch, *Commentary, ad loc.;* See Exodus 40:12; Leviticus 8:6.

11. See S. R. Hirsch, *The Pentateuch* (London: 1962), chap. 15.

12. Maimonides, *Yad, Tum'at Ochlin* 16:12; see *JT Sh'kalim* 3:5; *Sotah* 49a; *Avodah Zarah* 20b.

13. *Tana D'bei Eliyahu Rabah,* 7.

14. *Rashi, Shabbat* 68a; *Sifra,* Leviticus 2:26; Maimonides, *Sh'monah P'rakim* #6; *Hayei Adam* 86:18; see *Maharitz Hayot* to *Rosh Hashanah* 16a; Maimonides, *Commentary* to *Makot* 3:1; *Hovot HaL'vavot* 3:3.

15. A. Kaplan, *Waters of Eden,* 9–10.

16. See Maimonides, *Yad, Mikvaot* 11:12, *T'murah* 4:13, *T'shuvah* 3:14, *Moreh N'vuchim* 3:24, 31; see *Ramban* to Leviticus 19:19, Deuteronomy 22:6; see *Sefer HaHinuch* 545; see Ibn Ezra to Exodus 20:1; see *Tos'fot Yom Tov* to *B'rachot* 5:3; see *Etz Yosef* to *Leviticus Rabbah* 27:10, Deuteronomy *Rabbah* 6:1; see *Maharitz Hayot* to *Sotah* 14a; see *Tosafot, Sotah* 14a, *Hulin* 5a, "*Keday,*" Gittin 49b, "*R. Shimon*"; see *MaHaram, ad loc.;* see *Tos'fot Yom Tov* to *Sanhedrin* 8:6, see also *Bava Kama* 79b, *Bava M'tzia* 31.

17. Aron Barth, *The Jew Faces Eternal Problems* (Jerusalem: The Jewish Agency, 1965), 210.

18. S. R. Hirsch, *Commentary,* Leviticus 20:18.

19. See *Tosafot, Y'vamot* 62b.

20. *Responsa of MaHaram of Lublin* 53.

21. *Binyan Adei Ad* (Jerusalem: D'var Y'rushalayim, 1979), 52.

22. *Shabbat* 64b; *JT Gittin,* end; *Sifra, M'tzora,* end.

23. Maimonides, *Yad, Isurei Bi'ah* 11:19; *Sefer Mitzvot Gadol, Lavin* 111; *Tur Shulhan Aruch* XIV, 195:9.

24. *Nidah* 31b.

25. *Song of Songs Rabbah,* 7; see *Midrash* on Psalms 2:15; see also *Sanhedrin* 37a and *Tosafot.*

26. Deuteronomy 4:2, 13:1; Proverbs 3:6.

27. Norman Lamm, *A Hedge of Roses* (New York: Feldheim, 1966), 68–78.

28. Genesis 2:3.

29. N. Lamm, 76–78.

30. David M. Serr, *Israel Magazine,* Feb. 1972.

31. Moses D. Tendler, *Pardes Rimonim* (New York: The Judaica Press, 1979), 14.

32. Ibid., 13–14.

33. M. Coppleson, *British J. Hospital Med.*, 1969, 961–980, quoted by Tendler, 153–155.

34. *Ma'ariv*, Tel Aviv, March 3, 1984.

35. See Tendler, 15.

36. A. E. Kitov, *The Jew and His Home* (New York: Shengold, 1963), 153–155.

37. Maimonides, *Yad, Mikvaot* 11:2; *Sefer HaHinuch*, 175.

38. *Yoma* 85b.

39. Genesis 1:2.

40. S. R. Hirsch, *Commentary*, Exodus 29:4.

41. Maimonides, *Yad, Mikvaot* 11:2.

42. Ezekiel 36:25.

43. Leviticus 20:18.

44. Leviticus 20:17.

45. Leviticus 23:29.

46. Ezekiel 18:5, 6.

47. Naftali Zvi Yehuda Berlin, *Meshiv Davar*, 1:45.

48. *JT Hagigah* 1:8.

49. See Berlin, *Meshiv Davar*, 1:45.

50. J. H. Hertz, *The Pentateuch and Haftorahs* (London: Soncino, 1981), 492.

Notes to Chapter 10

1. From the text of the *ketubah*.

2. *Yvamot* 61a.

3. *P'sahim* 72b; see *Tosafot, Yvamot* 65a; see *Ramban* to Exodus 21:10; see also Maimonides, *Yad, Ishut* 12:2, 15:1; *Tur, Even HaEzer* 77:5.

4. *Magid Mishneh* to Maimonides, *Yad, Ishut* 15:1.

5. *Ketubot* 47b, 48a.

6. Exodus 21:10.

7. *Yvamot* 62a.

8. *Ravad, Baalei HaNefesh, Sha'ar HaK'dushah* (Jerusalem: Masorah, 1955), 139.

9. *N'darim* 20b; Maimonides, *Yad, Ishut* 15:18; *Isurei Bi'ah* 21:9.

10. *Eruvin* 100b; Maimonides, *Yad, Ishut* 15:17; *De'ot* 5:4; *Isurei Bi'ah* 21:11; *Shulhan Aruch, Even HaEzer* 25:2; *Orah Hayim* 240.

11. Maimonides, *Yad, Ishut* 15:17; *De'ot* 5:4; *Isurei Bi'ah* 21:11.

12. *Eruvin* 100b; Maimonides, ibid.

13. *Eruvin* 100b.

14. See *Magen Avraham* to *Shulhan Aruch, Orah Hayim* 240:7; *Shitah M'kubetzet, N'darim* 20b.

15. Exodus 21:10.

16. Deuteronomy 24:5.

17. *P'sahim* 72b.

18. See S. R. Hirsch, *Commentary,* Deuteronomy 24:5; *Sefer HaHinuch* 582.

19. Exodus 21:10.

20. *P'sahim* 72b; see *Rashi.*

21. Deuteronomy 24:5.

22. Exodus 21:10.

23. *Sefer Mitzvot Katan,* in *Amudei Golah, Mitzvah* 285, ed. Ralberg (New York: 1959), 316.

24. See *Sotah* 22b; see also *JT Sotah* 3:4.

25. Cited in David M. Feldman, *Health and Medicine in The Jewish Tradition* (New York: Crossroad, 1987), 63.

26. Ibid.

27. *Ketubot* 62a, b; *Shulhan Aruch, Orah Hayim* 240:1; Maimonides, *Yad, Ishut* 14:1; see also *Shulhan Aruch, Even HaEzer* 76:1.

28. Maimonides, *Yad, Ishut* 14:1; *Shulhan Aruch, Even HaEzer* 76:1.

29. Ibid.

30. *Ketubot* 62b; Maimonides, *Yad, Ishut* 14:7.

31. Maimonides, ibid.; *Shulhan Aruch, Even HaEzer* 76:5.

32. See *Ketubot* 61b; *Shulhan Aruch, Even HaEzer* 76:5, 76:7 and commentaries.

33. *Rama, Shulhan Aruch, Even HaEzer* 76:5, 76:7.

34. *Eruvin* 100b; *Rama, Shulhan Aruch, Even HaEzer* 76:5, 76:7, 76:4.

35. *Ketubot* 62b; Maimonides, *Yad, Ishut* 14:7; *Tur, Even HaEzer* 76:5; *Shulhan Aruch, Even HaEzer* 76:7.

36. Ibid.

37. Maimonides, *Yad, Ishut* 15:10.

38. Ibid.

39. *Ketubot* 63a; Maimonides, *Yad, Ishut* 14:15, and *Magid Mishneh* thereto; *Shulhan Aruch, Even HaEzer* 76:7, 77:1.

40. Ibid.

41. Maimonides, *Yad, Ishut* 14:8.

42. *Kidushin* 19b; *Ketubot* 36a; Maimonides, *Yad, Ishut* 12:7; *Shulhan Aruch, Even HaEzer* 38:5.

43. *Ketubot* 61b; Maimonides, *Yad, Ishut* 14:6.

44. Maimonides, *Yad, Ishut* 14:7.

45. S. Wolbe, *Hoveret Hadrachah L'Hatanim,* 26.

46. *Shulhan Aruch, Orah Hayim* 240:2; *Shulhan Aruch, Even HaEzer* 25:10. See *N'darim* 20b.

47. Maimonides, *Yad, Isurei Bi'ah* 21:12; see *Shulhan Aruch, Orah Hayim* 240:7.

48. *Gittin* 90a; Maimonides, *Yad, Isurei Bi'ah* 21:12; *Gerushin* 10:21; *Shulhan Aruch, Even HaEzer* 25:8, 10.

49. Maimonides, *Yad, Isurei Bi'ah* 21:12; *Shulhan Aruch, Even HaEzer* 25:8.

50. *N'darim* 20b; Maimonides, *Yad, Isurei Bi'ah* 21:12; *Shulhan Aruch, Orah Hayim* 240:10.

51. Jacob Emden, *Siddur Bet Yaakov* (Lemberg, 1904), 159a.

52. See *Baalei HaNefesh* 139.

53. *P'sahim* 72b; see *Rashi.*

54. Maimonides, *Yad, De'ot* 5:4; *Ishut* 15:17.

55. See *Shabbat* 30b; *Zohar* I, 180b; *Orhot Tzadikim, Sha'ar HaSimhah* 14:7.

56. *Eruvin* 100b; *N'darim* 20b; Maimonides, *De'ot* 5:4.

57. *Shulhan Aruch, Even HaEzer* 25:9; Maimonides, *Yad, Isurei Bi'ah* 21:12; *De'ot* 5:4.

58. Maimonides, *Yad, De'ot* 5:4.

59. Ibid.

60. *Y'vamot* 62b; *Shulhan Aruch, Orah Hayim* 240:1.

61. *P'sahim* 72b.

62. *Rashi, P'sahim* 72b; *Shulhan Aruch, Even HaEzer* 25:1.

63. Maimonides, *Yad, De'ot* 5:4; *Isurei Bi'ah* 21:9; see also *Rama, Shulhan Aruch, Even HaEzer* 25:7.

64. *T'shuvot MaHarit,* quoted by R. Joseph David Epstein, *"Kuntres Mishpat HaIshut," Mitzvot Habayit* (New York: *Torat HaAdam,* 1972) II, 28.

65. *Eruvin* 100b.

66. Ibid.; *Ran, N'darim* 20b.

67. *N'darim* 20b; *Eruvin* 100b.

68. *Eruvin* 100b.

69. Maimonides, *Yad, Isurei Bi'ah* 21:13.

70. See *Genesis Rabbah* 17:8.

71. *Eruvin* 100b; see Rabeinu Hananel.

72. Maimonides, *Yad, Ishut* 15:17; *Tur, Orah Hayim* 240.

73. Based on *P'sahim* 72b; see *Shulhan Aruch, Orah Hayim* 240:1; see *Mishnah B'rurah, Orah Hayim* 240:1.

74. Maimonides, *Yad, Ishut* 15:17.

75. *N'darim* 20b and *Ran* thereto; Maimonides, *Yad, De'ot* 5:4; *Igeret HaKodesh,* chap. 6.

76. Maimonides, ibid.; *Siddur Bet Yaakov,* 158a–159a.

77. *MaHaram* of Lublin, Responsa #53; see *Eruvin* 102b.

78. *P'sahim* 49b.

79. *Igeret HaKodesh,* chap. 6.

80. See *Zohar, K'doshim* 24.

81. *Siddur Bet Yaakov,* 158a–159a.

82. *Be'er Yehudah* to Maimonides, *Yad, De'ot* 5:4.

83. *Ramban* to Deuteronomy 22:24.

84. *Ketubot* 48a; see *Ritvah* to *Ketubot* 47b; *Shulhan Aruch, Even HaEzer* 76:13 and *Rama.*

85. *Masechet Kalah* 1; *Shitah M'kubetzet* to *N'darim* 20b.

86. *M'norat HaMa'or, Ner* III, Rule 6, part 5, chap. 2, 178.

87. See *Ezer M'kudash* to *Shulhan Aruch, Even HaEzer* 25:7.

88. See *N'darim* 20a and *Rosh* thereto and *Shitah M'kubetzet* thereto; see also *Tur, Orah Hayim* 240 and commentaries.

89. See *Shabbat* 40b; see *Rashi* and *M'iri* thereto; see *Lehem Mishneh* to Maimonides, *Yad, Ishut* 15:18.

90. See *T'murah* 17a; *Bava Batra* 10b; *B'rachot* 60a.

91. *Igeret HaKodesh,* chap. 6.

92. *Nidah* 31a.

93. *Shulhan Aruch, Orah Hayim* 240:1.

94. R. Moses Frankfurt, *Nefesh Yehudah* to *M'norat HaMa'or, Ner* II, Rule 6, part 5, chap. 3, 179; the *Igeret HaKodesh* explains: "His intention was not only for the pleasure of the act . . . for he perceived his motivation as fulfilling an obligation . . . that of the *mitzvah* of *onah* commanded in the Torah . . . and the intention and behavior of this pious man were elevated for the sake of Heaven and the *mitzvah.*"

95. *N'darim* 20b; *Masechet Kalah* 1.

96. *Megillah* 13a; see *Rashi.*

97. *M'norat HaMa'or,* part 6.

98. Proverbs 18:22.

99. *Sefer Hasidim* 509.

100. *Tos'fot Rid* to *Y'vamot* 12b.

101. *Mor Uk'tzia* to *Shulhan Aruch, Orah Hayim* 240.

102. Maimonides, *Yad, De'ot* 3:2, 4:9; Ibn Ezra to Leviticus 18:20; *Siddur Bet Yaakov,* 135–161.

103. *Siddur Bet Yaakov,* ibid.

104. Maimonides, *Commentary to the Mishnah, Sanhedrin* 7.

105. Maimonides, *Yad, De'ot* 3:2, 4:9; see *Isurei Bi'ah* 21:11.

106. *Sanhedrin* 107a; see also *Rashi;* see *Sukah* 42b; *Shulhan Aruch, Even HaEzer* 240:1.

107. Ibid.; see also *Sukah* 52b and *Rashi.*

108. Maimonides, *Yad, De'ot* 15:4.

109. See *Shulhan Aruch, Even HaEzer* 25:2.

110. Ibid., *Isurei Bi'ah* 21:11, based on *B'rachot* 22a.

111. *Ta'anit* 11a; Maimonides, *Yad, Ta'aniyot* 3:8; *Shulhan Aruch, Even HaEzer* 25:7; *Orah Hayim* 240:12.

112. Maimonides, *Yad, Ta'aniyot* 3:8.

113. *Rashi* to *Ta'anit* 11a; see also *Rashi* to Genesis 7:7.

114. W. H. Masters and V. H. Johnson, *McCall's,* Nov. 1966, 173.

115. *Shabbat* 152a.

116. *Ecclesiastes Rabbah* 12:5.

117. *M'norat HaMa'or,* chap. 1, 171.

118. See Genesis 2:24.

119. *Igeret Hakodesh,* chap. 6.

Notes to Chapter 11

1. *Kidushin* 2a.

2. Exodus 15:16.

3. *Avot* 6:11–13.

4. *Kidushin* 2b.

5. Maimonides, *Yad, Ishut* 4:1; *Shulhan Aruch, Even HaEzer* 42:1.

6. Maimonides, *Yad, Ishut* 3:19; *Shulhan Aruch, Even HaEzer* 37:11.

7. *Kidushin* 41a, 81a.

8. *Yvamot* 62b.

9. See Maimonides, *Yad, Ishut* 15:19.

10. Ibid., 12:1.

11. Ibid., 12:2.

12. Ibid., see *Shulhan Aruch, Even HaEzer* 69:11.

13. *Shulhan Aruch, Even HaEzer* 15:3.

14. Maimonides, *Yad, Ishut* 2:3; see *Shulhan Aruch, Even HaEzer* 69:1.

15. *Ketubot* 58b; Maimonides *Yad, Ishut* 2:3, 12:4; *Shulhan Aruch, Even HaEzer* 69:4.

16. Maimonides, *Yad, Ishut* 2:3, 12:4.

17. See *Ketubot* 58b.

18. *P'sahim* 50b.

19. See Maimonides, *Yad, Ishut* 10:7.

20. *Bava Kama* 89a; Maimonides, *Yad, Ishut* 10:10.

21. See *Shabbat* 14b; see *Ketubot* 82b.

22. See Mishnah, *Pe'ah* 8:8; S. R. Hirsch, *Commentary,* Exodus 15–16.

23. See *Ketubot* 11a, 39b, 54a; see *Yvamot* 89a.

24. Ibid.

25. Titus 2:5; 1 Timothy 2:11; 1 Peter 3:7; Ephesians 5:22; see Colossians 3:18.

26. Exodus 21:10.

27. *Gittin* 90a; *Yvamot* 12b; *JT Gittin* 9:11 (end).

28. Ibid.

29. Ibid.

30. *Rama, Shulhan Aruch, Even HaEzer* 119:2; see *Helkat M'hokek* and *Bet Sh'muel, ad loc.*

31. *Gittin* 90b.

32. See Genesis 2:24; 2 Samuel 3:11–6.

33. Ezra 10:3 ff.

34. Malachi 2:14-6.

35. See *Rama, Shulhan Aruch, Even HaEzer* 119:6.

36. Aron Owen, "Legal Aspects of Marriage," in Peter Elman, ed., *Jewish Marriage* (London: The Jewish Marriage Educational Council, 1967), 26.

37. Ibid.

38. Maimonides, *Yad, Gerushin* 2:20.

39. Ibid.

40. Ibid.

41. *Ketubot* 72a,b; Maimonides, *Yad, Ishut* 24:10, 11, 12; *Shulhan Aruch, Even HaEzer* 115:1-4; *Sefer Mitzvot Gadol, Ta'aseh* 48.

42. *Yvamot* 24b, 25a; Maimonides, *Yad, Ishut* 24:6, 10, 15; *Sotah* 2:13; *Shulhan Aruch, Even HaEzer* 11:1.

43. *Ketubot* 72a,b; Maimonides, *Yad, Ishut* 24:6, 10, 15; *Shulhan Aruch, Even HaEzer,* 115:4, 119:4.

44. *Ketubot* 72a,b; Maimonides, *Yad, Ishut* 24:12; *Shulhan Aruch, Even HaEzer* 15:4.

45. *Rashi* to *Ketubot* 72b.

46. *Ketubot* 72a,b; *Sotah* 25a; *Shulhan Aruch, Even HaEzer* 15:4; and *Rama.*

47. *Ketubot* 100b; Maimonides, *Yad, Ishut* 14:8-14, 24:5, 9; *Tur, Even HaEzer* 115; *Sefer Mitzvot Gadol, Ta'aseh* 48.

48. *Nidah* 12b; Maimonides, *Yad, Ishut* 25:7-9; *Shulhan Aruch, Even HaEzer* 39:4, 117:1, 2, 4.

49. *Yvamot* 64a,b, 65a,b; *Ketubot* 100b; Maimonides, *Yad, Ishut* 15:8, 24:1; *Shulhan Aruch, Even HaEzer* 154:10; *Rama, Shulhan Aruch, Even HaEzer* 1:3.

50. *Ketubot* 110a,b; Maimonides, *Yad, Ishut* 13:17; *Shulhan Aruch, Even HaEzer* 25:1.

51. *Ketubot* 110b; Maimonides, *Yad, Ishut* 13:19; *Shulhan Aruch, Even HaEzer* 75:3, 4. The Talmud adds (*Ketubot* 100b): "One should, under all circumstances, reside in *Eretz Israel*, even if in order to do so he must live in a city that is populated in the main with idol worshippers. A person should not live outside of *Eretz Israel*, even if he does so in a city mainly populated by Jews. For he who resides in *Eretz Israel* is likened to one who has a God, while he who resides outside *Eretz Israel* is likened to someone who has no God." The passage declares further that he who resides outside *Eretz Israel* is considered as one who worships idols.

52. *Rama, Shulhan Aruch, Even HaEzer* 154:1.

53. *Shulhan Aruch, Even HaEzer* 154:3.

54. *Shulhan Aruch, Even HaEzer* 154:1.

55. *Ketubot* 77a; Maimonides, *Yad, Ishut* 25:12; *Shulhan Aruch, Even HaEzer* 154:4.

56. *Ketubot* 77a; Maimonides, *Yad, Ishut* 25:11; *Sefer Mitzvot Gadol, Ta'aseh* 48; *Even HaEzer* 154:4.

57. *Ketubot* 63b; Maimonides, *Yad, Ishut* 14:8; *Sefer Mitzvot Gadol, Lo Ta'aseh* 81; *Shulhan Aruch, Even HaEzer* 77:2.

58. *Ketubot* 61b; Maimonides, *Yad, Ishut* 14:6, 7, 15; *Sefer Mitzvot Gadol, Lo Ta'aseh* 81; *Shulhan Aruch, Even HaEzer* 771:1.

59. *Shulhan Aruch, Even HaEzer* 76:19; *Rama* adds that if the wife insists on such an arrangement the husband may also compel a divorce.

60. Maimonides, *Yad, Ishut* 14:6, 7, 15; see *Sefer Mitzvot Gadol, Lo Ta'aseh* 81.

61. *Shulhan Aruch, Even HaEzer* 154:7, 76:19.

62. *Yevamot* 65a; Maimonides, *Yad, Ishut* 15:10.

63. *Ketubot* 77a; Maimonides, *Yad, Ishut* 25:13; *Sefer Mitzvot Gadol, Ta'aseh* 48.

64. *Rama, Shulhan Aruch, Even HaEzer* 154:3.

65. Ibid., *HaGra ad loc.*, 10.

66. *Ketubot* 63a, 77a; Maimonides, *Yad, Ishut* 12:4; *Shulhan Aruch, Even HaEzer* 154:3.

67. *Ketubot* 71b; Maimonides, *Yad, Ishut* 13:12.

68. *Ketubot* 71b; Maimonides, *Yad, Ishut* 13:13.

69. *Ketubot* 71b; Maimonides, *Yad, Ishut* 14:12, 13.

70. *Ketubot* 70a; Maimonides, *Yad, Ishut* 13:8; *Shulhan Aruch, Even HaEzer, op. cit.*, 74:1.

71. Maimonides, *Yad, Ishut* 13:15. Maimonides grants the husband a similar privilege.

72. *Ketubot* 102b; Maimonides, *Yad, Ishut* 13:19, 20; *Shulhan Aruch, Even HaEzer, op cit.* 75:3, 4; see note 49.

Notes to Chapter 12

1. *Sukah* 17a.
2. *Derech Eretz Zutah* 9.
3. *Avot D'Rabbi Nathan* 28:3.
4. *Yoma* 9b.
5. *Leviticus Rabbah* 9.
6. Psalms 19:11.
7. Genesis 2:18.
8. *Yevamot* 63a.
9. Maimonides, *Yad, Ishut* 15:19, 20.
10. Ibid.
11. Esther 2:7.

12. *Midrash* to Esther.

13. *Shabbat* 118b.

14. *Yoma* 2a.

15. *Bava M'tzia* 59a.

16. Genesis 12:16.

17. *Sefer HaMidot* (Warsaw, 1912), 98–99.

18. *Midrash Tanhuma, Vayishlah,* 6.

19. *Sh'lah, Derech Eretz.*

20. S. R. Hirsch, *The Wisdom of Mishle* (Jerusalem: Feldheim, 1976), 246.

21. *Ketubot* 59b, 61a; see Maimonides, *Yad, Ishut* 21:57.

22. *Ketubot* 59b, 61a; Maimonides, *Yad, Ishut* 21:3, 4, 6.

23. *Ketubot* 59b, 61a; Maimonides, *Yad, Ishut* 21:4.

24. *Shevet Musar,* chap. 16.

25. S. Wolbe, *Hadrachah L'Hatanim,* in *Binyan Adei Ad* (Jerusalem: D'var Y'rushalayim, 1979), 74.

26. *Ketubot* 16b, 17a.

27. *Tosafot* to *Ketubot* 16b, 17a.

28. Exodus 23:7.

29. *Rashi, Ketubot* 17a *("T'hay Daato").*

30. *Tosafot Rid* to *Ketubot* 16b, 17a.

31. See *MaHarsha* to *Ketubot* 16b; see *Korban N'tan'el* to *Rosh, Ketubot* 16b.

32. *Orhot Tzadikim,* "On Flattery."

33. *Hulin* 84b and *Rashi.*

34. Maimonides, *Yad, De'ot,* 5:10.

35. *Bava M'tzia* 59a.

36. *T'rumah* 16a.

37. *M'norat HaMa'or, Ner* III, Rule 6, part 4, chap. 1.

38. *Pele Yo'etz, Ahavat Ish V'ishto.*

39. Wolbe, *Binyan Adei Ad,* 65.

40. Wolbe, 111.

41. *Ketubot* 64b; Maimonides, *Yad, Ishut* 12:10; *Shulhan Aruch, Even HaEzer* 70:3.

42. Wolbe, *Binyan Adei Ad,* 111.

43. Ibid.

44. Ibid.

45. *B'rachot* 24a.

46. *Y'vamot* 62b.

47. *MaHarsha, Y'vamot* 62b.

48. *Horiot,* chap. 3; see *Tur, Yoreh De'ah* 251:78; *Hoshen Mishpat, Dayanim,* 15.

49. See *Hulin* 84b.

50. *Rosh HaShanah* 6b.

51. *Rashi* and *Tosafot, Rosh HaShanah* 6b.
52. Maimonides, *Yad, Ishut* 13:4; *Shulhan Aruch, Even HaEzer* 73:3.
53. Maimonides, *Yad, Ishut* 13:1–3; *Shulhan Aruch, Even HaEzer* 73:3.
54. Maimonides, *Yad, Ishut* 13:5; *Shulhan Aruch, Even HaEzer* 72:4.
55. Will Durant, *The Age of Faith* (New York: Simon and Schuster, 1950), 379.
56. *Esther Rabbah,* chap. 3.
57. *Ketubot* 49b.
58. *N'darim* 79b.
59. *Ketubot* 49b.
60. See *Aruch HaShulhan, Even HaEzer* 546.
61. Ibid.
62. *Likutei MaHaril.*
63. *Ketubot* 65a.
64. *Ketubot* 59b; see *Rashi, "L'tachshitei."*
65. *Biur HaGra* to *Shulhan Aruch, Even HaEzer* 1:1.
66. Proverbs 1:9.
67. *Biur HaGra,* Proverbs 1:9.
68. Maimonides, *Yad, Ishut* 13:4.
69. *Sanhedrin* 76b.
70. *Rashi, Sanhedrin* 76b.
71. *Torat Avraham,* quoted in *Mitzvot HaBayit,* 63.
72. See *Rama, Shulhan Aruch, Even HaEzer* 73:1.
73. See *Midrash Tanhuma* to *Vayishlah.*
74. *Responsa of Maharam of Rothenburg,* chap. 93.
75. Ibid.
76. *Bava Batra* 22b.
77. Exodus 38:8.
78. *Rashi,* Exodus 38:8; see *Ramban,* Exodus 38:8.
79. S. R. Hirsch, *Commentary,* Exodus 38:8.
80. *Pele Yo'etz, Ahavat Ish V'ishto.*
81. Wolbe, *Binyan Adei Ad,* 108, mentions that R. Joseph Hayim Sonenfeld (1849–1932), rabbi of Jerusalem, would study the *Shulhan Aruch,* the *Code of Jewish Law,* with his wife thirty minutes each day.
82. Ibid.
83. *Bava M'tzia* 59a.
84. *Deuteronomy Rabbah* 4:5.
85. *Ketubot* 61a.
86. *Nidah* 45b.
87. *M'iri* to *Bava M'tzia* 59a.
88. *Mitzvot HaBayit* I, 315.
89. Ibid.
90. Ibid.

91. Genesis 1:26; see *Rashi*.
92. *Mitzvot HaBayit*, 315.
93. *Ketubot* 61a.
94. *Shevet Musar*, chap. 16.
95. *Yvamot* 65b; see also *Perek HaShalom*, *addendum* to *Derech Eretz Zuta*.
96. *Shevet Musar*, chap. 24.
97. *Pele Yo'etz, Ahavat Ish V'ishto*.
98. Malachi 2:14.
99. Ecclesiastes 7:9.
100. *N'darim* 22b.
101. *Avot* 5:11.
102. *Sotah* 3b.
103. *Me'am Loez* to *Avot* 5:11.
104. *N'darim* 22a.
105. *Zohar, Korah*.
106. *Shabbat* 105b.
107. *N'darim* 22a.
108. *Orhot Tzadikim*, "On Anger."
109. Ibid.
110. Ibid.
111. Ibid.
112. Ibid.
113. *Shabbat* 105b; see *Avot D'Rabbi Nathan* 3; see *Zohar*, Numbers 189.
114. *Gittin* 6b.
115. *Sotah* 2b.
116. *Sotah* 47a.
117. *JT Ta'anit* 3:13, 67a; see *Taanit* 20b.
118. *Yoma* 23a; *Shabbat* 88b; *Gittin* 7a.
119. Judges 5:31.
120. *Orhot Tzadikim*, "On Anger."
121. *Zohar, Korah*.
122. Maimonides, *Yad, Ishut* 15:19.
123. Proverbs 25:15.
124. Proverbs 15:1.
125. Ibid.
126. *Orhot Tzadikim*, "On Anger."
127. Jeremiah 31:33.
128. Quoted in Wolbe, *Binyan Adei Ad*, 79.
129. *M'norat HaMa'or*, *Ner* III, Rule 6, part 4, chap. 2, 176.
130. Maimonides, *Yad, Ishut* 15:19.
131. *Bava M'tzia* 59a.
132. *Shabbat* 34a.
133. Ibid.

134. *K'tzait HaShemesh Bi-g'vurato,* cited by Zelig Pliskin, *Gateway to Happiness* (Jerusalem: The Jewish Learning Exchange, 1983), 194.

135. *Yvamot* 63a,b.

136. *Tur, Orah Hayim* 545:75.

137. *Kidushin* 31a.

138. S. Wolbe, *Hadrachah L'hatanim,* in *Binyan Adei Ad,* 74.

139. *M'norat HaMa'or, Ner* III, Rule 6, part 4, chap. 2, 176.

140. Proverbs 12:4.

141. See *Yvamot* 63a,b; *Eruvin* 41b; *Shulhan Aruch, Even HaEzer* 119; *Mitzvot HaBayit,* 394–401.

142. *Mitzvot HaBayit,* 394–401.

143. Pliskin, *Gateway to Happiness,* 390.

144. *Leviticus Rabbah* 9:9.

145. Ibid.

146. Exodus 23:4.

147. Exodus 23:5.

148. Deuteronomy 22:6.

149. Psalms 34:15.

150. *Leviticus Rabbah* 9:9.

151. Ibid.

152. *Birchat HaMitzvot U-Mish-p'teyhem.*

153. *Igeret HaT'shuvah.*

154. See *Avot* 1:12, *Avot d'Rabbi Nathan* 12:3,4.

155. *JT Sotah* 1:4; see *Sukah* 53b. As part of the procedure involving *sotah,* a woman suspected of adultery (Numbers 5:11–31), God's name is written and dipped in water.

156. *Shabbat* 32b.

157. *Kalah* 8.

158. *Yoma* 9b.

159. Ibid.

160. Ibid.

Notes to Chapter 13

1. Genesis 1:28.

2. *Yvamot* 61b, 62a; Maimonides, *Yad, Ishut* 15:4.

3. Genesis 15:2.

4. J. H. Hertz, *The Pentateuch and Haftorahs* (London: Soncino, 1981), 54; and *The Authorized Daily Prayer Book* (London: Soncino, 1976), 1006.

5. See Genesis 30:1.

6. See 1 Samuel 1:10; *Bava Batra* 117a; *N'darim* 64b; *Zohar,* Genesis 67a.

7. See Genesis 22:17, 32:13.

8. *Bava Batra* 117a; *N'darim* 64b.

9. Psalms 127:3,5.

10. *Zohar I,* Genesis 66a, 187a, 188a.

11. Philippe Aries, *Centuries of Childhood: A Social History of Family Life,* trans. Robert Baldick (New York: Knopf, 1962), quoted by Shoshana Matzner-Bekerman, *The Jewish Child: Halakhic Perspectives* (New York: Ktav Publishing House, 1984), 12.

12. Exodus 10:2, 13:8, 14; Deuteronomy 4:10, 6:20, 11:19. See Maimonides, *Yad, Talmud Torah* 1:1.

13. *Song of Songs Rabbah* 1:4.

14. S. R. Hirsch, *Judaism Eternal* (London: Soncino, 1959) vol. 2, 52–53.

15. Proverbs 22:6.

16. Exodus 10:2, 13:14; Deuteronomy 6:20.

17. Deuteronomy 6:7.

18. Ibid.

19. Genesis 18:19.

20. Isaiah 49:6.

21. *Song of Songs Rabbah* 1:4.

22. *JT Y'vamot* 6.

23. *Rama, Shulhan Aruch, Yoreh De'ah* 81:6,7.

24. Maimonides, *Yad, Talmud Torah* 1:6.

25. *Sukah* 42a; see *Tosefta, Hagigah* 1:2; see Maimonides *Yad, Talmud Torah* 1:6.

26. Deuteronomy 33:4.

27. Deuteronomy 6:4.

28. Psalms 111:10.

29. *Rama, Shulhan Aruch, Yoreh De'ah* 81:6,7.

30. Maimonides, *Yad, Talmud Torah* 1:6.

31. Exodus 20:12.

32. Leviticus 19:3.

33. *Sefer HaHinuch, Mitzvah* 27.

34. See Deuteronomy 32:6; *Bava M'tzia* 33a; *M'chilta* to Exodus 20:12; *Sifra* to Leviticus 19:3.

35. Philo, *The Special Laws,* II, sec. 229–231.

36. *Kidushin* 30b; *Nidah* 31a; *JT K'laim* 8:3; see *Tanah d'bey Eliyahu Rabbah,* 26.

37. *Kidushin* 30b; *JT K'laim* 8:3; *JT Pe'ah* 1:1; *Sifra,* Leviticus 19:3; Maimonides, *Yad, Mamrim* 6:1.

38. *JT K'laim* 8:3.

39. *Nidah* 31a.

40. *Kidushin* 30b.

41. Exodus 20:12.

42. Proverbs 3:9.

43. Leviticus 19:3.

44. Deuteronomy 6:13.

45. *Kidushin* 30b; see *JT Kidushin* 1:7.

46. Deuteronomy 14:1.

47. *Avot* 3:18.

48. Philo, *On the Decalogue*, sec. 106–107, 120; *The Special Laws*, II, sec. 225. Philo's ideas in comparing parents to "the gods" go beyond Jewish thinking and are undoubtedly influenced by Greek philosophy. See Gerald Blidstein, *Honor Thy Father and Mother* (New York: Ktav, 1976), 7, 8.

49. Ibid.

50. *JT Kidushin* 1:7.

51. *Kidushin* 31b; See *JT Pe'ah* 1:1; *Sifra, K'doshim* 1:10.

52. *Shulhan Aruch, Yoreh De'ah* 240:2.

53. *Hayei Adam* 67:11.

54. *Kidushin* 31a.

55. *Kidushin* 32a.

56. *JT Pe'ah* 1:1.

57. *Kidushin* 31a.

58. *Kidushin* 31b.

59. Ibid.

60. Maimonides, *Yad, Mamrim* 6:7.

61. *Shulhan Aruch, Yoreh De'ah* 240:19.

62. *Y'vamot* 55, 6a; *Bava M'tzia* 32a; *Kidushin* 32a,b; Maimonides, *Yad, Mamrim* 6:12; see *Yoreh De'ah* 240:25.

63. Leviticus 19:3.

64. *Rashi*, Leviticus 19:3.

65. See *Yoreh De'ah* 240:13,15.

66. S. R. Hirsch, *Commentary*, Exodus 20:12.

67. S. R. Hirsch, *Commentary*, Leviticus 19:3.

68. S. R. Hirsch, *Commentary*, Exodus 20:12.

69. *JT Bava M'tzia* 2:11; Maimonides, *Yad, Talmud Torah* 5:1.

70. *Bava M'tzia* 33a.

71. *Rama, Shulhan Aruch, Yoreh De'ah* 242:34; see *Bet Yosef*; see Maimonides, *Yad, Talmud Torah* 5:1; see *Yoreh De'ah* 242:1 and *Rama*; see *Sefer Hasidim*, 579.

72. *Shulhan Aruch, Yoreh De'ah* 242:34; see Maimonides, *Yad, G'zelah V'Avedah* 12:2.

73. *Zohar Hadash, Lech L'cha*.

74. *P'sahim* 113a.

75. *Genesis Rabbah* 49:4.

76. *Kidushin* 30a.

77. *Rashi* to Genesis 18:19.

78. *Sefer HaMidot* (Warsaw, 1912), 28–29.

79. *Sukah* 56b.
80. Proverbs 13:24.
81. *Midrash Rabbah,* Exodus 1:1.
82. Ibid.
83. S. R. Hirsch, *Y'sodot HaHinuch.*
84. Ibid.
85. See R. Akiva Eger to *Yoreh De'ah* 240:20.
86. *Rashi, Bava Batra* 21a.
87. *Shulhan Aruch, Yoreh De'ah* 240:20.
88. *Sotah* 47a; *Zohar* III, 177b.
89. S. R. Hirsch, *Y'sodot HaHinuch.*
90. *Even Sh'lemah* 6:5.
91. *Reshit Hochmah, Gidul Banim.*
92. *Kitzur Shulhan Aruch* 143:21.
93. *Sifri,* Deuteronomy 11:14.
94. *Leviticus Rabbah* 19:3.
95. *Avot* 3:17.
96. See *Avot* 4:15; *B'rachot* 6b; *Bava M'tzia* 87a.
97. See *Sifri* (103), Numbers 12:6.
98. *P'sahim* 3a; *Yoma* 86a.
99. See *Leviticus Rabbah* 34:3; see *Ramban, Commentary* to Leviticus 19:2.
100. *Shabbat* 113a, 114b; Maimonides, *Yad, De'ot* 9.
101. *B'rachot* 17a.
102. *Kidushin* 40b; *Derech Eretz Zutah,* 5.
103. See *Avot* 5:7.
104. Leviticus 19:32.
105. *Hagigah* 8a.
106. See *Gittin* 6b.
107. Ezekiel 41:22.
108. *Hagigah* 27a.
109. See *Hafetz Hayim, Ahavath Chesed,* trans. Leonard Oschry (Jerusalem: Feldheim, 1976), 189–193.
110. *Shabbat* 127a.
111. Leviticus 19:18.
112. *Tikunei Zohar,* Introduction, 6a.
113. Genesis 48:20.
114. See Ruth 4:11.
115. Numbers 6:24–26.
116. Numbers 24:5.
117. I. Zangwill, quoted by J. H. Hertz, *The Pentateuch and Haftorahs,* 935.
118. See *B'rachot* 57b.
119. *B'rachot* 47b.

120. Deuteronomy 11:19.

121. *Megillah* 27a.

122. Exodus 28:3, 31:3-5.

123. *Kidushin* 29a.

124. *Kidushin* 82a.

125. *Shabbat* 103a; See *Rashi*.

126. *Sefer HaMidot.*

127. *Sanhedrin* 90b.

128. *Judaism Eternal,* I, 171.

129. J. H. Hertz, *The Pentateuch and Haftorahs,* 366.

130. See Isaiah 61:8; *Sukah* 30a; *Sanhedrin* 6b; *Shulhan Aruch, Orah Hayim* 649:1.

131. *Eruvin* 18b; see *Sanhedrin* 92a; *Zohar* II, 149a.

132. *Commentary,* Genesis 28:10 and Genesis 18:22.

133. Will Durant, *The Story of Civilization, The Age of Faith* (New York: Simon and Schuster, 1950), 378-382.

Glossary

Aba — Father.

Ahavah — Love.

Aishet Hayil — Woman of valor, that is, the Jewish wife and mother; the title of the traditional song sung to the Jewish wife and mother at the festive Sabbath eve feast based upon Proverbs 31.

Am Ha'aretz — An ignoramus or boor.

Amorah — (Plural, *Amoraim*) Rabbinic scholar and teacher of the later talmudic period.

Ashkenazi/Ashkenazic — German; Jews of European, but not Spanish/Portuguese, origin.

Aufruf — (Yiddish) The "calling up" of the groom to the Torah in the synagogue on the Sabbath before the wedding.

Azut — Bold shamelessness.

Badeken — (Yiddish) The veiling of the bride prior to the marriage ceremony.

Baishanut — Modesty, or bashfulness.

Bar/Bat Mitzvah — Literally, "son/daughter of the commandment," that is, one under obligation to fulfill the commandments; a term denoting both the attainment of religious majority, and the occasion at which this status is formally assumed — age thirteen years and one day for boys, and twelve years and one day for girls.

Baraita — Rabbinic statement on Jewish law of the earlier (mishnaic) period of the Talmud not included in the Mishnah.

Bet Din — Rabbinical court. In ancient times, a court of law. In modern times, an ecclesiastical court dealing primarily with religious matters such as *kashrut* and divorce.

Birkat HaMazon — Grace after meals. At weddings and during the Seven Days of Feasting, it precedes the recitation of the *Sheva B'rachot,* the Seven Blessings of the newly married couple.

Chen — Grace, charm.

Derech Eretz — Literally, "the way of the land." Proper comportment and behavior in keeping with accepted social and moral practice: courtesy, politeness, honor of elders, good manners, etiquette, respect, and consideration for others.

D'rush — Method of textual analysis based upon close examination and investigation.

D'var Torah — (Plural, *Divrei Torah*) Torah discussion.

Eretz Israel — The Land of Israel; the Jewish ancestral homeland.

Erusin — Literally, "betrothal"; formal betrothal which requires a bill of divorce for annulment.

Gaon — (Plural, *G'onim*) Literally, "genius"; the head of the academy in the post-talmudic period.

Genizah — Storage room for old religious books, documents, and ritual objects.

Ger — Convert to Judaism.

Get — The Jewish bill of divorce.

G'mara — Commentary on and supplement to the Mishnah and, together with the Mishnah, forming the Talmud.

G'matria — The numerical equivalent of Hebrew letters.

G'milut Hasadim — Acts of love performed for one's fellow (see *Hesed*).

Hachnasat Orhim — Literally, "bringing guests into one's home"; hospitality to strangers — one expression of *g'milut hasadim.*

Halachah — Jewish law.

Halipin — A form of exchange which serves as a legal consideration.

Halitzah — A biblically prescribed ritual (Deuteronomy 25:9-10) conducted between a childless widow and her late husband's brother which obviates the necessity for levirate marriage.

Hasidism — In modern times, movement of religious revival founded by R. Israel Baal Shem Tov (1700–1770), which emphasizes finding God through joy and prayer. Followers are called *hasidim.*

Hatan — Groom.

Havdalah — Literally, "separation." The ceremony marking the end of the Sabbath.

Hesed — Acts of love performed for one's fellow.

Hezkat Kashrut — Presumption of Jewishness.

Hinuch — Education.

Horim — Parents.

Hupah — Marriage canopy.

Ima — Mother.

Ish — Man.

Ishah — Woman.

Lashon Hara — Derogatory speech about others.

Kabalah — Literally, "received" or "received lore." The term used for the esoteric teachings and mystic lore of Jewish tradition.

Kalah — Bride.

Kavanah — Proper intent; spiritual and mental concentration and devotion accompanying prayers or when performing a precept.

K'deshah — A harlot.

K'dushah — Holiness.

Ketubah — Literally, "her writ." The marriage document containing the husband's obligations and guarantees to his wife presented at the marriage ceremony.

Kidushin — Literally, "sanctification." Marriage betrothal.

Kinyan — Literally, "acquisition." A formal acknowledgment of an agreement.

Kittel — White linen robe worn by a groom.

Kohen (Cohen) — A Jew of priestly (Aaronic) descent.

Kohen Gadol — High priest.

Kolel — An institution for advanced Torah study, usually for married students.

Mamzer — (Plural, *mamzerim*) The offspring of certain prohibited adulterous or incestuous relationships.

Mazal Tov — Good luck.

Midrash — Rabbinic exegetical and homiletical literature forming a study of and commentary on the Torah, composed primarily during the first millennium of the Common Era.

Mikvah (Mikveh) — (Plural, *mikvaot*) Ritual bath.

Minyan — A quorum for Jewish public prayer. The minimum requirement is ten adult males.

Mishnah — The Oral Law, composed in six "orders" or divisions, originally taught orally. Codified, edited, and committed into writing at the beginning of the third century and, together with the *G'mara,* forming the Talmud.

Mitzvah — (Plural, *mitzvot*) A biblical or rabbinic precept or commandment; a good deed.

Mitzvah Dance — A dance with the bride at the conclusion of the wedding, when dignitaries take turns holding one end of a handkerchief held by the bride.

M'sader Kidushin — Literally, the "arranger" of the marriage; the officiating rabbi.

Musar — Jewish ethics and morals.

N'giah — Physical contact between men and women.

Nidah — Menstruant; the status of the woman from the onset of her menstrual period until her immersion in a *mikvah.*

N'suin — The nuptials; the completion of the marriage ceremony.

Olam HaBa — The world to come; paradise.

Onah — Literally, "season." The husband's obligation for marital relations with his wife.

Oral Law — The term used for the law which was originally transmitted orally and handed down from generation to generation, and eventually committed to writing as the Mishnah and *G'mara,* together known as the Talmud.

Paytan — Liturgical poet.

Piryah V'rivyah — Procreation.

Piyut — Liturgical poem.

P'sak Din — Rabbinic decision on Jewish law.

P'ru u-r'vu — Be fruitful and multiply; the biblical command to have children.

P'shat — The plain or literal meaning.

Prutah — Small coin.

Rahmanut — Compassion.

Sanhedrin — Assembly of rabbinic scholars that functioned as both rabbinical court and legislature in ancient Israel.

Savoraim — Rabbinic scholars in the period following the completion of the Talmud.

Sephardi — Spanish; Jews of Spanish/Portuguese or of non-European origin.

Shadchan — (Plural, *shadchanim*) Matchmaker, marriage broker.

Sheva B'rachot — The Seven Blessings to bride and groom recited at the marriage ceremony and during the Seven Days of Feasting following the wedding.

Sh'chinah — The Divine Presence; the Spirit of God on earth.

Shiv'at Y'mey Mishteh — The Seven Days of Feasting in honor of bride and groom following the wedding.

Sh'lom Bayit — The peaceful home; harmony between husband and wife.

Sh'ma Yisrael — "Hear O Israel." The first words of the prayer "Hear O Israel, the Lord Our God is One" (Deuteronomy 6:4), Judaism's confession of faith, which proclaims the absolute unity of God, that is recited twice daily by the believing Jew.

Shofar — The horn of an animal, usually a ram, sounded on Rosh Hashanah and following the Yom Kippur fast, and on other occasions.

Shoshvinin — Bride's and groom's attendants.

Shulhan Aruch — Literally, "The Prepared Table." The *Code of Jewish Law*.

Siddur — The Jewish prayer book.

Simhah — Festive occasion or feast.

Sofer — Scribe of Hebrew books and documents.

S'udat Mitzvah — Feast associated with a festive occasion, participation in which is considered a *mitzvah*.

Sukah — Temporary dwelling outside the home in which the Jew resides during the eight-day fall Sukot festival.

Taharat HaMishpahah — The Purity of Family Life; the laws that govern marital relations between husband and wife, especially those relating to *nidah* and *mikvah*.

Takanah — Rabbinical enactment.

Talit — Four-cornered, fringed, cape-like garment worn by the married man during the morning prayers.

Talmid Hacham — (Plural, *talmidei hachamim*) Literally, "a wise disciple," a person who is wise because he is always a student; a Torah scholar.

Talmud — Study; the oral teachings of the Torah, including the Mishnah and the *G'mara*.

Tanach — Acronym for *Torah, N'vi-im, K'tuvim* — the Hebrew Bible.

Tanah — (Plural, *Tanaim*) Rabbinic scholar and teacher of the early (mishnaic) period of the Talmud.

Targum — Aramaic translation of the Bible.

T'filin — Small leather cubes containing biblical passages, worn by Jewish males on the arm and upper forehead during daily morning prayers.

Tish — (Yiddish) Table. (*"Hoson's Tish"* — The groom's reception table.)

T'naim — Conditions; conditions of engagement, agreed to at engagement celebrations.

Torah — Literally, "the teaching." The Pentateuch, or the Five Books of Moses (*Torah she-bichtav,* the "Written" Torah); the Talmud (*Torah she-be'al peh,* the "Oral" Torah).

Tosafists — Rabbinic glossarists of the Talmud, mainly French and German, during the twelfth–fourteenth centuries who composed the *Tosafot* glosses to the Talmud.

Tosefta — Collections of rabbinic teachings on the Oral Law of the early talmudic period not included in the Mishnah.

T'vilah — Immersion in a *mikvah.*

Tzadik — Good or righteous person.

Tz'dakah — Charity; righteousness.

Tzelem Elohim — The image of God.

Tzitzit — Fringes on the four-cornered *talit* worn in accordance with biblical injunction as a reminder to perform God's precepts.

Tz'niut — Modesty; the way one is supposed to behave and dress.

Vort — (Yiddish) Literally, "word." An oral agreement between prospective bridegroom and bride executed at some engagement celebrations.

Yeshivah — Academy for the study of Torah.

Yetzer Hara — The evil impulse in a person; the tempter.

Yihud — Seclusion; prohibition against private, secluded association between the sexes among those unmarried to each other.

Yihud Room — The secluded chamber to which bride and groom retire immediately following the marriage ceremony to underscore their new status as husband and wife.

Yihas — Pedigree; lineage.

Yir'at HaShem — Reverence of the Lord.

Yir'at Shamayim — Reverence of heaven.

Zaken — Old man.

Bibliography of Selected Hebrew Sources

The works are classified by the principal texts, followed by the commentaries on them, listed chronologically.

Bible and Commentaries

Mikraot G'dolot. The text of the Hebrew Bible, with Aramaic Targum translations and various commentaries. Jerusalem, 1977.
Rashi (R. Solomon Yitzhaki, 1040–1105).
Rashbam (R. Samuel ben Meir, c. 1080/85–1174).
R. Abraham Ibn Ezra, 1091/2–1167.
Radak (R. David Kimhi, c. 1160–c. 1235).
Ramban (R. Moses ben Nahman—Nahmanides, c. 1194/5–1270).
R. Ovadiah *Sforno* (1470/75–1550).
Vilna *Gaon* (R. Elijah, *Gaon* of Vilna, 1720–1797). *Aderet Eliyahu.*
Shadal (R. Samuel David Luzzatto, 1800–1865). *Perush Shadal.* Tel Aviv, 1965.
R. Samson Raphael Hirsch (1808–1888). *Commentary to the Pentateuch.* Gateshead, 1976.
R. Meir Leibush *Malbim* (1809–1879).
Meshech Hochmah (R. Meir Simhah HaKohen of Dvinsk, 1843–1926), 1927.
R. J. H. Hertz (1872–1946). *The Pentateuch and Haftorahs.* London, 1981.

Targum — Midrashim

Targum Jonathan ben Uziel, first century B.C.E.–first century C.E. A midrashic translation of the Prophets into Aramaic. In *Mikraot G'dolot.*
Targum Onkelos, second century C.E. The standard Aramaic translation and paraphrase of the Bible. In *Mikraot G'dolot.*
Midrash Mechilta. Philadelphia, 1949.
Torat Kohanim.
Sifra. Jerusalem, 1959.
Sifri. Leipzig, 1917.

Midrash Rabbah. Tel Aviv, 1968.
Midrash Tanhuma. Berlin, 1927.
P'sikta Rabati. Vienna, 1880.
Tana d'Bei Eliyahu. Vienna, 1902.
Yalkut. Vilna, 1898.
Pirkei D'Rabbi Eliezer. London, 1916.
P'sikta D'Rabbi Kahana. Philadelphia, 1975.

Talmud and Commentaries

Mishnah. New York, 1963.
The Rambam (Maimonides — R. Moses ben Maimon, 1135–1204). *Shmonah P'rakim.*
    With most editions of the Mishnah.
Avot D'Rabbi Nathan. London, 1887.
Babylonian Talmud. Jerusalem, 1970.
Rishonim. Early talmudic commentators, tenth–fifteenth centuries.
Rabeinu Hananel (990–1055/6). With many standard editions of the Babylonian
    Talmud.
Rashi (see above). In all standard editions of the Talmud.
Tosafot. Analyses and commentary by French and German scholars of the twelfth
    and thirteenth centuries, among which Rabeinu Tam, *Rashi's* grandson, was the
    leading member. With all standard editions of the Talmud.
Ramban (see above). Jerusalem, 1928.
Mordechai (R. Mordecai ben Hillel, c. 1240–1298). With most editions of the Tal-
    mud.
Tos'fot Rid (R. Isaiah di Trani, thirteenth century). Jerusalem, 1931.
Ran (R. Nissim Gerondi, c. 1290–1375/80). New York, 1946.
Shitah M'kubetzet (R. Bezalel Ashkenazi, c. 1520–1592). Tel Aviv, 1954.
MaHarsha (R. Samuel Edels, 1555–1631/2). With most standard editions of the
    Talmud.
Palestinian Talmud (Jerusalem Talmud. All references to the Jerusalem Talmud in
    Notes are preceded with "JT"). Jerusalem, 1975.

Codes and Commentaries

Rif (R. Isaac Alfasi, 1013–1103). In most editions of the Talmud.
Mahzor Vitri (R. Simhah ben Samuel, d. 1105).
Even HaEzer (Eliezer ben Nathan, d. 1165). Prague, 1610.
Maimonides (see above). *Mishneh Torah* (or *Yad HaHazakah*). New York, 1956.
Hasagot HaRaavad (R. Abraham ben David, c. 1125–1198). With all standard
    editions of the *Mishneh Torah.*
Hagahot Maimoniot (R. Meir HaKohen, thirteenth century). With all standard
    editions of the *Mishneh Torah.*
Kesef Mishneh (R. Joseph Caro, 1488–1575). With all standard editions of the
    Mishneh Torah.
Magid Mishneh (R. Yom Tov Vidal, fourteenth century). With all standard editions
    of the *Mishneh Torah.*
Lehem Mishneh (R. Abraham di Boton, c. 1545–1588). With all standard editions of
    the *Mishneh Torah.*
Sefer HaRokeah (R. Elazar ben Judah, c. 1165–c. 1230). Fano, 1503.

Rosh (R. Asher ben Yehiel, 1250-1327).

Kol Bo (Anonymous, thirteenth century). New York, 1945.

Sefer HaHinuch (attributed to R. Aaron HaLevi of Barcelona, fourteenth century). Jerusalem, 1951.

Sefer Mitzvot Gadol (*S'mag* — R. Moses ben Jacob of Coucy, early thirteenth century). Venice, 1522.

Sefer Mitzvot Katan (*S'mak* — R. Isaac ben Joseph of Corbeil, d. 1280). Ladi, 1805.

Tur (R. Jacob ben Asher, c. 1270/80-1340/43). Vilna, 1900. This work has four divisions: *Orah Hayim, Yoreh De'ah, Hoshen Mishpat, Even HaEzer.* Vilna, 1900.

Bet Yosef (R. Joseph Caro, 1488-1575). With standard editions of the *Tur.*

Darkei Moshe (R. Moses Isserles, c. 1525/30-1572). With standard editions of the *Tur.*

MaHaril (R. Jacob HaLevi Mollin, c. 1360/65-1427). Lvov, 1860.

Shulhan Aruch (R. Joseph Caro, 1488-1575). An abridged version of the *Bet Yosef* commentary on the *Tur,* divided into four major divisions. Vilna, 1911.

Rama (R. Moses Isserles, 1525/30-1572). With standard editions of the *Shulhan Aruch.*

Turei Zahav (*Taz* — R. David HaLevi, 1586-1667). With standard editions of the *Shulhan Aruch.*

Helkat M'hokek (R. Moses Lima, 1605-1658). With standard editions of the *Shulhan Aruch.*

Magen Avraham (R. Abraham Gombiner, 1637-1683). With standard editions of the *Shulhan Aruch.*

Mor U-k'tzia (R. Jacob Emden, 1697-1776). With standard editions of the *Shulhan Aruch.*

Ba'er Hetev (R. Judah Ashkenazi, eighteenth century). With standard editions of the *Shulhan Aruch.*

Biur HaGra (R. Elijah ben Solomon Zalman — The Vilna *Gaon,* 1720-1797). With standard editions of the *Shulhan Aruch.*

Birkei Yosef (R. Hayim Joseph David Azulai — *Hidah,* 1724-1806). Vienna, 1860.

Pri M'gadim (R. Joseph ben Meir Teomim, c. 1727-1792). With standard editions of the *Shulhan Aruch.*

Mishnah B'rurah (R. Israel Meir Hakohen — *Hafetz Hayim,* 1838-1933). Tel Aviv, 1955.

Hazon Ish (R. Isaiah Karelitz, 1878-1953). Bnei Brak, 1958.

Igrot Moshe (R. Moses Feinstein, 1895-1986). New York, 1961.

L'vush (R. Mordecai Jaffe, c. 1535-1612). Venice, 1620.

Hayei Adam (R. Abraham Danzig, 1748-1820). Warsaw, 1908.

Hochmat Adam (R. Abraham Danzig, see *Hayei Adam*). Warsaw, 1899.

Kitzur Shulhan Aruch (R. Shlomo Ganzfried, 1804-1886). Lublin, 1888.

Aruch HaShulhan (R. Yehiel Michel Epstein, 1829-1908). Warsaw, 1911.

Extra-Legal Literature: Ethical, Philosophical, and Mystic

Zohar, Jerusalem, 1960.

Emunot V'Deot (Saadia Gaon, d. 942). Constantinople, 1562.

Hovot HaL'vavot (R. Bahya Ibn Pakuda, eleventh century). Tel Aviv, 1949.

Moreh N'vuchim (Maimonides — *The Rambam,* see above). Jerusalem, 1959.

Baalei HaNefesh (R. Abraham ben David — *Raavad*, c. 1125-1198). Warsaw, 1863.
Sefer Hasidim (R. Judah HeHasid, 1150-1217). Jerusalem, 1964.
Igeret HaKodesh (Ascribed to *Ramban*, R. Moses ben Nahman — Nahmanides, see above). Jerusalem, 1955.
Ma'alot HaMidot (R. Y'hiel ben Y'kutiel HaRofe, thirteenth century). Jerusalem, c. 1970.
Kad HaKemah (R. Bachya ben Asher, late thirteenth century-1340). New York, 1980.
M'norat HaMa'or (R. Israel Al-Nakawa, c. 1340-1391). New York, 1932.
M'norat HaMa'or (R. Isaac Aboab, second half fourteenth century). Jerusalem, c. 1970.
Nefesh Yehudah (R. Moses Frankfurt, 1672-1762). With many editions of *M'norat HaMa'or*.
Vikuah al Ahavah (Judah ben Isaac Abarbanel — Leon Ebreo, c. 1460-c. 1525).
Orhot Tzadikim (fifteenth century). New York, 1974.
Reshit Hochmah (R. Elijah de Vidas, late sixteenth century). Venice, 1579.
Pele Yo'etz (R. Eliezer Papo, seventeenth century). Jerusalem, c. 1970.
Shevet Musar (R. Elijah HaKohen Itamari, d. 1729). Amsterdam, 1734.
Siddur Bet Yaakov (R. Jacob Emden, see above). Lemberg, 1904.
Likutei MoHaran (R. Nahman of Bratzlav, 1772-1811). Ostrog, 1806.
Likutei Etzot HaShalom. Warsaw, 1913.
Hupat Hatanim (Raphael Meldola, 1754-1828). Venice, 1737.
Sha'arei Rahamim. Vilna, 1871.
Ahavath Hessed (R. Israel Meir HaKohen — *Hafetz Hayim*, see above), English translation by Leonard Oschry. New York and Jerusalem: Feldheim, 1976.
Sh'mirat HaLashon (R. Israel Meir HaKohen — *Hafetz Hayim*, see above). English adaptation by R. Zelig Pliskin, *Guard Your Tongue*. Jerusalem and New York: Feldheim, 1975.
Ta'amei HaMinhagim (R. Abraham Isaac Sperling, 1851-1921). Jerusalem, c. 1960.
Michtav MeEliyahu (R. Elijah Eliezer Dessler, 1891-1954). London, 1955. Abridged version published in English by Aryeh Carmel, as *Strive for Truth!* New York: Feldheim, 1978.
Binyan Adei Ad (R. Solomon Wolbe, twentieth century). Jerusalem, 1979.
Musar Avicha U-Midot HaR'iyah. Jerusalem: Mossad Harav Kook, 1973.
Ahavas Yisroel. Brooklyn, New York: Kehot, 1977.
Mitzvot HaBayit (R. Joseph D. Epstein, twentieth century). Brooklyn, New York, 1966.

Responsa

T'shuvot R. Meir of Rothenburg (R. Meir of Rothenburg, c. 1215/20-1293). Lemberg, 1860.
T'shuvot Rashba (R. Solomon ben Adret, 1235/45-1310). Several editions.
Tashbetz (R. Simon ben Zemach Duran, 1361-1444). Amsterdam, 1739.
T'shuvot Giv'at Pinhas. Lvov, 1837.
T'shuvot MaHarik (R. Joseph Colon, 1420-1480).
T'shuvot Radvaz (R. David ben Solomon Ibn Avi Zimra, 1480-1574).
T'shuvot MaHaram of Lublin (R. Meir ben Gedalyah, 1558-1616).
T'shuvot R. Akiva Eiger (1761-1837).
T'shuvot Hatam Sofer (R. Moses Sofer, 1762-1839). Vienna, 1855.
T'shuvot MaHarit (R. Joseph of Trani). Lemberg, 1861.
T'shuvot MaHaram Schick (R. Moses Schick, 1807-1879). Munkacz, 1881.

Bibliography of Selected English Sources

Barth, Aaron, *The Jew Faces Eternal Problems*. Jerusalem, The Jewish Agency, 1965.

Berkovitz, Eliezer, *Crisis and Faith*. New York, Sanhedrin Press, 1978.

Blidstein, Gerald, *Honor Thy Father and Mother*. New York, Ktav, 1976.

Boxer, B. D., *From the World of the Cabbalah*. New York, Philosophical Library, 1954.

Breuer, Isaac, *The Jewish Marriage*. New York, Feldheim, 1956.

Brown, Norman O., *Life Against Death, The Psychoanalytical Meaning of History*. New York, Random House, 1959.

Buber, Martin, *Tales of the Hasidim*. New York, Schocken, 1947.

Capellanus, Andreas, *The Art of Courtly Love*. New York, Norton, 1959.

Chavel, Charles B., *Maimonides, The Commandments*. New York and London, Soncino, 1967.

de Loris, Guillaume, and de Meun, Jean, *The Romance of the Rose*. New York, Dutton, 1962.

Durant, Will, *The Story of Civilization*. New York, Simon and Schuster, 1950.

Ebreo, Leon, *Dialoghi d'Amore* — The Philosophy of Love, translated by Friedberg-Seely and Jean H. Barnes. London, Soncino, 1937.

Elman, Peter (ed.), *Jewish Marriage*. London, The Jewish Marriage Educational Council, 1967.

Encyclopaedia Judaica. Jerusalem, Keter, 1971.

Epstein, I., *The Faith of Judaism*. London, Soncino, 1968.

Epstein, Louis M., *The Jewish Marriage Contract*. New York, Arno, 1973.

Falk, Z'ev W., *Jewish Matrimonial Law in the Middle Ages*. London, Oxford University Press, 1966.

Ficino, Marsilio, *Marsilio Ficino's Commentary on Plato's Symposium*. Columbia, Missouri, University of Missouri Press, 1944.

Freud, Sigmund, *The Standard Edition of the Complete Psychological Works of Sigmund Freud*. London, Hogarth, 1957.

J. H. Hertz, *The Authorised Daily Prayer Book*. London, Soncino, 1976.

———, *The Pentateuch and Haftorahs*. London, Soncino, 1981.

Hirsch, Samson Raphael, *Commentary to the Pentateuch,* rendered into English by Isaac Levy. Gateshead, Judaica Press, 1976.

_____ , *Horeb: A Philosophy of Jewish Laws and Observances,* translated by Dayan Dr. I. Grunfeld. London, Soncino, 1962.

_____ , *Judaism Eternal.* London, Soncino, 1959.

_____ , *The Hirsch Siddur.* Jerusalem and New York, Feldheim, 1969.

_____ , *The Nineteen Letters.* Jerusalem and New York, Feldheim, 1969.

_____ , *The Wisdom of Mishle.* Jerusalem, Feldheim, 1976.

Kaniel, Michael, *A Timeless Judaism for Our Time.* Jerusalem, Heritage Press, 1984.

_____ , *Guide to Jewish Art.* New York, Philosophical Library, 1989.

_____ , *Judaism.* Poole, Dorset, Blandford Press, 1979.

Kaplan, Aryeh, *Made in Heaven.* New York and Jerusalem, Moznaim, 1983.

_____ , *Waters of Eden.* New York, NCSY/Orthodox Union, 1976.

Kennedy, Emmet, *A Philosopher in the Age of Revolution.* Philadelphia, American Philosophical Society, 1978.

Lamm, Norman, *A Hedge of Roses.* New York, Feldheim, 1966.

Matzner-Bekerman, Shoshana, *The Jewish Child: Halakhic Perspectives.* New York, Ktav, 1984.

Meiselman, Moshe, *Jewish Woman in Jewish Law.* New York, Ktav, 1978.

Newman, L. I., *The Hasidic Anthology.* New York, Schocken, 1963.

Nietzsche, Friedrich Wilhelm, *A Nietzsche Reader.* Harmondsworth, undated.

Raz, Simha, *A Tzaddik in Our Time.* New York and Jerusalem, Feldheim, 1978.

Rosner, Fred, and Bleich, J. David, *Jewish Bioethics.* New York, Sanhedrin Press, 1979.

Russell, Bertrand, *Marriage and Morals.* New York, Horace and Liveright, 1929.

_____ , *Why I am Not a Christian and Other Essays on Related Subjects.* New York, Simon and Schuster.

Schopenhauer, Arthur, *The World as Will and Representation.* New York, Dover, 1966.

Shapiro, D. S., *Studies in Jewish Thought.* New York, Yeshiva University Press, 1975.

Tendler, Moses D., *Pardes Rimonim.* New York, Judaica Press, 1979.

Urbach, Ephraim E., *The Halakha.* Tel Aviv, Massada, 1986.

_____ , *The Sages.* Jerusalem, Magnes, 1975.

Index

Stendhal (Marie-Henri Beyle), 93
Survival. *See* Jewish survival

Talk, mate selection and, 59
Tallit (bride's gift to groom), wedding
    preparations, 166–167
Talmud
    bachelorhood and, 14
    child rearing and, 299
    divorce and, 235
    filial reverence and, 289–290
    Jewish traits identified in, 43
    joy and, 63
    love and, 85, 100–101
    mamzers and, 25
    marriage and, 4, 172, 248, 254
    mate selection and, 36, 57, 73
    parental marriage consent and,
        149
    sexuality and, 118, 134, 220,
        223–224
    Torah study and, 49
    women's fulfillment and, 8
    women's sensitivity and, 271
Temptations, sexual ethics and,
    134–136
Tendler, Moses, 207, 208
Thriftiness, mate selection and, 60
Thucydides, 281
Torah
    bride and groom as allegorical sym-
        bols for Israel and God, 125
    comportment and, 301–302
    family and, 282–283, 308–309
    family purity regulations and,
        195–106, 198–200, 212
    Golden Rule and, 77
    as guide for living, 127–128
    homosexuality and, 139
    Israel's betrothal to Torah, 126
    knowledge term and, 121–122
    love and, 78, 79–80
    mamzers and, 24
    marriage allegory in sacred institu-
        tions, 126–127
    marriage and, 3–4, 110
    optional marriage for women and, 9
    selflessness and, 12
    sexuality and, 115
    study of, and mate selection, 49–54
    truthfulness and, 60
    values and, 18

Trani, Isaiah di, 225
Troyes, Chretien de, 91
Truthfulness, mate selection and,
    59–60

Values
    assimilation and, xxi–xxii
    sexual liberation and, 18
Vaux, Roland de, 156
Veiling ceremony, marriage
    ceremony, 173–174
Vidas, Elijah de, 113
Violence. *See* Domestic violence

Wagner, R., 92
Wedding apparel, 161–162, 174–175
Wedding attendants, wedding prepa-
    rations, 162–163
Wedding ceremony
    breaking the glass, 188–189
    grace after the wedding feast,
        191–192, 200–201
    mikvah institution and, 197–198
    reading and presentation of *ketubah,*
        183
    recitation of marriage formula, 182
    ring presentation, 182–183
    sanctification (*kidushin*), 181–182
    seclusion room, 189–190
    Seven Blessings meaning, 185–188
    Seven Blessings reading, 183–185
    wedding feast, 190–191
    week following, 192, 200–201
    witnesses in, 182
Wedding day, rituals for, 163–164
Wedding feast
    grace following, 191–192, 200–201
    wedding ceremony and, 190–191
Wedding preparations, 149–167. *See
    also* Marriage ceremony; Mar-
    riage document (*ketubah*)
    bride's gift to groom (*tallit*), 166–167
    Conditions of Engagement, 150–151
    date setting, 151–152
    engagement, 149–150
    fasting, 165–166
    husband's guarantee toward wife,
        154–155
    locations for weddings, 153
    marriage document, 154
    music, 162
    rabbi selection, 153–154

About the Author

Dr. Michael Kaufman, a distinguished scholar and author, studied at Yeshiva and Mesivta Torah Vodaath, Telshe Yeshiva, Brooklyn College, and the University of Louisville. He has published numerous books and studies on Judaism and Jewish art and culture, including *The Art of Judaism, A Timeless Judaism for Our Time,* and *A Guide to Jewish Art.* He also served as a consultant to the *Encyclopaedia Judaica.* Dr. Kaufman resides with his family in Jerusalem opposite the Western Wall.